BEYOND

FRESH FEATHERED

EGGS

George D Bergen

2013

IN MEMORIAM

Sadly, before we could get this Book into publication, after a long illness my brother and co writer John passed away. Born on February 24, 1934, he died on July 23, 2012.

Over the years as John and I relived our childhood for *FRESH FEAHERED EGGS* and now for this *BEYOND FRESH FEATHERED EGGS*, we laughed and laughed as we recalled our many outrageous antics and learning experiences. Oh those were the days.

John spent his life working with and for others, in the financial services industry, in church work and in education. He loved most his time as a Doctor of Business Administration, teaching young people how to prepare themselves for life's challenges.

He loved music. You couldn't be in his presence without him pulling down his banjo or guitar and leading group singing, usually with songs from the heart.

We all join John's wife Susan, and sons Scott and Phil, and their families, in honoring husband, father, grandfather, brother and friend.

Rest in peace dear brother….

George D. Burgess

DEDICATION

Our inspiration for *Fresh Feathered Eggs* and now *Beyond Fresh Feathered Eggs* emanated from our parents, John Michael and Veda Helen Scott Burgess, who brought us up on the farm with firm direction and with an abundance of love. While they struggled with little money through the Great Depression and World War II, they always encouraged us to do our best with what we had.

They showed us who God is and they followed him throughout their lives. What they gave us was the best we could have wanted.

In their loving memory, we dedicate this book.

ACKNOWLEDGEMENTS

We have many to acknowledge and thank for their assistance with this Book. John's wife Susan and George's wife Carol offered encouragement, suggestions, and did hours of proof reading. Without them our task would have been impossible. Additionally, Susan was invaluable in sketching the maps and the cover art.

Classmates and friends who provided valuable fabric for the Book include Pat Clary Vining, Phyllis Carley Shelton and her collaborator Nonavee Taylor Howard.

We want to mention family members for their moral support, story ideas and encouragement. These include sisters Judy and her husband, the Reverend Steve Leonetti, and Joyce and her husband Doug Elcock (they live on the old farmstead). Additionally, Joyce ran down countless people, dates and events for our use. We deeply thank her for that.

We thank Cousin Bob Burgess for passing on his knowledge of the past. Carol's brother in law, Robert Fogarty, offered humorous scenes that we have adapted to our story. Bob Elder and John Lee (Buddy) Hableutzel supplied important dates and farming additions. Steve Bressler and Dr. Harry Haas helped with our baseball tales. Mrs. Dorothy Hupe Straub gave us a hand straightening out our grade school days. We are grateful for any others who helped keep us on track, especially those of whom we mention by name within the Book.

And, thanks to all who shared life with us in Pottawatomie County, Kansas during the time of this Book. Through our interactions with many of them, we truly have a story to tell.

PREFACE

When we published *FRESH FEATHERED EGGS* (Infinity Publishing, 2005), our goal was to share a story of typical young farm boys growing up in rural Kansas. We concentrated on what influenced them; e.g., family values and love, community values, their trust in the Lord and hard work, while showing their challenges and how they met them head on.

We were those boys.

That first Book brought our story from the 1930s to 1946 where Freddy (John) was finishing his 6th grade and George his 4th. Here we start again in 1944 and carry our story through John's second year in college and George's high school. graduation in 1954.

As youngsters we toted water and gathered eggs and by this Book's end, we'd grown into men, doing men's work.

During these 10 years with farm work, schooling, sports, FFA, 4-H, the Fairs and learning the essentials of cars and girls, we did some pretty dumb stuff. But in the end, we always ended up on our feet.

We've again called upon the fictitious *Brockman Family*—and a few others—to parody the craziest acts that we did or that we saw others do. These characters insure that no one will be embarrassed or offended. And we've taken the liberty of putting words into the mouths of classmates and friends, to add color to some scenes.

What is the origin of the titles? Dad's sister Helen Gordon raised six children during World War II while Uncle Houston was away building Victory Ships. While staying overnight with the Gordons, all Aunt Helen had for dinner were some eggs, crusty bread and Oleo Margarine.

Seeing George was balking at the eggs, she said to him, "Why Georgie, there's nothing wrong with those. You go ahead and eat them. They are real good cluckers. They don't come any riper. In fact they're *fresh feathered eggs*! I had to pluck the feathers off 'em before I cracked them in the skillet!" Aunt Helen was such a favorite of ours that it was natural to celebrate her life with our Books' titles.

Since so many of our activities overlapped or are recurring year after year, we found it necessary to shift back and forth to cover everything and give a fuller account. Oh we enjoyed those times, and have had fun putting our experiences on paper.

And so, ladies and gentlemen, and boys and girls, grab your knives and forks, and meet us at the table—for *(beyond) fresh feathered eggs*.

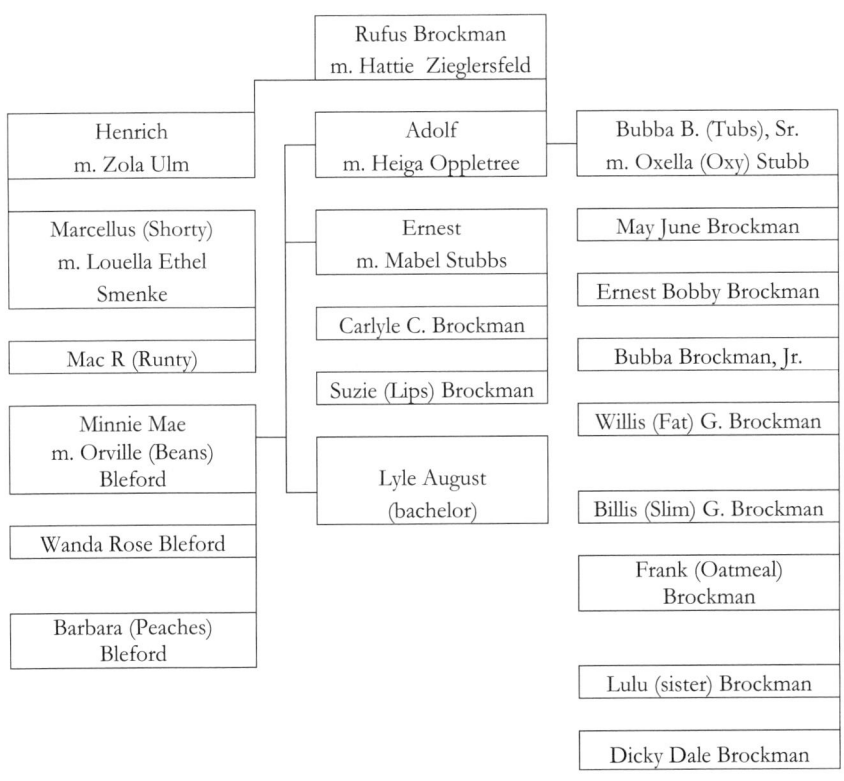

BROCKMAN GENEOLOGY
Pottawatomie County, Kansas,
circa 1940s and 1950s.
(This is a fictitious family) found in
FRESH FEATHERED EGGS
(pub. 2005) and in this sequel.

A TALE OF TWO BROTHERS

We close our eyes and in our minds visualize,
A story that begs to be told.
About growing up poor, yet with blessings galore,
And memories more precious than gold.

A story with charm of life on the farm,
Of pastures and clear sparkling streams.
A family with love and the blessings thereof,
Of two brothers and their plans and dreams.

Who learned early on that fine paragon,
That states your bond is your word.
And learned paramount that family does count,
With a love for the flag and the Lord.

Of Freddy, the one, that lived life on the run,
Whose curiosity reached to the sky.
Of George, the one who, reasoned things through,
Being reticent, quiet and shy.

As different all right as day is from night,
Embarking on different careers.
Yet loyal each brother, and true to each other,
With a bond that has held through the years.

So, just close your eyes and with us visualize,
This story that begs to be told.
Of boys' plans and schemes and childhood dreams,
And memories more precious than gold.

by Cowboy Poet and Rancher
Cousin Dwight Burgess
of Wamego, Kansas

Table of Contents

ONE

OFF THE MATTERHORN, DID SANTA INVENT RADAR? AND EVENING IN PHILADELPHIA

[*Wamego Reporter – December 7, 1944*] ~ NOW SERVING IN ITALY ~ Staff Sergeant William B. Owens, son of Mrs. A. E. Owens of Wamego is an original member of a B-24 Liberator group rounding out one year overseas.

His group has flown nearly 200 missions over strategically important targets such as Ploesti, Munich, Schwechat, Regensburg, Steyr, Vienna, Wiener Neustadt and Budapest.

1944

OFF THE MATTERHORN

Eight-year-old George dreamed in his bed. Something was wrong, very wrong. He thought, *Why am I so cold? I feel miserable. Why is there ice under me? Is this a glacier?*

Trembling, he looked up the slope. A Christmas tree hovered over presents like a brooding hen. Some were wrapped while others were still in Sears and Roebuck boxes. *Are those for me?*

Wide awake—he supposed—George tried to crawl to the tree but lost his grip, and in slow motion started slipping down the slope. *Whoa, I'm sliding. I can't hold on.*

His breath sucked in the icy air as he peeked over the glacier's edge. In the valley far below he saw Heidi's house where she lived with her grandfather and the goats. Flowers bloomed all around. *Am I sliding down a mountain? Are these the Alps? Listen to that wind. I'm freezing.*

His big ears picked up the sound of wind pounding against a wall. Huge gusts hammered at a window near his feet. He sensed flurries of dry snow moving to the east, forming small drifts behind bushes and grass clumps.

He shuddered again, and then looked toward the Christmas tree. There was the farm set he wanted for Christmas. Yes, it had the cardboard barn and a bag of animals.

1

And there he sensed his mother standing with her loving arms outstretched. With a tender look she handed him the bag. He pulled out a Hereford bull and four cows. Next came two big bay work horses, five Hampshire pigs and a dozen Leghorn chickens.

The animals seemed to warm him and just as he started to name the chickens after as many of the twelve Apostles as he could remember, he started to slide again.

Over the edge he went and plunged downward toward Heidi's house. The frigid air shocked him as the green meadow rose up to meet him. A hundred feet, then fifty, then…thunk!

George jolted out of his dream. His skinny and *broken* body lay sprawled on the cold, hardwood upstairs bedroom floor. *What happened to Heidi? Where's the Christmas tree? Where's my farm set?*

He stared at his breath in the 20 degree temperature room and scurried back under his covers. Another gust rattled the east window and a puff of snow powdered the sill white. Then he tried to doze. *I gotta find my dream. It's in here someplace ….*

IT'LL BE LIGHT SOON

"Come on boys, it's time to get up," George's dad called from somewhere. "It'll be light soon. Let's go. We have chores to do. Hurry down. We'll eat before we go out."

Get up? Why does the world torture me so?

Teeth chattering, George burrowed under the flannel sheet, the two wool blankets and the thick home-made brown and yellow sunflower quilt. Another gust shook his window.

Then he heard his brother flying down the stairs. *Oh no, there goes Freddy. I can't stall anymore.*

George eased his skinny arm out of bed and yanked his barn clothes from the eight-penny nail in the wall. Under the covers he pulled on his red wool, long underwear—after buttoning the flap left open from his last trip to the outhouse.

On went the long wool socks and a faded blue checked flannel barn shirt. Last of all he wiggled into his work overalls (everyone called them overhalls).

It's colder here than in the Meat Locker.

At that point, George's sensitive nose picked up the smell of frying bacon. It overpowered his nostrils.

Drawn like metal to a magnet, George grimaced, grabbed his shoes and barreled downstairs to the living room. There, the mantel in the *Aladdin* lamp glowed white and seemed to add warmth to the coal fire, inside the glowing *Warm Morning* Stove.

While he laced up his scruffy brown high tops, he sniffed the bacon and his hands shook. He tied his last shoe and sped to his chair at the wobbly kitchen table, steadied at one leg by a piece of shingle. A tired looking brown and green oil cloth draped the table. Worn spots marked territories for plates, platters and the boys' elbows.

When his dad finished the blessing, George dove into a breakfast of two slices of bacon, two scorched fried eggs—his mother's way—a mound of fried potatoes and a manly sized slice of homemade bread. *Oh boy.*

While he ate, his mind wandered. Then his dad said, "Hurry up now, we need to go feed and milk."

On cue, George's face took on a most pitiable look. "Dad, don't you remember what you said last week? You know, about the wind dying down when the sun comes up. Don't you think we should wait a bit to see if that happens?" he asked, cocking his head for effect.

"I don't know. The animals need food and shelter as much as we do, and a good farmer does his chores when they need doing. It isn't right to let the cows go hungry is it?"

"But, it's still dark, so don't you think the cows might still be asleep?"

"Yeah," George's brother Freddy added, "and won't they hate cold hands for milking? Their udders will be like icicles … and we don't want to break any of them off do we?"

"Okay, you guys win. It probably won't hurt to wait a few more minutes. While we're waiting, Veda, I might like to have another cup of coffee."

The boys' mom went to the wood burning *Monarch Range* for

3

the blue and white enamel coffee pot. As she poured she said, "You know maybe we should talk a bit about Christmas. It will be here before we know it."

George relaxed. *Christmas is good. I wonder if I'll get the presents from my dream.* Then his eyes widened as he thought, *Oh no, how will Santa find us?*

"How will Santa know we're at this new farm?" he asked. "What if he takes our Christmas gifts to our old house at Aunt Maggie's place?"

"Well, first of all, I wouldn't think Santa would leave gifts at the wrong house," George's dad said. "I expect Santa has our new address, just like the Post Office does. The old boy has to have some way of keeping track of kids doesn't he? Of course, you boys could send him a note just to be sure."

"That's a good idea," their mom said. "I'll get a penny postcard and a pencil. You can tell Santa where you live now. Why don't you address it to Santa Claus in care of the North Pole? We can mail it this morning."

"But what will we say on the card?"

"Just tell Santa the situation. You know, that you've moved and where the new farm is located."

Both boys nodded. Freddy took the card and after a couple of false starts and some erasing, he wrote out the message in large block letters using suggestions from George and his folks.

Dear Santa,

   My name is John Frederick Burgess. My brother is George David Burgess. We live on a new farm six miles northwest of Wamego, Kansas. It is on Route 1.

   Our barn is red and the windmill is named Aermotor Chicago. We invite you to come here at Christmas.

   Freddy and George

"That's a good message, boys. Now Santa will have your address for sure," their mom said.

Then their dad added, "I do hope he'll be able to make it

from the North Pole this year. What with World War II going on and all those soldiers overseas needing presents, Santa might have to ration gifts in places like Kansas."

Freddy and George looked at each other and then turned back to their father.

"And even if he does come, all this snow could make it hard to find houses, especially out in the country. Stormy weather could make him late, or he might not make it at all."

Oh, no, George thought. *What about my farm set? It wouldn't be Christmas without presents.*

§

Back in March, long before Christmas, our family left the big farm near Hartford owned by Dad's Aunt Maggie (the daughter of Irish immigrants, John I. and Margaret Burgess who brought our Burgess family name to Kansas) and moved ninety miles north to our own place near Wamego. Here we lived close to Grandpa David and Grandma Mary Burgess where our Dad grew up. And it seemed that we had aunts, uncles and cousins everywhere.

The new farm meant a house with our own bedrooms. Down at Aunt Maggie's the four of us slept in two beds—in one bedroom—in a tiny three room house. Now, the new farm's white house had a downstairs bedroom for Mom and Dad and the two of us had separate bedrooms in the unheated upstairs. By December we'd discovered the walls had no insulation and that the windows let in wind and powdery snow.

However, life on the new farm overshadowed the cold—to some extent. Our 185 acres sat in the rolling Flint Hills of Eastern Kansas and we wasted no time exploring every slope, shallow valley and stream.

In the summer, from the house's concrete porch, the prairie view stretched and moved in all directions. Prairie grass moved, the wild flowers moved, and the wheat fields ebbed and flowed like ocean waves. The continuous rows of Osage Orange fence posts seemed to be on the march. One after another, up and down the hills in single file, they separated one farmer's cows from another's.

Peaceful trees, large and small, lined the roads, and milkweed and buckbrush clogged the fencerows. Plants and grasses sparkled in the brilliant sun beneath the bright blue of God's great high-canopied sky.

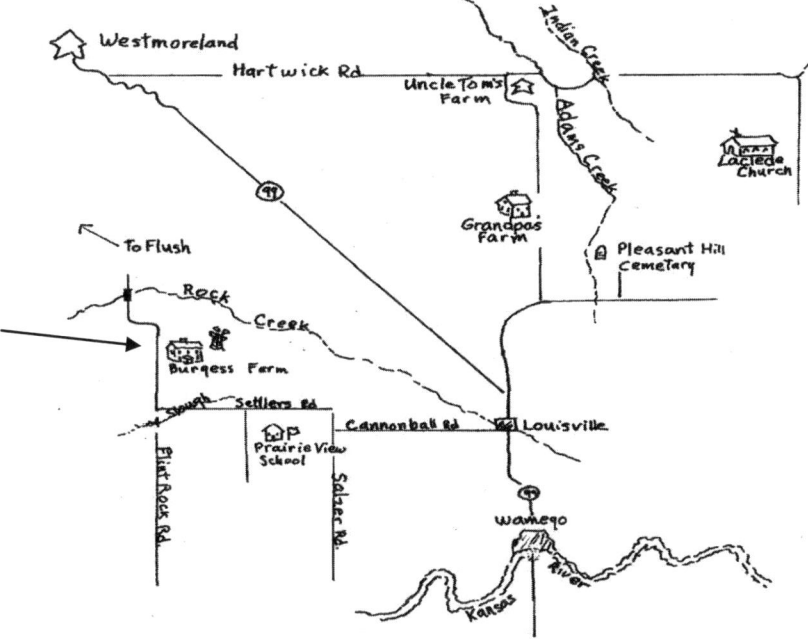

MAP 1 – To the new Burgess farm: (From bottom) Highway 99 to Louisville, left on Cannonball, north on Salzer, left on Settlers Road and north on Flintrock Road. (Note: County Road names added later.)

Now wintertime snow turned the clods and clumps of grass into miniature white mounds, and drifts built sculptured ledges. The drifts filled in the ditches and furrows pulling the landscape smooth.

Winter embraced the barren trees, stark against the white backdrop, while lonely brown stems of prairie grass poked through the soft blanket in golden-tan contrast to the sun-reflecting snow.

To avoid the cold, we spent a lot of time poking around in the two-story barn, the stand alone garage and the sprawling cattle shed with its three-bin granary and a farm shop attached. We inspected the tall, white smokehouse atop the tornado storm cellar that we found dark and scary.

During the summer we'd gone swimming in the clear brook we called the Slough where it meandered between the pasture hills. We'd walked along ever flowing Rock Creek on the farm's northern boundary and listened to redbirds and robins sing in the timber. We'd heard woodpeckers rapping away in the cottonwoods next to the water. In the hay field and along the fence rows we heard meadow larks whistle and we scared up coveys of quail.

During spring and summer, our farm was alive with sunflowers, purple cone flowers, wild roses, prairie potatoes, shooting star and Indian paintbrush. Big blue stem and slough grass waved in the breezes. Shades of green tinted the elms, cottonwoods, hackberries, willows and hedge trees that shared the land.

Now in winter, the huge barn and the cattle shed sheltered our livestock from the wind and snow. The animals seemed satisfied with their refuge, and with their grain, hay and water of winter, plus pasture of summer.

It dawned on us that the pasture contained dozens of cedars with branches outstretched to catch the falling snow and to offer protected perches for the birds.

Hey, a cedar would make a good Christmas tree, in case Santa does come ....

§

DID SANTA INVENT RADAR?

Back at the breakfast table, George stewed. "What if big snowstorms do keep Santa grounded? What if he can't find us?"

Freddy looked at his brother, shook his head and thought, *Dad's just teasing us. I'm sure Santa will find us.*

"Dad, are you saying Santa has problems with snow?" Freddy asked. "He's from the North Pole. Grandma Scott said they have lots of snowstorms there, like in Norway where she grew up. Snow wouldn't stop Santa, would it?"

When his father didn't respond, Freddy had more questions. "Anyway, don't you think he must have radar on his sleigh, like they have on Boeing B-17s? Then he grinned and asked, "Maybe Santa invented radar, huh Dad?"

His dad shook his head and took a deep breath. "Well, nobody knows for sure, but maybe so." Then he smiled. "Or Santa might hook-up that reindeer Gene Autry sings about. What's his name? Oh yeah, *Rudolph the Red Nosed Reindeer.* They say his shiny nose is bright enough to guide the sleighs."

The family sat in silence for a few moments and then the boys' dad walked to the window and looked at the gusting snow. "I sure hope he can make it, but Santa or no Santa, we need to get to work. George, you can drive the tractor for me to get a load of hay for the beef cows. When we're done with that, you feed the chickens while I tend to the hogs and break the ice in the water tanks. Freddy, you feed and milk the three cows. Okay, let's go before the weather really gets nasty."

George sighed, forced himself to his feet and grabbed one last piece of bacon. While his dad and Freddy pulled on mackinaws, corduroy caps with ear flaps, gloves and four buckle overshoes, he stalled.

Finally dressed for the cold, he stepped outside. An icy chill turned his head and stung his skinny body like needles. *I hate this cold. Maybe I'm going to die.* He scowled. *When they find me frozen, I'm at least going to look grumpy.*

"Hurry up you slow poke," Freddy shouted above the wind as he herded the dairy cows toward the barn. "The sooner we get to it, the sooner we can get back inside."

Chin to his chest, George shuffled against wind toward the tractor, its Allis Chalmers' orange exposed against the patchy snow.

Someday I'm going to live where it's warm.

"C'mon boy. Stop stumbling around and get up there on the seat. Open the throttle and give it half-choke," his dad instructed. "Hurry up so I can crank it up."

George grabbed the steering wheel and pulled himself up onto the ice-cold metal seat. His dad spun the crank while his son squinted from under his cap, pulled below his eyebrows, not unlike a freezing sparrow with its head tucked under its wing feathers.

Dang this old tractor. When's it going to start?

Around and around turned the crank. *Hey, it's finally sputtering.*

He adjusted the throttle and closed the choke. The four-cylinder engine smoothed into a purr and his dad hopped onto the drawbar. George could barely reach the clutch pedal, but once he got the tractor going, he drove over the frozen ground in low gear with the hay wagon jostling along behind. At the edge of the meadow, he stopped beside the biggest haystack and his dad starting forking on hay. George sat shaking with the wind piercing through his jacket and gloves. He could have helped load, but ….

For the next few minutes he shivered, until his dad hollered, "Okay, let's go. We'll be done in no time."

Savoring the little heat blowing back from the exhaust, George drove straight into the wind toward the feed lot.

"Look out for that disk!" shouted his dad as the young driver almost side swiped the implement.

At the first hay feeder George dodged two hungry Herefords whose steamy breaths sent cloud-puffs into the frigid air. He stopped and his dad pitched off the prairie hay while hungry cows pushed and shoved to reach it.

With the feeder full, three cows blocked his path to the second feeder. "Get out of the way, we can't feed you until you move." He inched the AC forward, almost nudging a cow. She sensed the threat and gave way.

About ten minutes later, his feet numb and his face without feeling, George drove the tractor and empty hayrack into the shed alleyway. He shut down the engine and went to the bin to fill a can with wheat. He dashed to the chicken coop and the hungry birds.

There he locked his right wrist, tipped the can and executed a rather awkward but speedy arm pirouette, splattering grain against the walls, floor and chickens.

He picked up the frozen watering pan, trotted to the well and grabbed the frozen iron handle. On the fourth pump, water poured down onto the pan and seconds later the ice dropped loose. Another few pumps and he hurried fresh water back to the chickens, just as Freddy and his dad started to the house with two pails of fresh warm milk.

There, they cranked the milk through the DeLaval Cream Separator and then all three farmers went inside to warm up.

Settled with hot drinks, the boys' dad stopped for a moment and then said, "We better go get a Christmas tree. We want a place for presents if the ole Boy does make it. You boys better bundle up again."

This time, Freddy and George were raring to go. And, while they put their cold weather gear back on, their mom gave them some strong Christmas tree recommendations.

THE FREE CHRISTMAS TREE

"Yes, we need a tree," she said, "but for heaven's sakes, if we have to use an ugly cedar, get one that's round and with a pointed top for the star. And, no more cedar limbs propped in a tub of sand, like last year. I can't imagine why I let you tie a bunch of boughs together with baling wire."

You don't understand Mom, it was a tree—and we got presents.

The threesome nodded and moved outside. At the barn, Freddy slipped a bridle and a collar onto the big draft horse Prince. Then the youngster climbed up and rode along a cow trail across the pasture. As the sun filtered through the thin clouds, it brightened patchy strips, with tiny snowdrifts behind each bush, rock and tree.

Overhead, a flock of blackbirds flew in ragged formation from a neighbor's feed bunks to freeload at the Burgess barn. Their black feathers contrasted against the sky.

Freddy announced, "Hey Dad, we should get a big tree."

"Maybe, but remember, we have to get one that will fit in the house. We don't want to upset your mother."

"Dad, look there," George said. "There's one with a nice pointy top like she wants."

Up close, however, that particular Plains Red Cedar, one of the thousands dotting Eastern Kansas pastures and rangeland, was a disappointment. It stood lop-sided with missing limbs.

In truth, most Red Cedars were flawed because of shape and by their dull, brownish-green color. However, Red Cedars had one over-riding quality, they were free, whether seedling size or 20-footers.

With the War in its fourth year, much of the country's resources went into the all out war effort, and not toward growing and shipping Christmas trees. People put any extra money into war bonds to help finance the Nation's arms production. Plains cedars would have to do, and after all they did smell like a Christmas tree.

After an hour, the three found an almost perfect tree. Though a bit small in the boys' eyes, their dad sawed it down, and Prince dragged it to the house. Their dad nailed 2x4s to the bottom to form a stand and inside it went, to their mom's "oohs" and "aahs." The free 1944 Christmas tree, though not a special spruce or pine, came at a very special price.

§

THROWING ON THE TINSEL

Out came our box of decorations from last year, with its Christmas ornaments of homemade items of wood and glue, tinsel and some paper chains strung together. We had no lights for we didn't get electricity until the Rural Electric Administration strung an electric line across Rock Creek after the War.

"George, you and I will set up the tree and put on the hanging things. Be careful with those glass balls," Dad

11

said. "Freddy, you help Mom pop some corn and string it on thread. When you're ready we'll wrap it around the tree along with the colored paper chains you made at school. We can put on the tinsel and the star last."

As the wind picked up and snow started to fall again, Dad stood on a chair and slipped on the tin star. Next, we looped on the popcorn strings and put on chains of colored paper rings in opposite directions.

Mom handed us the tinsel and we started draping the slivery, metallic lengths over the cedar needles, one at a time. The more we worked the more we thought about Christmas and how we wanted it to get here. Trying to rush the great day, we sped up our job, moving from single strips of tinsel to bunches, and before long, we were tossing on handfuls. That is until Mom shouted, "Stop!" We'd been caught.

"You boys quit that this instant! The tinsel is supposed to look like icicles. You go back and spread those bunches out, every last one of them. What's the matter with you two?"

Well, we could have told her Christmas was the matter with us, but we decided to be quiet and do as she said. Mom had been right, for the dangling icicles helped transform our cedar from an ugly duckling into a beautiful swan. To Mom's delight, and our peace, the lowly cedar tree smelled like a Christmas tree like those from her Michigan childhood.

That night, with the combat raging in two huge parts of the world, we sat around the supper table and talked about the sacrifices many were making to ensure the world's freedom. We prayed each night for those who were wounded or had died in battle and for their families, and of course for the end of the conflict. We knew thousands of servicemen and women would miss being home for Christmas.

We even prayed for Hitler and Tojo, asking God to

lead them to end the hostilities, for by this time in our lives, we knew God was all powerful, but that humans sometimes didn't listen and strayed off target.

Of course, as Christmas approached, we thought a little about gift giving and a whole lot about receiving. We couldn't wait to get presents and then share them with our cousins and friends.

What would Santa put under our tree? And how would the folks like the gifts we'd buy for them … when we got around to it? *Say, we'd better go shopping.*

§

EVENING IN PHILADELPHIA

"Dad," Freddy asked that Saturday, "don't you think this is a good night to take us to Duckwall's Five and Dime? We want to buy some Christmas presents. And … could we each have a dollar? That way we could get you something really nice."

The boys' dad took a deep breath and like slow-oozing honey gave each of his sons seventy-five cents. "Now be careful how you spend that. Money doesn't grow on trees you know. Think about what you want to buy. You don't want to regret it later."

Think about it? Okay, how am I going to get three good presents with less than a dollar?

Later, at Duckwall's, the first and only stop, George set a record. He did his Christmas shopping at what some people might call the junk counter. And in less time than it took to cook a soft boiled egg, he handed his selections to the clerk.

"This padlock is for Dad. See, it has two keys. And I got this deck of cards for Freddy. We'll probably play pitch. I know Mom will like this *Evening in Philadelphia* perfume. She'll smell so good. It cost thirty-five cents, but that's okay, because it's in this big bottle."

"Your family will really like their gifts. You made some very good choices," the clerk said and handed George a small sack and five cents change.

"Thanks," George said and smiled at the coin. *Maybe I'll go to the Drug Store and get an ice cream cone.*

A few minutes later, the skinny towhead sat at the soda fountain thinking, *I hope the family likes their gifts.*

§

CHRISTMAS AT ST. LUKE'S

We couldn't wait for the Day. Just next week the celebration would begin with the Christmas Eve service at St. Luke's Episcopal Church in Wamego. As in all coming years we'd sing carols and hear the story that somehow helped us understand that the gift of the Christ Child made gifts a good thing. We also knew that when the service ended shortly after midnight, just a few hours would stand between us and the long awaited Christmas presents.

When the time came, we arrived at tiny St. Luke's long before midnight. There we joined the fifty or so worshipers: the congregation, acolytes, choir and priest.

With the white candles glowing on the white-draped altar, the service started with the opening hymn, *Hark! The Herald Angels Sing.* The song resonated from the thick, white limestone walls, boomed back from the pressed tin ceiling and echoed from the rich wooden pews of the 1896 church.

Brimming with joy, we celebrated and gave thanks. We prayed for peace and for the needy. We remembered especially the soldiers and sailors overseas.

For almost two hours, we sang and worshiped, and sometimes fought to stay awake. Finally, after midnight came Communion and everybody felt the special warmth of knowing God. The service ended when organist Virginia Boyce played *Joy to the World,* with the thundering voices of Cus Johnstone and Jim Boyce floating above the rest. Joy, indeed!

On the way home, we nodded off before our '36

Chevrolet's heater warmed up, and at the house, we dashed for bed to get the night behind us. In a few hours, we'd have presents to give and receive, if Santa made it.

Sometime before sun up, Dad hollered up the stairs, "Boys … you better come on down. It looks like Santa made it after all."

Quickened by our anticipation, we exploded down the chilly stairs two steps at a time to meet Mom and Dad by the Christmas tree. The Aladdin lamp flickered white light off the cedar branches and decorations, and what looked like hundreds of presents around the tree.

"Looks like ole Santa found us all right," Dad said. "Maybe he does have radar. Let's see what he brought you."

For the next few minutes we tore away paper and opened boxes containing army men, a holster set, some books and some clothes.

"Look George, you got the cardboard farm set you wanted!" Sure enough.

Our smiles stretched from ear to ear. How could we be so lucky?

Somewhere along the way, Mom raved about her *Evening in Philadelphia* and the cookie cutter Freddy had given her. Dad thanked us for the padlock and the bottle opener. And of course, we said thanks for all our gifts.

Were we happy? You bet. We were so keyed up that we even saved the tin foil from the wrapping paper for the war effort. And there was more celebrating to come.

After chores—faster than normal—we had a Norwegian breakfast from Grandma Scott's recipes of warm stollen yeast bread with dried fruit and frosting, soft boiled eggs, and lefse potato pancakes. We ate until we could eat no more, and then played with our new toys.

In mid-afternoon, out came the roast chicken dinner with sage dressing, mashed potatoes and gravy, canned beets, more stollen, and for Dad, scalloped oysters with soda crackers. We finished off with pumpkin pie and fresh cream. What a day that was in 1944.

The cold and snow lasted for the next few days, so we had little work of any kind, except for the twice daily chores. We could take it easy and play with our gifts and eat special food with lots of leftovers. Time moved on.

By now we'd adjusted to our new one-room Prairie View School, our surroundings and our daily farm routine. Soon the New Year was upon us, and then spring and summer, when we'd get to know our neighbors better. In the process, we'd also find that one family—the Brockmans—were good people, but also downright peculiar.

TWO

CONVERTIBLE FIELD-WORK CAR, SIMPLE TRUTHS AND AT THE BOTTOM OF THE PILE

[*Wamego Times – May 17, 1945*] ~ AROUND THE COUNTY ~ One of the Oregon Trail markers to be put in Pottawatomie county was set in the Westmoreland Rural High School grounds and a short dedication program was held Tuesday.

A class of 27 boys and girls will receive their diplomas from the Onaga Rural High School on this Thursday evening. Dr. David McFarlane of Topeka will address the class on "It is Later Then You Think."

1945

CONVERTIBLE FIELD-WORK CAR

"Dog gone it," the boys' dad said. "This cultivator won't fit on our tractor. We drove all the way over here to Wabaunsee County for nothing. I wish that sale bill had been worded better. Looks like we're going to have to drag that old horse cultivator behind the AC for another year."

Shaking his head—the trip to the farm sale near Alma had been a waste of gas—he walked toward the gun-metal gray Chevy. "Don't they know there's a war on and we shouldn't do extra driving?"

He looked down for an instant and then said, "Come on boys, let's head to Wamego. We can't do anything about the cultivator, but maybe we can buy some new mower-blade sections."

As he walked on he said, "This War sure makes new parts hard to find. It's tough growing more food with worn out machinery. If we can't find new parts, we'll have to try filing an edge on those old worn down ones."

Listening as always, Freddy asked, "What about those broken sections?"

"Yep, they need replacing one way or another. Maybe we can find some used sections at the blacksmith's if we can't get new ones."

Turning, he looked at George, standing back up the hill fondly gazing at the food table.

"Come on George. We're burning daylight."

"But, Dad …."

George watched the VFW Auxiliary ladies load a table—a discarded barn door suspended on sawhorses—with hotdogs, hamburgers, potato salad, baked beans and more. The meal would be ready when the auctioneer gave the signal for a lunch break.

"George, c'mon! We have work to do."

At last the hungry boy turned and trotted toward the car. Though duty called, he'd give it one more try. "Ah, Dad…."

"Sorry George, we need to get going. Hop in the car."

George inched into the back seat, his nose twitching. His stomach hopped like a jackrabbit fleeing a coyote.

The car turned onto paved Highway 99 and headed north.

Ahead, three crows pecked at a road-kill cottontail. *At least they're eating.* George thought. The birds fluttered up and then settled back down when the car passed.

At the Kansas River Bridge—everyone called the river the Kaw—the car crossed between the high, graceful concrete arches while below a dead cottonwood floated in the muddy water. Heading up Lincoln Avenue past the Elevator and the Mill, the usual array of ton-and-a-half trucks, pickups and cars filled most parking spots.

Because of wet fields on this Saturday, lots of farmers were in town to shop and socialize. Many nodded hellos or waved.

§

In customary fashion, our Dad lifted his index finger from the steering wheel, offering his return greeting. A dirty windshield made some recognition difficult so he nodded at anyone he thought was waving at us; just to be sure he didn't snub anyone.

Across the railroad tracks we stopped at the red light at U.S. 24. We looked east to Abe Eddy's Allis-Chalmers dealership, the very place where Dad had purchased our 1938 Model WC tractor a few years back.

What a day that had been as we watched Dad make up his mind about which tractor to buy. And at noon we ate a store-bought man's meal of bologna, longhorn cheese and bread, and topped it off with soda pop and snowball cakes. Ah, that had been a time to remember. If only we could eat like that again ….

§

I hope Dad gets us something to eat, George thought. *I could eat the north end out of a south bound skunk.* He'd heard someone say that.

As if by magic, his dad pulled his round pocket watch from his overhalls pocket and said, "It's 12:00 o'clock straight up. That's dinner time. Anybody hungry?"

George grinned. He was always hungry, and his breakfast of Malt-O-Meal, toast and Ovaltine had worked its way through his stomach like fat through a stuffed goose. Besides, who ever heard of a farm boy turning down a meal?

"You bet," both boys replied.

Their dad eyed the Victory Café sign on the west side of the street, drove on past and looked back at the Café. Anticipating what might be in the works, George thought, *I'm going to order a hot roast beef sandwich with lots of gravy. I can smell it now.*

"Well, since your Mom's having Club at the house, what you say we grab a bite here?"

Freddy and George looked at each other, smiled and fidgeted.

The Chevy went around the block and then pulled into a slanted parking spot next to Shorty Brockman's '34 Ford. Everyone recognized that car. It stuck out like an elephant at a banquet table.

Shorty had modified his vehicle to use it as a tractor by hack-sawing off the roof and all of side metal above elbow height. On a sunny day things were fine. On rainy days he'd have to throw a tarpaulin over his head. Fortunately, there were enough rusty holes in his floorboard to drain off excess water. Springs showed through the deteriorated seat cloth, so he'd covered the driver's seat with a one by twelve inch board. The car's tires showed little tread.

The boys had seen Shorty plow using a 12" two-bottom John Deere model with the front plow share removed so the car could handle the load. The plowing was a two person job and while Shorty drove, either his wife Louella Ethel or their son Mac (Lulu and Runty) would ride in the back seat to jerk the plow's lifting hub rope upon reaching the end of a row.

Since cars weren't geared for such work, even with a single plow, the overworked flathead Ford V-8 regularly overheated. So Shorty kept a five gallon can of well water in the back seat to refill the boiling radiator. He went through a lot of water.

As the boys and their dad entered the Café they spotted the man himself. Shorty and Runty sat at counter stools, looking over the menu.

"How do, gentlemen? Mind if we join you?"

"Not at all," Shorty said.

"What brings you to town?"

"Ah, Runty … he had to get a tooth pulled. Boy, teeth-pulling is expensive these days. Next time I'm going to do it myself."

Young Runty's neck tightened and he shot a quick glance at his dad. Through his swollen mouth Runty mumbled, "He used rusty pliers to pull my baby teeth, but this is worse. Hope I can eat."

He said he'd try, and ordered the blue plate special with its roast pork, green beans, mashed potatoes, gravy and bread. *Maybe his mouth just healed,* Freddy thought with a grin.

Meanwhile, George went for the hot roast beef sandwich and Freddy ordered the fried chicken.

§

While we waited for our meals, we wondered why Marcellus Brockman went by the name of Shorty. Was it because Marcellus sounded peculiar? Was it because he was a shrimp? Or did his brain only give him short answers?

20

For sure, Shorty talked more than he farmed. If it hadn't been for his good wife Lulu, he'd have been on the County Poor Farm long ago. She kept Shorty in line most of the time, but his man-made convertible annoyed her, especially during foul weather.

Lulu's part-time job helping clean the High School paid most of the bills. She was a good saver, too, while Shorty liked to spend money … if he had it.

I wonder if Lulu knows Shorty and Runty are eating at a restaurant. Bet not.

Lulu even conserved the family's wardrobe with infrequent washings … and it showed. Shorty's heavily patched overhalls were stiff with axle grease, mud, milk, fly spray and several other contaminants. We wondered about his undershorts. Thankfully, on that day, the aroma from the kitchen overpowered Shorty's smell.

Besides foul clothes and odd farm equipment, we often laughed at the way he wore his cap cocked at a funny angle. His dirty, yellow and green *DeKalb Seed Corn* cap gave him an identity of sorts. He looked cocky. Did his swagger cover up his faults … like his dubious military record? He'd done just part of a year in the Air Corps—during wartime! Either way his behavior tickled us. What a character.

§

"Shorty, do you remember when you took me to the hardware store?" the boys' dad asked. Shorty just laughed.

"It was like this boys. I hired Shorty to help haul prairie hay. On the way out of the meadow, we broke the hayrack's tongue."

Freddy, George and Runty were all ears.

"I didn't have a way in to town since your Mom had the car and the truck had a flat tire. Shorty volunteered to drive me to Wamego in his convertible."

Shorty smiled again, nodded and shifted his hat some more.

"We got in Shorty's Ford and he drove us through that cluster of trees coming out of the meadow. To me, it looked like he was pretty close to a limb. I got concerned he might lose one of those fancy side-view mirrors he uses to watch out for cops."

Shorty's head bobbed and Runty smiled and nodded as well.

"About the time we reached the road it happened. Shorty clipped a 12-inch elm and—bang!—off flew the side view mirror."

Shorty reddened a little, lowered his head, then half-cracked a smile.

"And what do you suppose he said?"

A long pause and blank stares followed.

"Well Shorty turns to me and says, 'Oops, there goes another one ....'"

"Ah, that was an accident."

The boys grinned. It seemed like Shorty liked hearing about himself, whether good or bad.

For the next minute or so, no one said anything. During the pause, the café smells were overwhelming. The boys started twitching and spun on their counter stools. *Did the cook get sick?*

Finally the plates arrived and George dug into his meal as if it might be his last. Silence prevailed for a few minutes, and then ....

"You boys see those pies over there? That one looks like coconut cream, and there is a cherry and an apple. Should we have some?"

"Dad," Freddy said, "you know George always wants pie. I might even have a piece of raisin to keep him company."

"Make mine apple," George said.

§

A few minutes later we left the Victory Café and got into our car thinking about the good food … and Shorty Brockman. Pulling teeth with rusty pliers? Farming with a car? Knocking off side view mirrors? Messing up in the Army? No wonder people talked about him so much. Maybe, we'd hide under a cocked DeKalb Corn cap, too.

As Dad backed onto the street, we spied a can of water in Shorty's backseat … just in case. Would Shorty ever learn? And, what about us? What would we be like at his age? It was too soon for us to know; were still growing.

§

GROWING UP LIKE WEEDS

"I can't get over it … you boys are growing up so fast, I just can't keep you in clothes, and with the War on, we have to go easy on things. Just look at all those patches."

A slight frown crossed their mom's freckled face as she stared at her eldest. He stood with slightly rounded shoulders, red hair, freckles, well patched clothes, and for the past two months, wire rimmed glasses.

"Freddy, you look like the Sunday funnies."

Cloth-on-hand-at-the-moment patches—bits from an old tan shirt or from a feed sack—covered the knees and seat of his faded blue overhalls. Pieces of green dress covered the elbows of his Lee work shirt.

On the other hand, skinny George poked up through his overhalls, with his growing outdoing the design limits of his clothing. His ankles and lower shins lay bare below rising pant legs.

Under the weight of his suspenders, George's shoulders sloped downward fighting to contain a body too tall for his hand-me-down garb. Like Freddy, he had patches meant to extend the life of the overalls beyond common sense—or comfort.

"It just isn't fair," their mother complained. "Pretty soon you'll need new clothes. You're just *growing up like weeds*," she said, this time turning her head with a sigh.

The boys stood grinning near the chicken coop. A couple of white leghorns scratched in the damp dirt and a third ran helter skelter, chasing a grasshopper from spot to spot.

The clear and sun-bright sky formed a huge inverted blue bowl overhead. Everything grew in Kansas in the spring. Weeds, crops and the garden—and the boys!—rushed to grow in the warm, humid days and the rain that often drenched the land at night.

SIMPLE TRUTHS

When their mom said they were *growing like weeds*, Freddy looked at George and raised his eyebrows. *Here we go again; another old-fashioned lesson.*

Sometimes her phrases admonished her off-spring to change their behavior; other times she'd give warnings, and there were times of randomness when her words had little meaning.

Their mom's folksy sayings came often, so regular in fact that the boys had come to expect them. She used enough old-time phrases to *choke a horse*; they were *regular as clockwork*. Plus, she figured repetition of these simple truths would cause her sons *to get it right*.

Her sayings did offer them some helpful information and instructions, although Freddy and his mom might face off when she wanted him to do something and he had other urgent plans. Although he never balked outright or flatly refused to do a job, he'd quite often attempt to point out several perceived flaws in his mom's reasoning. For example, the evening it was pouring rain ….

"You go gather those eggs this minute," she said. "If you'd gone before supper like I told you, you wouldn't have to get wet. Sometimes you just aggravate me, you know that?" She tossed her auburn hair and glared.

Though Freddy wasn't too concerned about her aggravation, he did want to show where her logic was in error.

"Gee, Mom, don't I need to wait for this storm to pass? Look at those flashes. You don't want me to get struck by lightning, do you?"

"You won't get hit by lightning. Those streaks are landing clear over by St. George. They aren't even close. You just go get those eggs right now before they get broken. Take the flashlight."

"How are they going to get broken just sitting in a hen's nest? They're resting on straw and will be alright till morning. Anyway, I have to talk to Dad about a farm question. You want me

24

to learn, don't you?"

"Oh, alright, but you scoot to the coop first thing in the morning. And don't try to talk your brother into doing your job." Then she added, "If a skunk gets in there tonight and eats those eggs, I'm going to be really mad. Sometimes you're as *stubborn as a mule*."

This everyday saying implied that Freddy again needed to change his behavior. She wanted him to resemble her idea of the perfect son … which of course he wasn't. For example, to his mom some of his outrageous and unconscious antics made him a *silly goose*.

Mom never lets up, Freddy thought.

George, on the other hand, avoided most of his mother's ire. He did, however, get admonished about his slowness. He was the model of caution, and that lead to snail-like decision making when he contemplated speaking. When he headed to do an uninteresting chore, he'd slowly stumble along at a Three Toed sloth's pace.

"George David Burgess," she would yell from the house, "you just hurry up and feed those chickens and then go help with the milking. Sometimes you're *slower than molasses in the wintertime*. I don't understand how anyone can take so long to throw out a little corn. You just hurry up."

As it turned out, the boys accepted the corrections, directions and encouragements from the simple country phrases that were *meant to do the job* or to make a point. The boys made the most of them, including *growing up like weeds*. Ah, weeds ….

UNSAVORY REPUTATIONS

To Freddy and George, weeds were plants with unsavory reputations. For one thing, weeds showed up in places meant for corn or garden plants like onions and tomatoes. They infested rows of newly emerged seedlings like carrots or lettuce and outgrew those tiny plants. While the average stalk of corn poked along during its first few weeks, one could almost watch weeds grow. They rose like geyser steam. They popped through the ground and appeared to grow inches overnight.

Besides crowding out crops, weeds used up nutrients from the soil. For that reason, the boys' dad called weeds noxious, meaning they were unwanted and an enemy to farm production.

However, some weeds were more than noxious, they were narcotic. Marijuana and datura grew wild on the farm, although most people in Kansas called them hemp and Jimsonweed. Scuttlebutt had it that each possessed the ability to drug a person. In the past, Plains Indian medicine men had chewed Jimsonweed for special stupor-inducing religious rituals and also used them in the healing process, at least according to Freddy's *Four Centuries in Kansas* textbook.

"What does it mean when someone goes into a stupor?" George asked his equally naïve brother. "Get sick and puke?"

"Naw, I don't think so," Freddy said. "A stupor means they get stupid. Maybe …."

"You think Bubba Brockman from school chomped on some marijuana?" George asked with a grin. "He's Shorty's nephew and kind of dim-witted lots of the time."

Regardless of Bubba's behavior, Freddy and George weren't sure what happened if someone tasted datura or marijuana, but knew enough to avoid them. For one thing Jimsonweed grew very well in the manure of the barnyard, and who'd want to try that?

Other weeds offered challenges as well. For obvious reasons the boys avoided stinging nettles and cockleburs when they could. Any trip along the cool, damp banks of Rock Creek meant an encounter with nettles. Yelling, "Look out for the nettles!" was meant to warn the trailing brother to avoid getting whacked by a jagged leaf.

"Dog-gone-it, why didn't you tell me sooner?"

And while nettles were a menace, they seemed tame when compared to running barefooted through a patch of sand burrs. "Ouch, man that smarts. You can't even see them they're so small. I have to sit down and pick them out of my feet."

On the other hand, a few weeds had genuine self-redeeming qualities. For example, some were supposed to have bona fide medicinal properties. Various people said the beautiful purple coneflower, with its droopy petals hanging from the brown, pincushion center, relieved the flu. Black nightshade helped stop coughing, and Indian turnip and willow bark could be used for headaches ... or so the story went.

Some weeds were eye-catching. Pictured on the Kansas Flag, the highly majestic sunflower with its yellow and brown flowers dotted the fields and colored the roadsides and fencerows. The beautiful red-orange blooms of butterfly milkweed seemed to reflect the sun. Snow-on-the-mountain presented a cluster of tiny white cup-shaped flowers set atop stalks with vivid white and green leaves. Bunches of red Indian paintbrush, silver shooting star, and goldenrod also added to the scenic beauty of the prairie, and all bloomed in abundance.

Other fast growing weeds led vigorous lives in Eastern Kansas corn fields. The rains of spring and the heat of summer produced bigger and bigger cockleburs, button weed, smooth dock, curly-leaf dock, lambs quarter, milkweed, wild lettuce and more. Fast growing and deep rooted pigweed and sunflowers reached heights of six feet and beyond. Even hemp and Jimsonweed grew tall.

Regardless of size, weeds in the wrong places had to go. Either a tractor mounted or horse drawn cultivator or similar implement tilled the corn rows—or someone's muscle-power did the job with a hoe or a corn knife.

And, who do you think supplied most of the weed-whacking muscle power on the Burgess farm? Yep, for from the time Freddy was about ten, he and his younger brother did most of the hoeing and hacking. And, that took effort and perseverance. As a day drug on, it begged for diversion ... lots of it.

§

For us, the answer was cornfield swashbuckling that turned into a riotous distraction. We'd thrust and stab and slice our swords like Errol Flynn and other buccaneers, all the while screeching to high heaven.

We slashed our way along corn rows and inflicted physical harm on trespassing weeds, everyone a pirate intent on taking our ship. Some people would say we were playing, but we knew better. We meant to protect our crops for the good of the family, a chop at a time.

§

WE'LL SLIT THEIR GULLETS

"Arrrgh. The pirates are boarding! Draw your cutlass, Matey. We'll slit their gullets!" Freddy shouted as he stepped into a fencing stance with his trailing left arm curled up and inward, his right foot forward and his weapon pointed at the heart of a raider. He jabbed into the marauding button weed and followed that with a whistling slice. Green blood oozed down the severed stem.

"Take that ye blackguard. Yer a scurvy bilge rat, ya pompous gasbag."

"Aye, Captain, tis the rules of the sea they'll learn," Matey shouted back, "Off with their heads!"

Slash, whack, slash. Whack-a-whack. Pause. Whack, slash, whack.

Save the ship for the Stars and Stripes. Slash, whack, whack. Down went a dreadful pirate cocklebur, off went the head of a pillaging sunflower and to a bloody death went an attacking pigweed.

"We've got them now, Matey. Dead men tell no tales!"

"Look at those cowards, they're on the run!" George roared, chasing a cluster of Bluebeard's pigweeds into another corn row. "After them!"

Slash, whack, slash, went his saber and down fell the pirates, one after another and without a scratch on either Captain or Matey—except for the occasional corn leaf cut or a horsefly bite.

"Get that tall one with the yellow eyes, Matey," yelled the Captain. "Over in that row. They're coming over the larboard side. Quick, after them. No brigand shall live. They'll die like dogs," he added, as he took time out to rub corn-leaf scratches on his bare and sweaty left arm.

While Captain Freddy scratched in the heat, Matey George

chopped a pirate in the forward quarter and then dueled with two marauders amidships. Then he hopped backward toward the stern, and felled two more invaders. He cut his way zigging and sagging, that mimicked a demented grasshopper.

With this kind of erratic combat, Matey and Captain got most, but not all of the pirates. Some were missed in the tumult of battle. Maybe they'd die from loneliness.

In truth, the boys fought with sweaty efficiency until large numbers of intruders departed for Davey Jones' Locker, or until the good guys wore out … whichever came first.

"Tis time for grog, eh Matey? Let's swig some rum." the Captain said. "Drink ye fast, the second scoundrel horde is near."

§

In retrospect, our hot-and-sweaty game used lots of energy. For as ship's officers, we spent as much effort play-acting as weed killing. During a break, more frequent as the day got hotter, we sat swigging rum … as light as water … on the make-believe poop deck in the dappled shade of our fantasy ship's hedge tree sails.

Overhead we would often see small flocks of blackbirds heading where blackbirds go, or a cottontail rabbit might pause for a moment, balance on its rear legs, then flip its white bush and hop away.

Sometimes a warm, yet cooling breeze on a sweaty body flowed under the trees. There we'd sit, contemplating life, and our roles in it. Those July days, our jobs were that of weed whackers, and our weapons were corn knives, though we dreamed of when we'd take down the pirates with a cultivator like Dad and our neighbors. We craved to be regular hands, grownups, and we wanted it now. Maybe we did want to *grow up like weeds*.

But, like most farm kids, our first few jobs were unexciting. We'd feed the chickens, pick up eggs or milk a cow. That was farming perhaps, but it wasn't real men's work. We wanted to drive a team of horses or a tractor, but alas, we had to start at the bottom of the pile.

§

AT THE BOTTOM OF THE PILE

Farm kids started handling horses, tractors and trucks at about age ten. But as a rule, George did bottom-of-the-ladder jobs. He toted water to the house, gathered eggs, milked some cows, weeded the garden, and worst of all, he shoveled manure. How he sorrowed over his lowly position in life. It seemed the cows and horses—his enemies—defiantly generated mountains of muck, far faster than he could move it out of the barn.

Shoveling manure was pretty disgusting and heavy work for a kid of nine, especially the soft, wet stuff. Push the shovel into the mess. Fill the shovel, lift it, turn and walk toward door. Give a forward thrust; hold the shovel while the manure keeps moving. Repeat the process until the job is done.

This is ugly. Why do the animals go so much and why are the plops so big? There must be a better way.

In his frustration he searched for alternatives. Then genius struck *I'll use the wheelbarrow! I'll fill it, roll it to the door, and then tip it up. Great plan....*

He trotted to the shed and pushed the single-wheel barrow to the barn. With renewed energy and smiling at his shrewdness, he filled his vehicle and with extra effort struggled to the barn door. *This is so much easier, and look at all the steps I've saved.*

Straining, he lifted the two handles until the load reached center balance. With a deep breath, he flipped it forward to jettison its cargo.

"Fire in the hole!"

Like a boulder tumbling off a cliff, the load shifted away and so did the wheel barrow—and sorry to say, so did George. When he lost control, he hadn't let go. In a flash, wheel barrow, manure and George landed atop the dirty, slimy pile of dung next to the barn.

30

"Dang it."

Indeed, farm boys did start humbly ... and had much to learn about their every day jobs. George stuck with the wheelbarrow idea, but didn't fill it so full.

Beyond animal manure, farming was a rewarding but dirty job. The boys did their best to stay clean but it took lots of effort.

Their parents instructed the boys on washing up before dinner, bathing each week and brushing their teeth. School offered additional advice about cleanliness and sanitation, some of which was hard to understand. Downright hard.

THREE

HI GENE AND LEE SURE, CATCHING A WATER MOCCASIN AND JUST LIKE A HERO

[*Manhattan Mercury* – *August 15, 1945*] ~ PRESIDENT TRUMAN ANNOUNCES JAPAN SURRENDER ~ The world entered a new era of peace today. Along the enormous battle fronts of the Pacific and Asia the mightiest forces of destruction ever assembled rolled to a victorious halt around the prostrate, vanquished empire of Japan.

Throughout the entire Allied world, racked by war or threat of war since Germany struck Poland on September 1, 1939, it was a time for rejoicing and celebration.

1945

HI GENE AND LEE SURE

"Though the war is over, we need to continue doing our part to make the world a better place. For example, we should stay strong and healthy," said gentle Mrs. Draper. "That's why we study health. To avoid getting sick we must eat right, stay clean and use proper sanitation."

She taught the four third graders, George, Marilyn Wagoner and the cousins, Philomena and Pauline Straub, from her small desk in the front of District 82's, one-room Prairie View School House, about a mile walk from the Burgess farm.

George often wondered, *Why do we enter the front door of the school, and step into the back of the classroom?*

From the book *Health Studies for Home and Family*, Mrs. Draper read, "One should observe the standard rules of cleanliness at all times. That includes regular bathing and cleansing before handling food."

As she talked, the early September morning seemed normal. The sun shone in the east windows and high, thin clouds stretched across the blue sky above the tiny building. Down by the pond, a raccoon dabbled for crawdads in the shallow water.

Inside, everything seemed fine until Mrs. Draper's next statement. "It is very important to use proper hygiene."

That word jolted George from his daydreaming. *What did she say? Did she say, 'Hi Gene?' Who the dickens is he?*

George cast a questioning glance at Pauline and Philomena, who returned unknowing and blank-eyed stares. He cocked his right ear and grinned. *This is going to be interesting.*

"In addition, eating correctly is important to health. The government says that one should eat foods every day from the Seven Basic food groups. We need one or more cups of leafy vegetables, one or more cups of citrus or tomatoes, two or more cups of potatoes or other vegetables or fruit, two cups of milk products, one to two cups of meat or poultry or eggs, some dried peas and beans, some bread and cereals, and some butter or fortified margarine. That way our bodies get the needed vitamins and minerals that give us energy to live a healthy life."

Wow, listen to all that food. Every day? That'd stuff a bull elephant. Bet it'd even fill up Bubba Brockman. He glanced toward his oversized schoolmate.

"Furthermore," Mrs. Draper read, "it is very significant and essential to have leisure time; that is, taking time off every day."

Leisure? Time off? On a farm? Who is she kidding?

Another grin turned up the sides of George's mouth and he gazed out one of the windows. A red tail hawk circled in the bright fall sunshine. George could smell the dry grass and maturing corn.

Did I miss something? That book makes leisure time sound normal, like something a farmer should do. Ha, no farmer wrote that book.

As Mrs. Draper continued reading about the strange ideas of hygiene and leisure time, the other students in the tiny school listened as well. The words sounded pretty citified, like *coffee shops, cafeterias, skyscrapers and pie ala mode.* When would the good folks in farm country use words like that?

Just what is hygiene anyway? Like taking our baths?

Most farm families completed that weekend ritual in number 6 washtubs—near the kitchen stove in winter and on the back porch in summer—with a few inches of water that got pretty cool and gritty by the time the last got washed up—George.

We rinse our hands in a wash pan before we eat and change that water every day or two. Is that hygiene?

After class George slowly shuffled toward his seat feeling puzzled. Fourth grader Bubba grinned across the aisle and whispered, "Hey, Georgie, when ya go by that guy's farm, do you holler, Hi Gene?"

Bubba's joke drew a frown from Mrs. Draper, so he turned his head and mumbled from the side of his mouth, "You know … Hi ya, Gene. Do you know Lee Sure?" To avoid laughing, he assumed a wooden pose and seemed to study his social studies book; opened to pictures of Hawaiian hula dancers.

He cracks me up some times, George thought. Without warning George giggled and snorted … and sprayed his desk with moisture and other things. Mrs. Draper glared and assigned him the job cleaning the erasers after school. All this because of guys named Gene and Lee—and Bubba.

§

After school we walked the grassy pasture path toward home and talked about Hi Gene and Lee Sure. How could we keep clean on a farm and where would we find leisure time? All summer long, dirty field work came before time off, except on Sundays and a few holidays and even then we did morning and evening chores. We concluded our folks believed that *idle hands were the devil's workshop*, and to combat that, they kept us busy … and dirty.

We no doubt overestimated the amount of time we worked. Sometimes we hurried through our jobs to get to something fun. Other times, we ended up playing at the work and wasted time. Was that Lee Sure?

Besides whacking marauding weedy pirates, we often turned garden hoeing into clod fights. We even turned the disgusting job of beheading and butchering chickens into fighting off Viking raids.

However, sooner or later we finished our jobs and went off to play bare-handed catch, or other fun activities. We might have batting practice with broomsticks and gravel, play cowboys, tunnel in the hayloft, maybe take a horse tank swim or even enjoy such relaxing pursuits as fishing. Fishing and all such activities were great ways to find that guy, Lee Sure—even though Hi Gene sometimes suffered.

§

CATCHING A WATER MOCCASIN

Back in early summer, eleven-year-old Freddy had headed off on his first solo fishing trip. With a fresh cut 4 ft. dogwood fishing pole over his shoulder, he walked down the dusty road toward the ever-flowing Slough. Along the way finches and sparrows twittered in the hedge trees.

Striding along in the sunlight he reached the mailbox corner and waved to neighbor Frank Cotton, disking a small triangular patch of ground using his three-horse hookup. Behind the team the tandem disk cut through the rich slough-bottom soil.

To the east, like a dromedary's hump in the road, sat one of the slough's bridges. Freddy's dad, as a township board member, had requested this new bridge be erected with the surface set five feet above the water and the top even with the road. However, what the county workers built was a foot too tall for they measured the five feet to the bottom of the foot thick bridge and erected a twelve inch speed bump.

Beneath the bridge and for a ways downstream, shimmered a pool the size of four wagon boxes, full of fish—or so Freddy hoped. He sat on the bridge and looked into the old pork and beans can at the dozen night crawlers he'd spaded from beside the iris bed.

He lifted out a juicy wiggler and slipped it on the huge, double-aught catfish hook—he couldn't find a smaller one—and flipped it into the water.

In a flash, something knocked the line, first one way and

then in several directions. It danced like a fly on a cobweb. *Got one.*

He snapped the hook out of the water. *Drat, I missed him.*

The instant the hook hit the water a second time it wiggled and teased like flirting girls at a pep rally. Freddy jerked harder but still came up empty.

The third try brought more frantic nibbles and this time he gave his pole a violent yank, and again stared at the empty hook.

I've got to try harder. I can be faster than a fish, can't I?

Next try the fish hit the baited glob and Freddy executed a bone-jarring hook-set. Again the line had an empty hook as it snapped toward the sky. The jerking knocked his shapeless St. Louis Cardinals cap into the stained water. *Dang those fish.*

Shaking his head, he reached for the hat now floating away, and belly-flopped down into the Slough's pool. Splash!

"Arrrgh."

He rolled over and sat up chest deep in the cold water that back-washed against him. Disgusted, he waded out with his cap in one hand and his pole in the other.

Just as he stepped onto the bridge, a huge cottonmouth water moccasin gyrated under the bib of his overhalls!

Terror struck; Freddy's body jumped up and down and back and forth. Once, twice, three times, the snake's deadly fangs jabbed his stomach and then his hip.

Death seemed seconds away. The fisherman's body contorted out of control. He felt light headed.

Mr. Cotton pulled his team to a halt and ran toward the struggling young neighbor. "Freddy, Freddy, what's the matter?" Frank yelled, shaking Freddy by the shoulders. "Did something get you?"

Trembling, Freddy nodded yes and then stared as a wiggling, crawling lump worked its way out of his left overhalls leg. At his shoe top a shiny, slimy wet head poked out, followed by a slippery body. It plopped into the dust.

At that moment—he'd never seen a miracle before—the poisonous reptile morphed into a miniature bullhead catfish the size of a hotdog.

Its three tiny barbs pointing straight out had punctured like fangs. A miracle indeed.

Freddy took deep breaths, attempting to regain his composure. He, Mr. Cotton and the three horses eyed the dust-dredged fish not knowing what to do.

At last, the kindly neighbor said, "That looks like a real nice little bullhead. You know, that was an amazing catch, considering that you did it without a pole."

Huh? I did catch a fish didn't I? He smiled, but said nothing.

The horses said nothing, though perhaps the big gray, Dan, shook his head when Mr. Cotton said, "You must be a pretty good fisherman to catch a fish while sitting in the fishing hole."

As the horse nodded another horse fly away, Freddy took deeper breaths and realized he wasn't going to die. Bit by bit his brain came back to life, and then it hit him. He certainly had landed a fish without a hook or a pole. In a strange sort of way, his first-ever solo fishing trip had been remarkable..

He tossed the bullhead back into the stream. Maybe he'd catch it another day … and hopefully with a hook.

Freddy's Lee Sure adventure made for a good story to pass on to his friends and cousins. It was surely something to brag about. After all, he confronted a *mighty reptile*, like famed *Sea Hunt* actor Lloyd Bridges, and survived. Freddy felt like a hero. *Yeah, I'm just like a hero.*

§

JUST LIKE A HERO

At ages 11 and 9, heroes were essential to us. Being *like* our heroes kept us busy and out of trouble most of the time … although playing heroes could interfere with work.

Still, we hoped for chances to somehow save the day, and to do right. Our role models were men like Dad, Uncle Alfred, our Grandpas, Uncle Luther Andersen and Uncle George Scott. Another in our hero category was

Great Uncle Tom Burgess.

Raising six children made Aunt Helen Gordon, a hero and our Sunday school teachers rated high on the list. A special hero was Great Aunt Mollie, who opened up her home to children and adults alike.

We knew of war heroes like Gen. Jimmy Doolittle, and fellow Kansan, Gen. Dwight D. Eisenhower.

And neighbors like Wally Hoffman, Romanus Heiger and Frank Cotton—and later Herman Elder—Cousin George Burgess, Bill Mansfield, the Riats, John Habluetzel and Leo Scully and his boys inspired us. Big league ballplayers inspired us for sure.

We were so thankful to have the Heigers as our close neighbors. Romanus, Inez, Marie and Rose were on the scene to help us move in on that raining night in March of '44. That easily made them our heroes. The Graf family lived just south of us on the Daylor Place, but we didn't get to know them well before they sold out, moved to town and Frank Cotton and his mother moved onto the farm. During the ten years on our farm, on the Daylor Place would live the Grafs, the Cottons, Joe and Dorothy Straub and the Kensings.

As a young man our Grandpa David was heroic when he saved a lady with a runaway team of horses. Yes, Grandpa was a hero but, had we been asked who our favorite heroes were, they would have been movie cowboys.

When the family went to Wamego most Saturday nights to sell cream and eggs and to shop, the two of us dashed, with twelve cents apiece, for the Columbian theater. We'd climb the long set of stairs and sit through a double feature starring Tom Mix, Tex Ritter, John Wayne, Alan Hale or maybe Johnny Mack Brown. Sometimes we'd see Gene Autry, Roy Rogers or the Lone Ranger and Tonto. These heroes taught us the film version of right from wrong. And they showed us how to look good while doing it.

Each wore denim jeans, western cut shirts and most

had big, white Stetsons that never got dirty. Tom Mix could fight and fight and never lose his hat. Of course, the bad guys wore black hats and ended up fighting bare headed with their hair sticking out like the wet dogs they were.

Our movie heroes never lost because they upheld right … and … because their pistols never ran out of bullets. They shot and shot while the dastardly bad guys got caught when they'd stop to reload. Our heroes' horses galloped and galloped and never grew tired.

Our good guy heroes were fair and never acted rude or cussed. And they never mistreated women—or more importantly, horses—and they never failed to help the unfortunate. The real heroes always rode off into the sunset to save the girl with the red-gold hair. They simply hated wrong and always made things right. Many of our heroes could play guitars, sing and yodel.

Bad guys, on the other hand, were just that. They ignored the rights of others, were rude and even killed for no good reason. They robbed and rustled. They were hard drinkers in saloons and they cheated at cards. Maybe they deserved the fates that awaited them.

Through all of this, we learned unwavering rules of fair play, at least the movie kind. Only the lowest of the low would shoot someone in the back, or kill just to be killing. Every a quick draw hero routinely let the bad guy go for his gun first.

§

THEY'S GONNA PUMP YA FULL O'LEAD

"Did you see in the show last night how Hopalong Cassidy waited to draw until after that bandit fired?" Freddy asked. "That was dangerous. Why would you want to get shot by a bad guy who is going to hang next week anyway?"

"I don't know," George said. "Hoppy should have drawn

when the other guy went for his gun, like Randolph Scott does. He's the best quick draw … unless it's the Lone Ranger."

"They are both faster than Gene Autry, but that's alright because Gene sings," Freddy said. "Anyway, Gene will be in next Saturday's show with the Sons of the Pioneers. Man, they are good."

Music reached the older son. When Autry sang *I'm Back in the Saddle Again* or Roy Rogers crooned *Happy Trails to You* Freddy sat spellbound. He liked to hear Rex Allen and Jimmy Wakely too, but the blended voices of the Sons of the Pioneers moved him the most. He'd risk his dad's wrath and stay for the second showing to hear *Cool Water* or *Tumblin' Tumble Weeds* again.

While Freddy enjoyed westerns, any film with music touched his soul. He couldn't get enough of Spike Jones' band with songs like *Der Fuehrer's Face* from the sound track of a Walt Disney anti-Nazi cartoon. He liked the Andrews Sisters harmony when they played themselves in wartime movies and sang *Boogie Woogie Bugle Boy of Company B* and *Don't Sit Under the Apple Tree.*

George liked music, if the songs weren't too long. In fact he often 'entertained' his brother by strumming the large scoop shovel in the barn and singing Little Jimmy Dickens' creations like, *May the Bird of Paradise Fly up Your Nose.* But if the music came with dancing, hugging, and kissing, George sank low in his seat and moaned.

What he really appreciated were the old time movie comedies. His favorites were Laurel and Hardy, Abbott and Costello, and western comics Gabby Hayes and Smiley Burnette.

With puckered lips, wrinkled nose and gumming mouth, George imitated his hero Gabby. "Now, lis-en 'ear, yon' fella … you can't go fight with an empty gun. They's gonna pump ya full o'lead!"

Another of George's heroes came not from the movies, but from a comic book. Red Ryder rode his black horse Thunder from one adventure to another, through desert canyons and down the cactus trails, with his lever-action Winchester Model '73 at his side. In one frame he might hold it in his left hand as he swung his right leg across Thunder's back, or it might point the way when he scaled a canyon trail to search for outlaws.

Both boys traced and retraced Red's steps and those of his

sidekick Little Beaver until their single comic book wore dog-eared. Happily, the *Topeka Daily Capital*—it came a day late in the mail— also printed a Red Ryder strip in the funnies, and rain or shine, one boy or the other would volunteer to make the half-mile round trip to the mailbox to collect the paper and the mail.

The boys concluded Red *looked like* a real champion hero. In the colored comics of the Sunday paper, Red stood straight and tanned, wore a Stetson that turned up on the sides, and he had a square western jaw. He had strips of brown rawhide dangling from round silver fasteners of his wide scalloped chaps. When he walked from frame to frame, huge Mexican spurs left dotted lines in the dust.

Red wore a red cowboy-cut shirt across his broad shoulders, and a yellow kerchief circled his throat. Only a real cowboy hero would dress like that.

The boys thought soldiers, sailors, and flyers dressed right. In the Saturday night newsreels, they wore uniforms that made them look the part. Some servicemen and women home on leave came traveling through Wamego. Young people had to cheer for them, didn't they? The boys felt all service people were heroes, and that included schoolmate Bubba's uncle, Private Shorty Brockman—until the truth came to light.

SHORTY BROCKMAN OF THE ARMY AIR CORPS

On a Wednesday morning about two months before the war ended the boys' dad, his brother Alfred and neighbor Wally Hoffman bumped into each other at the Wamego Grain Elevator. Rain during the night put the brakes on field work and gave them an excuse to head to town for feed, machinery parts or maybe to get a flat tire repaired. A couple of blocks from where they talked, the Kaw flowed bank full carrying floating logs, downed trees and other debris. Dark, heavy gray clouds filled the sky.

"When I load up these salt blocks, I might go have a cup of coffee up at the Café. You fellows want to meet me there?" the boys' dad asked.

"Sounds good to me," Wally said. "Come on Alfred, you can get that case of oil after while."

Five minutes later, with farmer efficiency, all three drove a circuitous route and parked in front of the Victory Café. Inside, they ordered coffee.

"I'm telling you those donuts look mighty good. Maybe I'll have me a couple," the boys' dad said.

"Me too," echoed Alfred and Wally.

Soon all three sat sipping black coffee in squatty brown mugs and munching on hot and sugared raised donuts. "You know what I'm going to do one of these days?" the boys' dad asked. "I'm going to buy me a whole dozen of those donuts and go out in the alleyway and eat them all."

Both Alfred and Wally smiled, but said nothing. After downing half a donut, Alfred changed the subject. "Did you look at the lumps of mud dotting the streets? It looks like somebody marched cattle through here."

"You can't drive to town on unpaved roads and not pick up mud. Every fender that comes to town drops a load," Wally replied.

"The roads were a mess this morning. I was glad I had the chains on. The slough was over the road down by our mail box and water ran down the middle of the road in one place," the boys' dad said. "It's good for the corn though. We sure did need the rain."

"Well, we need the corn. America has a lot of hungry folks to feed when you think about the state of the world after all this War," Alfred said.

The other two nodded and the three talked on about the War, still raging in the Pacific Theater and about men they knew who had been in the service, including Leo Scully's sons, sailors all.

"Say, you know what I saw last week?" Alfred asked. "I saw Shorty Brockman strutting around like some kind of hero. Did he even serve in the Army? He had an Army belt around his overhalls."

"Yeah, he's strange." Wally said, "He got drafted late last year. I guess he didn't plant enough acres to get a farm deferral. Even though the War was over in Europe, the Army still needed men. He wasn't in very long though, and never went overseas."

"I hear they sent him over to Smokey Hill Field at Salina to learn how to fire the ball-turret machine guns on B-17 bombers," the boys' dad said. "Shorty, being small, was a perfect fit in that bottom turret; at least that's what the Army thought. But he never flew any combat missions. Do you know why?" Then he held up his hand to signal to the waitress that they needed more coffee. "I'll just have half a cup," he said.

As the girl poured, he unconsciously pointed his finger at the spot on his cup that he felt meant 'half.' For some unknown reason most coffee drinkers did that. An experienced waitress couldn't possibly know what a half a cup meant.

"Well, there are lots of rumors, but I guess Shorty never finished training," the boys' dad continued.

"Here's how I heard it," Wally said. "He did pretty well during Phase I of his training. They gave him a shotgun to shoot from moving flatbed railroad cars at stationary targets. This was to teach him how to lead enemy fighters, much like when you hunt ducks or quail."

"Then what was his problem?"

"Well he'd hunted his whole life, so he scored pretty high with the .12 gauge, though one day he got careless and riddled the red gunnery range safety flag. He had to go see the colonel, and ended up on the Parade Field walking off punishment tours with a full pack on his back."

The three men looked at each other, smiled and nodded understanding.

"Anyway, his troubles really got started after two weeks of ground school. Shorty was scheduled to make his first training flight in the Flying Fortress, but you both know he could foul up a one car funeral procession. For one thing, he had a fear of flying and of getting air sick, plus he approached his shooting kind of careless, like his farming."

"I think I'm beginning to get the picture," Alfred said.

"On that day of his first flight it was really hot and the air was bumpy. Shorty didn't like crouching on his knees with nothing but the ball-turret's glass between him and the ground, plus he was sweating like a dog. He'd also over filled his stomach with mess hall food and it was fighting to stay put."

"Oh oh," the boys' dad said.

"Well," Wally continued, "after takeoff he got to feeling sick, and just when the target tow plane rolled into position Shorty's stomach got worse. He was supposed to aim and fire at the towed target sleeve. About the time he'd figured out the lead point, his meal started up and out."

"Goodness," said Alfred.

"He reached for his airsick bag and pulled the trigger by mistake. His twin .30 caliber machine guns spouted flame as advertised. Shorty's aim was off and he hit the PT-19 tow plane square in the engine, sending oil spewing all along the fuselage. Thank goodness he didn't hit the pilot, who released the target, shut down the engine and glided to a safe landing at the Field."

"Was that the end for Shorty?" Alfred asked.

"Well no, but the colonel gave him another severe reprimand and more tours around the Parade Field. Due to the needs of the War, Shorty got still one more chance, though the colonel told him if he made one more screw up and he'd be heading to the infantry."

The story was getting very interesting.

"The end came just before his next flight. During preflight, Shorty started thinking about coyote hunting with machine guns, and as he fiddled with his equipment, he poured 20 rounds into an empty storage shed."

"Back in front of the colonel?" the boys' dad asked.

"Yep."

"More punishment tours?"

"Yep, plus Shorty ended up getting a psychiatric evaluation. When the shrink got done with him, the Army concluded he was more dangerous to the country than the enemy and sent him home to mess up farming again. So before he had ever learned how to put a good shine on his combat boots, he was back in Wamego strutting around and telling war stories of how tough it was in the Air Corps."

"I have noticed that he doesn't dwell much on the airplanes, or gunnery, or punishment tours, nor his general discharge," the boys' dad said, "but spends most of his time talking about his sleeping quarters, his uniform, the mess hall, and the latrines he got highly familiar with, although I heard he never passed an inspection. Finally the Army gave him the boot."

Each man took another sip of coffee in silence and paused. Then Wally continued.

"Shorty said he didn't earn any medals, but if the Army had *really* needed him, they'd have made him an officer … because the colonel kept asking for him."

In truth, no one but Shorty thought he was a hero, or could possibly be an officer—or even a PFC. He had trouble learning and didn't do the Army any good. Shorty's Army experience and his farming as well, left a lasting impression on the boys as how not to do things.

But, how would they learn the right lessons of life? Just where would Freddy and George gain this knowledge? It certainly wouldn't be from Shorty Brockman.

It turned out that the boys would be shown life's lessons by their family, neighbors and friends—and from an organization that would forever leave its positive mark on them, 4-H.

FOUR

TOE DANCING, BLACKJACK'S THE NAME AND CORN-STARCH SQUARE DANCING

[*Wamego Reporter – March 14, 1946*] ~ WANT AD'S: ~ FOR SALE ~
>115 acre Farm, immediate possession; 500 hen laying house; Grade A dairy barn; stock barn; silo; attractive 6-room house; electricity; good water. W. L. Haas, Wamego.
>Roan Milk Cow, 5-years-old, fresh soon. Price $80. P. M. Coleman, Belvue, Phone 1506.
>DeLaval Cream Separator in fine condition; wood or coal cook stove; Pure Bred Duroc Gilts. Chas. Banks, Phone 159 or 1614.

1946

TOE DANCING

"For our recreation tonight we will see some toe-dancing by club member Bubba Brockman's cousin," Blackjack 4-H Club Vice President Carol Harrell said. "Our guest, who has taken dance lessons for more than two years, will demonstrate something that takes a lot of effort and athletic skill … perhaps as much as basketball or even six-man football."

Huh? Freddy thought. *Toe dancing? How could that be like a football game? I'll bet this is going to be something.*

George thought, *Why would anyone want to dance on his toes?*

"Parents and boys and girls let us welcome our guest, Miss Wanda Brockman." Polite applause followed.

Up front, 4-H member Pat Clary cranked a Victorola and put the needle down on a fast turning 78 rpm record. It belted out scratchy longhaired music, with violins sounding like bagpipes, and what might have been tubas going rubba, tump, tump, tumpty, tump in an attempt to cover up the screech, or so the boys figured.

The boys thought, *A pair of fighting tom cats sounds better than that. How can nice people listen to it?*

The sound escaped through open windows of the St.

46

George schoolhouse into the warm June night just as two poor-wills—nighthawks of the goatsucker class—darted around gleaning moths that hovered near the single bare-bulb street light. A mongrel dog, several houses away, howled as the noise intensified.

"Man, that stuff is awful," George whispered. "That junk sounds like the time our cow Hazel stepped on that striped cat!"

Freddy nodded and as he started to make a wisecrack, his mouth snapped shut for through the door came Bubba's thirteen year old cousin, Wanda, wearing a ballerina outfit.

Holy cow, look at that, Freddy thought. Almost ten year old George squirmed and looked away.

The performance clad female inched toward them with little shuffling steps, then floated a bare arm upward, elbow first, with the forearm and wrist ratcheting along in increments. Once she extended the arm she flipped up her hand, only to let the fingers sag downward like leaves on drought-stunted corn.

MOVING AND SHIFTING

For the first time in their lives the two sheltered farm boys saw a girl dressed in a brief satiny get up. *Good gosh!*

As the music tumped, the young female pulled up onto the tips her toes and teetered for balance in pink satin slippers. After a few seconds, she seemed to lose her perch. In an attempt to regain her balance she took little mincing steps, similar to the tightrope walker at the Kansas Free Fair.

Over and over Wanda appeared to grasp at the air above her head to help pull up onto a toe-tip roost. Again and again, in night crawler fashion, she recoiled downward, landing with her feet flat on the floor. Once more she shuffled for control, and thrust herself back up onto the tips of her toes. Perch, titter, splat.

Throughout her perching and splatting, she undulated first left and then right and spun some, shifting her tiny pink outfit.

Speechless, Freddy's eyes stayed glued on the scene.

At last the record stopped, and so did Wanda, almost at the same time. Glistening with perspiration, she took a slow, strained bow and shuffled from the room. Soft applause followed, and a couple of adults shook their heads.

On the other hand, Freddy sighed while a couple of impolite kids snickered. The entertainment that began with shock and astonishment, ended with silence and some relief.

Could this be good for the younger children? Some parents appeared to wonder.

In the final analysis, even though Wanda had worked very hard, many in the room concluded that toe dancing fell far short of a good ball game.

§

Many years have passed since our first introduction to 4-H, and Wanda's toe dancing. However, what we've described here is how we remember that meeting's program and its impact on the two of us. Growing up in rural solitude, we were unrefined and naïve. In fact, the only girl we had ever seen in a swimsuit was our cousin Nellie Ann.

We realized later that Wanda did a superb job of dancing, and we now applaud her performance. She added culture to our lives, even if we didn't appreciate it at the time.

§

In truth, the cultural exposure for Freddy and several of the growing boys had been quite revealing. George? He was more flabbergasted than pleased.

Then George remembered how, a few months earlier, the family discussed 4-H for the first time. He never dreamed what it would be like. In fact, back then, he didn't have a clue what 4-H was.

WHAT IS A 4-H CLUB?

Before sunrise on Valentine's Day, their mom's birthday, the two boys had rushed downstairs and handed her a Duckwall's Store sack with an apron inside. "Oh my, what a pretty thing. Look at those flowers. Oh, thank you boys. You make me so happy."

"We knew you'd like it, Mom," Freddy said. "And it only cost 50 cents. Didn't we do a good job of shopping?"

"Of course you did. Now I'm going to make you a special breakfast, and I'll wear my new apron. So go help Dad with chores while I work on the meal."

An hour later, the boys and their dad came in from the cold. Their cheeks tingled in the warm room while the thin, late-winter sunrise highlighted the scene through the east windows. Together they sat down at the much-used kitchen table.

"Freddy," his dad said, "it's your turn to say grace, and then we'll dig into breakfast."

His eldest nodded and said the regular blessing, "Come Lord Jesus, be our guest, and let this food unto us be blessed. Amen."

During grace, George mouthed the words and sniffed the platter of buttermilk pancakes. His nose wiggled and twitched. Maybe his relatives' jokes of him having a tapeworm were justified.

Regardless, at the 'amen' George claimed two skillet-sized pancakes and passed the platter to his mother. "Thank you," she said. She then took one pancake and passed it on around the table.

At that point, well-mannered conversation ceased while the family savored the cakes covered with homemade butter and clear Karo syrup. They observed the farm-country rule: *Eat first, and talk later, if there's time.*

On this morning, the family could relax after breakfast for snow mixed with rain during the night modified the work plan. For a change, the four of them could talk together, and enjoy what there was of the February sunshine.

"Boys, your Mom and I have talked about getting you into a 4-H club," their dad said. He poured another cup of coffee from the old pot and added, "I spoke to Chet Harrell the other day and he said they're starting a 4-H club at St. George. Mrs. Lila Clary and Mrs. Edith Hofman of St. George have agreed to be the leaders."

The boys' mom added, "I guess 4-H is a good thing for farm

kids. I'm in favor of anything that helps young folks use the abilities God gave them. Nothing's worse than being useless."

"What is a 4-H club?" puzzled George asked.

Freddy said, "Bubba Brockman said it has something to do with four leaf clovers and heads and hands and herds ... things like that. It has meetings and helps you learn about farming, and there are lots of kids there, too. And you get to lead calves around the show ring at the Pottawatomie County Fair. And pigs, too. And you can be recognized for your efforts."

"Wait a minute, how are you going to lead a pig? With a rope? What kind of pig would let you do that?" George asked

"You don't lead pigs, you dope. Bubba says you guide them with a cane. If you make 'em look good for the judge, you might win a ribbon."

"I don't understand," George said.

"Well, we'll just have to find out, won't we?" their dad asked with a slight grin and a glance at his wife. "Why don't you let us take you to the meeting tonight and maybe we'll learn what to do?"

"Oh, doesn't that sound like fun?" their mother asked. "That way you can decide if you want to join. And isn't that a great way to celebrate my birthday?"

"I guess maybe I should go, I might learn some things," Freddy said. *Hey, this will be a great place to meet some kids my age.*

With some hesitation, George nodded yes. Many long hours later, after chores, supper and birthday cake, the family drove the six miles to the St. George Schoolhouse for the first meeting of the new 4-H Club.

FIRST 4-H CLUB MEETING

There, in the gymnasium, Pottawatomie County Agricultural Agent Harvey Goertz, several adults, and 27 kids milled around until Mr. Goertz asked for everyone to be seated.

"Thank you all for coming, and special thanks to Mrs. Clary and Mrs. Hofman for putting this meeting together," he said. "Tonight we'll form a 4-H club here at St. George, and you young people will join the more than a million and a half rural members across the country. Now, while we pass out these pamphlets, do you have any questions?"

Someone the boys didn't know asked, "Who can join 4-H?" After Mr. Goertz said members could be between the ages of 10-19, Freddy asked, "Do the 'H' letters on the 4-H clover symbol stand for Head, Heart, Hands and Herds, like Bubba Brockman said?"

"Well, your friend had it almost right though the last 'H' is for health. The green clover emblem means 4-H is to help improve farm and home practices with new ideas about health, safety, livestock, grain, gardening, homemaking and cooking. Each year, you'll have a project and experience the 4-H motto: *To Make the Best Better*. Another aim of 4-H is to teach excellence and to develop rural leaders."

"How does a 4-H Club work?" someone asked.

"Clubs hold monthly business meetings followed with a recreation period. There are also field days to teach members how to manage projects. Some projects can be exhibited at the County Fair in Onaga every August."

§

While Mr. Goertz talked we wondered about being in 4-H. Would we get to have a baby beef like Bubba had said and lead it around the show ring at the Fair? Where would we get a calf and how were we supposed to take care of it? The idea of leading a calf didn't sound easy.

We remembered when we'd run down our milk cow Maudie's big calf, looped on a make-shift halter and tried to lead him back to the barn. It turned out he was better at leading then we. After he dragged us around awhile, he escaped. We spent the next half hour trying to catch him, all the while calling each other names like 'dope,' 'sap' and 'stupnagel.' We even mentioned some bodily waste terms in creative ways. After a lot of running, we did retrieve the rope and let him go, but that made us question the whole

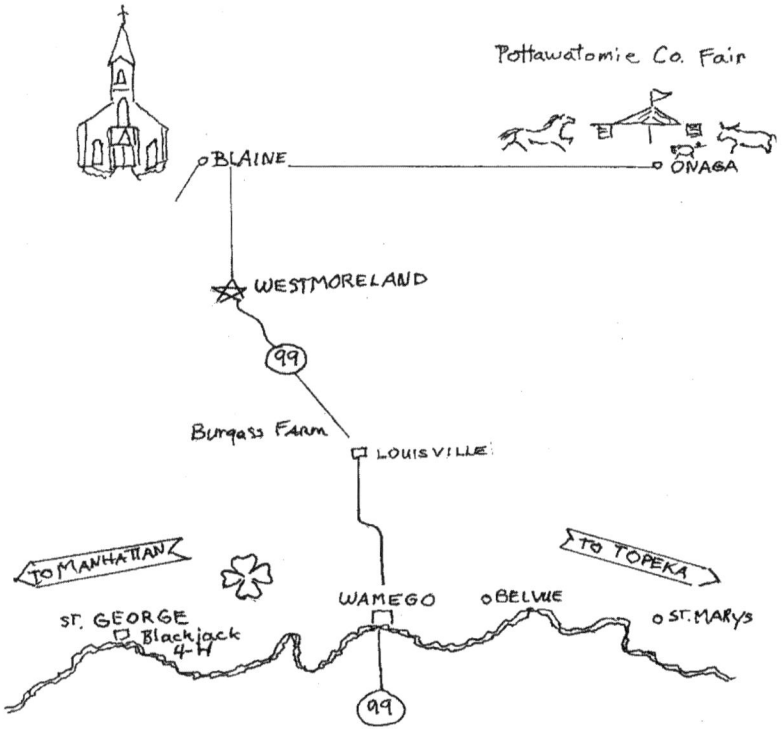

Map 2 – Shows St. George Blackjack 4-H Club birthplace, County Seat Westmoreland and Onaga, the home of the Pottawatomie County Fair.

idea of show ring calves.

Besides wondering about projects, we were curious about how a 4-H business meeting might run. This was our first one and it seemed like no one knew anything about it.

As we listened we heard that kids were to keep project records about feed costs and weights. How could you do that? If your calf is in with the rest of the herd, how do you track its feed costs? Things sounded complicated.

Mr. Goertz announced that Mr. Raymond Hofman and our Dad had agreed to be the adult male leaders, along with Mr. Don Clary. Then, when he asked for a show of hands of who wanted to be a charter member, everyone decided they did. So the next step was to elect officers.

Dean Duncan was elected President; Carol Harrell, Vice President; Marvin Hofman, Secretary; Mary Walters, Treasurer; and Tom Peters, Reporter.

We ended up voting for strangers. We only knew Bubba, and we sure wouldn't waste a vote on him. In the end, we just went along with the crowd.

§

BLACKJACK'S THE NAME

At that point, Mr. Goertz helped the president run the first meeting. They skipped the reading of the minutes and the Treasurer had nothing to report. Next, they skipped old business and went to new business. What should the new club be named?

"I think we should call it the St. George 4-H Club," Marvin Hofman said.

"Hey, how about calling it the Bombardier 4-H Club after my Uncle Shorty," Bubba said. "He was trained to be a bomber crew member." Several kids laughed. Some adults smiled while others frowned. Shorty's unflattering military record had spread throughout the County.

At that point, the new President said, "Let's call it the Blackjack 4-H Club after Blackjack Creek and the spring that you can hear flowing into the concrete horse watering tank outside. Someone stood and moved that the new name be the Blackjack 4-H Club.

Bubba hollered, "Second," and everyone voted in the affirmative. The Club had its name.

§

PLEDGING 4-H IDEALS

Though we didn't know it in the beginning, joining a 4-H Club meant we committed ourselves to some pretty heady and sometimes scary ideals. At each monthly meeting all of us promised to live by the 4-H pledge, "I pledge my head to clearer thinking, my heart to greater loyalty, my hands to larger service and my health to better living, for my club, my community, and my country."

At first the ideas of loyalty, service and better living seemed vague. And some wondered, why the pledge didn't mention anything about projects and fairs. After just a few meetings though, we understood we should better ourselves, our family, our community and our country ... and as was added later, "the world." And after we accepted the 4-H pledge, we'd learned how it all made sense.

Through 4-H, our lives took on some inspiring principles, and we wanted to use our talents. We promised to work to make things better, and at learning, doing, earning and serving ... though the earning part was slow in coming. After a couple of meetings we started catching on.

§

At a later meeting, the President ran the meeting according to the manual. The Treasurer reported the Club had $12.89.

When the President asked if there was any unfinished business, Donna Jean Cogswell moved that the club picnic be on Saturday August 24th and be held in the park across from Blackjack Spring. During discussion, someone said the date was just after the Fair and someone else said that was okay. Since no one else had anything to add, all the members said 'aye' and the motion passed.

Picnic setup details were approved, and then after the announcements about the following meeting and a County Fair update, the business part of the meeting ended.

Now it was time for recreation. Recreation could be a talk, a quiz game, singing, *toe dancing* and the like.

One evening Mary Howard led recreation and Donna Cogswell and Pat Clary served cookies and Kool Aid. Carol Harrell led the singing of *Home on the Range* from the 4-H Songbook while Donis Clary played the piano.

At each meeting, different members brought refreshments. One night, the Club had unexpected 'entertainment.'

CORN-STARCH SQUARE DANCING

The Vice President said, "Tonight we have a treat for our recreation. We're going to teach everyone how to square dance."

George squinted. S*quare dance?* He'd seen his folks do a few dance steps in the kitchen, but it didn't look square.

"May I introduce Mr. Loren Goyen of the State 4-H staff," Carol continued. "He will tell us about, and teach us how to square dance."

"Thank you Madam Vice President. Let me begin by talking about the history of square dancing. Some of you know square dancing is very popular at the moment. It is like a dance they used to do in France. Now a teacher from Colorado has even taken square dancing to Japan. In this form of dancing, four couples do the motions that the caller asks for in time with music. I'll explain that before we start the record."

George looked at Bubba who showed a laissez-faire attitude and then at his brother. Freddy seemed puzzled, and drew a square with his finger.

"As I call the dances, I'll say such things as, 'bow to your partner,' 'allemande left' or 'right,' 'promenade,' or 'dosey-do.' Also, you'll be asked to do things like swing your partner, form a square and move clockwise or counter-clockwise."

George pulled on his right ear, looked at his watch.

At that point, Mrs. Hofman spread corn starch on the gym floor to help the dancers' shoes move more easily. Donna Jean Cogswell, Carol Harrell, Dean Duncan and five other members volunteered to demonstrate how to dance the steps.

"Alright, take your partner's hand and move around the circle. Now dosey do, back to back."

Huh?

"Now let's try some of the dance moves." Mr. Goyen said to the volunteers.

"Let's begin with the dance, "*Backrack*" and then do *Birdie in the Cage, Seven Hand 'Round, Cotton Eyed Joe* and the *Texas Star.*

"In Backtrack, I'll call:

Allemande left like a hinge on a gate. . .

Right to your pard', and right 'n left eight.

Corns in the crib, wheat's in the sack . . .

Meet your honey and turn right back.

Up the river and around the bend. . .

The other way back, you're gone again.

Now you're right, you can't go wrong. . .

Take her this time and promenade along."

Finally it was time for others to try square dancing. George paired up with a much older girl, who did her best to keep him on the dance floor.

Then all of the sudden it happened!

In the middle of an allemande left, George lost his grip and spun into the open arms of a grinning Bubba Brockman, who shoved him like a coiled spring across the corn-starched gym floor. George spun on his high-top farm shoes and tried to stop. The next thing he knew he was skidding on his stomach toward the refreshments table.

"Look out!" he yelled just as he slammed into a table leg. Strawberry Kool-Aid and the punch bowl flew. Sweet red liquid soared, spread out and on the way to the floor drenched the hapless dancer.

Sploosh. In a flash, his white dress-up shirt turned a curious shade of scarlet. His mom looked on in horror. *That boy! I'll never get that shirt clean. And just look at that mess.*

George sat stunned, his face color matching the Kool-Aid.

The startled dancers stopped and stared, and though the music continued, the caller fell silent. Bubba laughed. When he laughed a second time, so did everybody else, except for George.

It wasn't my fault.

While not always a quick thinker, George felt a brainwave. He flipped off his shoes and started skating across the pink floor in his socks. Bubba and Freddy joined in and soon half a dozen younger kids took up the challenge to 'help cleanup.'

Finally, some parents found a mop and shooed the kids away while they wiped up the liquid. Meanwhile, the boys' folks headed for the stairs with their sons in tow.

"I'm really sorry about the punch," their mom said to the leaders. "I'm glad the bowl didn't break. Right now, we need to take these two scalawags home and give them a bath"

And so ended square-dance lesson number one.

§

When we analyzed it, we learned a lot of good lessons from 4-H, about square dancing and how to run a meeting. There were demonstrations about things like how to oil a saddle and about cooking. We did have the chance to experience some interesting and varied recreation.

On the more serious side however, we still had a great deal to learn about 4-H, and responsibilities—and life in general. As the months clicked off, we'd be taught many important lessons by many people.

One memorable lesson—not connected to 4-H— came on St. Patrick's Day, right there in Wamego.

FIVE

EVERYBODY IRISH, BABY BEEF DECISION AND I'LL HEAD 'EM TOWARD THE DOOR

[Wamego Times – March 14, 1946] ~ Wamego Wins Meet ~ Saturday night was the climax of the basketball tournament when the Wamego basketball team was proclaimed champion of the regional meet which was being held here. This entitled the Wamego team to place at the state tournament at Salina, which started last night with Wamego playing Garden City. If the game is won, Wamego will again play at 8:50 Thursday evening with either Smith Center or Iola.

After trailing 7 to 4 at the end of the first quarter, the Wamego Red Raiders walloped the Chapman Fighting Irish 50-32 in the Regional Finals.

1946

EVERYBODY IRISH

"You boys are up to something, aren't you? You look kind of ornery to me. Yep, you look mighty guilty."

The speaker was Great Uncle Tom Burgess, brother of the boys' Grandpa David. Uncle Tom lounged against a stack of oats in burlap sacks. "Of course since you're Irish, that's expected, isn't it?" The boys looked at each other.

The family character *full of himself* continued, "So what brings you to the mighty Wamego Elevator today? Are you buying?"

"We came with Dad to get some seed potatoes. He says we have to plant 'em today," Freddy said. "We wanted to do something fun, but now we have to work even though it's Saturday."

Yeah … and it's too darned cold to work outside, thought George

"Of course you have to work. This is St. Patrick's Day when everybody Irish needs to plant their spuds. Why my Pop, ole John I. insisted that we get ours in the ground on March 17th every year. Sometimes we stayed home from school to help."

"Why St. Patrick's Day?" Freddy asked.

"Surely you fellows know why St. Pat is so important to the

Irish. He's the guy who drove the snakes out of Ireland, so planting on his day makes sense, doesn't it?"

George cocked his head like their dog, Pep. *What do snakes have to do with potatoes?*

"Folks in the old country planted taters to honor St. Patty, and if it's good enough for them, it's good enough for us. What people say is that the potato eyes work really well today. That's important, too, because potatoes need to see which way to grow."

"Huh?" George asked. "Potatoes don't have eyes, do they?"

"Well, it might not look like it to you, but those little dimples on a potatoes are eyes. Once I even had one that needed glasses. Worked, too, as it grew tall after its vision improved."

That's hooey, Freddy thought. "Potatoes don't wear glasses."

"No, not many do, but if you find one that doesn't know which way to grow, you have a problem, don't you think?"

Watching and listening to this great story teller, the boy's dad looked at his kids, nodded his head slightly and masked a grin.

§

We laughed as usual at Uncle Tom's comments, and one joke led to another. He was another of our heroes. When he started to tell us about putting muffs onto corn ears we'd had enough and changed the subject.

However, we always puzzled most of all at his reply when we asked him which was better, Irish or English. He told us, "Well now boys, if a cat had her litter in an oven, you wouldn't call them biscuits would you?"

What in the world does that mean?

We asked him about our great grandparents John I. and Margaret Burgess. What were they like?

With a flourish, he related how they came from Ireland to America the month after their marriage and took up a homestead of eighty acres up along the Wheaton road. He said it had more rocks than any other farm land in Pottawatomie County, but it was good for raising kids. Most of their seven children had been born there.

We appreciated the coming-to-America story, of how John I. and Margaret had left home after the potato famine had killed more than a million people, one in four. He said the Irish, living on tiny tenant farms grew mostly potatoes and when the blight hit, it was deadly.

Our great grandparents had come by ship to New York and then by train and steamboat to north of the Kansas City area. Great Grandma Margaret's uncle and aunt met them and took them by wagon more than one hundred miles into Kansas to their place north of Louisville. The newcomers had been amazed by the size of their relatives' farm, but weren't so impressed with their tiny log cabin.

It wasn't long before John I. walked 50 miles to Topeka and filed a claim on the 80 acre homestead. He paid a $15 fee for the land.

They'd soon built a small cabin of their own—with an Irish-style thatched roof—and started their family. Their children were; Irving, John, and Alex who died at 18, followed by our Grandpa David, then Aunt Maggie, Aunt Mollie, and finally, Uncle Tom.

Our Grandpa David married Mary Anna Shea in 1897 and continued the Irish line. And although we had Scottish and Norwegian blood from our mother's side, our family looked to the Land of St. Patrick for our identity.

§

When the stories ended, the boys' dad loaded the seed potatoes into the trunk of the car and said goodbye to Uncle Tom. On the way home George daydreamed.

It's too cold to work outside today. I'll freeze my ears. Besides, I don't even like St. Patrick, but I better not tell Uncle Tom that.

"Dad, we're not from Ireland," he said at last. "Why do we have to do what they do? St. Patrick didn't drive away our snakes."

As he parked the car, his dad said, "Well, regardless, we need to get these potatoes in, so I'll disk the garden and George you go to the shed and get the spade and a hoe. Freddy, you plug that sack of seed potatoes into a couple of milk buckets. Be sure to leave a couple of eyes in each piece."

A few minutes later George traipsed to the garden with the hand tools. Overhead a skein of geese flew north and he eyed some sparrows, fluffed up against the cold. At the garden, he watched his dad steer the Allis Chalmers up and down the small field.

Gazing out the kitchen window, the boys' mom smiled. Her husband disked, her older son plugged potatoes and her younger son leaned against a fence post. She smiled again.

Unaware of his mom, Freddy sliced each potato into three pieces, leaving at least two of eyes in each plug. In ten minutes he'd filled one bucket and started on another.

"Bring that first bucket over here and we'll get them in the ground," his dad said.

The sun barely warmed George's ears and nose as he continued to take it easy against a fence post. His dad spaded out a row of holes and Freddy placed a potato plug into each, eye side up.

I wonder if cowboys plant potatoes, George thought.

After a couple minutes of his brother's idleness, Freddy thumped George with an egg-sized piece of potato.

"Ouch."

"That's what you get for not helping out. It's no wonder you get cold."

"Your brother's right. Grab that hoe and fill in these holes," his dad ordered. "Tamp the dirt when you're finished."

George shuffled to work and dragged some dirt into the first hole. He scanned the sky for more geese, and then bit by bit mounded the loose dirt over potato number two.

His dad wiped his brow and eyed his son's slowness. Shaking his head he said, "Son, those potato plugs are going to dry out if you don't work faster. Knuckle down."

George nodded and inched dirt into another hole. His dad screwed up his nose, then grabbed the hoe to finish the job. In another hour all ten rows were planted.

"Okay men. Now it's up to the Good Lord to send the rain and sunshine. With his help, we can eat new potatoes by May."

At the eat word, George stopped his mindless wanderings and sensed the stimulating aroma from the kitchen.

"It's almost noon, so let's go have some dinner and then you boys can clean the tools and put the things away. Leave the disk outside and put the tractor in the shed."

His sons nodded, and he added, "I'll be gone this afternoon. There's a regular Farm Bureau board meeting in Westmoreland."

§

After a quick wash up on the back porch, we sat down at the kitchen table to a meal of corned beef hash and vegetables. We topped off the meal with Mom's chocolate cake; she'd baked as her appreciation for a job well done.

All during the meal, we waited to hear Dad's afternoon work instructions, but none came. Instead, he studied over some Farm Bureau papers. He finished his cake and said he had to go.

"You boys do what I told you."

With that he informed Mom he'd be back by milking time and then steered the old Chevy out the lane. Would we have an afternoon without a farming project, or would Mom put us to work? She never said a word.

We were home free. Just a little clean-up and we would be on our own. Out the door we went.

§

JUST KILLING TIME

After the meal, George cleaned the tools and buckets and put them away, while Freddy drove the tractor to the shed and unhooked the disk. He parked the tractor and stood in the shade to watch a mother bobwhite quail lead her brood to drink at a puddle near the stock tank.

"You've got a lot of chicks, Mrs. Quail. You did a good job," he said as each marshmallow-sized bit of fluff dipped its beak, tilted back its head, and let the water run down its throat.

… nine, ten, eleven, twelve…. Your camouflage is good. It better be, nesting on the ground like you do. Do you lack odors like baby deer?

He watched the clutch file into the grass along the corral. Then he turned to see George coming. "Hey bird brain, what's up?"

"Maybe I'll go down to the slough and swim."

"In March? Dumbo, you can't even stand a cold bath."

George shrugged and headed toward the barn.

Freddy followed and both boys started throwing gravel at posts, at last year's dried weeds and whatever else made a good target. *We'll probably be Big Leaguers some day.* His next rock bounced off the gate post and hit George in the leg.

"Quit that. You are always throwing something at me."

"It was an accident. It bounced off the gate. Anyway, if you weren't so slow you wouldn't have been in the way."

George frowned and Freddy said, "Don't step on one of those cow pies or you'll blame them on me, too."

George dodged the barnyard manure and walked inside the barn alleyway. He maneuvered around some cobwebs and started up the creaky hayloft stairs.

SNAAA-KKE!

When his head inched above the hayloft floor he came eye to eye with the world's largest black snake, lying in the loose hay coiled like a rattler. George froze and so did the snake.

George gasped, his body went limp and dropped like a plane in a death spiral—whacking square into Freddy.

"Ooooof."

A huge spaghetti-like tangle of four arms and four legs landed in a billow of dust near the bottom of the stairs beside the hand-cranked corn sheller. "Uuumpf. Ouch. What the heck are you doing?"

"Snaa-kke. It's a snake."

"Where's the snake?" Freddy asked.

"In the haymow … right by the stairs."

"Ah, snakes won't hurt you. They keep mice and rats out of the corn crib. Let me look."

Freddy crept up the ladder with caution. Nothing.

"You're a coo-coo. There's no snake up here. What is the matter with you? Good grief."

"Well I saw one."

"If there was one he's long gone by now."

"Wait! Over there, under that hay, there's his tail!"

Freddy sidled over to the spot, and jerked up the end of a four foot length of black garden hose, and banged it against a beam.

"Here muffin head, catch!"

George threw his arms up to ward off certain death and dived onto the hay, only to watch the rubber hose plop lifelessly onto to the haymow floor. *Well I thought it was a snake.*

BABY BEEF DECISION

The excitement over for the moment, the boys moved across the floor to the big double-wide hayloft door and sat down facing the house. Their legs dangled outside. Below the light March breeze ruffled a Barred Rock hen's feathers.

She scratched with vigor at the barnyard litter. 'Cluck-a-cluck' commands coached her chicks to look for bugs and beetles.

George didn't see the hen for his attention was focused elsewhere. "Smell Mom's bread?" he asked, looking at the house.

"Yeah, it smells great … better than those cow patties."

Silence followed and up near the cattle shed a downy woodpecker knocked on a fence post. Below, a few flies warmed on the barn's south side.

"You know," George said, "this is better than work. I get tired of doing work all the time. I wish work would be easier."

"You want to work in a store or herd cattle with a horse?"

"Yeah, I'd like to be a cowboy, but we don't own a horse."

"Well, cowboys work with cattle, but it's not easy. But I think I'd like doing that, too. I like cows and calves. Say, maybe we could raise some steers for our 4-H projects."

"Is that being a cowboy?" George asked.

"Sure it is. It would be easy, too. Why I could raise a calf standing on my head."

Your head is certainly big enough, thought George.

"The 4-H calls them Baby Beef," Freddy said. "I read that in that brochure we got. It showed a picture of a guy washing his calf and one with a girl leading her calf in the show ring."

"I don't get it," George said. "Wouldn't a calf run away if you threw cold water on it?"

"Maybe you don't use really cold water, and all animals like a good brushing."

"I don't know …."

"Well, the first thing you're supposed to do is teach your calf to lead. Then you can tie it up, wash it and then groom it."

"Groom?"

"Yeah, make its coat look pretty. And you're supposed to feed it and care for it. At Fair time, you lead it around the show ring for judging. That sounds like fun. Let's do it."

George said. "A calf would drag me around. Besides, I'm not old enough to do a 4-H project am I?"

"You're old enough, and you have to do something if you want to be in 4-H. Projects are what 4-H is all about; they're good learning experiences. It says so in the pamphlet."

"I already did a project, I learned to square-dance at 4-H."

"That was just for fun. Projects are like raising animals."

Freddy dreamed. *I'm at the Pottawatomie County Fairgrounds and there's a big crowd cheering for my calf and me. Bet I'll get a blue ribbon for sure, and maybe even the grand champion purple.*

Meanwhile, George thought, *That bread sure smells good.*

"How about showing vegetables?" George asked.

"Yeah, we could grow vegetables like potatoes, but don't forget, you whined to hog heaven when we planted ours. I think a calf is the best idea. Dad can let us have a couple from the beef herd.

Let's talk to him tonight."

George didn't say no, which probably meant yes.

GETTING SOME HELP

After supper that evening, the boys found their dad reading the farm reports in the *Topeka Daily Capital*. He looked up when they entered the room and asked, "What's up?"

Freddy smiled and said, "We'd each like to raise a Baby Beef for 4-H, wouldn't that be good for us?"

"Well, that might be a fine idea if you'd really do it. Do you think you want the responsibility? Raising beef means you will need to buy a good feeder calf and raise it into a 1,000 pound steer."

"We can do it, Dad," Freddy said. "The 4-H project brochure tells us how and you can give us tips. And then in August we can take them to the Fair. And, I'll bet we win a ribbon or two."

"I see. Well, the first step is to find the right calf and then buy it. That's going to cost some money. How much do you have?"

"Oh, c'mon Dad, you know we don't have any money," George said. "But, maybe you could loan us some until we sell the calves in the fall."

Their dad looked down at his paper and said, "We don't have much cash lying around, but we might be able to find a couple of good young steers in our herd. There are some pretty good calves, if you know what you're looking for."

§

In truth, we didn't have a clue, including what we were getting ourselves into. We were penniless amateurs with no experience. Still, the small 4-H pamphlet made Baby Beef projects look easy. We could do that, couldn't we?

The next day the three of us stood in the feed lot with the sun giving some warmth. We struggled to tell which of the 15 young feeders would be the best. We finally relied on Dad's judgment.

"That's a good one there," Dad said, pointing at one of the biggest Hereford steers.

Okay, just how did he know that one's going to be alright? How do you know what a calf will look like in a few months?

To us, the calves looked pretty much alike. They snorted, and had runny noses and huge appetites. And there were messes all over the corral. *Is this a good idea?*

"You don't want that one; he's too small and won't grow as fast as the others."

Disregarding size, the only other difference we could see was the color. At least we had something to go on.

§

ALMOST HANDSOME IN CALF SENSE

At last Freddy—getting antsy and impatient—moved around the herd frowning and fidgeting. He had to make a decision. He didn't like looking dumb. This was taking too long. If only ….

Wait, there next to the fence.

Freddy zeroed in on a good looking steer … almost handsome in a calf sense. Intrigued, he grinned at the smallish, almost *white* Shorthorn. Freddy made a snap decision.

"I definitely want that white one. There won't be a prettier calf in the show. Everybody likes white," he said, trying to reinforce his fuzzy thinking with more words. "I'll get a blue ribbon for sure."

His dad stood still, and then taking a deep breath thought, *Well, I guess he's got to learn.*

"Are you certain that's the calf you want?" he asked. "Are you convinced it'll grow as much as that Hereford over there?"

"Sure, he will. He'll just have to grow faster that's all. I'll just feed him in a hurry-up way." Then he added, "I'm going to name him Don 'cause it rhymes with one. Yep, Don's the One."

While his dad sighed again, George eyed the remaining steers. Finally he pointed toward Don's twin, a somewhat bigger calf with lots of red and a few little white spots.

"That's the one I want."

"What you going to call him?"

"Irish Tom, after Uncle Tom. No I'll just call him Tom."

Now the boys owned Tom and Don—had some debts—and the fun began, according to the 4-H brochure. The first step: *Train your Baby Beef to be gentle.* That meant the calves' owners had to get close to their projects, a trick all its own, as they discovered the next day.

I'LL HEAD 'EM TOWARD THE DOOR

"I'll head 'em toward the door," Freddy shouted to George who stood on the other side of the barn. "You stay there and cut them off if they come your way. Better be ready, they're looking anxious."

He inched forward to pressure Tom and Don toward the open barn door. Eyeing Freddy over their shoulders, the stubborn calves edged into a walk—right past the door—then trotted and by the time they reached the barn's corner, they galloped.

"Look out, they're coming your way. You have to turn them back. Wave your arms or something."

With heads down and tails flying straight out, Tom and Don barreled around the next corner and straight at skinny George. Dust flew. In desperation, George flapped his arms and jumped at the bolting calves. "Hi-ya, hi-ya."

Zigzagging around the ten-year-old cowboy, Don moved left, right, left while George went right, left, right. Tom copied Don's moves and kicked up his back heels. They thundered to the far end of the huge corral.

George tore after them. "Dang you calves." He ran about 50 fast yards and gasped to a stop.

Tom and Don, in complete harmony, stopped when George stopped, and then moseyed to the northwest corner of the lot and began nibbling at the sparse spring-green grass.

"You have to be louder than that you noodle brain," Freddy yelled. "C'mon, give me some help."

"I'm trying to," George hollered back. "You've got 'em all worked up with your yelling. Calm down." *What a knuckle head.*

Red-headed and hot tempered, Freddy circled behind the calves to force them back toward the barn. It worked; however, peppy Tom galloped south and peppy Don dashed north.

"See, you can't make 'em do what you want either," George shouted. "We're never going to get them in the barn. We've been at this for forty-five minutes." *Is this really fun?*

Freddy adjusted his wire-rimmed glasses and then stood hands on hips, miffed at the calves and at his brother, while Tom and Don looked for more grass.

Maybe they'll come for grain.

So while the morning sun flooded the scene and several gray pigeons watched from the barn peak, he walked to the grain bin and scooped some ground corn and oats into an old tin bucket. As sparrows twittered in the hedge trees, he inched toward the calves.

Wide eyed, Tom and Don glared at Freddy, who moved nearer without making eye contact. Then, at about ten feet away he stopped. His farm-boy sense warned him to not move.

Don sniffed the air and Tom stuck his long tongue out the left side of his mouth and wiped his upper lip. They didn't budge so Freddy poured some feed on the grass and stepped away.

(Left) Freddy holds Don, his whitish steer. George has the twin Tom. Don earned a White Ribbon and Tom a Red.

"Okay guys, I'm backing up now so you can try that grain."

With Freddy outside of their discomfort zone, the projects went forward and sniffed the grain. Don nosed it and looked up with a grain covered yellowish-white muzzle. He swiped his wide tongue and tried another mouthful. Tom followed suit. Plan B was working.

During the next three days the calves moved, like Hansel

69

and Gretel along the crumb-trail in the forest, toward the barn door. On the fourth day the calves walked right into the milking parlor. They were nervous, but with more lunch, they let the boys touch them. While they dined, the boys slipped on rope halters for the first leading lesson.

In George's case it was like pulling a loaded farm wagon with an oblong wheel. Tom stood, legs locked and his weight leaning back. George jerked, tugged and sweated, until his steer moved a few steps. Then Tom balked again.

"Dang it Tom, come on," the frustrated boy said to the not-so-baby-beef. "You've just got to learn to lead. Come on. Let's go. This training is supposed to be fun for both of us."

Freddy struggled with Don, but before long both calves got the idea and started to act like pets. They followed, stood with patience, took to grooming and washing and accepted getting set-up—the manual explained all about it—with feet even and backs straight so they looked broad and full of muscle. The boys were proud. From a distance, so were their folks.

Everything moved slowly toward the August Fair, scheduled for a few weeks later. For Freddy and George and their steers, it would be the experience of a lifetime. But for now the boys had to contend with normal farm work, as well as training their projects. It was one of the most exciting times of the year on and off the farm.

The 4th of July was approaching, and Wamego celebrated Independence Day with pride and style. A carnival, fireworks, parade and displays captured those of all ages. What a time it would be.

SIX

A TOM CAT FROM THE SKY, CARNIVAL LURE AND THE LOCAL BOY

[*Wamego Reporter – July 4, 1946*] ~ VICTORY CELEBRATION IN WAMEGO ~ The mammoth Victory Fourth of July celebration is all set; and it's going to be the biggest and best ever held in Wamego. The Legion boys have been working hard for weeks.

The baseball game between Alma and Wamego will start at 2:30 P.M. Henry Eichman's fireworks committee has secured an unusually fine display of pyrotechnics. The popular Wamego Township Band will present a concert in the Bandstand at 7:00 P.M. with Howard Harms directing.

1946

A TOM CAT FROM THE SKY

Freddy wind-milled his pitching arm, rocked back on his right leg, kicked his left foot high and posed like his hero, Boston Red Sox pitcher, Tex Hughson. It looked like Tex was going to win 20 games during 1946 and his picture sometimes appeared on the *Topeka Daily Capital* sports pages. Who wouldn't want to be like him?

I might be able to look like that … but can I learn to pitch? Freddy wondered. *Will my name get on the sports page? Will I be a star?*

His imagination ran wild. He smiled, cleared his throat and *announced* a crucial Red Sox game.

"Ladies and gentlemen, we're in the late innings. The winner of this game will clinch the Pennant. The Red Sox are holding a one run lead, but the Tigers have the bases loaded with nobody out. It's time for a pitching change. All eyes are on the bullpen.

"Wait … well would you look at that? Red Sox Manager Joe Cronin is calling on his rookie relief pitcher, Freddy Burgess. This is Burgess' first game. Will he be up to the challenge?

"… it's all over, folks. The Red Sox have won the Pennant. Burgess tallied nine strikeouts! His team is carrying him off the field.

He's waving to a cheering crowd. The applause is deafening…."

Although twelve-year-old Freddy didn't pitch for the Red Sox that day, he dreamed of being a great pitcher. But for now he'd practice and practice. And on this particular day he could celebrate Independence Day at the same time.

Bunching the muscles he had, the young farm boy assumed his stop-action stance and, instead of throwing an imaginary baseball, he fast-balled a Silver Torpedo across the corral into a barn's sliding door. The fireworks exploded on impact, booming like a Fort Riley howitzer. The earth went silent, the hush deafening.

Swallows glided to perch unseen in the barn's high shaded alleyway. English sparrows dropped in mid-flight like stones to hide in the hedge trees and from the barn roof pigeons just disappeared.

At the hen house the White Leghorns and Plymouth Rock cackle-stanzas ended in half phrase. The chickens cocked their heads sideways, triangulating the blast's origin.

Every last bug froze in mid-crescendo and dived beneath leaves and litter, except the poor unfortunate flies near ground zero on the barn door.

"Whoopee! Isn't that something? Boy, those are loud. I heard that one echo clear down at Rock Creek."

§

This day was July 4th and we joined hundreds of others shooting fireworks. Year after year, we impatiently waited for the special chance to make lots of noise and leave evidence of the explosions.

Curious about the Silver Torpedo's impact, the two of us crossed the corral as wafting smoke drifted from the door into the hazy morning. With each step grasshoppers jumped and clattered, escaping the terror.

At the barn, we smiled at the black smudge on the faded red door and then talked more about fireworks; what we had and what we wanted … and of course how we should handle them.

"Do you think it's a good idea to throw Silver Torpedoes at the barn?" George asked. "Couldn't they cause a fire? You know we're supposed to be careful."

"Naw," Freddy said, once again justifying his actions. "They just explode. There is no flame."

"Well okay. But remember that the folks want us to think before we set anything off," George replied.

The folks had drilled their sons about safety and both boys tried to be careful, though with a few lapses. *I'm not gonna take risks like some kids do,* Freddy thought. *No, I've got to use common sense.*

Then he hurled a lighted Thunder Egg toward the barn. Boom! Smile! *If it's going to boom, make it a good one.*

Freddy then looked around and spied a Van Kamp's pork beans can beside the fence. "Hey, throw me that can. I'm going to send it to the moon," he ordered his younger brother

Frowning, George tossed over the can and then moved behind a skinny post. *I'm taking cover.*

"What you scared of? I'm not going to blow you up. Besides you are five times wider than that post." His brother said as he set up his next explosion.

Like Maxine Straub's hair, Freddy braided the short fuses of a pair of two-inch Thunder Egg firecrackers and slipped them under the dented can. With a steady hand he touched his smoldering cork covered punk to the fuses and stepped back a couple of paces. Sparks flew and a hiss sounded from his rocket propellant.

The wait was short. With a boom, the can bloused out like a nail keg and the space vehicle took flight. In knuckle balled up near the barn's crest.

Below, Freddy admired the launch crater. *See, that sure wasn't dangerous. How could anybody get hurt doing that?*

Meanwhile above him in the hayloft's double-wide door stood a spooked gypsy tomcat. Just minutes before he had felt secure where he'd established squatter's rights. Now however, Claws (as the boys' called him) stood with his back arched, eyes wide, body stretched basketball size, with his tail imitating a leafy elm tree branch in a heavy wind.

The rising tin can veered off course, bounced off the door frame and whacked the terrorized tomcat on the bridge of his tail. He bellowed, spit, snarled and true to his name, shoved forward every claw. He snarled again and leaped from the loft.

Below, Freddy crouched over his rocket's crater just as the bruised tomcat plummeted down. It's landing site? The highest spot below—Freddy's back!

Claws landed with full force, kicking and scratching. When the assault ended the gigantic gypsy dashed full speed down the road toward the Riat place, never to be seen again.

Beside the barn, Freddy swatted at his smarting back and hopped on one foot and then the other as if dodging a swarm of bees. He rubbed and hopped, and then hopped and rubbed, all the while clinching his teeth. Blood soaked through his T-shirt.

Dang! Where the heck did that cat come from?

Gazing through the kitchen's screen door, Freddy's mom saw the commotion. Seeing him flailing in pain and with blood on his hands, she did what mothers do. She grabbed the iodine bottle and a rag and headed for her son.

"John Frederick Burgess, sometimes you just amaze me with your carelessness. How did you get these scratches?"

"It was that wild tomcat."

"Well, just look at the rips in this shirt."

She's concerned about the shirt?

As she dabbed iodine on Freddy's wounds, he winced and tap-danced some more. "Stand still. You know this has to hurt, if it's going to work."

Yeah? Ouch!

She put the rag down and added, "Anyway you deserve this for being so dumb. Why don't you think before you do something? I hope you've learned a lesson."

"Yeah Mom, I have," Freddy whispered.

Likely story, his brother thought.

Freddy learned alright. *Iodine hurts, Mom is crabby and cats don't mix with fireworks. It was that stupid cat's fault. It's my patriotic duty to celebrate Independence Day.*

But we're getting ahead of ourselves. Earlier that day, their dad had given them a ride into town to buy fireworks, and that turned into an adventure all of its own. Indeed.

§

THE BATTLE FOR INDEPENDENCE

Why kids, boys in particular, liked to blow things up and make noise is anybody's guess. Perhaps we inherited a gene from the cave men, banging things together trying to make sparks or keep large predators away.

Anyway we reveled in any kind of noise on our isolated farm that had no traffic clamor, no construction racket or schoolyard din. Our solution came on July 4th. We used fireworks to bring noise to the farm, and in the process, crafted a celebration for the birth of our Nation.

Besides throwing Silver Torpedoes at the barn or rocketing up bean cans, we fought many imaginary battles and conquered army after army with noisy and smoky blasts. We did in the foul British, with their Red Coats and pointy hats, long muskets and little drummer boys. We fought the French and their Indian allies of the 1750s (a book at school told the story), and we charged up San Juan Hill with Teddy Roosevelt.

Our favorite enemies, however, were the Germans and Japanese of World War II … a War we'd lived through on the farm. Our rockets and roman candles torpedoed U-boats and brought down Messerschmitts, Stuka Dive Bombers and Japanese Zeros. Firecrackers, from ladyfingers to Cherry Bombs armed us for battle. Dastardly foes fell— we always won—when we had money to buy ammunition.

However, whether we could afford a huge sack of fireworks or small, our mock battles had risks that today have driven some locales to ban fireworks all together.

Besides battle-related cat scratches, we burned our fingers and sustained bruises when hit by exploding debris. We concentrated on being careful, though sometimes we just threw caution to the wind. Maybe good fortune and the Grace of God saved us from serious harm. Mom and Dad probably thought we'd never learn. In the end, we were just plain lucky. But we did discover that we fared much better than some, for example, Crazy Eddie.

§

CRAZY EDDIE

The annual Fourth of July activities actually started in mid-June when fireworks vendors set up makeshift board and canvas booths around the Wamego area. With them came thousands of explosions waiting to happen.

Customers could buy three-inch, two-inch, standard and ladyfinger firecrackers. There were also torpedoes, cherry bombs, rockets, roman candles, sparklers, spinners, showers, stars, snakes, cones and a whole lot more.

The boys' favorite display was at *CRAZY EDDIE'S HOUSE OF FIREWORKS,* just outside the city limits. Eddie said he came up from some little town in Oklahoma, all the while blinking his un-blinded eye and limping on his badly burned leg. His injuries resulted from his entire booth blowing up one year.

Crazy Eddie had little hearing, expecting his customers to point at what they wanted. His voice sounded pinched and guttural, something like a snorting sow. He seemed friendly and the boys liked him, although they didn't understand everything he said.

The boys had made their first stop at Crazy Eddie's a few days earlier and then made their last stop on this day. Eddie, standing slump-shouldered in front of his now partially loaded shelves, watched the two of them through his good eye.

"Hey, let's get a full dozen of those cherry bombs," Freddy

said, "each." Pointing at Eddie's top shelf, Freddy flashed the fingers of both hands, then added two. Eddie nodded understanding, when the youngster pointed to himself and to his brother.

"Yeeaah," smiling George said as Crazy Eddie added a dozen of the bombs to each pile. "With the fuse in the side, they explode louder than three-inchers. How many punks?"

George thought. *Punks are a whole lot safer than matches.*

Pointing his thumb at his brother, Freddy explained to Crazy Eddie, "Once before to save money, he skipped buying punks and had to handle lighted matches and firecrackers at the same time. A cherry bomb went off close enough to stop up his hearing for a while. He started a small grass fire, too."

Crazy Eddie's face remained emotionless. Blank.

Freddy raised four fingers, "We'll each have four punks."

Crazy Eddie said what sounded like, "Uh," and added the punks to the piles, and then scooped the piles into individual sacks. He took the boys money and handed them back a nickel apiece. With all his physical limitations, Eddie's mind was sharp, and he could make change … with his good hand.

"Let's go," Freddy said, "The quicker we walk up to Aunt Mollie's, the quicker we'll get home and shoot off some of our stuff. Dad's probably waiting for us."

§

Dad met us, and after giving Aunt Mollie some hurried hellos and goodbyes, we climbed into the car with our booty. On the way home, we heard yet another fireworks safety briefing.

"Look before you light something, don't light firecrackers under things, don't try throwing a lighted firecracker and never crouch over any fireworks you are lighting. And for goodness sake, don't set off anything near the animals."

When the car rolled to a stop, we scrambled out to start our noisy battles … first looking where the chickens and other animals were. The cows, Tom and Don and the horses were in the pasture, the hogs were in the upper pen and the chickens were near the chicken house. All clear.

Oops!

We missed our part-Collie, Pep, napping on the shaded concrete porch. At the first boom, he took off yelping like he'd been shot. Tail between his legs, he raced up to the tool shed and burrowed under a pile of empty feed sacks.

Pep might have been a good watch dog, but he lacked our courage in battle. We presumed he'd resurface—he finally did—that evening after we left for the annual fireworks show in Wamego ... and the carnival that beckoned us.

§

CARNIVAL LURE

After the war, a gigantic real-life carnival set up in the Wamego City Park and became a part of the city's Annual Fourth of July Celebration. This magical collection of booths, tents and rides curved around on the grass between the Old Dutch Windmill and Ash Street. It was the largest community gathering of the year.

Just a few days before the Fourth, the boys and their dad had stood at the service station at Highway 24 and Lincoln Avenue, watching the string of vehicles roll into town. This amazing traveling caravan—from who knows where—had semi-trailer trucks hauling rides and tents, and big Cadillacs, Hudsons and Terraplanes pulling streamlined sleeping trailers.

The 'carnies,' as everyone called them, unloaded the rides and equipment and then parked most of the trucks and cars across the street near the railroad tracks. They worked throughout the humid weather, sweating and swearing.

Crews assembled each ride, piece by piece. Like giant erector sets the Ferris Wheel, the Tilt-a-Whirl, the Kiddie Car track, the Floating Canoe course and the Zoom-de-Zoom came into being. Big canvas tents went up, and eventually, a midway of games, eateries and sideshows took shape.

In daylight, the scene seemed to be an ugly hodgepodge of booths and rides. Heavy electrical cables crisscrossed the grass and uneven, tilting light poles rose beside each booth where some vehicles sat among the tents. However, at night the sight turned into a thrilling assortment of lights, sounds and smells. If that night would ever come ….

Even with all the boys' activity, the day had dragged by with the carnival lure getting stronger and stronger. As evening approached, they rushed through the milking and feeding, and wiggled through supper. At twilight, cleaned up they climbed into the back of the old Chevy for a bumpy ride into town.

"You know boys," their mom said, "this year Wamego will have the best Independence Day celebrations around. They say the fireworks might be as good as they have in Topeka."

"Man, I can't wait to see when they shoot those big rockets up above the Lily Pond," Freddy said. "I'm going to lie on the grass and look straight up. I bet they'll have a thousand rockets booming right above us, echoing off the Kaw. Wow!"

"Yeah, those fireworks are great … and free," George said. "I can't wait to get to the carnival. With the two dollars Dad gave me I can take a few rides and still have something to eat."

§

Our plan was to learn our way around the Midway's circular pattern during dusk. We figured that when it got dark things might be a confusing jumble. By the time we'd made a few circles, the sun was below the horizon. Red and green and yellow lights blinked on and gave the grounds an eerie dreamlike brightness. Airport style tower beacons shot moving beams of light into the evening sky, beckoning people from miles away.

We continued circling around the Midway, weaving in and out among the crowd, stepping over electrical cables, past the rides and games and past tents offering incredible attractions. We made the circuit over and over, feeling like fish with all kinds of baited hooks of rides, games, sideshows and food dangling in front of us.

THEY'S HARD AS ROCKS

Then we saw it. The sign beckoned us to come in and see *THE PETRIFIED MAN*.

Huh? What does that mean? Has he really turned to rock? What's he look like?

We just had to see him. With little thought, we each plunked down a dime and walked into the dimly lighted sideshow tent. There we could see—though not well—an older man lying on his side on a cot inside a roped-off area. We were back five feet, but we could talk to him.

§

"Mister, are you really petrified?" Freddy asked after a long hesitation. George and others listened intently.

"Young feller, cain't you see? Jist look at them legs. They's hard as rocks," the man said, rapping on his left leg with the knuckle of his left hand.

To make his point, he dramatically reached down and scratched both legs with a wooden match forced into a yardstick's nail hole. Scritch, scritch, scritch, scritch. Scritch, scritch, scritch, scritch.

"I was born as normal as you fellas, but one time when I was near on to yer age ... I walked in front of a sulfur spring back home. An' from that time on, I've been slowly turning to stone." He sniffed and then sighed.

Again, scritch, scritch went the matchstick along his shiny, porcelain-like legs, tinted with clam-shell colors. Scritch, scritch again, while a forlorn look of sadness filled his face. He let out a deep and mournful groan into the silence. "Uhuuuuumm." Then came another sad, sad sniff.

After a long and distressing pause, he continued softly, "Boys, I tell ya something. Don't never go near none of them sulfur springs. They's deadly."

§

Let us tell you that right then and there, the two of us pledged we'd never have anything to do with sulfur springs. In fact, we didn't think we had any on our farm, or had we even heard of such a thing until that moment. However, it made good sense to avoid them at all cost. No one wanted to turn to stone.

How could we play baseball if our legs were rock? Who would go get the cows? No sir, there'd be no sulfur springs for us, we thought as we exited the sad man's tent … only to end up right in front of the, *BIG CITY DANCERS.*

§

BIG CITY DANCERS

The colorful dancers' tent sat just a few feet away from the petrified man's attraction. How ironic, the petrified man couldn't move and the long legged dancers were as limber as the famed Radio City Music Hall Rockettes.

Here a crowd listened to the barker. His girls stood on the outside stage. "Hey ya, folks, we got girls, girls, girls. They know every big city routine known to mankind." He paused and then continued. "If you're eighteen, we have a place for you inside."

Eighteen?

"Just look at these gorgeous creatures. Right there is darling Miss Daphne from Dallas, Lady Lillie from Chicago and redheaded Mimi all the way from Paris, France," the barker hawked with a practiced swagger. "They dance; they prance and crawl on their bellies like reptiles."

The boys thought, *Why in the world would dancers want to crawl*

81

around on the floor? They must be acrobats.

To the boys, the crowd seemed highly curious.

"Come on in and see them swing to phonograph music of the big bands. You'll enjoy their show and it only costs one thin dime. Don't push, don't shove, we won't start the show 'til you're all inside. Hurry, hurry, hurry," he bellowed, "Step right up."

To most of the crowd the ladies: Miss Daphne, Lady Lillie, and the beauty from Paris, France, were a remarkable sight among the rural folks of Eastern Kansas. Each lady had bright apple red lips, and their cheeks glowed the color of sweet pie cherries. They beckoned the crowd with curling fingers adorned with long fingernails, painted the same red as a new Farmall tractor.

The barker did his best to explain the show as people looked skeptical. Before long some paid their money and entered the tent.

"People are acting kind of funny, aren't they?" George asked. "I'm not eighteen, but I wouldn't want to watch any stupid girls dance around anyway. And, why are they wearing bathrobes?"

.

§

We stood there for a while until the show ended. Some left the tent laughing and rapping each other on the shoulder. Some seemed to sneak out.

They must have been good dancers.

THE LOCAL BOY

We then moved on down the midway. Near a big oak tree along the south side, we saw a huge tent with a large green sign with white letters.

> *GREAT MOUNTAIN MAN*
> *---WRESTLES HERE---*
> *WILL TAKE ON ALL COMERS*

While dancing shows were out for us, wrestling was

definitely in and this would be our first time to see a real professional match. And to think it featured this 'Great Mountain Man.'

We each spent a dime and walked into the tent. Once inside, the Mountain Man's size startled us. We had expected to see a giant, but this guy looked normal.

How could he be a great champion wrestler? We called the contest 'rassling.' After a time we decided he must be pretty good if he wasn't afraid of anybody. And, when he walked to mid-ring and beat his chest, we believed.

"Any of you yokels got the stomach to get in here and rassle me for five minutes? Or try to pin me? C'mon. Don't be bashful."

Will anyone have the nerve to get in the ring with him? Look how mean he is. Bet he'll bite and kick, too.

When the Mountain Man started jumping up into the air and falling loudly onto the mat, we really doubted if anybody would be brave enough to face up to him.

Still, with hope in our eyes—we'd already spend our money—we searched the crowd, wanting somebody to accept the challenge and earn the promised $15 prize. Most men's' eyes looked down. The more Mountain Man shouted and slapped, the more people examined the grassy floor. Nobody made a move. After a while, we concluded that however small his stature, he had scared everyone off. The tent fell silent.

We felt cheated that there would be no rassling and we would each be out ten cents. Then, as we turned to go, a farmer dressed in patched overhalls just like Shorty Brockman's, stepped from the back of the crowd.

We had never seen him in town before, so we didn't know his name or where he farmed. Nobody around us seemed to know the guy, although someone thought he might be from near Onaga or Blaine, each quite a few miles away. The fellow behind us wondered if the farmer might have come from Wabaunsee County across the river.

In reality, we didn't care where he lived. To us what mattered was that he was still a local guy. And he was big ... like he spent plenty of time at the dinner table. We had a good feeling about him. Surely, he would represent us well.

We watched our man move forward, shuffling toward the ring. His eyes looked left then right. Did he lack confidence? At the edge of the ring, he spoke to the Mountain Man in a whispering stammer.

§

"Mister, would you mind if I got in that ring?" Local Boy asked shyly. "I never been much for real rassling, but I did beat my brother a few times."

The Mountain Man stared back and shook his head. "Are you the best they got? Why I darn near killed a fat boy once. You think you have the guts to rassle me?" He laughed, pounding his chest and flailing his arms.

"Here, let me give you a hand," the professional said, grabbing Local Boy by the arm and jerking him flat on his face into the ring.

"Hey, watch it mister," someone hollered. "That's not fair."

"You can't cheat to win in our town," another fellow said. "Fight fair and square."

At that point everyone cheered as Local Boy—his eyes glaring—rose to one knee and then to his feet. With disgust in his face, he looked at Mountain Man and then at the crowd. It was obvious Local Boy was a fair fighter. When he shook his fist at Mountain Man, the crowd cheered and admired his spunk.

Somebody yelled time and the match began with a lot of shoulder slapping and grabbing. The two arm-wrestled some and then started to push each other around. Mountain Man had moves and holds and did things the boys had never even seen in the newsreels. To the boys' surprise, even Local Boy came up with grips and clenches that looked clever. The struggle continued until the two wrestlers crashed onto the mat. Wham. Slam.

For about the next four minutes or so, the bout went on with grunts and strains that only a real wrestling match would produce. Then Local Boy used a headlock and lifted Mountain Man to his feet, and with a flying mare—somebody called it—slammed Mountain Man to the mat. The pin came instantly.

§

Our home grown guy had won. He beat the professional at his own game. The crowd went wild, cheering and back slapping each other. We did the same. The match was over and our guy won. With broad smiles we moved out through the exit flap with the other fans.

At that moment, Mountain Man appeared in front of us yelling and waving his arms. He was shouting, "I demand a rematch. The fight wasn't fair." He roared even louder, "I have to have a rematch. I slipped on a banana peel somebody threw in the ring. I demand a rematch."

We hadn't seen any peel, but that didn't matter. Our local hero, now standing beside Mountain Man, grinned and gently nodded his head. The rematch was on. We just had to see that next match. We wanted Local Boy to win honestly. Out came another dime apiece, and in we went.

Slap, bang, flip. The noise and the effort went on for a few minutes and then in the blink of an eye Mountain Man had our guy pinned. We had lost. With sorrow we turned to go, only to see Local Boy standing in the ring hollering for a rematch.

"Mister, you gotta give me another chance. I gave you one. How about making it the best two-out-of-three? I'm sure going to beat you this time, fair and square."

You guessed it, Mountain Man agreed and a third match was on. We each spent another dime and once again stood nervously waiting for the match to start. Who would win? We'd find out.

When the third match ended in a draw we were in

a bad spot. We'd spent thirty cents, a big part of our spending money. We liked the rassling but realized we didn't have a clear winner. Should we spend another dime?

Then it dawned on us. Local Boy wasn't from Onaga or Blaine or Wabaunsee County or anywhere else close by. He was part of the carnival crew.

We wanted to be mad, but couldn't. We'd seen real professional wrestling.

So, feeling a bit tricked, but satisfied overall, we headed on down the Midway. As it turned out we followed our noses and ended up in front of a trailer marked *Eats*. Then, with each of us munching greasy hamburgers with pickles and mustard, we moved toward the fireworks display area. Once the hamburgers were gone, we used the green grass as a rassling mat and practiced a few head locks and hip rolls on each other. Later, we'd go home and try out the famous leg scissors, the half-nelson and the flying mare.

At the appointed hour, a boom sounded high overhead and a cluster of yellow and red sparks showered down. For the next half-hour we experienced mid-air explosions and watched the most magnificent fireworks display ever. What a great end to the Independence Day celebration.

We'd had a wonderful time that day. We'd tended to Tom and Don, interacted with a tomcat, fought mock battles, seen the night sky full of fireworks and learned the finer points of rassling. We also learned about sulphur springs, and of course, experienced some incomplete visions of big city dancers.

We wished Independence Day came more often. But—dog gone it—the *4th* was over, so we looked forward to our next adventure. It wouldn't take long, for just one day later there it was, harvest time—and in a few weeks, it would be Fair time.

SEVEN

HARVEST AND THE FAIR, LET THE COMPETITION BEGIN AND THEY LOOK PUNY

Wamego Reporter – July 4, 1946] ~ POTT. COUNTY BASEBALL ASSO. ~
Schedule for July 7th:

    Wamego at Cleburne.

    Westmoreland at Emmett.

    Flush at St. Marys.

    McFarland at Rossville.

    Louisville vs. Belvue (Wamego field).

Standings June 30:	W	L	Pct.
Flush	6	1	.857
Wamego	5	2	.714
Cleburne	5	2	.714
McFarland	4	3	.575
Rossville	4	3	.575
Westmoreland	4	3	.575
Emmett	2	5	.286
Louisville	2	5	.286
St. Marys	2	5	.286
Belvue	1	6	.143

1946

HARVEST AND THE FAIR

George poked a long foxtail grass stalk down into the ant hill. The tiny black insects scurried in all directions.

Hey, two are climbing up the stalk. "Ouch!" *I better move.*

Leaving the ants, George walked toward the golden-ripe wheat field and watched the roaring combine coming his way.

Sounds like a giant Buck Rogers wheat monster from outer space.

'Rooooaaarrr,' went the combine.

The old orange Allis Chalmers Model 60 harvesting machine followed behind the matching orange Allis Chalmers tractor. The combine's six bladed reel with its whirling over-bite swept huge swaths of standing wheat stalks up against the five-foot cutter bar. The triangle mower sections clattered back and forth through pointy sickle guards, clipping the golden stalks that dropped onto the broad conveyor belt. It carried them up into the fast spinning threshing cylinder.

George took in the scene while the high scorching sun sent heat shimmers dancing. In the air, dust and chaff flew as the threshing beaters whirred loudly and knocked the tiny brown wheat kernels from the straw. The combine's huge blower lifted the waste chaff and stalks onto the straw-walkers that floated them out a side opening to drop and form rows of ankle high stubble.

The five-year-old combine cut swath after swath as it followed the family tractor around the 80-acre field. The AC ran at full throttle.

When the *monster* reached the end of the field, George's dad eased in the tractor's clutch, shifted it into neutral and idled the engine. When he hopped off the pad less steel seat, he pulled a red bandana from his back pocket and wiped away the itchy grime and chaff laden sweat from his face and neck.

"Bring the truck over here Freddy, and we'll empty the bin. I'll grab a bite and then take this load to the Elevator in Wamego."

Twelve-year-old Freddy put the old International in its lowest and slowest gear and drove alongside the combine. His dad revved up the tractor and augered the new wheat into the truck's grain bed. The loading finished, he closed the spark.

As the four cylinder engine died, quiet ruled for a short time. The nearby clear-water brook reflected the noonday sun and silvery minnows flashed in the water below.

A few feet away, the boys' Mom laid out dinner on the car hood. In the stillness the whole family gathered in the shade of three giant oaks. High in a cottonwood across the road a crimson cardinal sang, its music moving among the trees.

"I'm going to sit on the truck's running board, Veda," the boy's dad said. "That way I can use the door for a backrest."

"Good. I know your back gets tired riding the tractor."

"We're about half done; we'll finish this by tomorrow."

"I hope you're right, John. The paper says there'll be rain by Friday," his wife said as she made sure their new baby, Judy, was cool on the shaded car seat.

"But now let's go ahead and eat. There's a whole fried chicken and there are bread and butter sandwiches, plus a bowl of potato salad and some dill pickles. There's cool lemonade in the bucket."

The hot wind rippled the remaining wheat. The family said grace and picnicked beside the little slough bordering the rented field. Overhead, a hawk flew in lazy circles.

"You know boys," their dad said, pointing at them with a drumstick, "we have the County Fair in three weeks. I hope you've got Tom and Don ready to show."

Freddy swatted at a pesky fly and said, "Both calves are gaining weight. I can lead Don pretty well and George can make Tom walk some. We've washed and curried them many times."

George asked, "How do we get the calves to the Fair?"

"We'll haul them to Onaga in the truck along with a sack of grain and some baled hay. You'll also need water buckets, halters and currycombs. You better take a pitchfork, too."

"What for?"

"You'll have to keep the manure out of the cattle barn alleyway. That's the rule."

George thought, *There I am again, back at the bottom of the pile.*

Freddy asked, "So Dad, what's a fair like?"

"The Fair lasts Thursday to Sunday and you'll leave your calves in the cattle barn the whole time. You need to wash and curry them each day so they're used to it."

"Will we get to stay overnight?" George asked.

"Not this year. We'll all sleep at home and go up to Onaga early each day to tend to the calves. You'll need to feed and water Tom and Don before we leave each evening."

"Ah Dad, can't we stay in the barn?" Freddy asked.

"I'm sorry; you are a little young to do that. Besides, Mr. Harrell, Mr. Clary and some of the older kids will be there."

At that point the discussion ended; however, there were many questions remaining. How did a person tend to and show Baby Beef projects at the Pottawatomie County Fair?

Freddy thought, *I wonder what the best way to win is. I hope ole Don turns out to be the champion. I just know the judge will like his white color. Maybe I'll get my picture in the paper. Yeah, I bet I win a blue ribbon.*

§

LET THE COMPETITION BEGIN

The Fair was on its way and we couldn't wait. But we were always working. We wanted to work less and play more. Maybe the Fair would be our chance.

Tom and Don just had to win. They were our friends, our buddies and almost every day we practiced sprucing them up and showing them. Every time we thought about ribbons we had to grin.

We'd never been to a county fair—all were cancelled during the War—so the folks kept giving us hints. There would be animals and kids. There would be judging of livestock and other projects. The carnival would have rides and attractions, and food to eat and pop to drink.

§

"I just can't wait," George said a day later. "We'll get to spend some money, too."

"I wouldn't count on that too much," Freddy said. "You know how tight Dad is. I'm anxious to see everything and be with all the guys from 4-H."

"Yeah, me too."

"Remember we're going there to compete in the show ring. Tom and Don are going to whip the pants off the rest of the calves. Just you wait."

If he only knew.

All farmers and their kids knew a lot about competing. Attempting to raise the best crops, the best livestock and have the best farm were unstated goals in the country. And farm families wanted their kids to excel.

Dad and farmers like him competed with each other, but they fought the weather, equally. Rain or drought dictated when to plant or the time to till or when to harvest. Too much wind, too much or too little rain increased the competitive odds. And, all farmers competed to earn the highest prices for their crops and livestock.

Where city dwellers might challenge each other for the best looking lawns, farmers competed for their livelihoods. Who could grow the best corn crop? Whose wheat would average more than 50 bushels per acre? Who raised the fattest cattle or hogs? And, whose kids would bring home the most ribbons from the County Fair?

It seemed to us that the Burgess family honor was at stake, and we had tried hard to make sure our calves could win. If effort counted, we'd surely be winners.

§

Very early the first day of the Fair, the boys' dad backed the old short-bed International truck up to the barn's highest door. "Freddy, you lead Don and have him step up into the truck. He might balk at first, but just keep pulling on the lead rope and talk to him. Stay calm and he'll follow you."

"Come on Don. Let's go to the Fair. You want to be a champion don't you? That's it, just step up. Now come up front so I can tie you to the stock rack. You don't want to get dirty."

"Okay George, now lead Tom on. He'll want to be with his brother."

"Come this way, Tom old boy. See, walk right up here. You're going to get to ride in the truck. It'll be fun."

Freddy and George loaded three bales of hay bought from neighbor Leo Scully. Next Freddy loaded a half sack of ground corn and oats and George put in two water buckets and two feed pans. Last in went a box with a currycomb, a brush and an empty coffee can for scooping feed into the pans.

With loading completed by 7:00 a.m., the boys' waved a happy goodbye to their mom and Judy and climbed into the cab. The old pre-war truck crawled out the rutted lane in compound-low with Tom and Don swaying in the back. *It's Fair time.*

This is going to be so great. I bet George and I have the best calves, Freddy thought. *I'm glad I picked a calf with a white coat.*

The slow moving truck drove through Louisville on Highway 99 and headed north. No one talked—all eyes straight ahead. During the miles on the Wheaton Road silence prevailed. As they moved east on the Hartwich Road and then north on the Onaga Road, George sweated. *My stomach feels funny.*

The rusty and faded red-brown truck moved along, a slow mile at a time. Before nine o'clock it reached the Pottawatomie County Fairgrounds, located in the northeast corner of the little town of Onaga. At the cattle chute, the three saw a line of other trucks waiting to unload. At last the old-International backed up to the chute and Freddy and George climbed in with their calves.

"Okay boys, lead them down the ramp one at a time. Good. Now walk them to the cattle barn over there," their dad said, nodding toward a huge building that held all of the beef and dairy entries. "You'll find the Blackjack Club's section to the left of the main door. Be sure to tie Tom and Don up well … we don't want calves wandering around. Then get the gear and the sack of grain from the truck and I'll carry over the hay bales."

As instructed, the two 4-Hers and their projects moved into the Cattle Barn. And what a tremendous barn it seemed to be. Tens of other calves, cows and a few bulls were tied in a long, neat formation, row after row. How could anything top this?

Man, look at the size of this barn. It's as big as a football field. There are calves and kids everywhere, Freddy thought.

§

We couldn't keep from staring. This show barn was the biggest building we had ever seen. It seemed wonderful, except of course for the multitude of flies and the reeking smell of fresh manure, enhanced by the sticky heat of the hot August morning. However, in some ways, the smells and the warm temperature seemed like home, and they were.

In our excitement, we dwelt on the optimistic qualities of the place, because like most Kansans we'd learned to see the optimistic side of things. After all the State Motto: *AD ASTRA PER ASPERA ("To the Stars through Difficulties.")* meant that people from our neck of the woods looked for ways to get things done in a positive way, regardless.

We took the motto to heart and tried to avoid the negative, although sometimes it was quite a struggle. It was tough when we compared Tom and Don to the other calves tied in the barn. Many of the other Baby Beef were mammoth and eye-catching. For a long moment we could do nothing but stand in the huge doorway and gawk. What in the world had we gotten ourselves into?

§

THEY LOOK PUNY

"Look at all those calves," George said. "Tom and Don look kind of puny."

"We'll just have to do a better job of showing our steers, that's all. Anyway, our calves look prettier. Can't you tell that?"

"I don't know …."

At that point, Mr. Raymond Hofman, who helped the Blackjack 4-H Club beef contestants, told the boys to lead their calves into the lounging area, covered knee deep with fresh yellow straw. He showed them how to tie the animals to the top rail as Tom and Don stood side by side next to the other club entries. This would be their home until Sunday.

§

Our calves secure, we completed our entry forms with Mr. Hofman's help. We wrote in our names and 4-H club, the names of our calves, their breed and their dates of birth, though that was a bit of a guess on our part.

While Mr. Hofman handed in the papers, we just looked at each other and grinned. We felt ready to bust wide open. We were at the Fair. This was the big time, with sights and sounds that almost overwhelmed us.

Everywhere we looked we saw calves, from one end of the big barn to the other, sleeping or eating. Some were chewing their cuds and others were snuggled down in the straw like they did this every day. What could be more fascinating than seeing our calves mixed in with the other entries?

Counting our two, the Blackjack Club had several Baby Beef entries. Tied on Don's right stood Bubba Brockman's Hereford named Bombardier, and then came Mavis Hooper's big Black Angus steer called Willis. Marvin Hofman had two nice Herefords next in line, and Lyle Harrell had a good sized Angus he called Spot.

From the Tannerville and Vermillion areas there were 15 entries lined up. Across the hard packed dirt alleyway stood another row of 15 calves.

Beyond them came the beef breeding stock of several heifers, young bulls and a few mature cows. Most were Herefords, with some Angus and a couple of Shorthorn mixed in. The rest of the barn contained two rows of dairy animals—Jersey, Holstein, Guernsey, and at least a pair of Ayrshires—heifers, cows and bull calves.

We kept beaming like we'd found a pot of gold. Humanity seemed to be everywhere and there was much more to see. And we still needed to explore the fair grounds.

§

"So do you dumb-dumbs wanta look around?" Bubba asked as he scraped manure from his shoe. "They got a lotta of stuff here."

"Well, yeah … what happened to you?"

"Aw, I didn't see that plop-plop until it was too late."

I bet he won't get that shoe clean. He never does at school.

"Why don't we go see what's going on at the carnival. Maybe I can win some prizes throwing at those milk bottles," Freddy said. "Boy, Bubba, you smell…."

George shook his head. "I think I better go ask Dad."

While Bubba went back to dragging his mucky shoe through the straw—little success—George asked permission to look around..

"That will be all right for a while," his dad said, "but come back right after noon because you have clean-up duty today. And don't go wasting your money."

§

Feeling full of excitement, we headed out to see what we could, with Bubba in the lead. Following him was like trailing a spooked garter snake. We went one way and then another as if we didn't have good sense.

First, we checked out the rides, the food booths and the games and sideshows, but most were closed until evening. Though this carnival seemed smaller than the one in Wamego, it excited us nonetheless.

After checking out the midway, we walked into what we later learned was the Home Ec building. It was infested with 4-H girls and their many projects, including homemade sundresses, pinafores, vests and skirts. Nothing appealed to us.

§

This place is pretty dumb, George thought. *Wait, I smell cookies.*

Nose in the air, he sniffed his way along until he hit pay dirt. He found dozens of food items, some on shelves and some locked inside of display cases. *Look at those things. Maybe I can get me a sample.*

Just as George reached for a cookie a giant hand came down out of nowhere. Whack!

"You leave those displays alone young man. The girls worked very hard baking them for the Fair," a booming voice belonging to a gigantic woman roared. "You rascals get out of here or you'll be sorry. Now scram!"

Understanding the huge woman meant what she said, the three boys hurried outside with Bubba and Freddy wearing sheepish grins, and George continuing to sniff the air.

"That old lady could have ripped us in two," Freddy said.

"Did you guys see that blue-eyed girl from Olsburg?" Bubba asked. "Boy, I'd like to get a holta her."

"How would you go about doing that you goof head? She's big, too. One look at you and she'd stomp you good," Freddy said.

"She wouldn't hurt me. I'd just turn on my charm and melt her like a candle. I know how to handle women."

"Bubba, you have the mentality of a dung beetle," George said. "The only thing you can handle is a pump."

Freddy slapped Bubba on the back and laughed. "Can you get a handle on a handle?"

Bubba looked at the boys and said, "Okay, enough time on this sissy stuff. Let's blow this pop stand."

He led them on toward the extra large farm machinery display. With the War over, manufacturers had begun turning out thousands of cars, trucks and farm machinery.

George said. "I can tell the color of paint by its smell."

Freddy shook his head. It was Bubba who spoke. "Man, you've gone off the cliff. You're nuttier than a fruitcake, you know that?" He sniffed for emphasis and then belched.

"Okay, well I think I smell Dad looking for us. We don't want to get in hot water. We'd better get back to the Cattle Barn."

"Maybe you're right. We need to clean our area and then

feed the calves. We'll need to go home in a while."

After the ride home, evening chores, supper and a good night's sleep, Friday morning came early with chores and breakfast. Before 8:00 o'clock the family, including two-month-old Judy, was back at the Fair. While their folks chatted with friends, the boys fed and watered Tom and Don. After that they did some barn clean-up. Then it was time to wash the calves.

And so the routine went, until the next day—*Show Day*. That morning George and Freddy washed their entries. A half hour later, while the projects stood drying in the sun, the boys currycombed horizontal lines along their calves' sides. After drying, Tom and Don looked wider and stockier. To improve the picture, the boys shined the calves' hooves and fluffed each of their tails into giant balls.

THE SHOW RING

The closer it got to the ten o'clock show time, the more nervous both boys grew. George's forehead dripped.

At show time the nearly twenty Hereford Baby Beef entries, including Bubba Brockman's calf, marched around the show ring. The cattle Judge, an Ag Professor from Kansas State College in Manhattan directed their progress.

At one point, he had them stand head-to-tail in the ring. He stepped back and studied each calf. After a while, he asked the exhibitors to lead their animals slowly one behind another. The entourage slowly trekked around and around. The kids did their best to keep their Baby Beef moving.

The kids would learn later that the judge compared the amount of quality flesh each calf possessed, including its type of muscling and finish. After about five minutes, he asked the circle to stop. One by one, he walked around behind the animals, and studied their width and depth.

Finally the judge selected the best calf and had it led to the middle of the ring. Next he ranked the remaining calves in order and had them stand in a neat row, best to worst.

The judge directed a Fair volunteer to present ribbons to

each calf owner. The five biggest calves got blue ribbons and the next seven calves got reds. The rest got whites, tied for third place, including Bubba's calf Bombardier.

The judge then sent all the red and white ribbon winners out of the show ring and picked a Champion and a Reserve Champion for the Hereford Breed. Later, these calves would compete against other breed winners for Grand Champion Baby Beef.

"Did you see the size of that big champion Hereford?" George asked as he and his brother waited for the Shorthorn competition. "Our calves look kind of scrawny compared to him. I think we're sunk."

"Yeah, those winners are big. But, remember we don't have that many in our Shorthorn class so maybe we'll come out alright."

After the Black Angus judging, six Shorthorn entries entered the ring. Freddy puffed out his chest and tugged Don along behind him. The calf's white coat gleamed in the bright sun. *This is great.*

Last in line came George tugging at Tom whose red and white roan coat looked clean and soft. Tom trailed sleepily behind his owner, who wore a forced smile with lumpy cheeks. While Tom seemed relaxed George didn't, until he saw his mom holding Judy, standing beside the ring. His mom smiled and his baby sister flailed her two-month-old arms and legs.

"You can do it George. Keep smiling and just walk straight," she whispered. "Pay attention to the judge."

He looks scared to death, she thought. *Thank goodness his overhalls look clean. I wish he had worn a cleaner ball cap.*

At that point, the Judge inspected each calf and then directed them to parade around the ring a couple of times. When the calves stopped, he examined each one. All animals seemed like giants compared to Don.

When the judge spent a long time examining calf two, Freddy felt glad Don was mostly white, still ….

Why is he taking so much time with that calf?

At last the judge walked up to Freddy and his project. It seemed like the whole morning had passed. As the Judge looked Don over, he shook his head just the tiniest bit. Following a sigh, he glanced back at No. 2, then back at Don, and then at No. 2 again. *What is this all about?*

The judge didn't spend much time with Don and then moved on to Tom. George flashed a scared smile and stood straight and tall. *I need to go to the bathroom.* Tom seemed to take the cue and squared up like he understood the art of showmanship.

In the end, the judge called out No. 2, then No. 1 and awarded them both blue ribbons. Next, he had Tom come to the center of the ring along with another calf. These got red ribbons.

That left Don and another smaller calf with a coat of mixed red and white. They both got white third place ribbons. No. 2 was the Champion Shorthorn and No. 1 was Reserve. Freddy's calf Don was neither.

At least he didn't call me out last. But maybe white wasn't such a good idea. Anyway I got a ribbon. That's what counts.

§

With the show over we did feel a lot of pride that seemed to offset most of our disappointment. We had competed and had been rewarded with ribbons for our efforts. And, though we didn't realize it, we had learned some things. Now we sensed we knew somewhat about what a judge looked for in a champion calf.

What's more, it was apparent that color didn't matter much but size did. Next time we'd pick bigger calves. And somehow we'd have to look for ways to help them grow faster. Bigger was better.

Of course our folks congratulated us and seemed proud of how we'd put in our effort with Tom and Don. We'd earned Mom's and Dad's admiration, and we were proud. Judy just cooed.

No matter where we'd finished, we'd done our best. The family honor was intact and that made it all worthwhile.

EIGHT

SHE'S PURDY CUTE, GAMES OF SKILL AND THE FORTUNE TELLER

[*Wamego Reporter – August 8, 1946*] ~ FLUSH PICNIC REACHES A NEW HIGH – The net receipts from the Annual Flush Picnic of last week passed the previous high mark made in 1944. The crowd was large and receipts would have been greatly augmented had more refreshments supplies been available.

The baseball game in the afternoon was a hard fought one, with Flush winning from Paxico in a ten-inning game by the score of 6 to 5.

Over 900 people partook of the chicken dinner, with 250 seated at one time and 450 can be fed in an hour.

The dance had the largest attendance of any since the Flush Hall was built.

1946

SHE'S PURDY CUTE

After the Baby Beef show, the boys returned Tom and Don to the Cattle Barn and spent time watering them and replacing the messy straw. For a couple of minutes George stood with his arms around Tom's neck and said, "You did good."

Meanwhile, Freddy joined Lyle Harrell and Bubba where they sat on bales of hay next to their calves.

"That was a good show, though I don't know about that college judge," Bubba said. "I think he should have put Bombardier up in the blue ribbon bunch. He's a dandy calf."

"Bubba, you must be joking. There was no way your calf was going to win a blue ribbon," Freddy said. "Not with a name like Bombadier. Who would select an animal with an aviation name?"

Changing the subject, George said, "I wonder if Judy will be in 4-H when she gets bigger? I bet she'll be a good cook and make champion cookies."

"Who is Judy?" Lyle asked, "Your girlfriend?"

George said, "She's Judith Gale Burgess, our baby sister. She was just born a few weeks back, on June the 20th. She's purdy cute, but she cries quite a bit. Most babies do, especially when they're hungry."

"She was born up at Westmoreland," Freddy said. "She seemed to like the livestock show."

Uninterested in babies, after Bubba told his tall tale about outrunning a blue racer snake, the topic turned to the fighter planes used during the War. George liked the P-40 Warhawk that the Flying Tigers used in China, while Lyle favored the P-51 Mustang. Bubba claimed the Corsair was best and Freddy argued that the Lockheed Lightning P-38 was the plane for him.

"Anyway, it doesn't matter. Our planes could beat a Japanese Zero and a German ME 109 any day of the week. Our planes were the best in the world," Freddy said.

At that precise moment, the roar of two mighty engines boomed from overhead, rattling the barn's roof and windows. Wide-eyed calves jumped to their feet and jerked at their halters. Some bellowed in terror and a couple of older cows yanked loose and ran.

The thundering noise propelled the boys outside. Overhead, two P-47 Thunderbolts streaked above the Fairgrounds at a couple of hundred feet. All eyes watched them bank right and circle back for another pass. This time they did two rolls right above the Midway. As they passed again, one of the pilots waved, and then with a waggle of wings, the planes climbed out toward Topeka.

"Hey, those are Thunderbolts," George said. "I flew one of them over Germany."

"You dreamer, you never flew a plane," Freddy said.

"I bet someday I will fly a plane," George said. "Yep, flying looks like fun. I might even build an airstrip on my farm."

"Ha, you ain't smart enough to fly a plane," Bubba said

"Well, I'm smart enough to not jump off your barn roof with a feed sack for a parachute. You could have ended up dead."

Freddy said. "I don't want to be a pilot. I'm going to play baseball for the Boston Red Sox and bat like Ted Williams."

"He's a great hitter, isn't he?" Lyle asked.

"Yeah, the newspaper said he hit three home runs and a

single during a game in July. Can you believe that?"

"Has anybody ever hit that many homers in a game before?"

"I'm almost sure somebody has, like maybe Babe Ruth or Johnny Mize," Freddy said.

"Our Dad has us bat rocks from the driveway with broomsticks. He says that will make us better hitters," George said.

The chatter went on until the boys' dad walked up with sandwiches from home. When he walked away, Lyle got out his homemade lunch, and of course, Bubba mooched off everyone.

The ham sandwiches disappeared one by one and so did the hard boiled eggs. Each boy had a drink from the water spigot and then the foursome decided to walk the fairgrounds again. For the next two hours they spent time watching the hog judging and then examined the farm machinery again. George again announced he could tell paint color by its smell. The others shrugged and laughed.

Upon returning to the cattle barn, the Burgess boys found their dad waiting. "Fellows you need to feed and water your calves. It's about time for us to go home. We have chores waiting; we will need to leave in about ten minutes."

"Ah, Dad, can't we stay a while longer?" George asked. "We want to go see the carnival."

"It's not fair to mistreat animals just to have fun."

Both boys sighed in defeat. They stood heads hanging until Bubba spoke up, "Mister Burgess, could you leave Freddy and George here for while? My dad and I could bring 'em home later. My Mom is doing our chores tonight so we don't have to leave yet."

§

The scene grew quiet. We both held our breaths. Maybe Bubba wasn't such a dunce after all.

We waited while Dad thought about Bubba's suggestion. Would he let us stay, just this one time? He could do the chores alone for one night, couldn't he? Why doesn't he say something?

After an endless pause Dad looked at Mr.

Brockman and nodded his approval. Without a word, a deal was struck. We'd get to stay and ride home with the neighbors. Wow.

As Dad prepared to leave, we stood by almost urging him to hurry up. First, he talked to the club leaders, and then he spoke to Mr. Brockman and finally turned to us.

Wearing his serious face, Dad gave us the usual instructions. We shouldn't get hurt, get into trouble or be disrespectful to others. We nodded and nodded. We had no intention of doing those things.

Then, Dad walked to the old truck and drove away. We were on our own. At last we were free to experience the nighttime wonders of the 1946 Pottawatomie County Fair.

Everything around us seemed to get bigger and brighter. Our nostrils came alive with the smells of the animal barns and the midway. All of these mingled together in a strangely pleasant way.

Somewhere from the Carnival we heard, "Come see this great show," and that sound tickled our ears. To this point the afternoon had been lazy. Puffy white clouds had dotted a deep blue sky that had served as a backdrop for soaring hawks. And, the Thunderbolts. A lazy time perhaps, but for now, our world sparkled with excitement.

§

GAMES OF SKILL

"C'mon, you guys. I'm going to wander around a while. It's only six o'clock so there won't be many people at the attractions. We can check out everything before it gets too dark," Freddy said. "Where should we start?"

"I've got a buck and four bits. I'm going to have me a hamburger. Man, they smell good," said George.

"Yeah, they do but we don't want to spend all our dough on food. We've scrimped too long to blow it all at once. C'mon Bubba,

103

let's head down to the midway," Freddy said and then led the way.

Any carnival offered adventure for the boys. Wamego's July 4th carnival had been Freddy's and George's first. Its sounds, smells, games and odd looking carnie workers seemed mystifying, and for certain, every red-blooded boy just had to take in the attractions. This Fair carnival had the same feel.

When the trio stood at east end of the County Fair Midway, they stared with a kind of reverence. As they gazed, a wood moth landed on George's shoulder and he brushed it away. While he wiped his forehead, the smell of frying hamburgers caught his attention.

The carnival layout formed an oval. Sideshow tents, food booths and game stands clustered along the sides. Clumped together at the far end were several rides, including a Whirl-A-Gig and a small Ferris Wheel.

"Hey, those rides are only a dime. We could do 'em a bunch of times," Bubba said. "I have four bucks."

Big spender, thought George.

The idea didn't work out very well, because when the Ferris Wheel stopped with Bubba in the top seat, he decided he didn't like the height. Freddy almost threw up during the Whirl-A-Gig spin.

For George's part, he knew he'd rather eat than waste money on dinky rides. "Hey, let's go take a look at the food booths."

Freddy said, "Maybe, but I don't feel like eating much."

The threesome first stopped at a hamburger joint called *BIG RED'S BURGERS AND CHIPS,* operated from a small trailer-like contraption with rubber tired wheels. It had a side window that folded down as a serving deck. The cooking meat wasn't visible, but the block buster aroma filled the air.

Big Red stood at the window. He looked to be the biggest … and maybe the dirtiest man the boys had ever seen—even in the fields. He blew his nose in a grimy towel and then wiped his hands on that same cloth.

"So what can I git you boys?" the huge red-head asked. "Want my special burger with cheese and mayonnaise on it? It'll only cost you fifteen cents."

George's nose wrinkled. *Mayonnaise on a good hamburger? That doesn't sound so good, and besides Big Red looks pretty grubby for a cook.* George shook his head and said, "No thanks."

"I don't know about Big Red, but you guys better make up your minds pretty soon. I'm hungry," Bubba said.

"I'm hungry, too. I wonder if Big Red serves hamburgers and 'cow chips'. Let's go see the place over there," Freddy said.

The other food stand, *MAMA GERT'S HAMBURGERS*, sent out its own aroma of browning meat and grilling onions. It was a small booth-like tent with a blackened grill in the rear, loaded with hamburger patties and onions. An older woman—Mama Gert the boys figured—kept flipping the burgers with a spatula.

I've always wanted to be a hamburger slapper, thought George.

"This is the place where we want to eat," Freddy said.

They walked up and Mama Gert met them, hands on hips in a soiled white dress with matching apron. She seemed somewhat cleaner than Big Red.

"You boys look like you're hungry," Mama Gert said. "Why don't I dish up a big hamburger for each of you?"

The three boys nodded at the same time. "Do you have pickles?" George asked.

"Honey, I got the best homemade dill pickles you ever tasted. They'll make you think you've died and gone to heaven."

Grinning George said, "Can I take my hamburger along?"

"You bet you can," Mama said, "after you plop down a dime and a nickel for me."

The three paid their money and Mama Gert said, "Much obliged."

Mama Gert's greasy burgers slathered with mustard, dill pickles, grilled onions and green tomato relish called picklelilly didn't last long. George wanted another, but decided to save his funds.

Wiping their mouths, the three said goodbye to Mama Gert and left to investigate the rest of the Midway, in particular the games of skill. Freddy felt an urgent need to try his abilities at winning something. His coming out on top loomed large in his life.

At the rail of the Ring Toss, he discovered that for only a nickel, he would get three rubber rings about the size of a turkey's egg. If he tossed a ring over an empty Coke bottle neck, he'd win points for prizes. And, the more points the better the prize.

"That table is just about three feet away. This ought to be easy. Look how close together those bottles are. I guess I'll get me that blue bracelet for Mom," Freddy said.

"Yeah, I'm gonna try it, too," Bubba said with an all-knowing grin. "Watch this."

Freddy and Bubba tossed their rings at the same time. Both rings hit bottles, bounced off and plopped onto the table. Rings number two and three, all missed.

The carnival man offered words of encouragement. "You almost did it. Try it again. Just look how easy these rings fit over the bottles," he said, gently dropping a ring over a bottle's neck.

More nickels purchased three more rings apiece, but none landed around a bottle's neck. Neither did each player's next set of three. While George watched and squeezed his money, his brother and Bubba experienced excitement and disappointment.

George said, "C'mon, let's go. You're never going to win. Maybe that guy has them booby-trapped or something."

Shaking off defeat as if failures in life somehow didn't count, Freddy and Bubba moved next door to the milk bottle throw.

"You fellas look like pretty good athletes," the man in charge said. "Maybe I'd just as soon you went to another game. I can't afford to have no pros throw here,"

"What are you saying?" Freddy asked. "You don't want us to throw at your bottles because we might knock 'em all down?"

"Well, I have to be practical," the carnie said. "Big strong guys like you can throw too hard. You might break something."

Freddy, eyed the stacked pyramid of fake milk bottles wrapped several times with adhesive tape. Each was a little more than two inches wide and almost five inches high. "Mister," he said, "I really want to try your game. If I get to costing you too much, I'll quit."

"Okay young fellow, it's three balls for a nickel, or five balls for a dime."

Freddy plopped down a dime and the carnie shoved five of

the smallish and lopsided balls his way. Like the pitcher facing *Mighty Casey at the Bat,* Freddy prepared for his feat of valor. Arm stretch … right arm windmill … a deep breath and another stretch … and with fire in his eyes, he reared back and hurled ball #1 toward the stack. Sadly, it missed everything by a couple of feet. Ball #2 missed and so did #3. Ball #4 barely touched a bottle and #5 hit the table.

George smiled. *Bet the Red Sox wouldn't be impressed*

Freddy thought, *Hey, that one ball slipped on me. I guess I might have lowered my aim too much on the last one. Maybe I have to throw harder.*

What followed was a true life experience. He plunked down another dime for five balls. Again, his mighty throws went over, around, under and even through the stack. Not one bottle fell.

"There must be something wrong with these balls," he said to the carnie. "I couldn't have missed them all."

"Naw, the balls are alright. You just had some bad luck. Watch your friend here for pointers and then you can try it again."

Bubba fired five straight misses. Then the bottle in the middle popped out, but nothing else fell. He said, "Darn, and I wanted to win that whoopee cushion for Aunt Lulu."

"That's too bad son. You don't win any prize points for knocking down just one bottle. You need to try it again."

Bubba slapped down another dime and this time had two hits, but only knocked over one bottle. He just shook his head, while Freddy paid his third dime for another set of five balls.

The guys are getting suckered, George thought. *Man they're dopes. Five bottles for a dime isn't as good as three for a nickel.*

Again, Freddy went through his warm-up exercise and concentrated hard. One after another, he fast-balled his tries toward the bottles. Again and again, he came close but missed.

"That's better young man," the carnie said. "Try it again".

"No thanks."

Bamboozled, Freddy and Bubba moved on.

Still there was hope, for just a minute later they came to the carnival glass toss. There a pretty looking young girl smiled at them and said, "Hey big guys, why don't you come win some of these pretty dishes for your girlfriends or your moms? Don't you think they'd like some of these pretty berry dishes?"

"What's a berry dish?" Bubba asked.

The girl batted her deep brown eyes and with an alluring smile said, "Why they are for serving strawberries or gooseberries. Their glass changes color in the light. They're from Denmark and are very popular. Every woman wants one."

Bubba moved closer. "What does it cost?"

"It's only five cents a toss. If your nickel stays in the dish you get to keep it. This game is so easy I don't know how my dad stays in business."

At that Bubba grinned and reached into his pocket.

Both boys breathed in and together flipped their coins toward the array of bowls on a low table. Freddy's nickel landed right in the middle of a glass dish … but bounced out.

Bubba's stayed put. "Hey, I won a dish for Mom. Now I'm going to try for Aunt Lulu."

At that Bubba and Freddy started tossing more and more nickels. None stayed in the flashy and slippery dishes.

"Can I borrow some money?" Freddy asked his brother, who stepped back, grabbed his wallet and shook his head sideways.

The gamers looked at each. They had spent too much. George just walked away, but would soon face his own problems.

THE FORTUNE TELLER

A couple of minutes later, George heard a voice hissing at him. The sound came from a strange looking woman dressed in shiny and fancy clothes. She was abundant, but her wide cloth belt kept her midsection in place. She wore a pirate's silk head scarf and a dangling necklace and earrings with huge blue stones. Her fingernails resembled hawk talons.

George stopped in his tracks and could only stare, first at the long hairs protruding from her chin moles and then at her face. It looked like crumpled newspaper.

Is she talking to me?

He looked up and noticed a large, hand painted sign that

read: *MADAM VADOMA ~ FORTUNE TELLER*. It pictured a crystal ball with three brightly colored moons and some falling stars.

George frowned and started to leave. The gypsy looking woman spoke again. He didn't understand, but he was too shy to ask for her to repeat it. *What do I do?*

He hesitated until the woman crooked her finger and motioned for him to come toward her tent. He didn't want to, still he knew he should be polite.

The woman beckoned him again and added a smile that revealed a missing front tooth. George walked up to the tent. Right away he noticed a musty smell similar to the potato bin in the storm cellar. As he moved closer, Madam Vadoma pulled back the canvas flap and motioned for him to enter the dimly lighted space.

At that point George's nervousness shot off the scale. *What does a fortune teller want with me? What is she going to do? Should I run?*

At first, his feet would not move, but then he followed her inside. The moldy smell made him woozy and his heart pounded. The only illumination came from the weak light of her fortune teller's crystal ball, and from her eyes. They seemed to glow and follow his every step.

"Young man, you were wise to enter Madam Vadoma's sanctum. That makes you a very brave young man, so I'll easily be able to tell your fortune. I will help you learn all and know all."

George gulped and his dry mouth froze shut. He couldn't say a word as he stood locked in place.

"Now just put your wallet on the table and let me help learn about your future."

George fidgeted and squirmed. His face turned chalky but he obeyed her commands.

"There now, just let me take this dollar out and we'll see what it tells us about you."

What is she doing? I don't want her to take my money. I wouldn't even loan Freddy a dime, and now ….

He stared at the total stranger with her fingers handling his spending money. Things were getting out of hand.

In a voice that came out too loud, he blurted, "Ma'am, I

have to go. My brother is probably looking for me. Thanks just the same."

The gypsy frowned. "You can't leave now. It is a bad omen. Something might happen to you, don't you see?"

George's jitters went staccato. With startling speed he grabbed his wallet—and the dollar—and burst out of the tent with more gusto than a frisky squirrel leaping between limbs.

"Young man, young man, come back …."

George ran all the way to the cattle barn, where inside he plopped down on a straw bale near his calf and tried to catch his breath. Thankfully, there was no one around so he sat in silence, pondering what had just taken place.

I think I feel sick.

After several minutes his breathing returned to normal, and so did his thoughts.

Yeah, like she said, I guess something did happen to me alright. For one thing, I learned how to keep my money in my own hands.

THE LEARNING PROCESS

Yep, Madam Vadoma taught George a valuable lesson. He decided that he wouldn't have had to run if he just hadn't entered her dark and musty tent in the first place. He thought, *In the future, I think I'll let Bubba predict my future. At least it won't cost me.*

George pondered, *At least I've learned how to train and show a Baby Beef. That's what's really important.*

For his part, Freddy had also learned the lessons of showing animals. And he'd figured out that throwing at milk bottles, ringing Coke bottles and pitching at carnival glass had a downside. And … he finally realized—too late—that he'd been gypped. Three balls for a nickel was a better deal than five for a dime. *I was cheated. Shucks. I guess Dad was right, but I'm not going to tell him.*

Both boys came away from their first county fair with a reservoir of information. They'd be back next August. In the meantime they had to return home and get back into the swing of thing, and there'd be many more lessons to learn.

NINE

IT'S ALL IN THE BAIT, TWENTY BUSHELS AFTER SCHOOL AND CORNFIELD BASKETBALL

[*Wamego Times – August 8, 1946*] ~ TRUMAN PROCLAIMS AUGUST 14TH AS VICTORY DAY – President Truman today proclaimed August 14—anniversary of Japan's surrender—as Victory day and directed the flag be displayed on all government buildings. It is not a legal holiday, however.

He called upon the people to observe the day as one of solemn commemoration of the devotion of the men and women by showing that through sacrifices victory was achieved.

1946

IT'S ALL IN THE BAIT

"Okay, the folks are leaving," Freddy said while he and his brother watched the family car head out the dusty lane early on a summer morning, "Let's do something fun for a while. Maybe we should head down to Rock Creek and do a little fishing." He smiled and added, "I can hear a big channel cat calling my name."

"Didn't Dad say we needed to chop the weeds?" George asked. "Shouldn't we do that first?"

"All he said is that we need to get it done today."

"You're right," George said. "Fishing sounds good."

"Sure, we can do weed whacking this afternoon."

With practiced ease, the boys put off farm work. Their dad would to be gone to a meeting in Westmoreland all day, and on the way he'd drop off their mom and Judy at the kids' Aunt Helen's.

The boys were on their own, even though the field was large and weeds plentiful. But after all, at ages twelve and ten, Freddy and George could figure out their work schedules couldn't they? In this case, the anticipation of catching a good sized fish easily trumped weed cutting.

"You go cut a couple of poles from that small dogwood at the calf pasture and I'll get the other stuff ready," Freddy said. He walked to the shop and nosed around until he found a few cents worth of heavy cotton line, a few over-sized hooks, some half-inch bolts for sinkers and a couple of jug corks for bobbers.

As George walked to meet him, Freddy finished unstitching a burlap potato sack. "This'll make a good seine so we can scoop up some minnows down at the Slough." Then, again using his status of bossy older brother, he added, "Bring our rock-batting broom handles and that lard bucket to put the minnows in."

George did as instructed and together the two walked the quarter of a mile down the dirt road to the small Slough bridge where Freddy had had his 'water moccasin' episode. "I know there are minnows in this hole," he said. "Stand back while I do the seining."

Again George did as he was told and watched from the bridge. Freddy removed his shoes and socks and waded into the water. When his brother got wet and muddy up to his knees George chuckled. *And he thinks he knows it all.*

Freddy wrapped the sack ends around the broomsticks and then pushed the homemade seine deep into the water. He spread it wide and scooped forward and up.

Four sunfish, a bluegill, two chubs and a little bullhead half the size of a sparkplug flopped and flipped in the seine. Two more sweeps netted about a dozen minnows. With the bait in the lard bucket, he wiped off as much mud as possible and put on his socks and shoes. The twosome then headed north the half mile to Rock Creek, the pleasant stream that ran a lazy zigzag course at the northern edge of the farm.

§

On our past fishing trips, when the channel cats were biting, we'd had fair luck using minnows. We'd also caught catfish with grasshoppers and angleworms.

We'd tried chicken livers with little success, and from the Western Auto store we once bought the most revolting stink-bait we could imagine. It came in a jar and smelled like rotten beef or chicken. The reek stayed in our nostrils for days.

We didn't catch a fish with the stink-bait, but we hadn't used it much because of the smell. We'd joked that it smelled worse than Bubba Brockman's feet on a warm day.

For this trip, however, we would rely on the tiny minnows from the Slough. So as the warm sun shone down from the cobalt blue sky, we ambled toward the Creek, kicking up some road gravel now and then. On top of a knobby fence post a colorful meadowlark sang.

Everything seemed just great. However, though we didn't know it right then, things were about to change in a dramatic way as neighbor, Wally Hoffman, drove up. As was country custom, he stopped his old truck to say howdy, and once he realized we were on a fishing trip, he seemed anxious to give us some friendly advice. That, of course, would alter our fishing trip … and a few other things as well.

§

"Going after some catfish, huh?" Wally asked and bobbed his head in understanding. "Looks to me like you're planning to use some minnows, is that right?"

The boys nodded yes. "Gee, that's too bad. Guess you boys don't know what to use this time of year, but it sure isn't minnows. No-siree-bob, not minnows. Besides the moon's just not right for them today."

What does he mean the moon's not right? George wondered.

"It's my belief that today stink bugs would be the only bait to use. Put a couple of them on each hook and bingo. Be sure you hook 'em from the bottom side up so they look right in the water. Bait 'em that way also lets out their smell and that makes the catfish go crazy."

Wally really knows fishing, both boys thought. *It sure sounds like stink bugs will work. Where do we find them?*

"See that bunch of milkweed growing in the fence row next

113

to Riat's cornfield?" Wally asked. "Those weeds are bound to have dozens of stink bugs just sucking out the sap. Here, take this empty Prince Albert tobacco can. Just fill it up with stinkers and you're in for an unusual fishing experience."

Then he added, "And when a fish takes your bait, be sure to wait until he munches on those bugs before you set the hook."

§

We could tell Wally felt good about sharing his knowledge, for his grin was a mile wide. He waited for us to head for the fence row and drove off.

For our part, we came face-to-face with dozens of the gray and green bugs clinging to stalks of many of the milkweed plants. The bug smell was revolting and we didn't want to touch them so we raked several into the can with the end of a fishing pole. After a few minutes, the horrible smell convinced us we had enough. We closed the lid and cut across the stubble toward the Creek.

When we started down the bank we could hear the water murmuring so we headed toward it. Look out fish.

§

"Don't brush up against those dang stinging nettles, they'll make you itch for a week," Freddy said.

"Right, so let's go down the path over there and we can miss most of them," his brother said.

"Okay, but be careful. That bank is going to be as slippery as an owl's droppings."

At the Creek's edge, the boys inched along and followed the water course a way down the stream. "Oops, watch the mud on the other side of that log. I sunk in a foot."

George avoided the mire and a couple of minutes later, the boys reached a likely pool, partially dammed by small limbs and debris caught on a huge, fallen cottonwood. The undercut bank looked like real catfish country.

"What should we do with these minnows? Just turn them loose?" George asked.

"We might just as well. Wally says that stink bugs are the best bait for now … though I never heard of that before today."

"Neither did I. He never did explain the moon thing."

"I sure hope he's right, because that smell is awful. I think I'm going to gag," Freddy said, peering into Wally's flat red tobacco can. Holding his breath, he picked up a stinkbug. He thrust the hook upward like Wally had said. In apparent revenge, the insect released a huge gush of more spiteful odor.

"How can you handle 'em?" George asked.

"This better work," Freddy said as he stacked a second bug on his hook. "If I was a cussing man, I'd say some words about stink bugs—and about Wally."

Armed with his pole and plenty of stench, he stepped to the edge of the creek, plunked in his line and stuck his pole in the mud. Next, he squatted down and tried to wash his hands. "This smell won't even rinse off."

"Well since you already smell, why don't you bait my hook for me?"

"No way!"

So while Freddy groused and grumbled, George wrinkled his nose in disgust and went through the same bait-up process at arm's length. *Wally is full of baloney. What kind of fish could stomach that smell?* He then flipped his bolt-weighted hook into the water.

After a minute or so the breeze carried away most of the smell, except from their hands, and both boys plopped down on the damp slope with their poles secured in the soft bank. They watched their cork bobbers drift a few feet from shore in the slow-moving current. Now it was up to the fish—and the stink bugs.

§

We passed half the morning in dank and somewhat

steamy air, as the sun flickered down through dozens of tall cottonwood branches. The air had a warm, sticky sauna like feel. Perspiration soon soaked our clothes as we lazily swatted the occasional fly or mosquito. Flies and mosquitoes didn't matter much to us. As farm boys we took all of nature's creatures in stride.

High in an old oak tree across the creek a red-headed woodpecker banged a rat-a-tat-tat rhythm. We heard a flashy-red cardinal whistle 'purr-die, purr-die, purr-die.' Looking up through the trees, the sky appeared gigantic, holding one big puffy cloud. It changed shape as we watched; first as a buffalo, then a baseball glove and finally as a large white horse's head with flowing mane.

Nearby a locust buzzed and far up the creek a dog barked. Above the burgling creek, a green dragonfly drifted on the breeze and landed on a tiny branch just above the water. Was our world peaceful? You bet, in spite of the stink bug smell.

§

The inevitable soon happened and George with his head cradled on his cupped hands dozed in the dappled sun. His breathing slowed and he slumped deeper into the soft grass.

Brothers being brothers, Freddy seized the opportunity to take a small bit of cottonwood fuzz and tickle the sleeper's nose. George wiggled his nose, then brushed, then wiggled, then brushed, and finally came awake with a glare in his eyes. The chase was on!

His laughing brother headed up the sloping bank and then turned back down with George in determined pursuit, until Freddy, crossing a log—oops—found himself in a foot and a half of water. It cooled him off and now it was George's turn to laugh.

When their panting calmed, the boys went back to fishing, a mostly waiting venture. Up the bank, the slight breeze rattled the cottonwood leaves, sending out a further message of solitude. The water sparkled as it spilled through the fallen tree limbs and driftwood, sounding musical in the stillness.

After a few minutes of calm, the sun did its magic and this time Freddy dozed. The napping went well until he groggily realized George—he thought—had turned the tables. Deciding to go along with the gag, Freddy brushed the side of his nose, expecting to find cottonwood fuzz.

"Uggggh! Right in my nose. It's a stink bug! I'm going to gag. You're in big trouble."

George threw up his arms and said, "Wait, I didn't do anything. The bug must have crawled out of the can. I'm innocent."

Not sure what to think, Freddy used his fingers and blew his nose. Again and again he expelled air from his nostrils and wiped his nose with his shirt-tail. In disgust he gave up, though much of the stink remained.

That Wally Hoffman sure played a good one on us. We haven't had a nibble and the smell in my nose makes me sick. I'm going to get that scoundrel the next time I see him, Freddy thought. *Stink bugs are not bait. My bobber just sits there. It hasn't moved in two hours.*

The question was, to quit or stay. "I guess we might as well leave. Stink bugs don't catch fish and we've dumped our minnows. We should have cut weeds," said George.

"I dunno," replied his brother.

The decision lingered in the boys' minds. As they stalled a while longer, monotony returned and their thoughts flitted away to wherever young boys' thoughts were likely to go.

Freddy started to sing and as usual added questionable verses of his own. His noisy song ended the peace. Insects went quiet and birds stopped twittering, perhaps because of the singing … or perhaps the lyrics.

You get a line and I'll get a pole hon..ey,
You get a line and I'll get a pole, ba..by.
You get a line and I'll get a pole,
And we'll go down to the crawdad hole,
Honey, oh, baby mine.

I came to see you 'cause you were so nice, hon..ey.
I came to see you 'cause you were so nice, ba..by.
I came to see you 'cause you were so nice,
Held you close 'n got a head full of lice.
Honey, oh, baby mine.

You caught me with a stinkbug smell, hon..ey
You caught me with a stinkbug smell, ba..by,
You caught me with a stinkbug smell,
Now our courting, ain't going so well,
Honey, oh, baby mine.

You went to a bush for to find your ring, hon..ey
You went to a bush for to find your ring, ba..by.
You went to a bush for to find your ring,
Poison ivy gave you a heck of a sting.
Honey, oh, baby mine.

All of the sudden Freddy's eyes drifted to his bobber as it floated gently in the current. Wait, did it move? It jerked and bobbed. *That has to be a fish, doesn't it?*

Fishing action at last. When the bobber went all the way under he whispered, "Hey, do you see that? Something is messing with my line. It's moving upstream."

"You have to wait like Wally told us. Set the hook after he gets it good," George said under his breath.

"There he goes," Freddy yelled, and jerked hard on the dogwood pole. "I got one."

The bending pole danced down and up as an unseen fish tried to shake the hook. After a moment, it moved downstream toward the fallen cottonwood. "Oh no, he's going to get tangled in those limbs!"

With a side-wise yank, Freddy slid the channel catfish up the slick bank and then belly-flopped on top of it, getting poked with fish barbs in the process. At that instant, the two-and-one-half pounder was his.

A few minutes later, George's two impaled stinkbugs attracted a three-pound catfish. It soon joined the first fish on the quickly whittled elm branch stringer and the two boys finally decided they had dawdled enough. Freddy, his nose still rebelling, dumped the remaining stink bugs into the Creek—*Good riddance.* Then the two fishermen headed up the bank and toward home.

It may have been a touch of guilt about the uncut weeds, but something had inspired the boys to go get to work. They decided that neither the stink bugs, stinging nettles, the marauding insects, nor muddy and wet clothes had dampened their great fishing adventure. Fishing was fishing and that was that.

And, maybe Wally was right, Freddy thought.

George surveyed the moon. *I wonder ….*

§

At the shed we and gutted and cleaned our fish. We walked to the windmill to wash them and then stored our catch in the family's coal-oil fired refrigerator. Fish for supper.

We thoroughly washed our hands with soap and water and then fashioned a noon day dinner from left-over Spam on buttered homemade bread.

Back up at the shed, we sharpened our two well used corn knives with the foot-pedaled grindstone and headed toward the field. For the next few hours we whacked and chopped and cut in the afternoon heat.

Late in the afternoon the folks got home and we went back to the barn to do the evening chores. About seven o'clock we sat down to a fried catfish dinner.

The folks seemed pleased with the fresh fish. They liked our efforts at the cornfield, too. All in all, hadn't we done a good job managing our Lee Sure time?

Mom looked at us and asked, "What in the world is that smell?" We were too embarrassed to tell her.

Time management grew to be a greater issue a few weeks later. The outside temperatures were cooling. Besides our normal work, we'd get yet another assignment.

Up to that point, our days began with early chores followed by a trek along dirt roads and across Frank Cotton's bluestem pasture to our classes. When we arrived at the tiny Prairie View schoolhouse we joined our classmates.

After school, we'd walk home, usually to do some small project like cleaning a stall or grinding feed before chore time.

However, on this weekend we were to get a new job. Some farms had mechanical corn pickers, but at our place, we still shucked corn by hand, with the help of our horses.

King and Prince pulled the wagon. The mammoth team were each big enough to each eat about ten acres of hay and grain a year. However, raising feed for a horse seemed like a reasonable trade-off when it came to corn shucking.

§

Freddy and George got their corn shucking assignment on the first Saturday in October. The morning sun dropped through scattered clouds as the family's old Chevy headed home. The boys and their dad had been to Lichtenhan's Hardware in Wamego to buy a couple pounds of eight penny nails and two new hinges for the corn crib door.

At the Slough Bridge, the car's tires crunched to a stop and the threesome got out. They walked a few rows into the cornfield as the wind whipped the tan stalks. The boys' dad pulled an ear from its stalk and stripped back the husk and dry brown silks to expose the yellow kernels.

"This looks like it's about ready to shuck," he said, as he removed the husks from several other ears. Matter-of-factly he said, "I want you boys to start shucking about twenty bushels every day after school starting on Monday."

That much? Starting Monday? By ourselves? Freddy wondered. *Who's going to harness the team?*

George thought, *It'll be windy and cold.*

"You two are old enough to do a little shucking on your own, and you've worked with the team before. It will get easier the more you do it."

And so, the boys had their new task and it demanded some honest time management. Were they up to it?

They had some misgivings. On the other hand, both boys secretly looked forward to the man sized challenge. Would they once again prove that farm kids could rise to the occasion?

§

LAMPOON CHARACTERS

Monday after school ended, in a forty degree temperature an easterly breeze pushed us toward home. Today the two of us would shuck corn for the first time without Dad's help. We could hardly wait.

Once inside we changed clothes, grabbed a quick slab of homemade bread, ate a warm bowl of chili and headed back out into the cold.

We'd dressed in our cold weather clothes with layer after layer, and before long we looked like a pair of lampoon characters. Our outfits … red-checkered caps with inner and outer ear flaps, ragged cotton gloves, heavy coats and sturdy high top shoes with overshoes … increased our size by half. And, thank God for the long-johns, flannel shirts and sweaters underneath.

As reality set in, we grew nervous about harnessing the team. How in the world would we manage it?

§

FORTY POUNDS OF HARNESS

Harnessing King and Prince was indeed a test. The big bay draft horses weighed almost a ton each. They stood as tall as George's reach. The horses looked similar to the famous Budweiser Clydesdales in terms of size, black manes and tails, white stocking feet and hooves as big as dinner plates.

Freddy used a bucket with oats to catch Prince and when he led him to the barn, King followed. Once in their stalls they ate more oats while the boys slipped on leather bridles.

The boys' next challenge was handling forty pounds of harness for each horse. Was there a best way to get the straps over the horses' backs? How about the neck collars?

Fortunately, the two towering behemoths waited patiently. Freddy pulled King's huge collar from its peg on the barn wall. Together, the boys placed it against the horse's chest, and while George held it in place, Freddy stood on the manager and buckled it around King's neck. Next, he fastened the hames, with bright brass balls on top, tight against the collar.

Now came the tricky part. Somehow, the heavy harness had to go up and over King's back. With all his might, George pushed and shoved the tangled leather straps up King's side. Freddy, lying flat atop the big animal's back, pulled and pulled.

"You have to push more. Get it up higher. I can't lift it," Freddy said.

"I'm doing the best that I can," George shouted back. *There has to be an easier way ….*

Inspiration hit and George took a new tack and simply shoved up a single strap. Freddy grabbed it and waited for a second one. A couple of minutes later he pulled the harness atop the horse and let half of it slide down the other side, almost tumbling down himself.

With many gyrations, the boys got every strap buckled in its proper place. So, the hard part was done … well not quite … for they still harness Prince—and shuck twenty bushels of corn.

With both horses harnessed, Freddy led King and George followed with Prince. They stopped the horses on either side of the wagon tongue. Together, the boys hooked the tongue neck yoke rings to the bottom of each horse's collar.

"You hook up Prince's tugs and I'll get King's," Freddy instructed as he attached the tug's trace chains to the wooden singletree. At that point, the wagon was almost ready to go under *two horsepower.*

"Help me get these reins hooked up right," George said.

Freddy nodded and cross hitched the two bridles, the last step in the harnessing and hooking-up process. Now, a pull on a single rein turned both horses in the same direction. The high-wheeled wagon stood ready.

Once aboard, Freddy clucked to King and Prince and the wagon moved out. The set-up resembled—no canvas though—one of the thousands of prairie schooners that had travelled west on the Oregon Trail, just a few miles north of the Burgess farm.

PRINCE DID THE WORK OF A KING

A huge horse, King, was large and beautiful. At the word "Giddup," this grand upstanding animal would step out smartly … for a few feet. Yes King was magnificent; however, he did have reliability problems. After taking only a few steps he'd drop back almost imperceptibly, with his tugs sagging just a bit. This let his slightly smaller teammate, Prince, pull most of the load. King continually needed urging to do his share. Does that sound like some people we know?

While King needed urging, the handsome though not majestic Prince willingly used his pulling power. He'd also accept a rider, but not King. Prince had a slightly turned down Roman nose and a somewhat droopy neck, but he did his share and more, on the left side of the two-horse team.

On the way to the field, the empty wagon rattled down the road while the good looking steeds strutted side by side. The wagon's tall iron rimmed wheels left parallel tracks in the dust.

To the excited boys, the crisp air smelled of fall and suggested an on-coming frost. The weak afternoon sun offered little warmth. Did the boys care? No, for today in the cornfield, they would be farmers, real farmers.

The evening before, their dad had said, "Be alert when you harness the horses. And don't spook them. Runaway animals have hurt a lot of people, and can ruin a wagon for sure."

"What causes a runaway?" George asked.

"Sometimes loud noises or even sudden movements can startle horses and cause them to bolt. The harness bridles come with four inch square leather blinders to block their side vision and keep the team looking forward."

The blinders for King and Prince were a good idea, because if the usually gentle horses had seen how the boys carried on once the corn shucking started, they might well have been alarmed. Fortunately, the well-trained team behaved far better than their young farmer friends.

Each horse lined up to walk between the two rows of corn. George shucked from the row closest to the wagon and Freddy husked the next row out.

The first step was to pull back the dry husks and then snap the kernel covered ear from the stalk. A quick toss sent it toward the wagon. After shucking ahead a few feet, one or the other boy would say, "Giddup," and the horses would walk forward until they heard the word, "Whoa." If necessary, the word 'gee' turned King and Prince right and 'haw' turned them left.

King and Prince are smart, George thought.

After tossing a few ears into the wagon, George asked, "Do you suppose horses talk between themselves?"

"I don't know," Freddy said, "but I know they 'neigh' to each other. I think maybe that is talking."

"I don't know," George said. "Maybe."

"Yeah," his brother said with a smile "I bet those grunts are saying you're a goofy looking kid who needs a better hat."

"I'm sure they're saying they don't like your dumb songs."

What if King and Prince really are laughing at us?

In truth, what the horses said had nothing to do with the job at hand, for the boys were in the field to send ear after ear against the four-foot high bangboard attached to the far side of the wagon box. Well tossed ears bounced off that board and dropped into the wagon. Little by slow little the yellow bushels piled up as the day got colder and each breath exhaled a crisp cloud in the air.

§

CORNFIELD BASKETBALL

As you might expect, it wasn't long before we realized that shucking corn was hard work. Fortunately, we'd also learned from other farming experiences that no matter how unappealing, tasks got easier when they were fun. We just needed to use our imaginations.

So in a flash, we turned the 10-foot long and 4-foot wide wagon box into our own private basketball goal. By now we were each shucking two rows at a time, so we had plenty corn basketballs to toss. We sent shot after arching shot to hit the bang board.

Making baskets in the large wagon box goal was easy. But of course we did miss some, when we tried to score with our eyes closed, or when we faced away from the wagon and tried circus shots.

With careless creativity we took full advantage of the wide-open field … and did a little of our own horsing around. But we didn't forget that we also had to shuck around 20 bushels.

We debated which type of shucking tool did the best job of scraping husks from each ear. Was it the husking peg that had belonged to our Grandpa Scott for some 40 years, or was it our dad's shucking hook that fit like a fingerless glove. The peg took three steps to get the ears out of the shucks and the glove only needed two.

Which shucking tool was the better? Of course it was the one that the other guy was using.

When at last we finished our job, we drove the team home, unloaded the corn, unharnessed and fed the horses, and then did the chores. We'd learned a lot that day, but tomorrow we'd have to shuck another twenty bushels. In the meantime, we'd have another day of school.

On the way to school the next day we were stopped in our tracks, stunned—shocked!—to see our neighbor Shorty Brockman, learning a highly valuable life and death lesson, courtesy of his wife Lulu ... and her butcher knife.

TEN

RUNNING FOR HIS LIFE, SHE'S IN TROUBLE AND IS THIS THING BUSTED?

[*Westmoreland Recorder* – September 5, 1946] ~ Wind and Rain Hits the County ~ A terrific wind and rain storm whipped out of the east and hit the county Wednesday morning, leaving considerable damage in its wake. The rain in Westmoreland measured 2.37 inches which fell in a two-hour period. Rock Creek rose some but did not go out of its banks.

Long distance toll lines were torn down out of Westmoreland, and, other damage was done to telephone and electric light lines. Raymond Hope, county engineer, reports that two county bridges on township roads were reported out.

1946

RUNNING FOR HIS LIFE

A half dozen turtle doves flew over us in level flight on that brisk fall morning. While the doves hurried by, we rushed along the road toward our Prairie View Schoolhouse. We were taking the roads all of the way rather than walking through Frank Cotton's damp bluestem pasture.

This was the morning, beginning precisely at 8:00 a.m. the three sixth graders were to take the County Scholastic Achievement test.

Suddenly, the doves veered left and then back right. *Hey? What's come over those birds?*

We followed their erratic flight for a few seconds and then scanned the fencerows and the hedge trees for signs of hunters. Or coyotes, always on the prowl.

To our amazement when we looked down the road we spotted a hat … bouncing up into view as it came towards us. *What is this?*

Then, rising beneath the hat in jerky increments

127

came the head and torso of our neighborhood character Shorty Brockman, huffing and puffing our way. *Look at that.*

§

"That's what spooked the doves. It's ole Shorty and he sure is in a hurry. He's acting like he's seen a ghost."

"That's no ghost chasing him," Freddy said. "It's his wife. And look, Louella Ethel's waving a butcher knife at him. Man, does she look mad. She's steamed about something."

Shorty's angry wife, head down with her stylish feed-sack dress flying, galloped after her husband. While Lulu ran with little effort, Shorty's gait seemed on the decline, after what the boys assumed was a late night in Younge's Tavern in Louisville.

Gasping with each step, Shorty ran a much less graceful pace than during his Air Corps training. His legs seemed rubbery. The boys thought that only fear drove him on.

Lulu seemed to be closing the gap, while Shorty looked to be consuming the last of his stamina. He was trying to run all out, but kept using up much of his precious breath by shouting some theological words in a non-theological manner.

"Oh, God, oh, God," Shorty wheezed. Then, just as he turned the corner, he almost stepped on a five-foot-long bull snake that had taken that moment to cross the dusty road. Shorty high-hurdled the snake and staggered on.

The reptile, alarmed by the low-flying human, coiled like a rattler. A loud, forceful and hurried hissssssssss sounded right as Louella Ethel approached him.

Gasping, she dug her heels in but her feet slid forward. The rest of her plopped onto her ample rump. She looked to be in panic as dust settled around her. Stopped in place she thrust and jabbed the butcher knife at the snake.

Trembling, she whimpered and closed her eyes. The bull snake seized the moment, uncoiled and headed into the hedge trees.

Meanwhile Shorty, seeing that his wife had her own problems, circled into Cotton's pasture and headed south on past the schoolhouse.

From a distance the boys watched Shorty head home, while the squinting Louella Ethel peered down the empty road. Nothing. No snake and no Shorty.

The boys stayed hidden behind some trees and watched her shake her head, make an angry face, stand up and slap dirt from her backside. As she headed back south the boys could hear her say, "I'm going to do some beheading if I ever catch that snake or that worthless husband of mine."

"What's she going to do now?" George whispered as he and his brother moved toward school, keeping well back.

"Darn if I know," Freddy said. "I hope she calms down by the time she sees Shorty again. Otherwise he's going to look like a mouse coming out of the back side of a combine."

"Yep, he's had it unless Lulu mellows out," George said. "But, c'mon. We need to get to school."

About thirty minutes after classes started, the saga took another turn. In walked Bubba Brockman and took his seat in the back row. The disturbed Mrs. Draper looked up from helping first-grader Delafield Straub with his reading. "Why, Bubba, you are very late today. May I please have an explanation?"

"Yes, ma'am," Bubba said, "but you ain't gonna believe it. I was almost to school on time when I met Uncle Shorty looking out of breath and all white. He said he was scared to death and he feared for his life 'cause Aunt Lulu wanted to slice him up. He told me to go home and send my dad to help cool her down."

§

The two of us smiled at each other for we knew Lulu could get pretty angry with Shorty. And today we'd seen it firsthand.

"Do you know what upset Mrs. Brockman, Bubba?" Mrs. Draper asked.

"I guess Uncle Shorty was getting ready to go hunting and started cleaning his shotgun in the kitchen.

Both barrels went off and he blowed a huge hole right through the linoleum and the floor under the kitchen table," Bubba said. "He'd forgot to unload the gun."

Bubba looked over at us and grinned. "Aunt Lulu thought he was shooting at her, so she grabbed a butcher knife and made for him. He dropped his gun and took off, and she chased him down the road right past this school."

Bubba stopped to take a breath—and to grin— milking the situation. "Uncle Shorty said only the Man Upstairs spared his life. He said he did a lot of calling on the Lord, and the bull snake was the answer to his prayers."

Is *'Oh God, Oh God,' really praying?* We wondered.

"Uncle Shorty said he thought maybe the snake scared the devil right out of Aunt Lulu and she lost her murderous intent. He said though, just in case the devil won after all, for me to go home and get my dad to help out. I did what he said and that's why I was late for school."

"My goodness, this is all very upsetting. I really hope the Brockmans can smooth things out. I don't believe your uncle would shoot his wife; he must have just been careless with his gun."

Yep, one could never be sure about Shorty Brockman.

"You know boys and girls," Mrs. Draper said to us, "there are two good lessons here. First, don't assume the worst about people or about what they might do. Usually, something good comes out of every situation. And the second lesson is to learn how to handle firearms safely."

She paused to let that sink in and then said, "We'll talk more about this later. Now I want everyone to settle down so these sixth graders can finish their achievement tests in peace. And, Delafield please read some more from your primer."

As we thought about it, we realized Shorty had shown yet another example of poor gun handling. It was no wonder the Army had kicked him out of the Air Corps.

Firing a gun in the house was something we would

never do. And, it was very obvious that we needed to do what Mrs. Draper told us and learn how to handle firearms the right way.

That gave us the excuse we needed to get our own gun. After all, hadn't our teacher practically instructed us to get one? In our minds, we felt obliged to learn how to use a firearm. Maybe we could even be like Red Ryder.

If we could just use a gun like he did, then we would do what our teacher told us to do. In fact, the more we thought about it, the more we convinced ourselves Mrs. Draper had *ordered* us to learn to use *our own* gun for safety's sake. So a few weeks later ….

§

POW, POW, PING

"Hey, look at this," Freddy said, "here's a Red Ryder BB gun in the Sears & Roebuck catalog. Boy, it would be neat to have that, wouldn't it?"

He aimed an imaginary gun toward the window and fired, "Pow, POW, ping." His bullets blasted through the glass and ricocheted across the calf pasture, dropping a bank robber hiding in the sumac. "Got him!"

Incidentally, mail order catalogs had two purposes on a farm. The first was for orders like BB guns. The second—at times a whole lot more important—was to serve as toilet paper in the outhouse. That's the way it was.

As Freddy finished his imaginary shooting, his eyes returned to the kitchen table. The fall sun lit up the full-color catalog page and spotlighted the lever-action gun with its curved trigger guard and ornamental leather thongs. The blue-black barrel and real-wood plastic butt made the gun look strong and sturdy.

"Let's ask Santa for it. Remember, Mrs. Draper told us we had to learn how to use one." Freddy said.

Later, their mom gulped when she saw the boys' Christmas

wish list. Worse yet, their dad flared his nostrils in disgust. "Boys, this list is mighty long. Did you forget the state the world is in? Santa will have a lot of needy kids this year. It might be a mistake to ask for too many things."

Freddy looked sad; George looked sadder.

"I think Santa gives more presents to poor kids who don't get presents from their folks," the boys' mom said.

"Do you suppose poor kids' teachers told them to get a gun so they could learn how to handle it safely?" Freddy asked.

"Well, I don't know, but we'll just have to see what the Santa brings," his dad said. "In the meantime, let's go do chores."

A couple of hours later, after cherry pie and listening to *Ma Perkins* and *Amos and Andy* on the old Philco radio, the boys went to bed to start the Christmas count down. *Only a few more days to go*, George thought. *I hope we get that BB gun.*

With an inch of snow covering the farm, Christmas morning arrived and under the red cedar tree lay an unwrapped Red Ryder BB gun with two tubes of BBs. Penciled on the box were the words: "To Freddy and George from Santa."

Thanks to Santa, the boys had their gun and could now battle packs of marauding wolves, possible stampeding buffalo and any misbehaving rustlers. The boys reckoned they could save many a day and, bring home much needed meat for the family.

COLD CHRISTMAS MORNING

"Let's go shoot some BBs," Freddy said. "We can go over by the windmill and find some good targets just like Red Ryder would do."

"Hold on boys," their dad said. "We have chores to do first. A good cowboy always cares for his stock before he plays around. You can shoot your gun afterward."

"Ah Dad, let us just take a couple of shots apiece before chores."

"Sorry boys. Listen to that ruckus up at the cattle lot. We better go check it out. Some animal might be in trouble."

"You want me to come with you?" Freddy asked. "George can start the milking this morning."

"Good idea. Get to it George."

George wobbled to the milking-parlor door, frowned and tamped down a small snow drift so the door would open. The big, almost pure white Holstein named Miss Bubbles led a quick-stepping parade of five cows to their assigned stanchions. While the cows started to munch away, George locked each stanchion bracket.

He picked up the milk bucket and eased up to black and white Louise who tossed her head. He settled down on his one-legged stool as the cow danced a reserved, yet shuffling two-step.

"Will you hold still?"

The cow stopped eating until she got used to George's cold and stiff hands. Then she resumed. For his part, George sent two alternating white streams into the empty tin bucket between his knees.

Take that … and that, he thought, crisscrossing the now moderate milky squirts to somehow eliminate a hiding enemy. *That's the way we'll do it with our BB gun.*

Then he squirted the cats, Zebra, Blackie and Four (sister of One, Two, Three and Five). They tried to take bites out of the warm white milk streams that George shot their way.

After a time squirting the cats seemed to irritate Louise and she stamped her right hind leg. George's mind caught the message as his left little toe got caught by her foot. "Ouch, dag nab it, Louise!"

Wincing, George examined his bucket. Just a couple of inches covered the bottom. He groaned, "Four more cows to go."

SHE'S IN TROUBLE

Up at the cattle shed Freddy and his dad found the older cows milling around a young heifer lying on her side, struggling to birth her first calf.

"Let's herd the older cows into the other pen so they will quit trying to help. They know she's in trouble."

With the other cows moved, the two returned to the prone

heifer. "It's no wonder she's having problems," Freddy's dad said. "Look at the size of those feet sticking out. This calf is too big for her and she's about done in. We'll have to help her. At least she's under cover. We need to use the stretchers."

Freddy ran to the alleyway and returned with the fence wire stretchers. He secured it to a corral post while his dad trussed the little calf's legs. "Go tie this other rope to the heifer's front legs and pull, and I'll work the stretcher tight in the opposite direction."

The exhausted young cow rolled her eyes at the rope but remained still until all was ready. "Okay, Bossy. Let's have some more pushes. You have to help us."

On cue, the heifer contracted and the compounded draw of the stretcher's pulleys inched the calf outward. This time it didn't recede. The third time as the heifer strained, out plopped a hefty looking bull calf. It didn't move.

"Quick. Let's drag the calf near her nose. Now help me turn her onto her legs. If she can get up and lick the calf, it might make it. C'mon lady, get up."

The new mother eyed the tangle of legs and struggled onto her front knees, and then she rose on her hind legs. With effort she wobbled erect and sniffed at the membrane covered calf.

"Look Dad. She's licking away the shiny sac. There, the calf shook its head. Is it going to be alright?"

"It could make it now if it gets to nurse soon. It needs some colostrum from the first milk."

About five minutes later the wobbly calf started looking for breakfast. "There it goes. It's looking for her bag," Freddy said.

"They're okay now; so go help your brother finish milking while I hay the other cows and feed the hogs and chickens. I'll check on the calf before I head for the house. Mom will be expecting us soon for Christmas breakfast."

Freddy nodded and hurried toward the barn. There he found George again wetting down the cats. "Is that the last one?" he asked.

"Well, there are still three to go."

"You mean Bubbles is just your second cow? Good grief!"

"Oh lay off," George said, sitting beside Miss Bubbles. "She always takes me forever because she gives so much milk."

Freddy just shook his head. He grabbed a pail and stool and moved along side Maudie, the old, hard-milking brindle cow. *She sure gives tiny streams.*

In a short while, Freddy finished Maudie and moved to the easy-milking Guernsey, Claudette. Five minutes later, he was milking Alma and finished about the same time George finished Bubbles.

"I'm taking these pails to the house. You turn the cows out and bring your bucket," Freddy said.

George unlocked each stanchion. He stood unmoving while each cow plodded outside. He went out and closed the door. Then he watched a single white cloud form into a large hippopotamus. After a minute the image changed into an alligator.

At the milk room on the porch he helped crank the cream separator. When done the boys went inside to the cheery warmth, shucked off their outside clothing and gratefully smelled the wonderful aroma of Christmas breakfast.

Hot cocoa or coffee, soft-boiled eggs and home-cured ham crowded the kitchen table. In the center rested a plate of warm Jule Kaga, the sweet Norwegian Christmas bread made from Grandma Scott's recipe.

Shortly, the boys sat at the kitchen table, the cold and chores forgotten, and woofed down their food. *Man this tastes good, but gotta hurry and go shoot our new gun.* They finished breakfast in record time.

Freddy smiled and said, "May we be excused? We're going to go shoot our new BB gun. Tell Santa thanks for getting it for us. Man it's going to be fun."

IS THIS THING BUSTED?

Like quail flushed from underbrush, the boys hurried from the table and donned their winter gear. George picked up the gun and this time pushed aside his thoughts of the cold.

"You know, I sure hope you two are careful. A BB can put shoot your eye out," their mom said.

"We'll watch it," Freddy said. "We handled BB guns with Ben and Rollie at Grandpa's farm. We know what to do."

"That's fine," their dad said. "Just don't shoot any animals or each other. And there's no need to shoot something just to kill it."

Nodding agreement, the boys shuffled out and dashed toward the windmill. Freddy cocked the gun, aimed at a dry sunflower stalk and pulled the trigger. The gun went 'poooff,' but the stalk stood unharmed. "Hey, I'm sure I hit it. A dry weed like that should crack or something. What in the heck is the matter?"

"Try it again."

Again went a 'poooff' and again nothing. "How could I miss it twice? Is this thing busted? I had to hit the stalk that time."

"Maybe you should read these instructions? Somebody took time to write them," George said.

"Oh, don't be so dense. Good grief, what's to read? We've seen cowboys shoot in the movies. You just cock the gun, aim and whammo, you blast 'em."

"Well, you can't seem to hit the broad side of a barn door. You got eye problems?"

"Okay, read that sheet to me."

"*Step One: Always use caution when shooting.*"

"Holy cow, everybody knows that. What else?"

"*Step Two: Move the cocking lever (Fig. A) downward. That motion loads a BB into the chamber and compresses air needed to propel it.*"

"We know all that. What else?"

"*Step Three: Place the stock to your shoulder and aim. Center the front sight in the vee of the rear sight (Fig. B) in line with your target.*"

"Okay."

"*Step Four: Gently pull the trigger.*"

Then he smiled and read, "*Step Five. Before cocking and firing, be sure to load the magazine tube under the barrel (Fig. C) with Daisy Brand BBs. You should enjoy your Red Ryder BB gun for years to come*—that is if you remember to load it. I added the last part." George giggled.

Unfazed by the facts, Freddy opened the BB tube, poured in BBs, cocked the gun and fired again. This time the dry stalk snapped off. *I guess the gun didn't come loaded.*

Next a dry button weed pod popped away and then he aimed at a high-hanging hedge ball in a leafless hedge tree. The dense Osage Orange gave a slight 'thunk' when the BB hit and a drop of sticky-white ooze seeped out. "Man, this is fun. Here, you try it."

George took several shots and most of them hit the target. By noon, the bulk of the boys' BB supply had flown to the land of expended ammo. By Christmas evening, every BB they owned had 'poooffed' away. With regret, they realized they'd have to wait until Saturday night before they could resupply.

After a couple of weeks, BB holes decorated every empty tin can on the farm. The pink fish pictured on a salmon can got plinked right in the heart from twelve feet. The red spot on the Calumet Baking Powder container vanished and dotted BB dents spelled out the readable word 'Van' on a Van Kamp's Pork and Beans can.

The boys' steady fire of either lead or copper BBs peppered many fence posts and weed tops.

§

Taking turns, we shot at anything that remotely resembled a target, but not at living animals or birds. We heeded Dad's rule of sportsmanship.

"Anything you shoot, you eat," he said, and we knew he meant it. Who wanted to eat a robin, a rat or—God forbid—a skunk?

Later, Dad relaxed the 'Shoot it and Eat Rule' so we could eliminate the free-loading starlings and blackbirds in the feedlot and sparrows feeding in the granary. *Sturlins*, *Blackers* and *Spatzie*s, as we called them, had to go. And some did, for it seemed we hunted every free moment.

Of course, flies, junebugs and beetles were targets and the side of the barn soon had plenty of BB craters. In season, we drilled many a ripe mulberry or chokecherry.

Still, two facts remained. We were always short of ammo—and money.

C'MON YOU DOOFUS, THE JOY OF SELLING SALVE AND WHERE ARE THE BULLETS?

[*Wamego Reporter* - January 27, 1947] ~ LEND LEASE PROGRAM FEEDS EUROPE ~ The world entered a new era today when tons of food and clothing began pouring into European ports to feed and clothe those torn by war. Several ships sailed from New York a week ago and arrived at London, Antwerp, and Bremerhaven in German.

Throughout the entire Allied world, racked by war or threat of war since Germany struck Poland on September 1, 1939, it was a time for rejoicing and celebration.

1947

C'MON YOU DOOFUS

"Dang it. We're out of BBs again. And out of money. We're always broke," Freddy said.

"Yeah, some kids get an allowance. They can buy anything they want, but not us," his brother said, shaking his head.

I sure wish Dad wasn't such a Scrooge, Freddy thought. *I hate trying to get money out of him. Hey, why don't I have George ask? Nobody can turn down his sad sack face.*

"Hey cuckoo, you need to go ask Dad for some money for BBs. Tell him we only need about a quarter."

"I asked him last time. It's your turn."

"Ah, c'mon you doofus, you know I'd be glad to do it, if it would work. But he turns me down easier than you. Tell him we need BBs to get rid of some spatzies and blackers."

George pondered. *Maybe he's right.*

Meanwhile, down in the field wind rustled dry leaves and tiny whirl-winds raised wisps of frost and dirt. Near the barn the windmill squeaked as it rotated on its high tower to face the northwest breeze. Pep barked at something near the shed.

At last, George meandered toward the granary. He watched

his dad tin snip a round piece from an empty coffee can and nail it over a rat hole in the middle grain bin wall.

When his dad looked up, George said, "You think our work has earned us twenty-four cents? We're short of BBs."

"Again? You two aren't wasting BBs are you?"

When his dad's face hardened, George grimaced. *Now I'm going to get another lecture.*

"You boys need to plan your shooting. Don't shoot at silly targets like icicles and snow banks. Anyway, we'll have to see."

George's shoulders sagged, his face twisted into a most sorrowful and cheerless image. Staring at two crows wrestling over a mouse, George sniffed.

"Oh alright, you two can get some more BBs in town tomorrow," his dad said as he reached in his pocket to fork over two dimes and four pennies, plus a couple of pieces of pocket lint. "Don't spend that foolishly."

Whew!

The next evening after supper the family made it into town to shop. "C'mon and we'll go get the BBs," Freddy said. "Hand me the money."

The boys entered the Western Auto store. At the sports counter they eyed the assortment of BB guns, .22 caliber rifles and shotguns. "Boy would I like to have one of those rifles," Freddy said. "What couldn't a guy do with one of them?"

"Well, let's stop daydreaming and buy what we came for."

At that point, the clerk Argyle Smith walked up and asked how he could help the boys. They relayed their request for two packs of lead BBs—the cheapest. Mr. Smith handed over the ammo and Freddy gave him the 24 cents. Transaction completed.

During the ride home Freddy thought, *Tomorrow those sturlins better look out. We're gonna knock 'em off one-by-one.*

During the next couple of days, the Burgess brothers 'poooffed' away shot after shot. Sometimes they actually aimed at pesty blackbirds or sparrows, but most often they sighted whimsical targets like clumps of grass, thrown walnuts and cow pies. By the third day all shooting ceased, and history, along with George's gloomy face and teary eyes, repeated itself. His performance again netted 24 cents.

One thing about all this shooting, the boys proved the adage that practice makes perfect. They learned to hit just about anything they wanted, even at long range.

§

In truth, it was a special time for being brothers, and springtime was upon us. The sun brightened and moved higher in the sky. Days grew warmer and the greening began. Because of Shorty Brockman's goofy carelessness we learned how to handle firearms. But in our case, due to our weapon, our education came with limitations.

Darn. That shot didn't even bust that apple. We need a rifle.
.

§

TIME TO MOVE UP

"It's time for us to move up a grade," Freddy said to the family dog, Pep, who lay motionless on the porch with one eye following the boy's movement.

"George, you know what we need? A rifle, for hunting."

"Think Dad would let us have one?"

"Yeah, what we need is a .22 caliber like Grandpa Burgess has. And the 4 Ds dad has one too."

"Yeah, I guess a .22 is a good gun," George said. "They probably shoot three times farther than BB guns. Maybe a .22 caliber bullet is the one Superman is supposed to have out run."

"Yeah, maybe. Why don't we go to the store when we're in town tonight? We can see what a gun costs."

"Why don't we ask Dad to go with us?" George asked. "I don't want to get a bad deal."

"Yeah, we can ask him. That way he'll know how serious we are and maybe start paying us more."

"What about the food we eat? We don't have to pay for that," George said.

"The folks are supposed to feed us. We're their kids, for heaven's sake."

George didn't reply so Freddy's thoughts turned back to the gun. *We have to come up with a smart plan to get the money from somewhere. Maybe tonight Dad will want to help us out.*

At the store, with their dad along to see 'something special,' the boys walked up to the sports counter and studied the rifles in the gun rack. "So this is what you wanted me to look at."

"Yeah, we think we're old enough to have a real gun so we can do some hunting for the family. Just look at those," Freddy said.

The boys' dad swallowed but kept looking.

"Hey, look at that one. It must be five foot long," Freddy said, turning to the clerk behind the counter. "May I look at that one, sir? It's a pump action .22 caliber Winchester, just like the one that won the West."

"It's a nice looking gun," his dad said, "but do you think you can afford fifty-five dollars? That's a lot of money."

While Freddy chewed on the high-cost angle, George shook his head. *Dad is right. We can't afford that much money.*

One by one, they examined the rest of the .22s on the rack. Some were a bit too long and heavy for George, but each looked good except for the price. Most sold for thirty dollars or more. Only a Western Auto Special at $21.79 was reasonable.

"Well, these are good rifles boys," their dad said, "but it's going be hard for you to come up with enough money for any of them. Why don't you check out the Sear's and Ward's catalogs at home? You might find something just as good that costs a lot less."

George turned to his dad and said, "Okay, we'll look in the catalogs tomorrow. We do want to pick the right gun."

After church the next morning George discovered a good looking, and much cheaper, single shot J.C. Higgins brand .22 rifle in the Montgomery Ward catalog. *It says it's a light weight, bolt action, single shot, with a solid oak stock. And, it's only fifteen dollars including shipping.*

At last the boys had a choice. But they didn't have the

fifteen dollars, and Freddy's idea to let their dad loan them the money fell on deaf ears. The only solution was to start saving change, and any Christmas and birthday money, and deposit it into their bank, a Maxwell House coffee can on Freddy's tiny dresser.

Even after getting birthday money, the can held only seven dollars. "We'll never get the cash we need this way," Freddy said. "We have to figure some way to earn something."

THE JOY OF SELLING SALVE

"Hey, how about this?" George asked, pointing to the back of a *Ladies Home Journal*. It says it's a sure way to add to your bank account in your spare time. All you have to do is get some salve and sell it and make twenty-five cents profit a tin. I can do that and I'll have four bucks in no time."

"Good idea. Now I have to find something. Say, wasn't there an ad in the *Earl May Seed Catalog*? Yeah, here it is. Okay, you sell salve and I'll sell vegetable seeds. We only need another eight dollars. This will be easy."

The boys' venture into commerce jumped into action two weeks later when Freddy started selling seeds to the neighbors and folks at church. Since most planted gardens, and because his timing was right, he sold lots of packages of carrots, lettuce, spinach, squash and beans. He earned a nickel profit from each sale.

George thought, *Hey, selling salve sounds easy. Everybody needs salve don't they? It'll be a snap to sell a case.*

With confidence, he took money from the coffee can and placed his order. In a couple of weeks, a case of *Waterloo Brand Quick Drawing Salve* arrived in the mail.

"Draws out inflammation from minor cuts, scrapes and boils, ingrown toenails, insect bites, splinters and more," he read aloud from one of the containers. *This is miracle stuff.*

Now all George had to do was sell.

Earning a quarter profit from each tin seemed like a handsome return. However, there was nothing handsome about the reactions he got from his neighboring farmers when he offered 'drawing salve.' His job turned out to be downright tricky.

The startled neighbors seemed blindsided when George went into his sales pitch, regardless of the salve's advertised promises. Reactions moved through predictable patterns.

"Huh, oh, so you're selling salve are you?"

A few let out a big sigh, and followed that with a slump of the shoulders and statements like, "Well, I suppose I could maybe use some salve … if it works."

John Habluetzel seemed pretty cautious, "What's this stuff for, anyway?" All asked, "How much does it cost?"

Of course every neighbor—kindly or wary—had the same comment after hearing the price, "That much for it, huh?"

Bill Mansfield said, "Ah well, you might as well sell me a tin. Maybe I can use on my dog—"

To the young salesman's distress, most said, "Sorry, George, not this time. We have all the salve we need."

One reply or another came presentation after presentation. Though a few did buy a tin, George grew curious about his customer's peculiar expressions and stilted smiles.

Mrs. Ted Straub shook her head, rolled her eyes back, wrinkled her brow, and looked at her feet. After several deep breaths … she slowly dipped her hand into her purse. Then she shucked out her money for the unwanted tin, the price of being a good neighbor.

Slowly walking down the road toward his next 'victim,' George wiped sweaty palms on his pants. *Hey, I sold one, but Mrs. Straub sure had a funny look. Hope she isn't sick.*

However, George now had another sale, one of the few. Before long, all the neighbors and most folks at church had been offered their chance of a lifetime. Still, after covering his territory, more than a half-case sat on the living room floor, and George hadn't yet recouped his investment.

I'm letting down my end of the bargain. What am I going to do with all this salve?

As the sun dropped and the nighthawks started sweeping the dusk for insects, a defeated George sat on the couch, his unsold salve resting at his feet. Head down, he stared at circles in the linoleum. His forlorn look told the story.

"What's the matter, George?" his dad asked. "You look kind of down in the dumps."

"What's wrong with people, Dad? They don't want to buy this good salve. I tell 'em it's a chance of a lifetime, but mostly they say no. We're never going to get that gun."

"How many have you sold?"

"Eleven."

"Humm, just eleven? That leaves thirteen, doesn't it? Well, maybe we could use some more, don't you think, Veda?"

"Whatever would we do with it? Good heavens, we already bought two tins. I just don't understand whatever possessed that boy to order a whole case of salve. Who in the world would want that much of the stuff? It's just ridiculous."

"Now Veda, he did what he thought was right. We can help him out this time, can't we? The boys do enough around here to earn a little help from us … as long as they don't make it a habit."

"Well, that might be, but why in the world would he buy all that salve? And the stuff smells like an old goat. I hope it doesn't attract flies."

"Yep, it does have an odor. But we'll buy what you have left George—if you think you've learned from this."

"Thanks a lot Mom and Dad. You've taken a whole load of hay off my mind," he said. "You're really going to be glad you have extra salve. It'll last a long time, don't you think?"

"You're the one who should think, George," his fiery haired mom said. "But maybe this will be a good lesson for you."

"I'm glad you helped George," Freddy said. "He's looked like a droopy faced dog for three whole weeks."

George gritted his teeth. *That stupid salve.*

"You know boys, when you look at it, you worked really hard to earn for what you wanted, even if you did need a little help. If you'll give me the cash you have, I'll write a check for the order. That's a safe way to mail money, and your rifle will be here before you know it."

Fifteen minutes later, the boys dashed the quarter-mile to

the mail box with an envelope, and a donated three cent stamp, addressed to Ward's in Chicago. After pitching the envelope into the box, they raised the flag to let the mailman know he had something to pick up. Soon the gun would be on its way.

I can't wait, each boy thought.

§

While we waited on the mail, Dad explained yet another bit of homespun philosophy. "You boys are pulling your weight around here more and more. And that's good. I always say, 'If a person doesn't work, he doesn't eat.'"

Yep, you better work or you don't get anything.

As if hearing our thoughts, Dad added, "And why shouldn't a person earn his keep if he's able? People have to be responsible. That's why God gave them abilities."

But we never get done. Oh well, some people are worse off.

As we waited for the gun's arrival, we shifted our thoughts from BB guns to the rifle. And, it all happened because our folks had an unexpected need for salve—much of which was still unopened when we went off to college.

The gun order seemed to take forever. We watched and waited, and waited and watched hoping that each day would bring our Ward's package.

After more than two weeks, the RFD Route 1 mail carrier, Lawrence Buatte, drove our way with a cloud of dust rooster-tailing behind him. With an 'ahooga,' 'ahooga,' on his Model A Ford horn, the car clattered into the yard. He saw us and pointed to the big, long package on his back seat.

"Is this the package you've been asking me about? It was too big to fit in your mail box down at the corner, so I brought it up. Hope you boys don't mind."

Mind?!?

The scene around us—cats staring from the hayloft and Pep trotting to sniff and investigate—seemed to stand still while we opened the package. Grinning, the mail carrier

145

and Mom watched. When we pulled out the gun, we smiled until our faces hurt.

"Hey look at this! Man-oh-man, look at this! Let's take it out and give 'er a try. Thanks so much Mr. Buatte. And you too Mom."

"Now you be careful," Mom said.

§

WHERE ARE THE BULLETS?

"Dag nab it. How could we have forgotten shells? This is plain stupid," Freddy said. "Why didn't you remember them?"

"I didn't forget them, you did."

"I wanted to blaze away. It'll be Saturday night before we get to town … and today is only Wednesday. Blast it," Freddy said. "Let's go hunting anyway. We can pretend to load and shoot. We'll learn about the gun that way."

They lined up the .22's sights and practiced firing at tin cans, rocks on fence posts, perching blackbirds and even at far away hedge balls and sunflowers. The more they worked, the easier it got to hold the front ball sight steady in rear sight's vee. With each shot, they pulled the trigger guard instead of the trigger for their dad had told them firing empty would damage the firing pin.

"Hey, I got a direct hit in that coyote." Freddy said.

"Once we get bullets, we'll see if you can hit everything."

Saturday came at last and the boys rode in back of the two-door Chevy to Wamego. At the curb, Freddy pushed the back of seat ahead and squeezed out. "Excuse me mom, we're hurrying to the store to buy bullets."

"Boys," their dad said, "be sure to start with a box of shorts. They'll cost you less and are good for practice."

"Okay."

"Oh, and bring the shells to me after you buy them. You don't want to take them to the picture show."

In short order, the young hunters examined the boxes of

146

shells inside a glass case. The first shelf held the .22 shorts marked 29 cents in black crayon. They bought a box and headed to find their folks at Ince's Save Way Grocery Store. They gave the shells to their dad and left for the Columbian Theater to see, *Dick Tracy vs Cueball*, staring Morgan Conway and Anne Jeffreys.

Sunday came with chores and church. Once home the boys changed clothes, and on the run grabbed Velveeta sandwiches and headed outside to start shooting the new rifle, for real.

"Remember, you aren't shooting BB guns anymore. Be careful," their dad said. "Even .22 shorts can travel a mile, if you aim high enough."

As the boys headed for the door, he added, "And unless you're aiming at something, point the barrel down. Never point it at people or livestock, and put the gun down when crossing a fence. Also, don't cock it until you're ready to shoot. Uncock the rifle if you don't take the shot. And, never ever leave a bullet in it when you put it away."

Then he added, "Just because Shorty Brockman was careless doesn't mean you have to be."

At that point, he imparted his best advice, "Just use good judgment and make sure no one gets hurt."

§

We took Dad's warnings to heart, and didn't kill a living thing unless it was for the table, or a declared pest. We ate the occasional rabbit or squirrel, and we somewhat diminished the pest population; however, we had many other time consuming activities.

4-H had become one of our favorites and a highly important part of our lives. It offered us many challenges, some of which were more exciting than target practice.

For one thing, we'd have steers again. They would take lots of our time and effort, but hey, this year we knew what we were doing. Off to another meeting ….

TWELVE

BABY BEEF LOTTERY, BOBBY AND RENO AND HOW TO FIT AN ANIMAL FOR THE FAIR

[*Wamego Reporter* – *March 13, 1947*] ~ At the Columbian ~ Friday-Saturday, March 14-15, comes a double bill. First there is the Bumstead family with Daisy in "Blondie Knows Best." In this picture Dagwood fires the Boss. It was time.

Then he thinks he is Romeo—but Blondie holds all the keys. Then there is "Dangerous Millions," featuring a woman as dangerous as the fortune they sought, as the thrills they found. Shorts and Serial. Owl Show Saturday night.

1947

BABY BEEF LOTTERY

One after another, arctic blasts rattled the windows of the St. George School House and cold, drifted snow glistened under the weak light from bare-bulb street lamps. The central heating worked fine and nobody wanted the meeting to end for that meant braving chilled air and cold cars for the ride home.

During *New Business* one of the parents, Chet Harrell, asked to be recognized. "This is a special announcement for those of you who are planning to have Baby Beef projects this year. Thanks to the efforts of John Burgess, Raymond Krause and others, you'll be able to get an Angus calf at a lottery sale at the Wamego Stockyards on March 22nd."

"Are they good calves?" Bubba Brockman asked.

"I understand they come from a prize herd of Angus up near Belleville, the County Seat of Republic County. They are mostly January calves so they'll have some size," Mr. Harrell said.

"Do you want me to pass out these flyers?" his daughter Vice President Carol asked.

"Yes. Make sure everybody gets a copy. You kids and your parents need to look them over and decide if you want to have a calf from this group. If you want to buy one of these, let us know so we can let the rancher know how many calves to deliver."

While members looked over the notice, Mr. Harrell explained the details. "Here's how it'll work. If you participate, you will be able to buy a young Angus project calf from this select herd. We'll employ a lottery system during the selection. First, you draw a number out of a hat and then you look for a calf tagged with the same number. That animal will become your calf as soon and you pay for it. The lottery will give everybody an equal chance."

"I don't get it. What's a lottery?" George asked his brother.

"Well, it'll be kind of like drawing a certain kid's name

∞ **COUNTY WIDE BABY BEEF** ∞

∞ **LOTTERY AND SALE** ∞

WHO: 4-H MEMBERS & PARENTS

WHAT: ANGUS CALVES FOR SALE

WHERE: WAMEGO STOCKYARDS

WHEN: SATURDAY, 3/22/47 – 9AM

WHY: PROVIDE 4-H BABY BEEF

HOW: CALVES CHOSEN BY LOT

- PRICE PER POUND - GOING RATE
- NOTIFY OF INTENT – PURCHASE
- PAY ON DAY OF SALE
- ALL SALES FINAL

for the Christmas gift exchange at school. The big difference is you'll have to pay a whole lot more than the 32 cents you spent on that handkerchief you gave Pauline."

"How much money do you have now?" asked George.

"Our rifle took all that I had. We'll need the folks' help if we're going to come up with enough capital."

"Yeah, we're going to need the folks help alright."

In a loud, guttural tone, Bubba Brockman threw his head back and said, "I'm sure my old man will help me get a calf, 'cause he told me he'd do *anything*, to get me off my good for nothing, lazy backside and turn my life around *360 degrees*."

The boys' dad stared at Bubba, sighed and shook his head. *Those Brockmans.*

Mr. Harrell also shot a glance at Bubba, hesitated and then continued, "Let's take a few minutes so each family can talk this over. Bubba, you can ask your dad when you get home. We don't need your final decision until our next meeting."

The boys looked at their dad. "Well," he said, "what do you guys think? You did a good job raising Tom and Don. Are you game to try raising a couple of Angus?"

§

That was a good question. Were we ready to accept another 4-H challenge? Could we do it again?

Although we knew Dad and Mr. Krause had been working to buy calves for some time we hadn't paid much attention. Now we had to.

This would be different than talking things over with Dad and picking from his herd. He wouldn't be able to help us because the number we drew from the hat only matched one calf. Did we have the guts to jump in with both feet? What if we got a bad draw? We did know the calves coming were top quality, but were we ready for a black colored steer? And would the folks loan us the money?

Problems, problems … but then again, maybe we'd get lucky and draw the Grand Champion right off the bat.

§

Mr. Harrell cleared his throat and said, "I think this is a great opportunity and when the sale ends you'll be able to see much of your Fair competition right then and there. My son, Lyle, is going to participate. Now, if there are no further questions, Mr. President, I turn the meeting back over to you."

About a half hour later the business meeting was out of the way and the recreation and refreshments were done. All the families braved the cold and headed home.

The family's old car churned east and then north along the bumpy back roads. Light snow flittered in the car lights. Ruts were iced over and slick.

"If you fellows are each serious about owning and showing an Angus, you'll need some funds. Though Mom is home with Judy tonight, I suspect she'll agree with me to help you finance your projects. You can pay us back when you sell your steers."

In the headlights a snowy raccoon scrambled across the road. Its eyes showed as bright as embers. In quick order it disappeared into the underbrush.

At least that 'coon knows what the heck he's doing, Freddy thought. *What if I don't get a good calf? Would I end up finishing third again?*

A while later the Chevy pulled up to the house and soon both boys were in their unheated rooms snuggled in their beds, probably dreaming about calves and ribbons.

The next morning they hurried through chores and breakfast and were at Prairie View School by eight o'clock. The day flew and that evening they sat with their parents at the supper table.

Together the family decided Freddy and George would take part in the lottery and they worked out a plan for purchasing, feeding and showing what would be the newest members of the barnyard. A few weeks later, *Sale Day* arrived.

"Time to get up boys," their dad called up the stairs. "Let's get our stuff done. If we can leave here a bit early we can get a good look at all the calves."

As directed the boys hurried with the milking and feeding and soon came in for breakfast. There they got another hurry up as their mom said, "Hustle up and eat your food. I cooked up a lot of pancakes that'll stick to your ribs. It's going to be cold at that sale."

BOBBY AND RENO

At 8:00 o'clock the boys and their dad, donned warm coats and climbed onto the cold seat of the old three quarter ton

International. With the stock racks clattering from the rough road, they headed for the Wamego Stockyards. The truck's growling rear end gears sounded over the engine noise, a fact of life for well used trucks. Still, this vehicle kept on going.

I wonder if Dad added some more sawdust to the differential, Freddy thought, w*ould that muffle the grinding noise?*

Ignoring the sounds, their dad said, "Next month the county road maintainer will grade out this road, but for now we have to live with the ruts."

No one else said anything for a while until Freddy asked, "What do we do if we get a bum steer?"

"These are pretty good calves, but if you draw a smaller one, I guess you'll just have to live with it," his dad said. "Not everything in life is what you hope for. But if you put extra effort into caring for your animals you should do fine."

Again there was quiet, and in short order they had made it into Wamego and started looking over the calves corralled in the stockyards southeast of the city park. More than a couple of dozen young Angus steers milled around, each with an ear tag.

What's the point of looking the herd over? Freddy thought. *We're just going to get what we draw.*

The boys and their dad talked with other 4-H members and parents about what buying a calf this way would cost. As always in farm country, everyone was concerned about not overpaying. Would buying this way be worth it? Each calf would be weighed, and paid for at the going price per pound listed for the big K. C. Stockyards.

"I think you're getting the calves at a good price. It looks like you boys will soon be in business," their dad said.

Freddy and George took stock of the calves, and though they'd seen some professional judging, they still had lots to learn about comparing steers. But even though they both found a favorite calf, it'd take blind luck to draw it.

Bubba Brockman came with his brother Dicky Dale and their father Tubs. Bubba's Uncle Shorty had also tagged along, and trying to impersonate an animal husbandry professor, he stood there expounding on his special knowledge of livestock.

"Well now you take that there calf," Shorty said, pointing with an elm branch to an animal that stared back at him. "You can tell it'll be a winner because, look, it has a wet nose."

All calves have wet noses.

"Yeah, that one will bring top dollar when you fatten it up. You don't have to worry that it's kinda small. You feed it proper and it'll grow like a sapling into a giant oak."

Tubs nodded his agreement.

"Come on boys, the water's getting a little deep around here," the boys' dad said.

At that point the sale started. "Okay boys and girls," County agent Harvey Goertz said, "it's time for you to draw your numbers. Gather 'round."

One of the Sale volunteers stood on a flat bed truck and said, "Now come up one by one and pick a number out of this hat. When everyone gets a number, we'll see what animal goes to whom."

Freddy drew number 11 and George got number 17.

§

Once we'd drawn our numbers we raced to the corral fence to check out our calves. *Which animals did we get? Did we get winners?*

At that moment along the east fence, we spotted both #11 and #17. Together, we wrinkled up our noses. To be very honest, we were disappointed with what we saw.

§

"Well those calves don't look so bad," their dad said. "We'll take 'em home and you guys can get to raising them right."

Freddy slowly nodded as he stared at his smallish lottery draw. George cocked his head trying to figure out his calf's appearance. Though bigger than his brother's calf, it seemed out of proportion, longer and narrower than a prize steer. *It doesn't look all that great. Well, at least it has a wet nose ….*

"Dad, I don't think I can win much with this calf," Freddy said. "It's so small it won't be classified a Baby Beef by Fair time."

"Now you never know," his dad replied. "Some of the little ones grow pretty big. You'll have to feed him lots of grain and hay."

"Dad, my calf looks like a wiener dog," George said. "Do you think it'll be okay?"

"Sure," he said, "now don't you guys go getting excited. We'll make sure they grow into real Baby Beef."

After paying for their calves, they loaded the two Angus into the truck and headed home. On the way their dad asked, "What are you going to name your calves?"

"I don't know for sure, but maybe Bobby," Freddy said.

"I'm going to call mine, Reno," George said. "I saw an ad in Life Magazine that said Reno, Nevada is the 'Biggest Little City in the World.' I want my Reno to get big like the other Reno."

Freddy then settled on Bobby because he liked it. Their dad's thought? *Kids. Who can you figure them?*

§

That day at the Lottery Sale, we learned a good lesson about the real world. We found that sometimes even Dads didn't have control over all things, and we would just have to make the most of what we got.

Maybe it was good that we were farm kids and knew how to make do. For example, we could repair a fence with baling wire and use binder twine like a rope. We often straightened crooked nails to avoid paying good money to buy new ones. Scrap boards could repair many things from feed lot gates, to barn walls and even cover holes in the grain bins. Shucks, we could splice the mower's Pittman arm and even rivet in hand sharpened cutter bar sections.

Dad taught us to be resourceful, so we guessed we'd just have to find a way to make our calves competitive. Regardless, we'd find out at Fair time.

Meanwhile, we had school, the usual farm work and were involved in ever so many other things, one of which came out of the blue. *Thanks, Mom….*

HOW TO FIT AN ANIMAL FOR THE FAIR

At our Mother's urging, we agreed to give a demonstration at the next Blackjack 4-H Club meeting.

"Oh that won't be hard at all" she had said.

Hey, she doesn't have to do it. Anyway, what will we do?

After several dinner table discussions, we finally decided we'd demonstrate how to show a Baby Beef … the proper way. Now all we had to do was to figure out how to make the demonstration interesting and believable.

We gained some show experience at last year's Fair, and had garnered some ribbons, but now we were in a different situation, and we weren't too confident.

§

Once again the boys' mother had put them into a challenging predicament. She'd said this would be a good way for them to overcome fear of the unknown, by doing something in front of people.

"I've got it," Freddy said, "you just be the calf and I'll demonstrate to everybody how to show off your fine beef qualities."

"Why do I have to be the calf? I'll feel funny," said George.

"Don't be a chicken; most of the folks will be watching me anyway, so don't over react."

"I don't like it."

"Now George, it won't be that bad. And it will make a good presentation. You'll have fun and Freddy will do all the talking," his mom said.

"Okay … I guess."

So there the boys were. They had a month until the next meeting to polish their demonstration. But as so often happened, they put things off. Freddy had conjured up some ideas how to liven

155

things up, but he didn't share them with his brother. When the time came, George would learn what they were—the hard way.

The night finally arrived and at the proper time the Club Vice President introduced the Burgess boys and explained that the evening's recreation would be their demonstration of, "How to Fit an Animal for the Fair.".

Freddy immediately grabbed a small willow stick he had hidden under his chair and boldly walked to the center of the room. George sat for a moment, lowered his eyes, trying to think of a way to postpone his expected agony of being in front of people. Finally his mom jabbed him hard—he'd been jabbed before—and he slowly got up and walked to the side.

"There are many important rules to follow if you want to fit your animal for the Fair, and earn a blue ribbon," Freddy said. He walked toward his younger brother and continued, "First you have to lead him into the ring."

Once he reached George he whapped his 'calf' hard on his shins with the switch. George fell onto all fours, glared at his brother and pretended to be a Baby Beef. With skill, Freddy slipped a rope halter over his brother's head, wrapped it over the nose and cinched it tight. Chuckles came from the crowd.

"This is going to be some interesting recreation," some parent was heard to say. Bubba Brockman just snorted.

Freddy jerked on the rope and his brother flinched and followed on hands and knees to center stage. "Notice how I firmly lead my calf to let him know who is boss?" Freddy jerked again and George flinched again.

"Now you want your calf to stand up straight to show off his good qualities and present a level back-line," Freddy said. To make his point, he again used the willow switch and tapped his brother hard under his stomach. George responded and straightened his back. Another glare; and more chuckles.

"See how easy that is? You'll have to teach your animal ahead of the Fair, but he'll learn. You also have to find a way to get his feet as far apart as possible." As he spoke, Freddy whapped George's arms and legs. The chuckles turned to laughs.

By now George looked abused. *Freddy didn't poke me like that when we practiced. What's the matter with him anyway?*

Freddy eyed his calf and smiled. His parents looked at each other and shook their heads.

"To get your calf to stand even straighter, just before the judge approaches you, tickle your calf's belly." As Freddy rubbed his calf's stomach with the stick, George just couldn't hold back any longer. He started to giggle and squirm. The laughter got louder.

"If your calf gets unruly, just flick your fingers on his nose." Yep, Freddy flicked George's nose. The Baby Beef twitched his head and sneezed. The crowd roared.

Finally finished with his litany of does and don'ts, Freddy asked if anyone had any comments. When no one asked a question, the demonstration ended—almost. Freddy whapped his animal one more time, for good measure.

George, still on his hands and knees, looked at the crowd, paused, and with a painful face voiced his only speaking part, "Mooo."

The room exploded with laughter and applause. The demonstration was over. The boys' parents weren't sure if they approved, but everyone else—except George—thought it was a brilliant way to explain the proper technique of fitting an animal for the Fair. Even Bubba slapped George on his back and said, "You done good, pilgrim."

On the way home George sat staring out the window. His mom asked him if he was okay. He nodded yes. To Freddy she said, "Well you can thank your lucky stars that you didn't hurt your brother." Freddy just laughed under his breath. *That was fun.*

George thought, *Well if the audience thought the demonstration was good, it must have been. Next time we'll use a jackass—and it'll be Freddy!*

THIRTEEN

CHIEF NEGOTIATIONS, THE HORSE TANK SWIM AND BUBBA DIES ALMOST

[*Wamego Reporter* - JULY 17, 1947] ~ BLACKJACK 4-H PROJECT MEETING ~ The 4-H project Meeting was held July 10 at the St. George High School in the Home Economics room. Some of the girls were working on their hand towels and tea towels, while others worked on dresses.

There were twenty-three 4-H members, two leaders, and four mothers present for the meeting.

The next sewing meeting will July 17th in the Home Economics room at 1:30 p.m. Refreshments were served by Carol Harrell.

1947

CHIEF NEGOTIATIONS

The boys spent extra time caring for Bobby and Reno. The young men were determined to overcome their animals' shortfalls.

Freddy thought, *How can I make Bobby grow faster? George hasn't done anything special for his calf, but Reno keeps on getting bigger.* Freddy ran the currycomb over Bobby's back. *Maybe I need to take on another calf. Bobby is just too small.*

A few weeks later Freddy saw an opportunity when he and his brother went with their dad to check on the cattle herd in the big pasture. They drove across the pasture's bluestem onto a slight knoll where their dad stopped the car and honked the horn. Across the way, the herd of cows, each with a calf alongside, stopped grazing and began running toward the car.

"Look at 'em come. Ole Maudie sure wants to know what we've brought her, doesn't she?" Freddy asked. "Look at those calves hop and run."

"Yep, the cows know we have some salt and minerals for them and the calves don't want to be left behind," his dad said. "You get the bag of minerals out of the trunk and George you get that salt block. Put 'em in the wooden boxes over there."

Following instructions, George lugged the heavy block to the cattle salt box. He stared at what remained of last month's block and thought, *Their tongues sculptured tunnels in the block.*

Freddy poured out the minerals and soon the former milk cow Maudie, led the Herefords and a single Shorthorn cow to the boxes for a taste. The calves watched the jostling, but stayed back.

Freddy looked at the youngsters and thought, *These Hereford calves look much better than Bobby. I wonder if Dad could part with one.*

At that point his dad said, "Okay, let's go. The cows and calves all look fine. With more warm weather, they'll go through the salt a lot faster. We'll now need to check on them every week."

The threesome climbed back into the car and drove to the barbed wire gate. Freddy got out and opened it and his dad drove onto the Wheaton Road. Freddy closed the gate—a must on a farm—and they headed home.

That evening the family sat around the new G.E. radio powered by electricity brought to the farm by the REA. First, they listened to songs and jokes from *The Grand Ole Opry*, with Little Jimmie Dickens and Bill Monroe. Next came an episode of *The Shadow* followed by *Duffy's Tavern* with the classic lines, "Duffy's Tavern, where the elite meet to eat, Archie the manager speaking … Duffy ain't here … oh, hello Duffy." At nine o'clock the boys headed upstairs to bed.

After Freddy snuggled down on top of his covers, he thought about the group of beef calves in the big pasture. He remembered one in particular, a well proportioned Hereford steer. To Freddy it appeared better than Bobby and Reno in all respects.

I wonder if I could use him for my Baby Beef project. I'm gonna ask Dad if I can have that calf for 4-H.

Next morning the family gathered at the table for breakfast. . Just a few minutes into the meal, George's Mom spotted him dawdling with his meal.

"George, you quit playing with your food. Hurry up and finish," she said. "You boys need to clean out the barn."

George nodded and again stabbed at his hard fried egg with its chemical smell. *Could I get petrified legs eating these eggs? I hope our hens haven't been near a sulfur spring.*

While George struggled with his breakfast, Freddy cleared his throat and asked his dad, "Don't you think my Baby Beef calf is kind of small and maybe not the best for a 4-H project?"

"Well, he isn't as big as he could be. My guess is he was born in February instead of January like we expected."

"What if instead of taking Bobby to the Fair, I took that biggest Hereford calf from the beef herd? He's larger and has better conformation," Freddy said.

"We might consider that, but what about your Angus calf?"

"Well, suppose I trade Bobby to you for the Hereford?"

"I can see you might want to do that, but do you think that would be good business on my part?"

"What if I kept Bobby then and raised the Hereford besides? That way I could make more money in the cattle business," Freddy said. "Of course, you'd have to be my banker again."

Shaking his head, Freddy's dad said he'd think about it. When Freddy left the table a big smile crept over his dad's face. *That boy sure can get things done.*

So at a family meeting that night, Freddy agreed to all the conditions his dad proposed. He would be advanced enough money to buy the calf at market price, he would pay off that loan when he sold the calf and he's also show Bobby at the Fair.

A couple of hours later, Freddy lay on his bed and thought, *It's going to be a good deal to have two calves.*

The next morning Freddy's mom asked, "Have you come up with a good name for your calf?"

"I thought of a lot of good names. But, you know I think I'll call him Chief. With his red and white coat he kind of looks like he's wearing an Indian outfit. Chief will be a good name for him."

"My guess," his brother said, "is that by Fair time your Chief will look like a papoose. My Reno is going to be huge."

And so the good-hearted teasing started with assurances from first one boy and then the other about the slim possibilities of losing to his brother.

Through the night the Kansas skies had opened and savage rain poured down. The wind blew and lightning flashed everywhere, with thunderclaps rattling the windows. In a little over one hour, more than two inches of rain fell.

Each lightning bolt lit up the road, yard, fields and corral. The rain ran in all directions. These little watercourses would later come together to head for the Slough or Rock Creek.

Next morning, pools of water were everywhere, reflecting in the morning sun. It would be a while before things dried out.

DIGGING AND DAY DREAMING

"Man, it's hot." Freddy said as he struggled to spade a shallow ditch from the big puddle in front of the house. Although the storm was long gone—luckily the wheat had been harvested—it left a small lake three or four inches deep near the steps.

Even the casual observer could tell by Freddy's pursed lips and the sweat dripping from his sunburned face that he was annoyed. "I hate hot weather, wet soil and high humidity. But most of all, I hate the heat. I can't wait until fall."

George, leaning on his shovel, shook his head. He glanced at his brother. *He's nuts. I love this heat. Better than cold weather for sure.*

"Well," George said, talking while his brother worked, "you'll just have to put up with hot weather for a while longer."

"You're right, so let's finish up so we can get in the shade."

In about fifteen minutes Freddy's trench started draining the puddle of water down the lane. With the job finished, he headed toward the house. "I'm going to get a drink of water."

For his part, George walked to the stock truck parked under a shady elm. He climbed onto its bed and lay back, cupping his head in his hands. While staring at the scattered clouds, a whisper of a breeze cooled him some—enough—and he was soon lost in thought. As his mom often said, "He's a thousand miles away."

Heat doesn't bother me. I can wear a flannel shirt all year round. When I sweat I cool right down.

George wasn't hot this morning because he'd spent his time daydreaming while his brother spaded. Lying looking into the heavens, his mind floated far away … into the realm of philosophy.

He swatted away a fly and thought, *Yep, it's like Mrs. Draper said. A lot of things can make us rich.*

His teacher often told her students that a person could get rich by reading books or by looking around at the wonders of nature. After she explained what she meant, George had caught on.

I think people are richer when they live and work in the country and sweat a lot. Cities are all cramped up. Man it's peaceful out here. He dreamed on … in no particular direction.

It sure feels good to sit in the shade and let the hot wind blow across my face. I like to watch grasshoppers jump across wheat stubble. It's funny how mud cracks when it dries. Weeds sure have crazy shapes when they get all brown and full of seeds. Dry pasture grass ruffles when the wind blows. I like to see cows huddled in the shade, whipping their tails at flies.

When it's really hot at night and I get sweaty in bed, I like to stretch out on the floor near the window and feel the puffs of air. They cool me, most times. Sometimes I see the Moon. I wonder if it really is made of green cheese.

He shifted his body some and had more thoughts. *Darn, I wish the folks would buy me bigger overhalls.*

I love it when the family gathers at the Cemetery on Decoration Day. It's always hot. I like those jars of peonies and iris we put on Grandpa's and Grandma's graves. And, when the grownups head to a shade tree to visit, us kids can explore or play tag. No one seems to notice the heat when we're having fun.

The annual Memorial Day get-together at the Louisville Cemetery was a tradition. The family went there every year to meet the boys' dad's siblings to honor Grandfather David Samuel Burgess and Grandmother Mary Shea Burgess and other deceased relatives.

George took a chew on a piece of straw and continued to contemplate his world. *I guess I don't like chiggers or flies or bugs that much. Yeah, and mosquitoes make me itch. But that's a part of the summer.*

When it's hot, I sure like to swim in the Slough. The leaches I got didn't bother me. Why do the red tail hawks call so much? I wonder why heat waves on the highway look like pools of water. Doesn't the country smell good?

His mind paused for a few seconds and then moved on. *When we fish down in Rock Creek, it's always humid and still. It feels sticky and damp there on the bank, but I feel cooler when sweat pours from my face. I like baseball and playing catch … except when Freddy throws too hard. I really like playing Mumbly Peg, though I did stick my foot with my pocket knife once.*

More out-of-the-blue thoughts popped into his mind. *Another thing I guess I like is to hear tractor noises in the distance. One thing I don't like is cutting cockleburs and sunflowers out of the corn … except when we fight the pirates.* At that point he grimaced, remembering the many cuts and scratches he suffered from the cornstalk leaves and the weeds.

I guess we just have to put up with the hot sun and the weeds and the bugs. It's all part of farming. It doesn't matter much because it's still nice out here, no matter how hot the weather is. And we do have plenty of elbow room. I think when I grow up I'm going to have a big farm of my own.

He looked up and spotted two turkey buzzards circling high and away to the west. *I wonder what the farm looks like from the sky. I'd like to fly like a bird. In that school book I read that Amelia Earhart said 'You've never seen a tree until you've seen its shadow from the sky.' Wow.* Then he squinted through the clouds toward the sun overhead.

I guess we need sunlight to raise crops. Maybe that's one reason I don't mind the heat. Boy, there sure are a lot of ways to get rich out here. Then ….

"George, where are you? It's time to do chores. George!"

"Huh?"

And so ended George's reverie.

THE FUN OF PROJECT FORMS

As far as 4-H went, there was one nuisance that couldn't be avoided. Having a project entailed painstaking record keeping.

"Man, these records stink," Freddy said as he sat at the living room table with his brother and dad. *I'll never get this done. Keeping track of the weights and dates is bad enough, but how do you know the cost of all the grass a calf eats?*

"Dad, how do you figure the cost of the grass for a calf?"

His dad said. "You get the rental price for an acre and times that against the number of acres you need for your animal."

"Yeah," Freddy said. "I'll enter that for both of my calves."

"What about the corn you feed them? You probably average about a coffee can of ground corn twice a day for each calf don't you?" their dad asked.

"Probably. They'll eat more toward the end and not so much at first," Freddy said. "How much does that cost?"

"Five months is about one hundred fifty days. So figure out how much corn there is in a can and then how many cans it takes. Calculate how many pounds that is. Now let's look in the *Capital* and find what corn prices are. It looks to be about $2 a bushel

Under the light of the single bulb dangling above the table, the boys worked their 4-H project forms. Freddy asked, "Dad, how many pounds of corn are there in a bushel?"

"The standard is 56 pounds."

Freddy nodded and did some calculating. He stared at his sheet and wrote down what he'd figured. George completed Reno's form and handed it to his dad to check over. Then Freddy finished his form for Bobby. The paperwork was done, for now.

What a relief.

Over the next few weeks the boys turned their full attention to training the three calves to lead, stand and get groomed.

"Dang it, Reno, come on … just come along," George said to the balking, big boned Black Angus steer. George couldn't erase the memory of their demonstration at the 4-H Club meeting. *That darned Freddy.*

Barn cats scurried out of the way when the parade of two boys and three calves circled through their territory. Again and again the entourage marched and marched. Soon the weeks of work paid off, for Bobby, Chief and usually Reno would lead as commanded.

Both boys felt relieved for they knew that in the show ring well mannered calves tended to get higher awards. And little training just welcomed trouble.

And, it was trouble that Bubba Brockman's big black steer would give him at Fair time. Bubba, like his Uncle Shorty, sometimes struggled to get things right, and when Bubba trained Rocket, he did a pretty shabby job. We'll get to that later … at Fair time.

THE HORSE TANK SWIM

A few days later, the morning started out warm and humid, but without regard for the weather, there were things to be done on the Burgess farm.

"Well fellows, we need to clean out the horse tank today. It's been a while. Let's go," the boys' dad said.

When the three gathered beside the windmill, sunlight reflected off the round metal tank. Against the blue sky, sparrows flew overhead, some landing on the fence posts to sing and twitter. In the barn, mice darted to find grain and avoid the cats. Pep barked and surveyed the activity from his citadel on the manure pile.

"There's moss growing in the tank so we need to get rid of it. Bucket out all of the water you can and then we'll tip the tank on its side. We can scrub it with that old broom and flush it out."

I guess 'we' means George and me. Freddy thought.

§

We called the common animal water tank—some nine feet across—the horse tank, even though cows and calves used it too. All our animals needed water, so the tank sat just across the fence from the windmill. A float released the windmill's brake each time the water level got low.

That worked fine for adding water, but it didn't address the growing algae and moss. This slimy plant matter encroached on drinkable water. So occasionally we needed to scrub the tank.

On this day, while Dad worked up at the machine shed, we spent considerable time scooping out bucket after bucket of the fouled water. A little before noon, he helped us tip the tank on its side and out came the remaining water full of slippery gunk that smelled like newborn calf poop.

§

When their dad went back to his tasks, George stood back stalling. "That smell is getting to me," he said, wrinkling up his nose.

"Ah, quit whining and bring me another bucket of fresh water," Freddy said. "The faster we wash this out, the faster we'll get done. I want to toss some balls. Plus, I have to practice leading Chief and Bobby some more."

165

"Well I don't want to touch that stuff. It might turn me green like that movie guy in *The Monster of the Hidden Swamp*," George said, using his mind to add color to the black and white film. "You saw what happened to him."

"C'mon and just keep working, we're almost done." That turned out to be an understatement for it took the boys almost an hour to get the tank scrubbed out.

While Freddy gave the tank a final rinse, George asked their dad to come help right it. Once in place, they released the windmill brake and fresh water flowed into the clean tank.

"The more the wind blows, the more water comes into the tank. It's going to fill up in a hurry today," George said. "Hey, look how the water swirls."

"Yeah, that's a real eddy. I wonder if the wind spins and turns like that," Freddy said as he and his brother pondered eddies and wind currents and admired their work.

§

After chores that evening, while the setting July sun cast long shadows from the west to the east, Dad asked us to follow him. Together we walked to inspect the now filled horse tank.

At the tank, a hot breeze rippled the clear water and he said, "You know, that looks pretty inviting. Why don't we take a swim?"

We stood amazed and watched him. First, he looked out toward the road, then paused and took off his overhalls—and everything else. We were flabbergasted.

Sure we'd taken swims with Dad in the creek, but then he'd worn his underwear for a bathing suit. We'd never seen him in the buff.

We shouldn't look down, should we?

Timidly, we looked at each other and then tore off our clothes as well. Kersplash!

Before long the three of us circled the tank round and round, laughing and splashing water on each other. We wondered if Mom was watching from the kitchen. She never said.

That indeed was a special time for us. We'd worked hard doing what had to be done and then we ended up cooling down, albeit under unusual circumstances.

We'd talk about that swim with Dad for a long time. Would we ever swim like that with our kids? We'd have to wait and see.

Our thoughts slowly drifted to the next day, for the County's 4-H clubs were to hold a Field Day. We planned to attend, and that would be another time to remember.

BUBBA DIES ALMOST

That morning, by seven o'clock Dad and the two of us left the farm to pick up Bubba Brockman for the ride to the Field Day at a ranch in the Vermillion Valley south of Onaga.

Of course, when we drove up to Bubba's house he wasn't ready. Dad didn't say anything, but his nose curled. With Bubba in the car, Dad headed the car north on the hour long trip.

About half way to Louisville, Bubba started telling jokes. "Did you hear about the cow that fell in the washing machine? Well, she came out giving butter that tasted like Rinso."

We smiled. Dad said nothing.

Did you hear about the couple arguing as they drove by a field full of mules? The husband asked his wife, "Are these your relatives?" "Yep," she replied, "my in laws."

We smiled. Dad said nothing.

When we drove through Louisville on Highway 99, Bubba told the one about a hen and a rooster. Along the Wheaton Road we heard about a pet skunk getting switched with a wild one. And, during the drive on the Onaga Road he told about a cow's afterbirth. Dad didn't say anything, but we watched his neck muscles bulge out.

When Bubba started seeing how long he could belch, Dad's composure failed. Though seldom stern with others' kids, this time he clenched his teeth and said, "Bubba, you may think that is funny, but in most people's estimation, that's pretty rude." Then he said, "I prefer not to hear that in my car."

Bubba mumbled something like an apology and then tried to be funny again. When nobody laughed, he turned silent for the rest of trip.

When we arrived at the ranch not far from Onaga, we joined about 25-30 4-H club members, parents and leaders from around the county. County Agent Harvey Goertz greeted everyone to start the program.

"Hello everyone. It is good you could come today. We have a fine program planned to give you information about quality beef cattle programs. Let's walk over to that pen and 4-H member George Wayne Walker will demonstrate how to select quality breeding stock. Then we'll have a judging contest and before lunch we'll take a tour of the livestock buildings," Mr. Goertz said.

"When you look for breeding stock try to find animals with true breed characteristics. Bulls need masculine heads and females should look feminine. Regardless of the breed, look for depth of chest, width, stockiness and a level back," George Wayne said to those of us sitting on the top of the big pen fence rail.

We tried to understand his ideas, but nothing seemed clear. "See how this heifer has a lady's face? And, she has a fine calf-carrying capacity."

All of the heifers looked the same to us.

"You can tell this bull calf is going to be much sturdier than the one over there," he said.

Again, we could spot little difference.

Over and over, for the next few minutes, County Beef Champion, George Wayne made comparisons by pointing out worthwhile traits.

We stared with marginal understanding.

168

After the demonstration, Mr. Goertz said, "That was well done, George. Now, each person should take one of the judging scorecards that are being passed around and you'll have a chance to put what you learned into practice. Okay boys, herd those four Angus heifers into the ring and we'll have a judging contest."

Both of us looked and studied the calves, but just couldn't see much difference. In desperation, we picked the biggest calf for first place. About ten minutes later, the judge agreed. Hey, maybe we were learning after all.

§

On the other hand, Bubba missed them all. Clowning around, he'd closed his eyes and stabbed the ballot with his pencil. It didn't work, but it got the laugh he wanted.

With the judging over, everyone toured the big red cattle barn with its indoor stock pens and a huge hay mow overhead. Built next to it were two open sided hay sheds with a hay-moving elevator system. In front were two huge watering tanks with float systems, and submersible electric heaters to handle winter ice.

"Man, this is something. Look at all those buildings," Freddy said while the group moved onto the lawn for a picnic lunch.

About thirty minutes later the crowd piled onto a rubber tired hay wagon hooked to a John Deere B. The tour circled around the pastures to look at the grass, the salt boxes and the three water storage ponds, each with a large earthen dam.

As the 4-Hers rode across the dam of one pond, Bubba stood up and pretended to dive into the water. The wagon wheels hit a rut and Bubba sprung airborne.

To his grief, the base of the dam was wider than his jump. He landed almost headfirst in the mud. He didn't move.

The tractor braked to a stop and several adults ran down the slope. The boys' dad reached Bubba first and turned him over.

Bubba took a breath and inched open his eyes. Their whites shined brightly out of the black mud-pack. "Am I dead?"

Everyone laughed. At that the boys' dad wiped Bubba down with some straw and told him to wash up in the pond.

Noticing Bubba's open mouth, George thought, *I think Bubba has some dental issues.*

About an hour later, people left for home, and in the Burgess car, the boys' dad lectured the entire way about the need for farm safety. Was Bubba listening? You couldn't always tell.

The boys' dad continued his safety theme for all forms of activities. Even in sports, he said, a person must be vigilant to the dangers waiting to happen.

Freddy said, "Yeah, and when you're playing baseball, you have to watch how you slide or you'll get a real strawberry on your thigh."

"And a batter has to be alert so he doesn't get hit by a pitch. Some day I'm going to get a real ball glove and play on a real team," George said.

Freddy nodded his agreement.

Bubba never messed with sports. Too strenuous.

Regardless of the boys' activity, whether working with their Baby Beef, whacking weeds, doing chores or cleaning out the horse tank, baseball was always in the front of their minds. They watched the town teams play, practiced with their broom sticks and gravel, and tossed a ball back and forth.

After all baseball was the *American pastime*, for those who knew Lee Sure.

FOURTEEN

MANY FORMS OF BASEBALL, MOWING 'EM DOWN AND THE OIL DRINKING POSSUM

[*Wamego Reporter* – July 21, 1947] ~ BLACKJACK 4-H PROJECT MEETING ~ The 4-H project Meeting was held July 10 at the St. George high school in the Home Economics room. Some of the girls were working on their hand towels and tea towels, while others worked on dresses.

There were twenty-three 4-H members, two leaders, and four mothers present for the meeting.

The next sewing meeting will July 17th in the Home Economics room at 1:30 p.m. Refreshments were served by Carol Harrell.

1947

MANY FORMS OF BASEBALL

All through the summer of 1947, the grand old game of baseball filled much of the boys' leisure time. That is, if you counted listening to games on the radio. Sometimes, if the signal made it to Kansas, they heard Cubs games on WGN from Chicago or the Cardinals on KMOX from St. Louis.

Most often, however, they settled for ball games over the newly created Liberty Broadcasting Network. Announcing those games, broadcast by KMBC in Kansas City, was Gordon McClendon who recreated many old time major league games from the 1930s, and some as far back as the 1890s.

The Old Scotchman, as he called himself, used box scores for a guide and broadcast the play-by-play of full nine-inning games as if they were live. These games included crowd noise, the crack of the bat smacking the ball and the pop of the ball into a glove. The sound effects seemed so authentic that McClendon fooled listeners for a long time, including the boys.

The announcer had a knack for telling about how teams back in the early days played with one ball for an entire game, even if it landed among the buggies and horses or got lumpy. The

Broadcaster went into detail how the players caught the ball barehanded and explained that the bases were posts in the ground.

Could that be? Posts for bases? Baseball bare handed? The boys wondered. *Well, that is for the birds. Why didn't players use gloves?*

By the boys' time, all players had their own baseball gloves of some kind … except for the Burgess boys. To play catch, Freddy or George wore the tiny glove their dad played with during the late '20s, while the other brother wore a leather work glove. Both felt to the boys like catching bare handed.

§

During the late spring and early summer of that year, our baseball craving grew and grew. Besides hearing live or recreated games on the radio, each Sunday after church we travelled with the folks to see a town team game in Wamego, or Westmoreland, or Louisville or perhaps, even at Flush, a tiny spot in the road a few miles north.

Dad's cousin and best friend George Burgess pitched for Louisville. He was our hero as was Red Machin who played second base, and knuckle-balling Wally Ubel, another star pitcher. Bob Burgess, George's brother, used his new bat to smack the ball into the outfield. Local character Roy Weaver did the catching, and he was a great hitter. It seemed to us our favorite team, Louisville, always won, even when they lost.

Louisville played on a field next to the big limestone schoolhouse. The infield had a high backstop, but outfield had no fences. Weaver would drive smash hits that rolled and rolled into left field. If the ball got past the left fielder, these shots often turned into homeruns—if hit in the early innings.

However, Roy and his brother Sam had a habit of visiting Sam's car between innings. For some reason, Roy's ability to run weakened after a few of these trips. Sam, who announced the games from a modest booth, also seemed influenced. For one thing, he got funnier and funnier and slurred his words by the ninth inning. By the later innings some of those in the crowd got more and more annoyed, although they had to fight back laughs.

After a few innings, when it came Roy's time to bat, he'd leave his catcher's shin guards on. If he connected with the ball—he very often did—he'd jog down the baseline with the leather guards just a flapping. This really irritated Dad and he'd shout—very unusual for him—at Roy to take the gear off. It didn't do any good.

There was no admission charge for these games, but during a late inning someone would pass a hat to those in the stands to collect a little money for balls and bats. The average contribution was around 20 cents, although we occasionally saw a big spender drop in 35 cents.

A highlight of that summer came just after the 4th of July in Wamego when a county All-Star bunch played an exhibition game with the Topeka Owls—who played their home games at Community ballpark in North Topeka—of the Class C Western Association. Two of the Owls' star pitchers were right hander 'Fireball' Lee Dodson, Topeka's 'Mr. Baseball,' and left hander Ross Grimsley who later played for the Chicago White Sox. Though a good team, the Owls had problems because their owner, Ray 'Fido' Murphy, didn't pay his bills and was later suspended from baseball.

The Owls won that exhibition game, but we didn't care. We'd seen real baseball with a professional baseball team. Now we knew for sure what we wanted to be when we grew up.

Our lofty goals were fine, but the lack of baseball gloves nagged at us. How could we practice? How could we improve without real gloves? Without baseball gloves we would always be amateurs … wouldn't we?

§

The boys' baseball itch just had to be scratched and so they saved birthday and special jobs money for the day they could buy their own gloves. They had baseball fever and longed to approach the game at the higher level.

They began an earnest study of their problem. To view suitable gloves, they poured over the J.C. Penny and the Montgomery Ward Catalogs. The more they studied the less sure they felt about which to buy. They had two constants, the need for gloves and the miserable sum of thirteen dollars between them.

"Hey Dad," Freddy asked one day, "can you help us get a couple of ball gloves? We need 'em awful bad."

"What's wrong with my glove? It worked for me."

"It's too small, and we need two gloves," George said.

"You want us to get good like you were when you played, don't you?" Freddy asked, using just a touch of persuasiveness.

"Okay, let me take a look in the catalogs. Have you spotted any good gloves you can afford?"

"Well, maybe. See the gloves on this page. I'd like to get that Lou Boudreau glove that costs $6.00. He plays shortstop for the Cleveland Indians. I like the glove's shape."

"And I want that Joe Gordon glove for the same price," George said. "Shipping only costs a dollar, so we can afford that. We have $13.00."

"I wish we had seven more dollars and then we could get this Joe Garagiola catcher's mitt. You know, he's the Cards' star behind the plate. That would be good if you wanted to play catch with us," Freddy added.

"Humm. Well, maybe it would be good for you to have the mitt. Why don't you order all three. I'll pay for the catcher's glove."

Can you believe that?

The next day the boys handed over their funds and mailed the order and their dad's check for $20.00 to Wards … and the wait began. Each day seemed longer than the one before, but still no package arrived.

Will they ever get here?

Almost two weeks later, Mr. Buatte, drove up to the house with a large cardboard box. Since it wouldn't fit in the mail box a quarter mile away, he claimed he brought the box up just to be sure it didn't get stolen. Then again, he may have just wanted to share the boys' joy with their new possessions. And of course, the contents thrilled the young ballplayers. *Baseball gloves at last.*

I'm never, never going to leave my glove unattended. Someone might walk off with it, George thought.

§

Have you ever smelled a brand new baseball glove? The delicious aroma of tanned leather and oil almost overpowered us. Something about the smell in the box jumped out and caused our hearts to beat a little faster. We now knew complete happiness. We'd be playing catch in minutes.

At first, almost every ball popped out of our gloves. They needed breaking in. Dad had us work linseed oil into the leather, and then alternate between pounding our fists and throwing a baseball into the pockets. We worked and worked, wanting very much to do things right. Over time the leather softened.

At Dad's urging we practiced and practiced. After chores most evenings, we threw fly balls or grounders to each other until dark. Cracked smokehouse wallboards proved that we also chucked some wild pitches in the dusk. And there were other hazards from late-in-the-day baseball.

Swollen knuckles and jammed fingers showed that we sometimes failed to catch balls. We'd learned that a good popping pull would un jam a finger, so we'd go back throwing and catching until it happened again.

We sometimes could talk the Louisville Town Team out of a used ball. It might be a ball with popped stitching or be dirty from landing in the mud.

We got pretty good at sidling up to the players on the bench and asking if they had any old balls that were too banged up for practice. For us, a baseball was a baseball.

§

The boys played catch as often as they could. They came up with rules, on the spot most often, to make their games civilized. There could be no hard throws from up close and if either boy threw wildly, he chased the ball down.

Of course, this caused some disputes. What was catchable or a bad throw or an overpowering one? Most often the arguments were settled without either boy quitting the field, though the charge of cheater did generate some loud debates.

A bruised hand, a pitfall for young baseball players, always lurked nearby. When a baseball—hardball as many called it—banged the bottom bone of an index finger it was instant pain. Once that spot bruised, it stayed that way all season. Some players put sponges inside their gloves. Some just put their index finger on the outside.

Freddy favored the exposed finger, but not George. Oh well, they also differed on which was better, the shucking glove or the peg—and for many other reasons. They were brothers.

Hard throwing Freddy liked to practice pitching. Using their Joe Garagiola mitt, George played catcher. This satisfied Freddy for the most part, but George hated his brother's wildness. As history would show, Freddy would never become a pitcher … though he tried a couple of embarrassing times.

George really liked another game they played. While imitating Brooklyn Dodgers outfielder Duke Snider, he shagged high fly balls his brother threw. George moved with grace and caught anything thrown his way. So while Freddy liked the infield, and pitching, George found he was a natural for the outfield.

In reality, much of the time games of catch were just that, simple back and forth tosses. This was supposed to be easy.

"Hey you creep, why did you throw that ball over there by the fence? I'm standing right here. What's the matter with you?" Freddy asked and walked across the lane to pick up the wild toss.

"It just slipped," George said.

"What do you mean slipped? It came out of the side of your hand. C'mon, think. Put some dirt on your hand."

"Maybe it's the grease from Mom's fried chicken. Anyway, I'm tired of throwing; let's hit some rocks."

§

Over time, we deposited a hundred pounds of gravel from the lane to the barnyard with our broomsticks. And sometimes we'd 'broadcast' our games.

§

"Hello once again, everybody. It's a bee-yooo-tiful day for baseball," said Freddy, mimicking St. Louis Cardinals Broadcaster, Harry Caray, while redoing a 1946 World Series game between the Cards and the Boston Red Sox. "It's the last of the ninth and Dom DiMaggio is up with the score tied," Freddy said.

With his left hand, Freddy tossed up a bit of gravel and swung. The broomstick and rock collided. 'Twick!' The small rock sputtered away, falling down toward the dust just beside the horse tank.

"It's a tall can of corn to left field. The left fielder isn't going to get there. It's falling into short left for a double. Hole … leee cow! What a great piece of hitting," Freddy continued as he reached down for another small rock.

"That brings up the Splendid Splinter … Ted Williams, with third baseman Vern Stephens on deck. The Red Sox have a good chance to score and win the game. Here's the stretch and the pitch."

Again the broomstick and a rock met. A sharper hit headed toward the barn wall.

"Williams swings and lashes a shot down the right field line. It is all the way to the corner and off the wall. Here comes the winning run. Williams has done it again, and won it for the Red Sox. It's another one-run victory. Oh my, oh my, the Cardinals better get busy."

The Cards did get busy and won the Series 4-3, George thought.

Cardinals pitcher Harry 'The Cat' Brecheen had won three of the games. Joe Garagiola, had batted .316. Injured Williams hit

.200 for the series. Freddy's hero Tex Hughson pitched in three games, and didn't win a game but lost one.

Both boys read the daily box scores in the Sports Page of the paper. They followed the exploits of their favorite players and kept track of who was on top of each League. They knew a lot about most every big league ballpark including the parks' names and the distances to its outfield walls. No doubt about it, Freddy and George were immersed in baseball. They played when they could.

Baseball was their favorite game, but as you've already seen, they could make a fun game out of work. And they had many opportunities to make believe and do a real job at the same time.

MOWING 'EM DOWN

Could farm work be as fun as baseball? Well no, but—

One of the most labor intensive projects on the farm featured man and beast working together. At haying time, neighbors worked together for a couple of weeks ... cutting, curing and building huge stacks containing big bluestem, side oats grama, and little bluestem prairie grasses.

At the Burgess farm, haying took place in the seventeen-acre meadow between the barn and the field next to Rock Creek. This meadow was original prairie and had never been tilled. Some of the grass would be four feet high by haying time and among it grew purple cone flowers, Indian paintbrush, and prairie potatoes, or in the boggy areas near the old buffalo wallows, the white and red lady's thumb water weed.

Tall grass prairie at its finest, this meadow presented a real challenge to an excited Freddy as he prepared to drive King and Prince pulling the steel-wheeled McCormack mower. His dad mowed the first swath counter-clockwise around the outside of the meadow while his son walked along and listened to instructions.

"Never let the horses spook and be sure to keep the cutter bar and wheels away from the fence. Try to mow straight. If the heavy grass balls up on the mower, you might have to stop and clean it off. Always tie the horses' reins to the mower seat and disengage the cutter bar before you hop off. And stay behind the mower while you work on it. Okay, on you go. You'll do fine."

Freddy breathed deep and rubbed palms on his pants. He climbed into the iron seat and smiled. This was his first time to mow.

While his dad watched the young farmer said, "Giddup," and flipped the reins across the backs of the huge team.

When the horses moved, the knobbed mower wheels turned, driving power through connecting gears to move the pitman rod and send the cutter bar sections back and forth. As the mower cut the grass it fell backwards. *Redcoats, marching on a frontal attack into the Minute Men's blistering fire*, Freddy thought.

Around and around man and beast mowed, leaving fallen grass in neat five-foot swaths. If the rains stayed away, it would take a couple of days to cure the hay.

This is great. It's not hard at all. Mowing this meadow is easy as pie.

However, as the day wore on the sun got higher and hotter and the sameness of mowing got to be a bit humdrum. So what did this baseball player, 4-Her, fisherman, cattleman and farm boy do to stir things up? He fired up his imagination.

"Onward ye mighty war horses, move this chariot thither. We shall mow down those advancing Roman Legions who threaten our island," he said, urging on his team just like he'd seen in a Cecil B. DeMille movie.

Round after round and hour after hour the battle continued, with Freddy on the one hand feeling grownup and earning his keep, and on the other hand, finding ways to turn a big job into a game.

Just listen to that cutter bar click and clack. It's like a Tommy gun.

Before long it was time for the dinner for both the mower driver and the pulling team. And then it would be back to work.

Two days later, the morning dawned bright with only a few puffy clouds in the west. Somewhere a pheasant called in the early morning heat. It would be a great day for haying.

At the meadow the boys' dad crushed a blade of bluestem between his teeth and said, "This has cured enough to rake and before that job is finished, we can start stacking."

Freddy also stuck a blade of grass between his teeth and

thought, *Does he mean I get to rake?*

At the barn, George, whose haying duties included fetching water for the men and horses, and "staying the heck out of the way," watched as Freddy and his dad harnessed King and Prince and hooked them to the old ten-foot-wide dump rake.

In the meadow, perched high on the steel seat the fun began. When King and Prince moved out the rake tines clawed along the ground and with marginal precision Freddy dumped a ten-foot bunch to start the winnow, though most everyone called them windrows. During the trips back and forth across the mown hay, he added another section, and another, and another.

In a few hours, more than half of the meadow's sweet hay lay gathered in rows. Now, the hay could be stacked.

STACKING HAY

Not long after noon, neighbors Wally Hoffman and Bill Mansfield brought their eight-foot wide buckrakes into the meadow. Behind them came Mark Riat with his pitchfork. They stopped where the boys' dad had hitched his second team of horses, Rocky and Dolly to either side of his tall Jayhawk Stacker.

"Well John, it looks like you've got a good crop," Wally said as the men stood beside the stacker. "We should get a good start on the first stack today and maybe finish tomorrow, don't you think?"

"If we don't have problems we might get it done tomorrow and then we can start on yours. We need to get started now though. I wonder where that Shorty Brockman is. He said he'd be here to help Mark tamp the stack," the boys' dad said.

"Don't wait on him John," Mark said, "I can tamp by myself until he gets here. With him I end doing most of the work anyway."

"Shorty's not a great worker, but two people on top of the stack can manage better. But, you're right, we need to go ahead."

"C'mon Bill," Wally said, "Let's fill up these buckrakes."

Wally clucked to his team and drove them to the nearest windrow. Here he levered down the rake's long, two-by-four teeth and their rounded ends slid under the hay, piling it up against the frame. After about fifty feet the rake held a mammoth bunch of the cured grass.

Wally raised and locked the teeth off the ground and turned his team back to the stacker. There, he placed the hay on the stacker's two-by-four teeth. Wally backed away and the stacker moved forward and in the process winched up the loaded hay. At the appointed spot the loader tripped down and the hay dropped to the ground.

Bill Mansfield drove up with his load and the process repeated. As the men worked, the stack started to take shape and after an hour stood about three feet high.

About then, Shorty Brockman showed up and the boys' dad just nodded and pointed to the stack. Shorty did as directed and climbed up to help Mark spread and tamp the hay.

Needing a drink, Freddy drove King and Prince into the shade of the big cottonwood near the stacker. "Hey bumpkin, hand me that water jug. I have just a little raking still to do."

George nodded, and handed over the jug.

§

We watched the men work throughout the day, slowly building a high domed stack. Haying took plenty of effort and used strange implements and lots of labor. It was a hot, tiring and thirsty job.

§

THE FRATERNITY OF WATER DRINKERS

"Here, let me show you," Bill Mansfield said to a struggling George, when the crew stopped for a break and a drink. "You have to sling the jug up from behind like this, and then cradle it on your arm and shoulder."

Bill really knows what he's talking about.

Bill took a swig of the cool water from the big stone jug perched on his right shoulder. He'd shown George the proper way.

Stone-jug water drinking seemed to be a rite of passage for farm boys, and especially George, who struggled to lift the water-soaked burlap wrapped jug. With Bill's help, he hoisted the heavy jug to his shoulder and took a struggling swig. Then George ceremoniously flushed the jug—a splash out the neck—cleansing the spout for the next guy, and unspoken rule of farm etiquette.

To George, this was a giant moment. He felt like hot stuff, joining the fraternity of water drinkers.

Stacking hay called for real hands. Neighbors helped each other. The boys' dad, the Skullys, Wally Hoffman, Mark and sometimes Leo Riat, Romanus Heiger, John Habluetzel, and Bill Mansfield traded work until each farm's hay was ready for winter. Shorty Brockman helped out, if there was no one else available. Shorty did a slightly better-than-nothing job. Whenever he showed up.

The boys' dad always operated the stacker, for he was especially adept at jobs requiring skill and exactness. In reality, the men spreading the hay atop the stack had the hardest job, wading through knee-deep loose hay and muscling it around by pitchfork.

Hot and tiring work, it made good sense for the haying crew to take water breaks. When the Kansas sun pushed temperatures into the nineties, men and horses needed a breather now and then.

Some men pushed themselves hard regardless of the heat and the effort required, not wanting to be the first to 'cry uncle.' One was Herman Elder. He became a friend and fellow worker after he and his wife Onie and their children, Viola Mae and Bob, moved onto the Scully place in November of '47. Herman would drop in his tracks before he'd let anyone out work him. A somewhat shorter but very strong man, the boys found he seemed to relish out working any man in the county … breaks or no breaks.

"Let's take another breather," the boys' dad said a couple of hours later. "We need to drink some water and get in shade. We don't want any sunstrokes"

THE OIL-DRINKING POSSUM

Everyone headed for the shade under the huge tree by the

182

fencerow and plopped down on the cool grass. A slight breeze stirred the waxy cottonwood leaves. The fun was about to begin.

"Would you look at George's feet?" Bill Mansfield asked the men. "They're bigger than a mule's."

"Yeah, and for an eleven-year-old, that means he has *good understanding*," Wally Hofman added. Everyone laughed.

Wally asked if anyone had heard about the guy working in the noon day sun. "A lady was watching him and said, 'Sir, you'd better get out of that sun or it'll cook your brain.' The fellow replied, 'Lady, if I had any brains I wouldn't be out in the sun.'"

While the men relaxed and passed the stone water jug around, they talked and teased. As a result, the boys—and others—ended up getting sucked in by some of the banter.

"Did you hear about Beans Bleford?" Wally asked. "He always seems to have bad luck, including his being married to Shorty's cousin. Right, Shorty?"

Shorty nodded but didn't answer.

"It seems," Wally continued, "that Beans started his car the other day and heard noises."

"What was wrong?" George asked.

Several men looked curious.

"Beans hadn't mentioned anything to me," Shorty said.

Wally grinned and said, "He found the tail of the dumbest possum he'd ever seen. The best Beans could figure was that it had crawled on top of the motor to get a drink of oil. Apparently he got part way sucked into the engine, with just his tail sticking out."

"Gosh," George said.

"Yep, and ole Beans had to take the whole engine apart."

"That's not true, is it?" Shorty asked shaking his head.

With a sly grin, Wally looked slowly around the circle of men. Then he said, "Beans doesn't lie, does he boys?"

"Beans usually tells the truth," the boys' dad said.

"That possum probably got in through a spark plug hole," Bill Mansfield said, adding more credibility to Wally's tale.

At that point only Shorty hadn't caught on. He said he couldn't wait to get home and ask his wife Lulu about it.

And so it went; men and boys laughing hard, and along with the horses, working hard. Soon all of the neighborhood haying would be done and the scene would shift to something else.

In the boys' case, it was time again for the County Fair and another try at winning Baby Beef ribbons. They'd done well with the haying, but would they do well at the Fair?

That was a good question.

FIFTEEN

FAIR TIME 1947, ROCKET'S LAUNCH AND THE PERILS OF HAND CRANKING

[*Westmoreland Recorder* – September 4, 1947] ~ OVER THE FARM FENCE by Harvey Goertz, County Agent ~ Lawrence Orsborn, Wamego, donated a registered Duroc gilt to help the 4-H Club building fund. The gift was auctioned off during the dedication program at the Pottawatomie County Fair. 4-H Club members were very happy to receive this additional help to pay for their new exhibit building at Onaga. Mr. Orsborn farms in Center Township; his family has been very active in the Tannerville 4-H club

1947

FAIR TIME 1947

"Are you gonna take Chief's horn weights off today?" George asked his brother, referring to the round, lead-ball devices attached to each of the calf's horns. "They'll look funny to the judge."

"Yeah, I guess I better. They're not going to curve his horns anymore. I don't know why judges think curled-down horns are better," Freddy said. "The problem is Chief's horns don't look even to me. The left one looks lower than the right. See?"

"They don't look too bad to me," George said. *I think Freddy has one ear lower than the other, but nobody says anything.*

"Well, you're not the judge now are you?"

"No, but I still think Chief looks good, though he's pretty small. You'll probably have to settle for third place again."

"Wait, Reno won't even get a white. He's all lumpy and his hind end sticks up too high. You said it; he does look like a wiener dog. On flat ground he looks like he's sliding downhill. You better clip the hair on his pin bones and tail head so he'll look more level."

"I'm going to do that after we get to Onaga tomorrow."

§

The next morning the big day arrived. After the chores, we dug into bowls of Kellogg's Cornflakes, fresh cream and homemade applesauce, except for Judy who sat in her highchair eating mashed peas and carrots and not necessarily enjoying them. We slipped her some applesauce and she smiled.

Near the end of the meal, Dad said, "As soon as we finish here, I'll get the truck down to the barn and we'll load the hay and grain and the other gear. Then you can lead your calves straight on. George, you go first with Reno, he's the calmest. Freddy, your two can come on together after that. Be sure to tie them all looking forward so they won't kick each other where the road gets bumpy."

"Don't forget your suitcase," Mom said. "You did put in clean underwear, didn't you?"

"We have that, plus clean pants and shirts to wear during judging. And we have our toothbrushes."

"Good," she said and left the room. A minute later she returned. "Here are a couple of old blankets to cover up with at night. You can use a little straw for pillows. You'll have to sleep in your clothes though."

§

In a few minutes, the old truck backed up to the highest barn door. First, their dad loaded a partly filled gunny sack of ground corn and three bales of hay.

George carried on an old wooden Hire's root beer box— "Hire's to you!" it said on the side—containing two hand brushes, the currycomb, shears, a pair of scissors, a couple of big rags and part of a can of Dura Seal paste wax for the hooves. *Should I take some salve? Naw, I guess not.*

Freddy used twine to tie the pitchfork up high on the outside of the stock racks.

When George tugged on Reno's halter rope the calf stepped right from the barn into the truck's bed. Bobby and Chief walked calmly aboard right behind George's black calf.

186

Smiling George hopped into the cab and slid to the middle of the seat. Freddy trotted ahead to open and close the corral gate and got in the right side next to the window.

"Don't forget your suitcase. You'll need your extra clothes. I put in some Lifebuoy soap, a towel, and a tube of Ipana toothpaste," their mom said as she passed the cardboard case through the window for Freddy to hold on his lap.

Both boys stretched to the window for a kiss from her and from Judy, who gurgled and smiled. "You boys be careful and don't get into trouble. Judy and I'll come up with Dad tomorrow."

"We'll be careful and we won't blow our money on dumb stuff. Money doesn't grow on tree you know." *That ought to hold her.*

"Bye Mom, bye, Judy," George said with a wave.

"Yeah, bye," his brother said. And with that the old truck groaned out the lane and onto the road that would start the boys and their projects to the 1947 Pottawatomie County Fair. The boys' dad smiled and thought, *They're growing up.*

The trip was a long, slow ride under cloudless blue skies. A hot wind blew in through the windows and the threesome wiped sweat on their shirt sleeves.

A few times a thrush or a robin flew across the road, and one meadowlark sang from a fence post. Other birds looked down on the scene as the rusty looking vehicle crept along with its load of Baby Beef and their excited owners.

Later the truck backed up to the Fairground's cattle chute to unload the calves. From there, the boys led them to the cattle barn. After getting the animals settled alongside other Blackjack 4-H Club entries, the boys brought in all of the feed, grooming materials and their suit case and blankets. Beside them, other club members gathered and started discussing each one's animal.

"You've got some good calves," Lyle Harrell said. "You know George that big Angus of yours might win something."

"He'll never win, with that ugly face," Bubba said.

Bubba ought to look in the mirror, George thought.

"Of course he'll win something you dingbat," Freddy said with a frown. "All calves get a ribbon of some kind, don't they?"

"You've got a good calf, too, Lyle," George said. "And so do the other guys, except for yours Bubba. It looks like a starved hippo with horns." He grinned and nodded toward Bubba's calf.

"Rocket is a sure winner," Bubba said. "I had a fortune-teller figure that out. She said with his kinda blue nose, he will be a blue ribbon winner for sure. You know that's the truth. And it only cost me a buck to find that out."

Umm, Madam Vadoma? George wondered.

"Bubba, that calf doesn't have a blue nose. It's just shiny black 'cause he's mostly Black Angus," Freddy said. "You're dumber than a stink bug." *And sometimes Bubba smells like one.*

"Ah, pipe down," Bubba said.

The back-and-forth chatter continued for a while. Then the collection of boys spent some time trying to guess where each calf might place. Everyone agreed Reno and Chief looked like winners, although Bubba compared Bobby to an Orangutan.

A few minutes later the group toured the rest of the Cattle Barn, the Swine Barn and the new machinery display. George took particular notice of the green John Deere implement smell.

Next they strolled through the carnival, mostly closed until evening, except for Big Red's greasy spoon and the Coin Toss. Since nobody wanted to spend any money, they continued on through the sewing and baking displays of the many 4-H girls.

At the end of the afternoon the drifting bunch of young men went back to the Cattle Barn and forked messed up straw to the manure pile and watered their calves. Then, the boys' dad walked up.

ALONE AT THE FAIR

"Okay boys," he said to his sons, "I have to go home now. I'll come back about mid morning. Tonight you can sleep on the straw in this empty stall next to your calves. You'll be all right because Mr. Clary and Mr. Hofman are sleeping on those cots over there. If you have problems, they can help you out."

Then he added more instructions, "Remember, don't get silly and your money has to last."

"Oh we'll be careful. And we'll take good care of the calves. You can count on us," Freddy said. "Bye."

"Why don't you feed your calves now and then go check out the carnival?" With that he walked to the old truck and drove away.

"You look like you're constipated," Freddy said.

"I'm just nervous," George replied.

The fact was both boys were excited. To that point in their lives, the only time they had slept away from their folks was at a supervised church camp and a couple of times with aunts and uncles—including when their Aunt Helen fed them lard fried *Fresh Feathered Eggs*. This was their first time sleeping with livestock, except for a couple of naps in the haymow.

At that point Mrs. Clary called the Club's Baby Beef project members together and said, "Well, the Leaders are all here and we'll have a fine time. But we do have some duties each day as most of you remember. We must keep our stock in water and feed. Also, we need to keep the aisle and the stalls free of manure. This group can do the cleaning tomorrow; that group the next day."

"That's not fair," Bubba said with a snicker. "What if Freddy's calf goes plop plop more than mine?"

"Oh, Bubba, you do ask some strange questions. I imagine things will even out over time. Let's take a break and eat these ham sandwiches we brought for everybody."

Each club member also got an apple and a glass of Kool Aid. All the members thanked Mrs. Clary for the food. The meal was fine for the girls, but Freddy and George and some other boys still felt hungry. Maybe a carnival hamburger would do.

Off the boys and Bubba went to MAMA GERT'S HAMBURGERS with the same good results as the year before. She still wore a huge flowered sack dress, but now bigger and … tighter.

After two hamburgers a piece, Freddy and Bubba tried the carnival games with the same results as last year—nothing. George left them to waste their money and walked through the midway, giving a wide berth to MADAM VADOMA'S place. *And Bubba thought he got his future told. His calf Rocket it too wild to win anything.*

A while later Freddy convinced Bubba to quit the games and the three boys walked in the warm evening back toward the Cattle Barn leaving the carnival to others.

Overhead the moon shone brightly in spite of the Fair's lights. Big moths and night flying insects circled lights and in the grass crickets made their presence known. Somewhere a locust buzzed, stopped and buzzed again.

"Man, I like being here," Freddy said. "Everything is really exciting, and listen to all those sounds and the smell in the air."

"You dope, what you smell is cow dung. It smells just like at home and doesn't seem all that great to me," Bubba said.

"But you live in your barn," said a smiling Freddy.

George changed the subject. "Hey, let's go again and see if we can get some cookies. They might give us samples this year."

The trio got up and wandered toward that building. Sadly, they saw that same large lady from last year, so they kept on moving.

After that they toured the new machinery again where once more George insisted he could tell a color by its smell. Nobody believed him, but the other two went along with the gag.

In one corner of the Swine Building, they spotted a few sheep and goats. "Can you smell that?" Bubba asked. "Man they stink. I don't see how anybody could have them things around."

"The smell's not any worse than your B.O. Besides those little goats are cute," George said, "and you're not."

"Yeah Bubba," Freddy said, "you should have a sheep instead of that wild steer Rocket."

Bubba grinned and then asked, "Did you hear the one about the guy that offered his buddy a smart pill?"

"No," said George.

"Well the friend tasted it and said, 'This tastes like sheep manure.'"

"See, you're getting smart already."

The boys had to laugh.

The teasing and joking continued until George yawned and headed back to the Cattle Barn. When he started that way, the other two followed. They flopped down on the straw in the empty stall and while Bubba and Freddy bantered away, George brushed his teeth, pulled up his blanket and went to sleep.

The conversation got slower until finally Freddy stretched out and a couple of minutes later so did Bubba.

FAIR IS THAT DANISH

About daylight the noise of hungry animals, talking people and chattering sparrows roused every Cattle Barn sleeper. This was the big day to get the Baby Beef ready to show the next day. There was much to be done. But first there was the need for breakfast. And no one was hungrier than Freddy and George. But the question was, where to eat?

§

To us, the Pottawatomie Fair was grandiose. It had a life of its own. It was a community unto itself.

There were 4-H kids, leaders, parents, officials, carnival workers, and fair goers. We all grouped together into a unique social setting that made interaction easy for even the shyest person.

We 4-H kids had our own identity … talking and laughing, tending animals, preparing them for the show ring and just being together, even when cleaning the barn.

We were good citizens overall. And, what could be more fun than running helter-skelter among the barns and the many carnival attractions.

Before the Fair opened for the day, a few of us ventured to the three-block long business district of Onaga, to get breakfast. Our stop for the day was outside the big glass window of the Onaga Bakery. There, we would experience what to us was heavenly.

§

"That peach one sure looks great," George said, his mouth watering. For the first time in his life he stood staring at Danish pastries, dozens of them inside the bakery's glass display case. "Man, I bet that'll taste good. It makes my taste buds tingle."

Freddy and George thought the golden, butter-laden crust looked like it would melt in their mouths. The pastries had preserves and white icing layered. The bakery case held a grand group of morsels—peach, cherry, apple, blackberry, apricot—each calling to the boys. The smell of fresh baked Danish and donuts lured the boys like catfish to angle worms.

§

It was time for us to make some decisions. Out came our imitation leather cardboard wallets and we surveyed our money. We'd left home with $3.65 each and that was to last us throughout the Fair. Could we afford a sweet roll?

We reasoned of course we could and crossed the step-up threshold into the bakery. We made our selections of a peach and a blackberry.

Even before we exited the bakery, we dived into the breakfast goodies. Chomp, chomp and they were gone. By the time we reached the sidewalk we had nothing left.

"Let's have another."

And we did.

One thing seemed odd to us. Two other 4-H boys saw the bakery and smelled the fresh baked goods, but kept on walking downtown to buy cigarettes. How very weird— indeed a strange choice—we concluded.

We returned to the Fair Grounds, did barn duty, washed and curried our calves and then spent the day waiting, watching and talking. Mom, Dad and Judy arrived in late morning. They spent some time touring the Home Ec displays and the livestock barns. In late afternoon our family returned home. They'd be back on Saturday for the judging.

We felt we would be short of cash, but didn't have the nerve to ask Dad for more money. In truth, our money went mostly for food.

That night we tried to sleep. During the little sleep we got we dreamed of Danish rolls—and the Big Show.

§

THE BIG SHOW DAY

Noisy activity in the Cattle Barn the next morning roused the boys. Excited voices and nervous giggles signaled this was it. This was the day every Baby Beef owner had worked for all summer long. It was time to present the projects the best ways possible. Some would win, and some would lose.

After another quick trip for sweet rolls the boys washed their animals again and combed parallel lines along the sides and back. After the hair dried, they used the currycomb to fluff it up, hoping to make their steers look wider and stockier. The boys combed their calves' tail switches into puffs, and in Chief's case, his horns and hooves got a good cleaning and a touch of the paste wax.

The anticipation built when the boys' folks and Judy showed up. "Oh, your calves look so smart," their mom said. "I just know you'll do well. And George, look right at the judge and don't be shy."

Though young, George had experienced the show ring the year before so he wasn't as anxious, but he still had butterflies.

On the other hand, Freddy usually didn't worry much about anything. That is, until he saw George Wayne Walker and the Rezac sisters lead their mammoth calves by.

The K-State judge instructed that the calves should slowly circle the ring. At this year's Fair, all Baby Beef entries were shown together, so Freddy led Chief and asked the Blackjack Club President Dean Duncan, to lead Bobby. George followed with Reno.

If you've ever been to a Baby Beef show, you'll remember the drama. Every calf is led by a 4-Her dressed in clean clothes with his or her head high. The young people and their calves parade around and around the ring in what parents, friends and most Fair goers consider majestic fashion, while the judge eyes each entrant and silently compares it to a mental image of the ideal calf.

Each person showing a Baby Beef watches the judge for instructions and tries to anticipate his every wish. Lead ropes are held high so the calves look tall, whether walking or standing. Most contestants carry a cane or long stick that they can use to move their calf's feet to square it up. The stick can also be used to scratch under the animal's belly to level its back. Blocky, square, wide, erect and large all count to the judge, and of course, how much quality meat is on the carcass. The animals color? Sorry Freddy.

(Left) *4-Her George and his big Blue Ribbon calf Reno. Freddy holds Bobby and Chief (before getting horn weights). The family barn is in the background.*

The boys did their best and felt proud. Every Baby Beef owner would never forget the Fair experience, especially, Bubba.

His big crossbred, but mostly Angus steer, turned out to be a menace in the show ring. Sadly, Bubba always struggled to get things right, and once again when Bubba trained Rocket, he apparently did a pretty shoddy job.

ROCKET'S LAUNCH

In fact, Rocket got little training and so on occasion elected to go in a direction opposite to the other calves. Rocket also had a bad habit of tossing his head, snorting and periodically locking his legs. Only a severe yank on the lead rope would get him moving.

Plus, Bubba had made a mistake when he washed and curried Rocket for the show. Currying close under Rocket's tail, the steel comb's teeth sent Rocket into orbit. He had leaped high and landed balanced on top of the stall partition with all four feet pawing thin air.

After a bit, Rocket calf-paddled forward only to find himself standing in the opposite stall alongside Mavis Hooper's calf Gentile. Neither calf liked the situation.

The calves kicked and butted each other until several adults separated them and led the still upset Rocket back to his stall. Although Bubba seemed undaunted by this whole incident, Rocket unfortunately long remembered.

During the show, trouble brewed again when Rocket once more demonstrated his lack of training as the entrants paraded along the outside rail of the show ring.

The well meaning judge, in an effort to encourage Rocket to behave, thumped him gently with a cane right on the top of Rocket's tail head. You guessed it, Rocket launched!

He took off again and ran smack into—who else?—but Mavis' Gentile, who let out a bellow and hightailed it with Rocket in close pursuit. Away they went, two disgruntled calves with two owners in tow, zig-zagging through the other animals and causing turmoil of enormous proportions.

After three erratic trips around and across the ring, the judge and two adults from Onaga jumped in, and finally brought the animals under control.

Bubba stood with his hands on his hips, displaying no detectable emotion, except maybe a faint grin while Mavis stood shaking and rubbing away tears. Bubba thought the whole affair had humor, while Mavis, Gentile, and Rocket were all sorely put out.

During the rest of the show, Gentile kept looking back over his shoulder. The boys noticed that the judge looked a little sheepish too, for his part in the episode.

Neither calf placed high. In fact, Bubba's Rocket, Mavis' Gentile and Freddy's Bobby all got honorable mentions. Chief earned a red while Reno, on this day looking flat across the back, judged just right and earned George a fine blue ribbon.

Ten year old Larry Riat had the grand champion in his first 4-H Fair. Indeed, it had been a memorable fair and featured a show within a show ... as often happened.

§

We later realized that what we showed was limited by what we had raised for the Fair. That was that better stock won better ribbons. And, we knew Larry Riat had drawn his Grand Champion steer from the same lottery as we drew Reno and Bobby. Oh well, that was the way things went sometimes, and so we learned another lesson.

Sure we had disappointment, but it only lasted a short time. We felt good about competing and earning our strips of colored ribbon, even white. Hopefully, we'd do better next time and maybe draw a better calf, show it better or have better luck. Anyway, we'd learned things about beef judging and even about Danish pastries.

When the Fair ended, our calves went home in the old truck and moved into our feed lot for more grain and growth. In early October, Dad hired a long haul truck to transport the family's group of grown steers the 120 miles to the Kansas City Stockyards. There all the calves sold at a good price, and we had some profit to show for our efforts.

Both of us could now open checking accounts at the First National Bank in Wamego. Bobby and Chief made a $45 profit and Reno $24.50.

We had money, and that tempted us to spend—another lesson in the making. We felt flush and as such enjoyed little rewards for all our Baby Beef efforts. Instead of single dip ice cream cones, treats like milkshakes and sodas became realities. A brand new baseball turned up and lots of .22 caliber ammunition made its way home, and quickly disappeared. We bought new shirts and cowboy belts.

We tasted the rewards from the hard work of farming and liked what we felt.

Our money didn't go very far and by the time we needed to buy Christmas presents we were down to only a few dollars apiece. We again faced financial stress.

As we thought about our predicament, we realized two things. The first was that we spent our money too fast, and second, we hadn't earned enough. We needed to think of ways to remedy those problems.

Not spending our money seemed easier, now that we were low on cash. We just wouldn't buy unneeded items. The other way to solve our financial dilemma was to find more money. Maybe we could expand our 4-H options, but how? We'd better start planning now.

§

"I think I'll raise a bunch of hogs next year. I'd like to have some of those red Durocs to show and then sell," Freddy said. "And, I could raise a Beef Breeding Herd. That would take five heifers. Yeah, that's more like it. That'll help me get some more money in the bank."

Will Dad go for this? George thought.

"Of course it'll be a lot of work," Freddy continued. "If you want something in life, you have to earn it."

Both boys stood deep in thought. "I guess I'd kind of like to do some wheat. If dad will rent me some land I'll be set," Freddy said. "A person can make money on wheat."

"Maybe you can, but how are you going to plant it and combine it?" George asked.

"Yeah, that's a problem; I guess Dad would let me use his equipment. I'm his son after all."

During the next few months continued planning didn't resolve much. Still, both boys tried to come up with ideas that would make them some money.

In the mean time, they had school and work. The Fair was over and the baseball season ended. And before long, Mother Nature turned on winter. But farm work doesn't stop when it is cold.

THE PERILS OF HANDCRANKING

Cranking the Allis Chalmers tractor—no starter—in the cold, was a problem for anybody, but especially for the boys. It often took a number of tries before the engine fired up. And if, in the process it backfired—once in a while—the crank kicked back in the opposite direction with enough force to snap a careless person's arm.

"Let me show you how to handle this crank," the boys' dad said. He slipped the crazy 'Z' looking crank onto the cranking shaft sticking out from the front of the engine. "Tuck your thumb inside your fingers. That way if the crank kicks back, you automatically release it and you won't get hurt."

The boys nodded understanding.

"That's the only safe way. And, always pull upwards on the crank so that it doesn't kick back against your body. Always!"

He then adjusted the throttle and choke, and placed the crank in the seven o'clock position. After a couple of hefty upward pulls, he brought the sun warmed engine to life … whrrrr, sputter, chug, chug, whrrrr.

End of lesson. Now it would be up to the boys.

§

The following morning, our turn came because Dad needed to head to town, but not before giving us our Saturday morning job. "I want you boys to haul a trailer load of that brush down the road and throw it into the canyon to help stop erosion"

The canyon, as we called it, was a highly eroded ditch beside the road. It served some specific purposes, including as a setting for games of cops and robbers with our cousins and a place for unwanted debris. Today we'd add more brush.

From the porch, we watched Dad scrape off some windshield ice and snow, start the car and drive away over the shallow covering of new snow. Engine exhaust trailed him out the driveway. When he turned toward town, we turned to do our job. We first had to start the tractor in the 20-degree weather.

Cranking the engine would be tough because we were lightweights and didn't have Dad's strength to pull upward. What could we do? Well, we did what farmers have always done. Luckily, Dad didn't witness our mistakes.

§

Freddy, always intent on driving brushed off the steel seat and hopped on. He set the choke and throttle and nodded to his brother and said, "Crank her up and let's go."

George hesitated and shivered. *I can't pull the crank up the way Dad does.* Then inspiration hit.

I'll jump up and come down on the crank with all of my weigh.

What else could he do?

Quickly he pulled up a cinder block to stand on, removed the crank from where it nestled in the frame and slipped it on the cranking shaft at the two o'clock position. Tucking in his thumbs, he gently threw his weight downward against the crank. Nothing moved.

"Put more weight into it," Freddy directed.

George jumped up again, almost begging the crank to move downward. Even his extra weight from his winter clothing wasn't enough.

"Stand on you tiptoes. You have to hit it harder if you want it to turn."

Too short and too skinny, George couldn't get the knack of it. Even his mittens—the crank was too cold for bare hands—worked against him, giving him a slippery grip.

He would jump higher this time. With a mighty leap, he landed square on the crank—it moved.

'Ker-clatter.' The engine turned one revolution. And then nothing.

With irritation and impatience, Freddy pumped the choke. He'd give it more gas.

Again George jumped and dropped on the crank. Spurt, sputter, and sputter. Then nothing.

Freddy pumped the choke again. *That ought to do it.*

Once again George jumped, forcefully throwing his weight against the stubborn crank. Sputter, sputter, pop! Pop!

"Dad gum it."

George, with his brother's goading, decided to try one more time. When he came down this time, he lost his balance.

"Look out!"

Ker-pop … pop! The magneto shot high voltage energy to the spark plugs and the AC's engine primed with the extra fuel, gave a mighty belch and forcefully backfired. The backward rotating crank caught George in his midsection and sent him flying.

He fluttered like a rag doll. Only his tee shirt, long john shirt, chambray shirt, sweatshirt, summer jacket, long scarf, mittens, and heavy outer coat saved him from real pain.

Luck was on George's side, for as he came to earth, he landed some ten feet away in the middle of a four-foot snow drift. That cushioned his fall some, but also drove snow inside his clothing. *Good grief.*

"Are you alive or dead?" asked Freddy

"I think I'm alright. I guess."

George got up slowly and walked around shaking his arms and rubbing his midsection. Nothing seemed broken.

"I don't think we should tell Dad about this," he said.

I'm not about to, thought Freddy.

Freddy realized that he needed to do the cranking. In short order the engine was idling. End of drama.

The Allis Chalmers always started sooner or later and through the years, the boys often spent long monotonous hours herding it from one end of a field to another.

More new things always seemed to await the boys; this time they had a surprise waiting at Prairie View School.

SIXTEEN

MRS. DRAPER, JUDY GARLAND AND YOU'LL GET A KICK OUT OF IT

[*Westmoreland Recorder* – September 4, 1947] ~ **DOCTORS MEET IN ONAGA** ~ Wednesday evening the Pottawatomie County Medical Society met at Onaga, with seven members in this society. Dr. Eugene Walsh, associated with Dr. C. S. Fleckenstein in Onaga, was admitted as a new member. After the business session, technical motion pictures were shown. Dr. Thos. Dechario, of Westmoreland, is president of the Society, and Dr. A. H. Bressler of Wamego is secretary-treasurer.

1947

MRS. DRAPER

Back in early June of 1947 we completed grades five and seven at Prairie View School. Our teacher Mrs. Draper announced that she was retiring. We hadn't expected that.

She had been with us for the past three years and we'd be sorry to see her leave. She had inspired us and taught us well, and we liked her and she liked us.

Mrs. Draper had plenty of energy and dealt well with the often unconventional behavior of her seventeen students. By teaching all classes in one room, we were allowed to hear each story every year, or hear third grade spelling again, or fifth grade grammar, or sixth grade geography. Sometimes groups of students moved to the front of the room, and we could listen in to hear two or three—first and second graders together perhaps—attempt to read, discuss and understand, *The Tortoise and the Hare,* or do math problems with chalk—always messy—on the blackboard.

As a result, we literally learned, and relearned, the lessons of every grade. All of this helped some students get smarter and, unfortunately, some got bored—Bubba.

Spring, 1947
Mrs. Draper's
students during
her last year in
front of the one
room school.
Freddy, is at the
right next to the
back row;
George sits on
the concrete steps
in front of his
brother.

Because of her love for children, her pleasant demeanor and grandmotherly ways, most of the kids eagerly listened and learned. She taught us, kept the peace and extended a personal interest in each of us.

§

SCHOOL SUPPLIES ON THE CHEAP

Through the school years, Mrs. Draper taught the younger Prairie View students how to mold clay into farm animals, how to draw, cut, paste, and clip paper, and how to pass scissors to one's neighbor, handle first for safety.

Back when George had been one of the little ones, he learned about art using his box of crayons with a dozen colors.

Truthfully, he envied his classmate, Pauline Straub's jumbo box with 30 colors. Surely, a person could be a better artist with more colors from which to choose.

Many kids had large, translucent erasers with that great smell—according to George's nose. However, his folks thought those used up too quickly, so he had to settle for the smaller, solid, uninteresting ones. He had also longed for a real glue bottle with a rubber-topped dispenser, but his frugal parents insisted that he use small jars of foul smelling white paste. If he had pasting to do at home, he had to make his own paste by mixing water and flour.

To communicate a request to go to the pump for a drink of water, or to the outhouse, students used sign language. Silently holding up one finger meant one thing and two fingers meant something else.

Of course, all schoolmates watched as a student left the room. Many a time George suffered until recess because he didn't want the embarrassment of leaving with everybody watching.

Interestingly, years later a Port-a-Potty company's motto, "We're Number 1 in the Number 2 business," gave George a flash back to his early days at Prairie View.

SCORCHED CHILI

Toward the end of Mrs. Draper's last winter, the Prairie View students put on a Chili Feed & Talent-Show Fundraiser that featured such songs as *Nita Juanita, The Atchison, Topeka and the Santa Fe* and *Don't Fence Me In*, with a pitch pipe as the only instrument. The idea was to entertain—the parents loved it—plus sell bowls of donated chili and homemade cakes and cookies. The proceeds would be used to buy more books for the library shelf and needed supplies.

This particular event turned out to be unforgettable. There was an abundance of leftover chili. What to do with the excess?

"Well, why don't we just leave the leftover chili at school and the eighth grade girls can warm it up tomorrow for lunch?" one of the mothers asked. "The temperature is cold enough."

"I think that is a good idea," another said. And so it was set.

Next morning, the temperature hovered below 30 degrees and the big pot-bellied stove struggled to heat the whole room. Someone set the flue wide open. The room warmed and everyone went about his or her business throughout the morning. The stove duty crew poured in more coal as needed to keep the room cozy.

Some time before noon, Mrs. Draper said to the eighth grade girls, "Okay girls, this is a good time for you heat up the chili."

"Let's pour all the chili into this big metal pot and put it on top of the stove," one girl said. "It will be ready by noon.

By now you're probably getting the picture. Cold day, heaps of coal fueling a roaring fire, chili on the stove, the girls returning to their desks, getting preoccupied, and then….

"What's that smell?"

"Oh my goodness," said Mrs. Draper, "just look at this. Girls, you need to come see to this chili. I think it's burned."

The eighth grade kitchen help ran to the stove and stared blankly at the blackened chili disaster."

"Ah, it looks and smells awful. How does it taste?"

"I don't think I want to try it."

Since every student expected to eat the chili that day, no one had brought sack lunches. They were stuck with burned lunch or do without. Most picked at it and ate every cracker they could find.

Finally, Freddy—the oldest boy—threw the remaining scorched chili over the south fence. The pile of blackened beans lay lifeless for weeks. Even the varmints wouldn't touch them.

What started out as a harmless chili feed fundraiser ended up as a bona fide calamity. However, kindly Mrs. Draper used the event as another object lesson, about attentiveness.

ROAD RUTS AND ONE PEANUT

Mrs. Draper certainly earned her pay teaching so many grades so many subjects, plus riding herd during recess and lunch all by herself. It must have been exhausting, yet she willingly helped out when the boys asked for a ride part way home after school.

They were in hurry one day during her last spring at Prairie View School. She nodded okay when they asked for a ride to the corner. They walked toward her old, mud splattered, and forlorn looking '39 Plymouth coupe. The car was unique.

First, the driver's side door didn't unlatch and the passenger's inside door handle was broken. Mrs. Draper, as always, entered the passenger side. This day as she slid across the bench seat, she tossed a single Spanish peanut into her mouth.

Nibble, nibble, nibble.

"Get in boys and slam that door hard so it will stay closed."

George marveled as she drove the half mile to their corner still munching on that one peanut.

"Is it all right if I leave my window down?" he asked, thinking ahead about an emergency escape. The kindly teacher nodded yes … and nibbled some more.

She probably didn't sense the boys' concerns for she was just heading home, tired from a long day of teaching.

Mrs. Draper taught the boys well. Who says a one-room school couldn't provide a good education? The boys got most of their grade schooling at Prairie View and it carried them forward. But, unfortunately, she was leaving.

Indeed, Mrs. Draper's approach would be missed … but her leaving meant a new teacher for next year. Would that person be like Mrs. Draper? Everyone would have to wait and see.

The boys' dad was on the School Board. They reluctantly accepted Mrs. Draper's retirement letter and immediately began the search for a replacement. The teacher they selected to replace Mrs. Draper wasn't ready for retirement nor was she matronly

§

JUDY GARLAND

During the summer, the School Board hired Miss Dorothy Hupe to teach at Prairie View. She was engaged to Joe Straub. The connection couldn't be missed, since Joe was the brother of schoolmates Maxine and Pauline, plus the first cousin of the Louise, Philomena, Delafield and Rayfield. Beside Joe, members of the Straub families who had already graduated from Prairie View were Brother Dale and Sister Rita, and Cousin Lorene.

With or without the Straub associations, Dorothy Hupe had earned a Teaching Certificate and was ready to begin her teaching career.

We wondered what it would be like to have a younger teacher. Would she fit in?

§

A few days before school began, the boys ran into Bubba in town. "Have you seen our new teacher?" Bubba asked. "She looks just like Judy Garland."

"You mean she's a movie star? Does she know a wizard?" George asked.

"I bet she could dance and sing and be in the movies if she wanted. Too bad she's going to marry ole Joe Straub."

George added, "Why's that? Our Dad says Joe's a real go-getter, one of the best farmers around."

Bubba's a real bird brain. For sure he'll have to go out of town to get a wife, because all the girls around here already know him, George thought.

"Dad and the rest of the School Board met with Miss Hupe, but he didn't say she had a dog named Toto," Freddy said.

Lots of speculation surrounded the new teacher's arrival. Was she a good teacher? And, did she really look like Judy Garland?

On the first day of school, the boys arrived early. She had a beaming smile for the students when they walked through the door.

"Good morning. You must be Freddy and George Burgess. I'm Miss Dorothy Hupe and I'm very pleased to meet you. We'll have a grand year together, won't we?"

Freddy said, "We're glad you're our new teacher. Dad said you are very nice."

"Well, thank him for me. He's a good man."

The boys nodded and smiled at her and then at the other students standing around. The room looked the same as last year with columns of desks that grew in size from front to back. As students grew, they'd move to a seat farther back.

"Can we sit anywhere?" Freddy asked.

"Well, why don't we group the grades together since most will be about the same size? You eighth graders can sit in the back two rows, and the rest of you ahead of them. Will that be alright?" Soon everyone had a properly sized desk and sat down for the day to begin.

At that point, Miss Hupe asked everyone to stand and say the *Pledge of Allegiance*. All of the students placed their right hands over their hearts and recited *the Pledge*.

"Thank you, now take your seats. Next, please rise one at a time and tell us your name and an interesting personal fact about yourself."

Maxine and then Louise giggled and acted embarrassed when they said their names. Everyone knew who they were. Georgette Talley said her real name was Babe, but she liked Georgette and that she lived with her grandmother.

"My name is John Frederick Burgess," Freddy said. "Because my Dad's name is John, I get called Freddy. I don't like that name much and wish people would call me John. And, I'm going to play professional baseball for the Boston Red Sox."

"Thank you, John," Miss Hupe said. "We'll all call you by that name, won't we class?"

When it was George's turn he said, "I'm George Burgess and I'd like to have a big farm, or maybe I'd like to be a ball player, or be a mailman … or … maybe I'd like to drive a Pepsi truck."

After Pauline and Philomena said their names and that they would soon be related to our new teacher, it was Bubba's turn. He stood, cleared his throat and looked around the room. "I'm Bubba Bleford Brockman, Jr. and I live down the road. I'm going to work in the Columbian Theater so I can watch all of the movies for free."

Everybody laughed and Bubba sat down.

"My name is Dorothy like in the Wizard of Oz. When Joe and I get married in the summer, I'll be Dorothy Hupe Straub. And I've always wanted to be a teacher and have students just like you. We'll have such a good time this year."

And a good time they had. Miss Hupe like Mrs. Draper, worked at keeping everyone interested and had winning ways. She enjoyed teaching and the hodge-podge bunch of farm kids learned from her. Her sparkling personality and quick wit set well with her students, plus her high energy kept everyone on their toes. She sometimes joined in recess ball games.

George thought, *I hated it last year when Rita Straub played softball. She always hit the ball clear over the south fence. I wish I could do that.*

Miss Hupe related well to the eighth graders that had always been the largest class at Prairie View. Maxine, Louise, Georgette and Barney Gava were Freddy's—John's—classmates as they moved through the grades together.

1947 was a memorable year for John the younger and George. They had a new teacher, new studies and new farm responsibilities. This was the year they got another surprise that would remain in their minds for a long time.

YOU'LL GET A KICK OUT OF IT

Oh boy. This is gonna be fun, thought Freddy—still his name at home—when his dad handed him the old Remington .12 gauge pump-action shotgun. He tried to remember the safety rules. *Point the barrel down except to shoot, never aim at any person, think where the shot will land and keep the safety on until ready.*

When he looked, his dad nodded toward an unsuspecting brown sunflower stalk standing in front of a small mound of dirt. *Oh man. Is this going to hurt?*

Despite the cold day, Freddy rubbed his hands and gripped the gun. His heart threatened to leave his chest. "How do I aim?" he asked. "Is it like our rifle?"

"Well, you notice there is no rear sight, just the bead in front, so you have to aim along the barrel. Remember the pattern of shot will keep widening until it reaches its limit."

"How big will the pattern get?"

"That depends on just how far away the target is. Aim for the top part of that sunflower. It's about 35 yards away so your shot will spread to be about the size of a galvanized washtub."

While Freddy worried the dried sunflower vibrated stiffly in the late autumn gusts. The weak fall sun reflected muted sparkles from the thin cover of snow. Nearby, a red squirrel, in its high nest of sticks and leaves, scurried from its cottonwood home in search of acorns beneath a leafless oak. The two boys and their dad awaited the shotgun's roar.

After plenty of uneasiness, Freddy squinted along the barrel, past the sight-bead and on to the sunflower. He released the safety, gritted his teeth and pulled the trigger.

BLAAMMM!

The exploding shell was as loud as a car crash. Pellets burst from the barrel in an ever-increasing pattern. Much like an ant under the blow of a sledgehammer, the withered top of the sunflower just disappeared. Then came silence where not even a sparrow moved.

Freddy's first sensation was wonder, for the flower top was gone. The mighty .12 gauge's blast just blew it away. His second sensation emanated from the acrid smell of gunpowder that puffed out the barrel. The third sensation was a concentrated feeling of pain. The blast had forcefully jammed the gun butt into his shoulder.

He grimaced. *I feel like I got hit by a baseball bat.*

Silently aching, he turned away and flexed his arm like an old-time baseball pitcher. *I forgot to hold the butt tight to my shoulder.*

His dad had told him, "It has some kick, so keep the butt tight to your shoulder."

I think my shoulder is broken. What if I have to walk around with a sling? What will I tell the kids at school?

In a while Freddy's pain started to subside and he reckoned he wouldn't need surgery or a sling.

Then the boys' dad said, "Alright George, now it's your turn. Do like your brother did, only hold the gun tighter against your shoulder."

George wanted to shoot. He rubbed his left eye to remove some dirt that wasn't there. He rubbed his nose and sighed. Then he rolled his head to stretch his neck muscles.

Is it going to break my shoulder?

Running out of patience, his dad gave him 'that look.' Sheepishly, George took the gun into his hands and inched the barrel upward. *This thing is heavy.*

Struggling, he leveled the gun, pulled the big wooden stock tight against his shoulder and sighted along the wavering barrel at a hedge ball 25 feet away.

The breeze seemed to calm as George took a few shallow breaths. Then closing his eyes, he pulled the trigger.

BLAAMMM!

The exploding shell startled him as much as the kick of the gun. He felt some pain, but he didn't dance around like his brother. It was over, he was still on his feet, and he'd done it.

The knobby green hedge ball lay some ten feet from its limb. Sticky white mucus leached from a dozen punctures. Yes George had done it. What a day ... and, what a relief.

Dull pain set in, still, he'd made his first shot ... and it was worth it. Both boys got a kick out of it.

§

How we boys strutted when the three of us headed toward the house. We were big stuff. What would Mom say? Dad didn't share his thoughts, but we sensed he felt proud of us for taking another a big step toward growing up.

We couldn't wait to tell our friends. What envy we'd see on their faces, though we knew Bubba would try to top our story.

Dad had once again helped us overcome our fears and we gained confidence and understanding about hunting and shooting. Nothing was said about our getting only one shot apiece, in part because that would have wasted shells and, just perhaps, because Dad understood about our soreness.

He also understood about our apprehension. All of this was a part of maturing he'd say. But the shooting incident was supervised and controlled.

What he may not have known was that we often adventured off, on our own, using dubious judgment and sometimes throwing caution to the wind. If he had, he might have challenged whether we were truly maturing.

The frosty Saturday morning started as usual. We did the milking and then Dad asked us to get a load of ensilage for the beef herd. At the shed, we started the forlorn looking truck. It had a tiny engine and needed very low gears to get enough power to haul a load. In motion its gears whined to high heaven.

We listened to the high-pitched growl as we started toward the pit silo dug into a pasture hill. At that point, the slick, snow-dusted grass proved to be a temptation.

What happened next progressed from assigned duty to questionable recreation. And, what we did could have perhaps caused real harm to the truck and to us. Fortunately, though the truck was noisy, it was also very slow-of-foot.

§

"This thing is slow as a snail," said Freddy, as he herded the truck across the pasture. "I going to see if I can spin the tires." He gave the foot feed a couple of heavy stomps.

All of the sudden, the groaning, plodding truck spun its back tires and sashayed. "How about that?"

"Can you do it again?" George asked.

Freddy gunned the engine and drove with increasing speed in an immense circle around the treeless section of pasture. With the fresh snow it took a few seconds to reach cruising speed. Now what? *This is going to be fun.* "Hang on."

With a sharp left turn of the steering wheel—full throttle; second gear—the truck spun three slow revolutions on the slickened grass. What a sight to see the truck's backend spin faster than the front.

"Whoopee! Will you look at that?"

Let off the gas, the spinning slowed. More gas, the rear wheels shoved the rear wide. Crank it to the right then left … a figure eight. Medium gas equaled a slow spinning arc. Speed up, fishtails.

What sport and what fun. Did the boys get in trouble? Their dad never said a word. Maybe he never knew as the noonday sun melted the evidence.

In any event the sometimes 360-degree spins were—long before the boys knew what to call them—'wheelies.'

As the boys grew older it was not uncommon for them to start across a feed lot in low gear, climb up over the truck's stock racks, pitch out hay and as the truck approached the far fence, climb back over the racks, get inside and turn the truck around. Farmers do what they have to do. There's no other explanation.

What else did the boys do in wintertime? Well it wasn't always dangerous, although it could be painful.

SEVENTEEN

HAYLOFT BASKETBALL, BARN CAT GAMES AND THE NEW 4-H CLUB

[*Wamego Times* – January 15, 1948] ~ Notice of Sheriff's Sale of Stray Domestic Animal ~ You are hereby notified that I the undersigned, Sheriff of Pottawatomie County, Kansas, will sell at public auction to the highest and best bidder for cash in hand, one certain whitefaced steer, weight about 700 pounds, which has been taken up and held as a stray animal, according to law; said sale will be held at the John White farm, one mile east and one mile south of Laclede, Kansas on the 10th day of February, 1948 at 2:00 P.M. of said day; the proceeds of said sale to be disposed of according to law.
Wiley Taylor, Sheriff.

1948

HAYLOFT BASKETBALL

Eastern Kansas winters changed our leisure activities. Gone were the baseball games. Cold weather fishing had little appeal. We needed to be inventive if we were to amuse ourselves out-of-doors. For example, beside wheelies in the old truck and the shotgun practice that ended with sore shoulders, we hunted rabbits or squirrels with our rifle. Snow meant snowball fights and sometimes building snowmen.

However, most winter activities were technically indoors. Every day, whether we wanted to or not, we braved the Kansas winter wind while doing morning and evening chores. Why would we want to go back outside just to play? Surely there was plenty to do inside.

After church on cold winter Sundays we stayed inside and played regular checkers, Chinese checkers, or a Draw Pitch card game with Dad, and sometimes, Mom. Checkers wasn't our favorite game because when Dad used his logical mind he was always a few jumps ahead of us.

213

These games might have been good learning experiences, but our competitive spirits took a beating.

If it was just the two of us, neither regular checkers nor Chinese checkers were much fun. We could easily get bored, especially when our opponent took forever to make a move, tried an illegal move or we felt the need to accuse the other of cheating.

Sometimes Dad read to us from a Max Brand western pocket book or *Skeezix Goes to War* from a *Little Big Book*. We all enjoyed those special times, which let us stay in for a few hours where it was warm.

On many a Sunday afternoon, the whole family sat together in the living room eating popcorn while 'watching' the radio and listening to *Mr. District Attorney*, *The Lone Ranger* or *The Lux Radio Theater*. We spent many happy hours listening to favorite shows, including *Jack Benny* with skits like: *"You want I should start the old Maxwell now, Mr. Benny?"* Rochester asked in a gravelly voice.

"Not now, Rochester, because I don't want to waste the gas. We won't leave for another minute," answered the always frugal Jack.

At that we heard the studio audience laugh and so did we. What a great show and great time for our family to be together.

Some Saturdays we heard radio shows like *Jack Armstrong* and *Sergeant King of the Royal Mounted Police*. Mom liked to hear *Inner Sanctum Mysteries* with its squeaky-door opening and Dad was a *Mr. First Nighter* fan.

We most always read our day late newspaper sports page and the comics. We took pleasure in knowing most of the big league baseball players. During football season, we could name the Kansas State College—later to become Kansas State University—star players and we knew all of the basketball players as well.

Dad listened to every K-State basketball game, and so did we. While few people would say the words apple pie and basketball in the same breath, we did. Dad told us again and again how he'd played at Louisville High. We very much wanted to learn to play it, but sadly we had major handicaps. No basketball, no goal and no court to play on.

What made things worse was that we had gone with Dad a couple of times to Wamego High games and watched the school's 1946 team that played in the Kansas High School finals. Names like Erv Buzzart, Ed Peters and Jim Sackrider inspired us. If we just had a ball ….

No question about it we learned to love the game by watching the high school team, listening to K-State on the radio and from hearing Dad's tales of how he and Cousin George Burgess played together in the tiny Louisville gym. According to Dad, it was so small the walls were declared inbounds and, as a guard, he'd bounce-pass off the wall to George who played center. The way Dad told it, they fooled the opponents and were a mighty effective combination.

Listening to games and stories only whetted our desire. We just had to have a ball and a goal and a place to play.

After a lot of suggesting, asking and pleading, Dad bought us a pathetic looking used leather basketball from K-State. It was tired, but still held some air, and we assumed the price was right. Back then our farm had no blacktop or buildings with concrete floors, so we'd either have to play on dirt or gravel outside, or in the barn's hayloft.

With enthusiasm we moved the loose hay around and exposed a wooden floor with several warped boards. Now we needed a goal.

Dad came to our aid and took us over to see the Louisville blacksmith who said he could make us a hoop. To this day, we believe that the blacksmith was good at making iron horse shoes, welding broken implements and the like, but that his basketball savvy was limited.

As a result, he made a smaller than regulation, almost-round black ring, and welded it directly—no offset— to a strap-iron mounting bracket. There were no net hooks, just the almost smooth ring. Still, that wasn't the biggest problem.

Dad took charge of installing the goal and mounted it flush against the north wall of the hayloft. That wall served as the backboard, but because of the lack of the normal six-inch off set, bank shots were nearly impossible. He also placed the goal about 8-feet high to compensate for the sloping roof on the right side. The good news was we now had court, a ball and a goal. "Let's go play basketball."

In that hayloft above where we milked Claudette, Wilma, Bubbles and their friends, we played *Horse, Twenty-One*, and a lot of hard-nosed one-on-one. We competed, again and again. Without a net, we often—often!—argued whether a shot went through the hoop.

Loosely nailed high-rise boards made dribbling iffy. After a time we played with a sad-sack, lop sided, lumpy, leather ball that would never regain its shape. The irregular floor had been just too much for it.

In addition to these hindrances, the right side of the barn roof had sharp nails protruding. It sloped across that half of the court, forcing only the flattest trajectory shots.

To surmount these obvious drawbacks, we formed some hayloft-basketball innovations. Generally, we observed standard basketball rules, plus we agreed that it was illegal to knock the other player into the hay on either side, and since we didn't have a teammate to pass to, the player inbounding the ball had to dribble at least once before he could shoot.

We knew no self respecting snake would dare invade our court while we were playing, so we just disregarded the threat. We did send some cats into hiding during our battles.

§

With a fake from the knife-marked inbounds line, John slammed the lumpy ball on one of the few solidly nailed pieces of flooring. He picked up his dribble and jumped and fired a low arching shot. It dropped through the tipped down ring.

"Hey, that makes it 16 to 14," he panted, his competitive character now in full charge.

George took the ball to the end line, took a deep breath and burst forward one dribble, stopped, faked, jumped and let fly. "Now we're tired." George had a desire to win as well..

"Okay, but look out this time," his brother said. Even in the near freezing barn he needed to wipe sweat from his eyes. Now he was ready.

John faked left, right and left, bounced the ball once and this time drove past George—mostly through—on the way to a layup. The drive took him crashing into the barn wall while the ball ricocheted down and through the goal. George ended up in the hay.

"That was charging. You ran right into me and that's illegal."

"No, it wasn't, it was a foul on you for hacking. Anyway, that makes it 18 to 16."

And so the games went, with John using his quickness and weight and George relying on his long arms and grace. And, since the playing surface was only about seven feet wide, there was little finesse. It was fake and shoot over your opponent or fake and try to dribble around—or over—him.

Truthfully, the games were a bit rough at times. When that carried on for a while, one or the other boy would have to call off the fun and they'd go back to work—at separate jobs.

Did all this basketball practice help? Not much. John never did play on a school team, except for intramurals, and George, after Prairie View School, made his Louisville Grace School 8th grade team, and scored a few points in games that ended with scores like 15-11. George never made his high school team.

Basketball, hayloft style, offered a place to play out of the wind. There were many days, however, when the sun shone brightly and the weather warmed. Then, John and George looked for outside activities. They created several sports that gave them exercise, competition and exercised imagination. Bows and arrows and slingshots consumed much of their Lee Sure time.

The boys liked to play medieval heroes, especially archers. In particular, they'd imitate Robin Hood, the good outlaw of Sherwood Forest. Homemade bows and arrows regularly dispatched the Sheriff of Nottingham's men and saved Lady Marian.

"Come on, Little John," shouted Robin Hood (George) as he ran behind the big haystack castle at the edge of the meadow.

There stood the famous Robin Hood and his sidekick, John Little, called Little John, firing arrow after arrow at the fleeing Sheriff's men. With unerring aim, bad guys fell, impaled by arrows cut from willow trees.

Cut a flexible willow branch, tie on some twine, and presto, a long-bow emerged. Reasonably straight reedy willow twigs served as an unending supply of arrows. The boys fired at will, and watched the flimsy shafts wobble toward targets.

"Did you see that, Little John? Your arrow went deep into yon foe's chest?" Robin Hood asked.

"Aye, that it did."

Pulling his arrow from the bad guy's haystack chest, Little John said, "Volley we must until our quivers are empty,"

Acting heroic against the evil Sheriff didn't cost any money. The boys didn't require money for slingshots either, for when the Sherwood Forest battle ended they moved on to do war against the Philistines.

Find a hackberry branch from which to cut a perfectly formed Y-limb, attach old rubber tire inner tube strips and a piece of a discarded leather shoe tongue and a weapon was born. Thus armed, John and George moved to the David and Goliath story from the Bible.

Slingshots launched rocks or bits of gravel that fell many a soldier and of course, the mighty Goliath. The Biblical giant often masqueraded as a big hedge tree or a dried sunflower stalk.

Ah, this is great.

Sadly, not all shots hit chosen targets. Giant Goliath—this time impersonating a big fence post—'ducked' and the small rock missed. Into the barnyard it sped and went … 'ker-thunk' … square onto the rump of another giant … the big Hereford bull, Domino.

Domino—his whole name too long to remember—bellowed and took off, glaring at the boys while he plowed right through the fence into the calf pasture. He jumped, kicked, broke wind, and ran to the far corner. While the bull usually intimidated the boys, this day he didn't seem so tough.

Oh dog-gone-it, now we have to herd him back and fix the fence.

The boys also had to explain to their dad why Domino ran through the fence. The story didn't impress him.

Hadn't John and George complained about not having any free time on the farm? It seemed after all that they kept pretty busy with extracurricular activities. Maybe they did know Lee Sure a lot better than they realized, although Hi Gene continued to be an obstacle. However, work responsibilities never ended, so sometimes the boys would extend their fun by taking their weapons with them as they fed the hogs or brought in the cows for milking.

MUDDY MILK COWS

"Don't go in there," eleven-year-old George hollered at the milk cows. "Yaa, Yaa, Yaa. Stay out of that marshy stuff. I said don't go in there. You make me so mad."

I hate these dumb ole cows. And Dad keeps buying more.

George grimaced under his badly worn turkey feathered winter corduroy cap with ear-flaps drooping down over both ears.

Why do I have to get the cows every night?

Frustration showed on his face. He stared at the big, mostly white Holstein named Bubbles.

She turned her black eyes toward him, gently lifted her head and then daintily tiptoed into the watery-muck created by a series of side-hill seeps. Weaving between the tufts of blue-green slough grass, she led the way and Louise, Claudette and the others followed.

At that point, whitish Bubbles and her friends stood knee deep. Their partly immersed milk swollen bags contrasted with the black sludge.

Waiting in the swampy mess amid the grass covered hummocks, the cows posed like statues. Slick, black goop covered the cows' legs. The late-winter winds were near freezing while George steamed.

He pondered his problem. In frustration, he yelled again, "Yaaaa. Yaaaa," and ran back and forth on the uphill side of the quagmire. "Hey you good for nothings, get out of there."

I'll show 'em.

He waved his arms and hippety-hopped in his most threatening manner. On each jump, his ankles flashed white between the short legged overalls and his scuffed high-topped work shoes. He edged toward the cows, jumping from one spot to another, trying to avoid dropping in the mud.

This place stinks to high heaven. It smells like that slimy snapping turtle we caught last year. We couldn't wash the crud off for weeks.

I've got it; this'll fix them.

As George frowned he aimed his slingshot at Bubbles' flank and let a pebble fly. 'Smacko.' She jumped a little, looked at her tormenter and—unlike 'big brave' Domino—slowly led the cows out the other side and headed toward the barn. As George stepped back to circle the swamp, a blade of slough grass sliced a three-inch scratch on his exposed left shin.

Howling, he jumped back onto solid ground. "Darn you cows. Just look at this." In anger he fired another piece of gravel at the cows, by now far out of his slingshot's range. "Darn you."

Trailing the cows, George splashed across the shallow slough bloodying the water and hurried after the now trotting cows. When he neared the trench silo his brother met him. "Where in the heck have you been? Mom sent me out to find you."

George walked on and repeated, "Those darned cows."

"Hey, how come you're bleeding? You didn't drive the cows through the slough grass, did you?"

"I didn't drive 'em anywhere, they just went."

"Haven't you learned anything about cows?"

George's face hardened and he spit toward the cows just going out of sight into the corral. .

"Well, come here. We need to have Mom take a look at that cut, but first I'll put some of this jumping spider web on it. That's what the Indians put on wounds."

"I'm not an Indian."

"I know that, but it is supposed to stop the bleeding. I read that at school in my *Four Centuries in Kansas* book."

He pulled some web from the grass and put a stringy, matted wad on George's wound. "This doesn't hurt, but you're going to yell when Mom puts iodine on that cut. Anyway, you wouldn't get cut if you'd lower your overhalls down to the tops of your shoes."

"I can't do anything about it. These overhalls didn't grow with me. I've let my suspenders all of the way out."

George thought, *Oh for two pairs of overhalls—and shoes—a year. Every spring I have to curl up my toes.*

Leaving the pasture, the boys locked the milk cows in the barn lot and walked on toward to the house. Their mom took the iodine bottle from the cupboard and poured some on a piece of cloth. With a sigh, she moved it toward George's injured leg.

"Ouch!"

"I haven't done anything yet."

When he did feel the medicine's sting he gritted his teeth.

"Stand still, you know it has to hurt if it's going to work. Everybody knows that. How did you get this cut anyway?"

"He chased the cows into the mire by the slough and got cut on slough grass because his pants don't cover his legs. He always walking around with highwaters," John said. "He looks like Li'l Abner in the comics."

"Yes, his pants are short. I can't get over how you boys just keep growing," she said. "I just can't keep you in clothes."

Both boys looked at their clothing. They had been new last September, but would they last through the summer? Only with extreme modification.

Every summer every year the boys' dad cut the toes out of their work shoes to extend the leather's life until the fall. Overhalls often got shoulder strap splices. John had filled out and George had filled up.

"I wish you boys wouldn't grow so fast. It doesn't seem right," their mom said.

Her eldest son shook his head. *I want to grow. I need to be bigger to play football this fall. Why doesn't she understand?*

John said to his brother, "It's time to do chores. Go feed the hogs and chickens and I'll start the milking." Grabbing two galvanized buckets, he walked to the barn.

Once there, he stared at the mud-covered cows. *What a mess. It's going to take forever to clean those dirty bags. That brother of mine—*

BARN CAT GAMES

Twenty minutes later George ambled in to help milk. Looking at the clean cows he smiled. *Maybe next time he'll offer to go.*

George glanced at his brother sitting on a one legged-stool with his head pressed into Hazel's flank. John sent white streams of milk, alternating between right and left hand pulls, into the three-gallon tin bucket squeezed between his knees. At first the squirts had made tinny music, but as the pail filled and foam formed, the swishing sounded like crumpling cloth.

"C'mon, help me milk. Grab that other stool."

Without comment, George settled down by Bubbles and began making his tin bucket ring. *I hope Bubbles doesn't hold a grudge.*

Then he said, "See that old the gray and yellow mama cat? Watch this." He sent a long spray of warm milk in a rainbow arc directly from the cow to the cat.

"She looks like she's just trying to bite the stream. Hey … she's drinking it. Man is she ever soaked." John joined in the fun. They were once again playing barn cat games.

The drenched cats licked milk from the edges of their mouths and waited for another squirt. Once more, white streams arched across the five-foot distance to within a few inches above the cat's heads. Pawing the air to maintain their balance, the cats stood on their hind legs with their jaws biting sections from the flow. Finally, when the milk stream disappeared, they dropped down to all fours.

"They sure like it. Let's see what the kittens think."

"Aim for the little yellow one, and I'll squirt the gray and white," John said.

Splish, splash, and two rounds of milky artillery squirted towards the two partially grown kittens. Both streams landed and splattered their intended targets and the milking parlor floor as well.

The little gray and white kitten zoomed out of the room with the little yellow one following.

"Look at those kittens run. They're afraid of the milk," laughed George.

"They haven't figured out what their mama knows, but they will. It's a good thing the cows don't jump like that," John said and went back to putting milk in the pail. The fun was over—for a while.

§

In those days, we still milked by hand. Thankfully, a year later Dad bought a milking machine. But for now we sat with our heads against the cows for balance. As we pulled and squeezed, the milk ricocheted off the inside of the pail. Each squirt slowly added to the volume.

Flies were everywhere on a farm. Besides lining the walls of the milking parlor, they pestered the cows and the milkers. There could be as many as 50 horn flies, green-bottle flies, house flies or giant horse flies hovering nearby.

The flies sat on the cows' withers out of reach of the switching tails and slobbery head tosses. And with so many flies present, they often congregated on our sweaty necks.

That's the way milking went.

§

About 6:30 on a cool March morning young John stood facing the parlor wall, emptying three gallons of Hazel's milk into a big 10-gallon milk can.

Without warning, his dad sent a strong, wet stream of hot milk right onto the back of his neck. Before the unsuspecting eighth grader could say a word, his dad took the offensive.

"George, dad-gum-it, I've told you not to squirt your brother. Don't forget, boys, we are here to get this milking done. George, when you squirt someone, you're being wasteful," his dad said with a calm, lighthearted smile on his face.

"Hey, I didn't squirt anybody," George said.

"Well, someone did," his dad said, grinning broadly.

John picked up on the joke. "Darn you George, I'll get you good one of these times."

Again, George claimed his innocence and the game of words continued, with the both boys and their dad laughing and teasing each other. Here it was, early in the morning, with lots of chores to be done, including the milking, but instead of anyone feeling abused, it was a time to have fun together.

§

Those were good times in our milking parlor. While WIBW radio sent us the music of Little Jimmy Dickens and Edmund Denney from Topeka, we milkers and the cows and the cats just seemed to blend together.

Cats served as a necessary line of defense against an infestation of mice and rats. Without the cats, these rodents would rob grain bins and potentially carry diseases onto the farm. Even with cats, we had more mice and rats than we wanted, but our cats helped keep things in balance.

When some cats died off replacements always arrived. Each spring, at least two new litters of kittens came along, born up near our hayloft basketball court.

We wondered if Claws, *The Tom Cat from the Sky*, fathered any of these kittens. After the 4th of July incident, we'd never seen him hanging around although he could have come by for an occasional late night liaison.

Mama cats normally had five or more kittens in each litter. Though born blind, the kittens grew some every day and soon the little multicolored fur balls opened their eyes, began to romp and run and, after a while would come downstairs to visit the cows and us.

Besides cats, the farm had lots of animals including our dog, the horses, the milk cows, the beef herd, the hogs and the chickens. We were supportive partners. At another level we were always in need of information about how to care for animals to make them worth their care.

To supplement what Dad taught us, 4-H was a never ending supply of worthwhile knowledge and we trusted what we learned. 4-H and Farmers were natural partners, each serving a role *To Make the Best Better.*

§

THE NEW 4-H CLUB

In October of 1947, some people had talked to the boys' dad about John and George joining the new 4-H club in Louisville. Although the boys had already learned much from 4-H, many kids in the Louisville area hadn't.

Just like at the Blackjack 4-H Club in St. George, the new club would be offering kids the opportunity to learn practical skills like raising and showing animals, sewing and cooking, project management and record keeping. The kids would also learn how to run meetings, do public speaking and give demonstrations.

Once parents of prospective members got familiar with the 4-H ideals, they realized 4-H taught skillfulness, citizenship and trustworthiness. Indeed, this would help their kids learn how to be productive and mold character in positive ways.

The Burgess family discussed the Louisville club idea. Unfortunately, they'd have to leave the Blackjack 4-H Club.

That's when Owen and Reva Stratton came to visit to talk to the family. "We want to add to our initial membership," Owen said, "and wonder if you would be interested in joining. We have several farm kids involved, plus some from the town. It's a good mix."

"Yes, so far we have Lois and Larry Riat, our kids Raymond and Donna, Doris Lintz, Florence and Mildred Blankley, Dean Ebel, Phyllis Carley, and we think Nonavee Taylor and Harold Wilson will join," Reva said.

"That sounds like a good start," the boys' dad said as he glanced at his wife. "And you think our boys might want to join?"

"We know they like the Blackjack Club, but we are hoping they wouldn't mind giving us a hand with our new group. Their 4-H experience would be valuable," Reva said.

"What do you think, boys?" their dad asked. "And Veda, how about you?"

"Maybe we could move to the new club. It'd be fun to help out," John said. "What do you think, George?"

"I just don't want to make Blackjack Club kids mad at us."

"I'm sure they'll understand," Reva said, "especially when they figure out that you kids could really help us out with new members. And, maybe your dad would be a leader."

The boys' mom said, "Well, it's up to you two."

After a couple of days the boys agreed to move to the new Club. On January 1, 1948, a new 4-H club was born.

At the first meeting, some 15 young people joined and John was elected President and George Recreation Leader. The group selected *Louisville 4-H Club* as its name.

Thank goodness Bubba Brockman decided to stay with the Blackjack 4-H Club, the boys thought. *Too bad for them though*.

The Louisville 4-H Club soon became a well respected group. Mrs. Stratton was good at teaching cooking and sewing classes and her husband and the boys' dad helped with the farming projects.

PROJECT PIG

Everyone in the new 4-H Club wanted to make his or her mark which meant members needed to work hard to learn and manage their projects. If they fared well at the County Fair, they might also be entered at the Kansas State Fair in Hutchinson.

As with most clubs, girls did mostly sewing and cooking and the boys did livestock or crops. John decided to raise two Market Hogs of the Duroc Breed and also enter a garden project.

George also raised a market hog, and he picked a Hampshire. The boys' dad once again helped by *selling* them the pigs. George also chose to raise about five acres of wheat in the south field, as his own.

Why did the boys decide on Market Hogs? The logic was that since pigs were smaller than beef, they'd involve less work.

I hope nobody asks us to demonstrate, 'How to fit a Pig for the Fair,' George thought.

In reality showing hogs properly, required considerable training. Unlike beef, swine had to be directed in the show ring totally with a cane.

Pigs, though highly intelligent, are also independent and very much like to make their own choices. "I can't get Oscar to stand still," George said with hands on his hips and throwing a frown toward his project. "What's the matter with him?"

John said, "He's just a pig. Anyway, you should have bought a Duroc. They are easier to work with."

George scowled again but didn't comment. *What does he know? He's having the same problems that I am.*

"Why don't you get an ear of corn and let your hog eat on it while you brush him down? He'll stand still until he finishes."

George did, and Oscar seemed to enjoy the treat. George brushed the finely bristled black back. Next he worked over the white shoulders and down the white front legs. When the hog finished his meal he trotted off. "Come back here you brute!"

"Snort," went Oscar as he flopped into the muddy wallow beside the hog water trough.

You crazy pig, now I'll have to wash you again.

While the boys at times questioned the sanity of showing pigs, they soon found that with lots of corn bribes and rub downs Oscar, and John's Bud and Ike grew more gentle.

For certain washing a hog was a truly iffy process. Pigs normally liked to wallow in dampness, not get sloshed with it.

"We've got to figure out a way to keep them still while we wash them," John said. "Let's make s chute in the corner and then give them their normal feeding."

It worked. Once confined, with their meals, the pigs grew fairly content and washable. Still, the process was slow.

But ... we've jumped ahead of ourselves again, because earlier in 1948 the family experienced a much more important event. On February 22nd a second baby sister was born. She turned out to be a blessing ... and a real corker.

EIGHTEEN

SHE'S A CORKER, THE JOHNNY POPPER AND TONY THE PONY

[*Wamego Reporter* – March 3, 1948] ~ Flush News ~ John Straub, Sr., John, Jr., Walter and Norbert Straub helped Carl Straub saw hedge posts last week.

We are sorry to report that Theo. Dekat was taken to the Dechario hospital, Saturday afternoon.

Mr. and Mrs. Charles Pinnick spent Sunday evening with Mr. and Mrs. Carl Straub and family. Herman and Louise Zoeller spent Sunday evening with Miss Rose Dekat and Ed Dekat.

1948

SHE'S A CORKER

On Valentine's Day, the 14th of February 1948, the Burgess family celebrated the boys' mom's 37th birthday and on the 24th they recognized young John's 14th. However, the big event that month was the arrival of a second baby girl on the 22nd, and indeed it was momentous.

The baby came into the world at the Dechario hospital in Westmoreland with Dr. Dechario in charge. During delivery the boys stayed home and waited for their dad to bring the news. When he finally did arrive, he said everything was fine and the baby was healthy and lively … although she didn't have a name yet.

In the weeks before the birth, the family had discussed many boy and girl names. If the baby was a girl, the name Joyce found favor with all. The boys' mom also wanted to use Sigrid, her Norwegian mother's first name.

"You remember Grandma Scott came to the U.S from Norway at age 19," the boys' mom reminded them. They had.

When their dad got ready to return to Westmoreland the next morning he asked, "How about Joyce Sigrid? Mom likes it."

"That's great," the younger John said. "It sounds pretty high brow. I'll bet she'll be smart with a name like that."

"Yeah," George said. "What do you think, Judy?"

The not yet two-year-old girl smiled and tried to say the name. Out came, "Way-ce."

"Alright then, Joyce it is," their dad said. "And, if Mom hasn't changed her mind you three have a baby sister named Joyce Sigrid." Then he added, "She's really cute and very lively."

"When can we see her?" George asked.

"Why don't I come get you after school? You can see your Mom and Joyce for a while then," he said. "Judy you can stay home today with Lucille."

The boys' dad left for the hospital and John and George walked off down the road toward school. The day at Prairie View School seemed long. At home, Judy played and napped under the care of recent high school grad Lucille Kufahl who had come to stay and help out for a few days.

About three days later, baby Joyce and her mom came home and she was indeed a corker. Even as a tiny baby she tried to follow the action in the room with her eyes, and seemed to smile a lot … although John junior said he thought she just had gas.

Regardless, the family was now complete with John age 14, George soon to be 12, Judy at 20 months and now Joyce. And, what made things so interesting was that Judy and now Joyce were irresistible to their big brothers, and the start of a loving relationship.

§

With four offspring in the family, there was a constant need for food. Of course on the farm we raised meat and garden vegetables. Still, trips to the store were necessary.

NEW PROSPERITY

Although World War II had ended two years earlier, in March of 1948 America was still getting back on its feet and there was pent-up demand for goods and services. Also, everyone who wanted to work had a job and that meant money to spend. Rationing was over and production that had been dedicated to turning out war machines for more than four years now switched to producing consumer goods.

Dad toyed with the idea of buying new farm machinery—another tractor?—and maybe trading in the heavily worn twelve-year-old Chevrolet for a new car.

Mom wanted changes, too. During the War she had used a coal oil fired refrigerator. In 1946 the REA brought electrical lines across Rock Creek to the barn, house and 'yard light' at the end of the walk. Dad had bought a used Nash-Kelvinator refrigerator, but now Mom wanted a newer, larger one. Maybe she'd get a new washing machine to replace the old Maytag with its small gas engine.

We sensed Mom's excitement each time she talked about the situation, knowing she wouldn't have to use Mason jars to can vegetables and meats anymore. She glowed when she discussed this new prosperity.

"You know," she said, pointing to the pantry, "We can keep the shelves well stocked by buying most of what we need in town. That way I'll have more time to do other things … like caring for two little girls."

§

Glancing at his wife and smiling, the boys' dad said, "I think it's just great to have another girl. Now, Judy has a playmate."

"I guess we sort of have two families with the older boys and baby girls." their mom asked. "It's just wonderful."

On the next shopping trip the old car rattled down the road into town and ended up at Trivett's Grocery Store. There, the boys' mom moved up and down the aisles, lost in her own world, all the while filling her cart higher and higher. While she shopped, the boys' dad stood back smiling. Of course, in their admiring way, the boys—tending their sisters—laughed at both parents.

To this point in their lives, John and George had only experienced the privation and cautious spending of the Great Depression of the 1930s and World War II of the 1940s. While the U.S. generously gave aid to the war torn nations, the Country's conservative attitude had now changed to a sense of abundance.

Like the rest of the U.S., the boys felt like they'd entered a time of luxury that no one could have imagined.

The boys now got more than one pair of overhalls and shoes each year, and occasionally, their dad bought them a *Coca-Cola* or a *Grapette* or a *Nehi Orange,* or maybe an *Oh Henry!* candy bar—or his favorite—a *Snickers.* The youngsters had a little more money for rifle shells and they went to movies every Saturday. They could spend for leisure activities without guilt, though they still got frequent advice about overspending.

During this exciting period, one thing moved to the head of the boys' most wanted list. They almost ached for the taste of store bought *Rainbow Bread* or *Wonder Bread* in the cellophane wrappers. The soft, uniformly sliced white bread seemed sweet and feathery.

I just love baker's bread, John thought.

Life was good, and with the new economy, their dad went ahead in expanding his farming operation, and made a purchase that to the boys seemed magnificent.

§

THE JOHNNY POPPER

Dad had toyed with the idea of a second tractor. He'd rented extra ground to almost double our grain-crop acreage and by then knew he needed bigger and better equipment to farm it.

Besides more small grain land, he'd also inherited a quarter-section of bluestem pasture when Grandpa Burgess passed away in 1946. That meant he could now run a large herd of beef cows and sell feeder calves. With more cows, it also meant that he'd need more hay, silage and grain to feed them during the winter months.

The whole expansion decision came about in part because the two of us could function as effective farm hands. Besides doing chores and tending livestock, we could drive a tractor to plow, disk, plant, cultivate, harvest and haul grain or hay. With three machine operators in the family, it made sense to add another tractor.

While we were still in school that spring, Dad started comparing tractor brands and models. The local area dealers sold Allis-Chalmers, Farmall, Massey-Harris, Ford and John Deere, and each was considered trustworthy.

He finally settled on the John Deere A model, because he said it was reliable, easy to repair with just two cylinders and he could buy it right. His choice was rated a 2-3 plow tractor and it easily handled the new two-bottom 16 inch John Deere plow he bought. For its part, the AC was rated to pull two 14 inch plows.

When the John Deere dealer's delivery truck turned into our lane with the new A aboard you'd have thought we were floating on clouds. What excitement and what a sense of pride. In that one action, our farm converted into an up-to-date and modern operation.

While we watched excitedly, the delivery driver dropped the ramp from his trailer and climbed into the A's plush vinyl seat. He pushed the starter and instantly the two giant cylinders roared to life with a low rumbling Pop-pop, Pop-pop, Popity-pop. The tractor backed down the ramp while we stared with delight.

At last our brand new tractor stood parked beside us at the edge of the lane. The bright green paint reflected the sun and the yellow wheels and trim smacked of tasteful design and high-style indeed. We had arrived.

§

"Can you smell that green paint?" George asked his brother. "I smelled the tractor coming our way."

"Are you sure you didn't hear the truck's noise?"

"Man that is some tractor. I can't wait to drive it."

"Me neither. See how tall the back wheels are? They're 38 inchers and that will give it a lot of speed. They say it will go about 14 mph in road gear."

"How about that hand clutch?" George asked, "And the lights?"

"Yeah, this is probably the best tractor ever made. And … it has a starter. Wow. We have a *Johnny Popper*, I want to drive it."

And drive it the boys did day after day, enjoying its extra power and speed. They never—almost never—got tired of driving it.

All through the year, the big A handled implements with ease. It did everything asked of it, with the old Allis-Chalmers attempting to keep pace. A new day had dawned in the Burgess farming situation with the boys a big part of it.

Incidentally, four years later the A's paint had dulled so through Wamego High Vocational Agriculture George repainted the machine. He swelled with pride when neighbors asked if his dad had bought another new tractor.

AGRICULTURAL ART

High bulging clouds dotted the spring morning's pale blue Kansas sky. Along the road and fence lines greening trees showed fresh leaves and buds. New vegetation sprouted everywhere. Busy finches and sparrows hurried back and forth to their nests with food for their hungry offspring. Overhead a huge vee of geese moved north. Rabbits were everywhere.

At the north field alongside Rock Creek, John disked with the John Deere. Back and forth he went, cutting up swathes of the rich bottomland with the new disk. The field would soon have planted corn.

This sure is easy to drive. Turns on a dime.

And so it went for the next couple of hours until sometime before noon the newness began to wear off and the disking started to feel like a job.

At the east end of the field he cranked the steering wheel left and hit the left brake hard. *Oops. Almost too much!*

234

The disk's hitch strut nearly slammed into the tractor's left rear tire. Quick reflexes saved the day as John jerked back on the hand clutch and hit both rear brakes. The big tractor slid to a stop with just a few inches clearance between the wheel and strut.

Gotta watch it.

Recovering quickly, his uneasiness waned as he swung a corrective loop across the plowed soil. He was turning right, and then decided to turn the other way. *Hey, I could paint a picture in the dirt with this. Yeah, let's see what I can do.*

Across the fallow ground he drove first one way and then the other. He was creating agricultural art, for art's sake.

As he finished his last pass, George arrived at the end of the field ridding bareback on the family's newly acquired pony named Tony. With an exaggerated gesture, George cupped his left hand palm up and dipped the other hand into it. Up went the right hand to his mouth again and again.

Dinner time, John thought.

He did a vigorous up and down head dance and disked to a stop at the west end of the field. He stopped the tractor and unhooked the disk.

As he finished, his brother asked, "How was disking with the A? What the dickens is all that stuff over there?"

John grinned and stared at his agricultural art. "Can't you tell what that is?" he asked. "Look close, can't you see what I drew?"

"What do you mean drew?"

"What's the matter with you? I'll bet the birds understand. Can't you see how I disked a picture of that new girl at church?"

"Huh?"

"Yeah, you know about that wheat field down by Topeka where the crop spells the word Kansas, right? I did the same thing with the disk. This is agricultural art."

"Are you sure that's a girl? It looks to me like a peacock."

"Look over there. There are her feet and toward the east that's her head."

"Oh yeah, I see," George said.

"Yep," John grinned. "I'm going to hate to disk her under this afternoon, but I doubt Dad would appreciate this art."

In truth, both boys did waste considerable time drawing and painting the fields with machinery. They sometimes used up an acre or more creatively writing their names, or drawing a girl—or a peacock. How many artists could turn a tractor and disk into usable artistic tools, as John had done that day?

§

In fact, turning the soil during normal fieldwork did make us feel artistic. It was as if we were slowly brushing out the pale browns and beiges of last year's stubble and replacing them with linear patterns of moist, sandy brown loam, and in some fields black gumbo.

Hour after hour this landscape canvas altered as our disks or plows flipped over the debris. And, though we'd sometimes just peel off and do some curly-cues in the middle of a field to momentarily overcome monotony's clutch … we got the job done.

In the meadow or the alfalfa patch, we worked on canvases of a different sort. There we'd watch our mowers cut down prairie grass or alfalfa in five-foot swaths. Fields slowly changed from an array of grass and wild flowers swaying in the wind, to a blanket of colorful cuttings lying motionless on the ground.

In similar ways, the orange Allis-Chalmers Model 60 combine drew five-foot wide patterns in fields of ripened wheat. It swallowed the stalks, then separated the grain and chaff and spewed waste straw out like a huge Serengeti elephant … leaving mounds across the expanse. And we were amazed by the beauty on other farms.

We were stunned by the occasional field with precisely planted check-row corn that showed symmetry in any direction … a picture of superb orderliness.

Maybe it was the orderliness—ultimately—that we cherished. Any way you cut it, when we prepared the soil for the next crop, we took pleasure in directing the power of our machines to transform the chaos of straw, corn stobs, or weeds into smooth, well-manicured fields.

Looking back, we were more accustomed to agricultural art than real oil or watercolor paintings, although we had studied the few oils in Aunt Mollies' house. And as much as we appreciated them, we thought the pictures drawn by our machines had indescribable beauty. We were farm boys don't you see? This was our environment, this was art to us, and to others like us.

We sensed how real farmers appreciated the productive tidiness of their fields. There was something about working the soil that brought a sense of closeness to God and nature. Maybe that's why farmers understand other farmers and often spend hours admiring each other's handiwork.

As we grew older, we came to appreciate certain farmer's artistry. At the Eckart farm east of Wamego, we marveled at the corn fields. Mr. Eckart was surely a master craftsman, as his rows were always as straight as *The Petrified Man's* a yard stick.

We've wondered if non-rural folks could possibly appreciate the beauty of agricultural art.

But, where did all of this start for us? How did we go from six-year-olds toting pails of water and gathering eggs to teenagers working tractor drawn equipment? We started learning as all farm kids learned, a little at a time … and not just in the fields.

ADDICTED BOVINES

At the trench silo, the steamy alcohol odor told us when the field chopped corn and sargo fodder had cooked and fermented enough to be called ensilage—silage—a prized feed for cattle.

After only a few weeks in the silo, material baked enough for the sugary sap to change from green to brown and from sweet to heat. Twice daily, when wintertime came, we loaded sixty steaming bushels onto the tractor drawn trailer and hauled the feed to the cattle.

The animals loved the pungent, alcohol smelling silage. These bovines seemed addicted to this fermented feed … and maybe they were.

§

Watching the cattle eat, George said, "Hey, wouldn't it be funny if the cows got drunk on this stuff?" He nodded toward the big Holstein Hazel, who along with her friends, stood side by side with the Herefords gulping down huge mouthfuls that reeked like Shorty Brockman's breath, following a stop at Younge's Tavern. Apparently, the cows enjoyed these daily nips, for they buried their noses in the stuff, all the while madly switching their tails to shoo-off a crowd of blackbirds joining them for a meal.

"Yeah, wouldn't it be a blast to cow-tail ski behind a tipsy Holstein?" John asked.

Just then Hazel tossed her head, sending a stream of saliva and silage over her back, some of which landed on George's shoes.

Darn. Maybe she's under the influence already.

When spurred on by the cold, there was no table etiquette at the feed bunks. George thought the ensilage smell was as overpowering as AWOL Bertha-the-hen's rotten eggs he'd accidentally stepped on in the haymow the night before.

That night at the supper table George grinned and said, "I guess I found out where Bertha laid her eggs when she wandered off a few weeks ago."

The rest of the family thought, *He found them all right.*

"They exploded like gun shots, and scared the tar out of me," odiferous George said.

The egg and silage smell on his pant legs drove his mother to say, "You throw those overhalls into to the laundry right after we finish here. Do you hear me?"

The boys would have more accidents and more smelly clothing, but that was farming.

However, when they got their new saddle pony, both boys wondered if farming was such a great idea.

§

TONY THE PONY

We called her a pony though she was really a small horse about 11 or 12 hands high. Black except for a very small white star on her forehead, she had the distinguished name of Antoinette though we always called her Tony.

Dad brought her from Herman Elder to be our saddle horse to help bring in the milk cows for milking and sometimes herd the beef cattle. Herman said Tony was about three years old and fairly well broken. He said she was a bit frisky, and as we found out, really hard to catch.

§

"Will you come here, Tony?" George asked one day in a pleading voice. "Please." This was his third request.

Tony, at home in the three-acre pony pasture beyond the barn corral, had other ideas. She'd let George move up close only to inch away when he got near. Then she stopped and nibbled grass. When George moved, Tony moved.

At last, ingenuity came to the rescue. *Oats!*

After George shared his idea with his brother, they always took oats when they wanted to ride her. The oats melted most of her resistance and Tony grew more cooperative.

The boys just knew she was thinking, *Eat, duck and run.*

Once one of the boys got her to eating, "Gotcha!" When she'd finish her snack, the rider would swing up onto her back and away they'd go at a gallop. Sometimes the boys would use the saddle.

One warm evening George took on Rex Allen's persona. On went the small saddle with its very narrow girt strap buckled in place. *Rex* climbed aboard and rode along singing, *Streets of Laredo* while admiring the beauty of the *Old West*.

At the slough Tony waded the stream's three foot wide clear, cool water and started up the steep far side bank. As she jerked to get up the hill, the narrow saddle strap broke and *Rex* went sliding, saddle and all, off the horse's back and into the water.

'Kersplush!' Tony ignored her rider and trotted on.

Dad-gum-it.

So picture if you will, a very wet cowboy walking home carrying his saddle with its broken strap. Due to the circumstances, on this day, *Rex* drew his six gun and put his horse with a broken leg out of its misery.

Tony came back to the corral a couple of hours later. George decided he'd fix the saddle strap before he rode out into the *prairie* next time..

While John the younger wasn't involved in this pony adventure, he and his brother shared many others, and they dreamed of even more.

Tony the Pony, Baby Beef, Fat Pigs, field art, new machinery and a host of other goings on kept the boys busy and fascinated. But for recreation, baseball may have fascinated them more than anything else. They just knew someday they'd be big leaguers.

Finally one day ….

NINETEEN

GET IN THE GAME, SNAKE PANIC BUTTON AND POOR DEAD LAST

[*Wamego Reporter* – August 26, 1948] ~ **WAMEGO LOST LAST SUNDAY** ~ The Leonardville baseball team came to Wamego Sunday and won 5-0. Riat and Hoferer were the Wamego pitchers.

Next Sunday, Aug. 29, Westmoreland will be here for a game.

1948

GET IN THE GAME

As we've alluded to, in the booming times after World War II, baseball solidified its place as American's national pastime. Everyone played or talked baseball and at the Burgess farm in rural Kansas the game took top honors. If we weren't working, tending to our 4-H projects, in class at school or weren't in church—sometimes there too—our thoughts and minds lived baseball. You've seen how we played the game whenever and wherever we could.

Baseball images flitted in our minds while we milked, while we drove the tractors, during recess at school or just about any time we were awake. Baseball obsessed us. We saw ourselves racing across the outfield grass and making a catch against the wall, or in the bottom of the ninth slamming a fastball to the fence for a triple and knocking in three RBIs for the win.

Again and again we clearly pictured ourselves as starting spectacular double plays, sliding on our stomachs to spear an infield line drive, or pitching a curve that snapped down at the plate hard, baffling the batter. In our minds we continually broke our ash bats with smashes to the outfield or bunted squeeze plays for the winning runs.

We saw ourselves in classy uniforms, streaked with dirt and grass stains. We went all out. We gave the game 100 percent, all of the time. Baseball enthralled us, as it did most of the country.

The Major League Baseball had eight teams each in the American and National Leagues. There were also twelve Negro Major League teams. Sometimes in the paper we could find information about other baseball leagues of various classifications. With the majors on top, other leagues followed at the Triple A, Double A, Class A, Class B, Class C and even at the Class D levels.

The Topeka Owls, of the Western Association played teams from Joplin and St. Joseph in Missouri, Fort Smith in Arkansas, Muskogee in Oklahoma, and Kansas teams from Leavenworth and Salina, plus a team that split its time during the summer of 1948 between Hutchinson, Kansas and Springfield, Missouri.

We knew of pro teams in tiny Kansas towns like Iola, Independence and Chanute in the KOM (Kansas, Oklahoma, and Missouri) League, and other leagues called the American Association, the Pacific Coast League with San Francisco and Los Angeles, the Midwest League, and the Sally League (South Atlantic). Texas had a league. California and other states or combination of states had leagues.

The American Negro League had a squad called the Kansas City Monarchs. Founded in 1920, the team was recognized as a highly successful franchise. We all marveled at exploits of Satchel Paige, Buck O'Neil, Sug Cornelius and Cool Papa Bell. The legendary Jackie Robinson of the Brooklyn Dodgers, the first African-American player in the majors, had played for the Monarchs.

Even the island of Cuba had a league and so did Japan. Across the U.S. there were maybe 50-60 leagues in all.

Besides the professional teams, most communities had an amateur town team. These players were farmers, section hands, clerks, teachers and from almost every walk of life. That meant most games had to be played when the players weren't working, Sunday afternoons.

Besides the players, it seemed that most everyone else in the country attended baseballs games at some level. In the days before television, people were in the stands avidly watching baseball, and that included us.

Along with our folks and our friends, we attended town team games. Judy and Joyce tagged along although they played with their dolls while we watched the games. Dad loved the games. We'd get a nickel for any foul ball that we brought to the umpire. Cokes were a nickel so we sprang from our seats when we saw a ball go over the back stop.

When we weren't watching a live game or listening to one on the radio we continued honing our skills. We now had gloves, but what we needed was to get in a game. That opportunity finally arrived in June with the formation of a kid's baseball program that included a Louisville team. We had organized baseball at last.

Dad took us to the first practice, and to our surprise some 13 other boys were there, including three of the 4Ds: cousins Danny, Denny and Deane Burgess (Dwight was too young and the 5th D, Dwayne, hadn't yet been born.). Before that practice ended we realized we had someone to play all nine positions. We were a team!

§

Along with the 4Ds' father George, the boys' dad served as a coach. "Okay boys, gather round," he said. "We need to talk about a few things." In a group, the players bunched on the sideline.

"We have some pretty good players here and I think we can develop into a fine squad. I talked to Virgil Haas in Wamego and he said their team would like to play us. What do you guys think?"

A cheer went up and the decision was made. There would be a Louisville youth team, playing games just like the adults.

"For now," the boys' dad said, "George and I would like to try this line-up. Danny, you're big so you can be the catcher, and

Crawford you've learned to pitch pretty well from your Uncle Wally, so why don't you be our pitcher. Denny you're tall so you be the first baseman for now and Johnny Lolley, you look pretty good at shortstop. Freddy, you've got quick hands so you play third. George, you're not overly fast, but you seem to catch anything hit toward you so you can try centerfield. We'll try some of the rest of you guys at the other positions."

§

Can you imagine our excitement? We were on top of the world. Not only were we on a baseball team, but we had positions that we wanted to play.

There wouldn't be a clinic for early training, so we'd just have to jump right in and practice and practice.

Dad and George put up the money to buy catcher's shin guards, a face mask and chest protector, and three or four bats and two or three balls, plus some of us brought a bat or ball from home. We saved one of the new balls for games and we used the rest for practice. They quickly got stained and damaged. Town team discards were well used, but acceptable.

Did we care? Not in the least. A ball was a ball, and if one of the bats cracked, we just taped it up.

Uniforms? You've got to be kidding. No one could afford one, and although we envied teams with smart looking outfits, we were more interested in playing the game.

We practiced hard right on the Louisville diamond, with Dad hitting grounder after grounder to the infielders and Cousin George hitting fly balls to the outfielders. Infielders and outfielders alike learned to stay in front of the ball, hit the cut-off man and be ready to field the ball at every swing of the bat.

Did it work? Sure it did. We played Wamego and teams from St. George, St. Marys, Westmoreland, Rossville and Silver Lake.

In the final analysis, we played the real thing against real teams. Were we good? In our minds we were. Would we do it again? Darn tootin'.

§

WE'LL GET THOSE GUYS

"Hey … batter, batter, batter. You can't hit what you can't see. Chuck it in there, Crawford. You got him now," third baseman John said as part of his constant chatter to encourage his team and discourage the opponents. "One more out and we got 'em."

"Plop it right here. This guy's no hitter," catcher Dan said while he squatted behind home plate. He pointed his right index finger down between his knees indicating he wanted a fastball.

At the mound, Crawford nodded and began his windmill windup. After he was set he let it go.

'Kerplop!' "Stee … rike!"

Flash the sign for a curve. Repeat the windup. "Here's the pitch."

"Ball two." Even Danny's pulling the glove over the plate didn't fool the umpire.

"Hey umpire, you need glasses," shouted a local fan.

After the umpire frowned toward the crowd, Crawford threw another fastball. 'Whack.' The bouncing ball two-hopped toward the hole between third and shortstop. John moved to his left, scooped up the ball about ankle high and fired it toward Denny at first.

The throw sailed way over Denny's reach. *Error. Darn.* The runner tore from the batter's box to first.

"Safe."

Groans erupted from the home team's bench and from the smattering of parents and spectators. "Sorry guys," John said. "We'll get the next one."

And so the games went with some good and some bad plays on both sides. Getting an out seemed spectacular; a hit sparked jubilation. The teams relied heavily on a single pitcher and if that guy

245

had a bad day, hits started coming. This season was a learning experience, but it was baseball ….

LEARNING THE INS AND OUTS

The teams learned that a left hander pitcher had an advantage for a first base pickoff.

Sometimes a pitcher would throw to first. The runner would casually step off the bag only to get tagged out by the first baseman. *Hey, I thought he'd thrown the ball back to the pitcher.*

A run-down play taught hard lessons. Out of instinct, a runner might start to the next base because a fielder fumbled the ball. The runner ended up in no man's land. "Ooout!"

John batted right handed and did a good job. When he came to bat, the other team's manager often moved his outfield to the gaps to which John usually hit. Over and over his deep hit fly balls merely ended up as outs.

George settled on hitting left. His problem was that he was weak—perhaps from leaning on his pitchfork or shovel. Even the lightest bat, choked up as far as he could, seemed as heavy as a sledgehammer. This often resulted in George crossing up the opponents as he hit—often—to the opposite field. He got a lot of hits that way. Incidentally, there were no batting gloves in those days so players let Mother Nature's infield dirt serve the same purpose.

With only a few possible opponents, the number of games was limited. And, with the mass of inexperienced players, some contests were drubbings with scores like 14-3 or 11-2. Others had big scores for both sides, maybe 12-11.

Why the high scores? Usually because of errors. The reality was that if the batter swung and hit the ball, inexperienced fielders had to make competent plays to get the out. Many innings lasted throughout a batting lineup.

The quality of baseball played during the boys' rookie season in some ways mirrored all baseball games in that good pitching trumped what hitters could do.

For the boys, it was a happy time. Teams practiced and played hard, regardless the competition or obstacles. And in baseball—as in farming—there was a host of obstacles.

FLIES AND BUGS AND BEETLES

What could an outfielder catch in the outfield besides batted balls? Insects. In those days, the old joke was, "What has six legs, wings, and lives in Kansas?" The answer, "Flies and bugs and beetles."

There were chiggers and flies and grasshoppers and crickets and mosquitoes and stinkbugs and butterflies and moths and Junebugs and chinch bugs and on and on. They all lived in vast abundance at every ballpark in every town..

Around a farm, besides barnyard annoyances, there might be corn borers infesting the corn, tomato beetles sucking on the tomatoes, spinach-leaf-hoppers on the spinach, apple maggots in the apples, potato bugs in the potato patch and cut-worms cutting just about any vegetable that came through the ground. With no insect sprays, farmers and gardeners picked bugs off, plowed them under, and in the case of chinch bugs, dug a shallow trench and filled it with creosote. That trap caught the migrating hoard of the bugs heading from a destroyed area to a lush, green one.

On rainy summer evenings Junebugs, beetles the size of a robin's eggs, bombarded the screen doors to get to the lamp light. Moths, as big as oatmeal cookies, fluttered around any street light or near the bare bulbs in the milking parlor.

And flies. Were there ever flies. They were the scourge of the milk cow and the person doing the milking. Many a milker's head got whacked by the three-foot, bony section of cow's tail or was face-whipped by the not too sanitary tail bush When bitten by a two-inch long horse fly, a cow's jump could dump the milker from his one-legged milk stool.

Insects bugged ballplayers. However, most farm folks accepted them as a part of nature's profusion.

As mentioned before, most Kansas snakes were not pests. In fact, many fed exclusively on rats and mice and helped control those populations. The blacksnake, garter snake and bull snake, to name a few, ate hundreds of the real pests and were highly beneficial. With a little caution man and snake avoided each other. However, sometimes—

§

SNAKE PANIC BUTTON

Though beneficial, we found snakes in locations we didn't want. One such place was in our cool, dark storm cellar. Somehow, those conditions, plus occasional mouse, made it an ideal home for a medium-sized blacksnake.

Technically, Kansas storm cellars served two official functions. They protected us from tornadoes—we never saw a twister—and they served as a cool storage place for a good part of our food supply.

Our storm cellar, a limestone dome built below the smokehouse, served with distinction. In its depths, we stored Mason or Kerr jars of 'canned' fruit, vegetables, and meats. In the far corners of the cool cellar sat bins of potatoes and onions that gave the cellar a musty, decaying smell.

Our storm cellar was also home to *Blackie* the blacksnake. We never did find out how he got in when the cellar doors were closed, or where he went. But we were always cautious in the storm cellar.

§

SNAKES AND THE PONY

The boys were always on guard for snakes, especially John due to his solo fishing trip with its water moccasin scare, and seeing Shorty Brockman and his wife confront the bull snake. .

248

Fortunately in those days, few poisonous snakes lived in that section of Kansas. However, the real water moccasin was local and that led to extra caution near streams.

On more than one occasion, the boys fled their skinny-dipping swimming hole in a hurry when a long, gray snake swam slowly their way.

The boys weren't the only ones who disliked snakes. Woe to the bareback rider when Tony the Pony met one.

This time it was young John at full gallop while the April sun painted the low western clouds crimson and orange. Astride the mare bareback, he tore down across the pasture, until the pony spied a coiled brown bull snake about three gallops down the path. Tony hit the brakes, but her rider sailed over her head and landed with a great and painful "Woooof!"

He landed on his right shoulder with the side of his face, coming to a stop about three feet from the snake. In self-defense the reptile coiled and sent out mammoth hiss. The now horseless rider's eyes bulged and his breath stopped. A non-poisonous snake bite would still hurt.

The snake hissed a second loud bluff and slithered off. John got up slowly and rubbed his hands on his dirt caked face. He shook his head and picked up his hat.

He then adjusted his mangled wire-rimmed glasses and looked around for his horse. By now Tony was grazing quietly a good quarter-mile away. *That doggone horse. That doggone snake.*

There was no end to country kids' experiences. And there would always be another time. And now as the Fair approached again, the boys had to concentrate on their 4-H projects. More lessons. They'd toiled through the summer getting ready and once again they had to produce. Their hogs did pretty well for being hogs; however, it took loads of repetition to train the animals.

FAIR TIME AGAIN

By August, the boys' consistent effort was paying off and they felt their projects were ready for the show ring. Before long they'd be showing Oscar, Bud and Ike and trying to win blue ribbons. John would also exhibit garden produce while George would display a sample of his wheat.

On Fair day, John said, "Okay, let's herd our hogs down to the barn so we can load them. I'll back the truck up to that high door at the horse stall."

George nodded and guided Oscar out of the pig enclosure. His brother's Ike followed along nicely, while Bud suddenly turned obstinate and needed special attention.

When the pigs finally reached the barn, a bit of corn bait encouraged the threesome to enter through the horse stalls. At the door, the newly acquired used ton and a half Chevrolet truck awaited the hogs.

"C'mon you pigs. Walk into the truck and we'll get this show on the road," John said. "C'mon on Bud, what's the matter with you?"

"He seems a little nervous. Ike and Oscar are acting okay," George said. "Let's give them some more corn."

With that, he tossed a handful of kernels into the truck bed and Oscar and Ike walked right on. Bud would have none of it. He turned away and ran back into the milking parlor to hide.

"We have to get him on board," John said. "Come hold your herding panel along one side of his head and I'll cover the other. That way he'll go where we want."

On that day and in that place, Bud did not do as expected. He'd move toward the truck and then like a bulldozer, shove through the panels to get away. Over and over the boys ran him down and moved him toward the back of truck, where he'd snort and burst through the panels again.

About then the boys' dad showed up with yet another panel. With the three of them working together, they finally forced Bud onto the truck.

The boys soon had their pigs gated into the right front corner of the truck bed, and feed, water troughs, buckets, plus the boys' bedding and a small suitcase were laid in the back end.

On this day, John the younger would drive his brother and their hogs to the Fair. The boys said their goodbyes to their dad, mom, Judy and Joyce. Then John steered the truck out the lane and headed down the road with everyone enjoying the ride, except for Bud, who continued to grunt, snort and try to jump over the gates.

Later, as the truck headed north on the Onaga Road, the boys realized the hogs were sounding distressed. The pigs' grunts sounded as if they were moaning. Their mouths were frothing.

"Stop, over there," said George, pointing to a windmill beside a fence near the road. "I'll get some water from that horse tank and cool them down."

John complied and George soaked the project pigs with buckets of cool water. That calmed down Oscar and Ike, but Bud still acted agitated.

Once at the Fairgrounds, John backed up to the livestock chute and the boys unloaded all the gear. By this point, Bud seemed to be quite over-wrought. He didn't want to move or follow his friends the short distance to their stalls, and only extra pressure forced him to move.

"C'mon Bud, get a move on," John said.

"He's getting all hot and worked up again," George said. He then spoke to the hog, "If you go inside we'll give you some water."

John shook his head and strained to push the stubborn pig along. Froth poured out of Bud's mouth.

"Grunt … grunt," from the pig.

"He's getting way too hot," George said.

"That's why I'm pushing him inside you blockhead. Move, you darned hog … move."

The struggle continued for a couple of minutes more, until the determined pig finally stumbled into the barn's shaded alleyway. Just inside, Bud collapsed and stopped breathing. In panic, John started pumping on the hog's chest … and for an instant the heart restarted. Seconds later it stopped again … and Bud was dead.

It didn't seem like anyone knew what to do at that point, but someone must have taken action for in about a half-hour the Rendering Plant truck (they processed dead animals) showed up and hauled the deceased project away. Just like that.

What could the boys do? They weren't expecting all of this. Once again though, the farm kids had to accept reality.

Bud's demise put a damper on John's Fair experience for sure. While Ike earned a blue ribbon and John's garden produce also won a blue, he felt sad about his dead pig. What had gone wrong and why did Bud die? Most people said the hog had probably gotten too hot, and since pigs have weak hearts, it died of heart failure.

Knowing the cause didn't help ease John's discomfort, but time helped. He'd won a couple of blue ribbons and in the end he'd had fun bunking in the Pig Barn with his friends. And the carnival offered some relief for he actually won at the milk bottle throw and earned a Kewpie doll for his mom.

Then it hit him. *Oh my gosh, how am I going to pay Dad?*

As usual the boys' folks knew there wasn't anything anyone could have done, so they absorbed the loss. Good parents always seemed to come to their children's rescue.

By the time the boys got home from the Fair, the memory of the Bud episode was starting to fade. Life went on. The next Sunday, in the Guild Hall after the church service, the boys' friend and long time church member Hank Schroeder asked them how they'd done at the Fair.

"My hog Oscar got a red ribbon," George said, "And I got a blue for my wheat."

"That is a job well done," Hank said in a grandfatherly way. "How did you do John?"

"I got two blue ribbons at the fair," he answered. "You would have liked my garden project.

After a pause he continued, "My Duroc Market Hog named Ike won a blue ribbon. He really looked good with that blue draped across his red back. He was almost a champion, but a Spotted Poland China won that, even though it was smaller than Ike. Maybe his missed his buddy."

"What buddy?" Hank asked.

"John took another Duroc to the Fair but when he got it to Onaga and unloaded it, the pig died," George said with a grin. Then he added, "I guess that pig finished dead last."

In the end, both boys gained valuable know how from farm work, baseball, a couple of snake scares and their 4-H fair projects, especially what hogs needed. In reality, the boys had some good and some not-so-good experiences during their summer. But all of this made the young farmers stronger and wiser.

For John the summer of 1948 was demanding physically, but this time it would pay off. In a few weeks when he enrolled as a freshman at Wamego Rural High School, his world would take on a new perspective. For one thing, when he tried out for the Red Raiders' football team he'd use every muscle he had.

First though, he had to do the haying and other duties, to build those muscles.

TWENTY

BETTER WAY TO PUT UP HAY, OFF TO HIGH SCHOOL AND "GET THAT COYOTE!"

[*Wamego Reporter* –August 26, 1948] ~ Draft Headquarters Now in Wamego ~ On this present draft, the headquarters will be in Wamego. The large meeting room at the Fire Station has been made available. This is nearer the center of population than Westmoreland and facilities and accommodations will be better.

1948

BETTER WAY TO PUT UP HAY

The best word to describe the boys' summer of 1948 was busy. Besides baseball, fishing and other *Lee Sure* activities, they disked, plowed and cultivated with machinery. And, they cut and whacked cockleburs, pigweeds and sunflowers, and tended to their 4-H projects.

That year the family harvested nearly 300 acres of wheat and oats. They stored some of the grain on the farm—plenty of shoveling—and sold the rest to the Wamego Elevator.

The two things that took up most of August was the Fair— poor *dead last, Bud*—and haying. In former years, the family had gone from stacking hay to baling it with Leo Scully's stationary baler, but by now neighbor John Habluetzel owned a new mobile baler that did the job more quickly and with a smaller haying crew.

Although someone still had to cut and rake the grass, finishing the job with a moving baler made the operation more efficient. No more stomping around on a haystack and no more bucking the hay to the stationary baler. Now the guy who had the hardest workout was the one who stacked the completed bales onto a trailer trailing behind the moving baler.

John the elder believed John the younger would benefit from that job. So when a bale worked its way out, John grabbed it with a hay hook and pulled it onto the trailer. He'd then heave the

70-pounder—more or less—on top of other bales until they were stacked four high.

Young John handled every bale of prairie hay and alfalfa harvested on the Burgess farm that summer, while several people stored the bales in the barn. A portable hay elevator carried the bales to the hayloft, and then a couple of men dragged each bale across the slick wood floor and stacked them—leaving ample room for the basketball court.

So while the yet-to-enter-high-school farm boy handled every bale, it took three or four others to finish the job. While John worked on the bouncing trailer in the dust, sun and heat—character building the boys' dad said—George mowed and raked.

Riding on seats on either side of the baler, one guy poked the baling wire through and another guy tied the wire.

The actual work each day started when the sun burned off the overnight dew. Like for hay stacking, some days started by 8:00 a.m., while after heavy dew, it might be as late as 10 or 11 before the mown hay dried enough to bale. Timing was critical, as there was a danger of the hay eventually igniting, if stored before drying out.

The routine varied for the farmers waiting to get to work. Some looked for make-work while others just gabbed and joshed and enjoyed the idle time, and the camaraderie that went with it.

"So, did you hear that George Burgess threw a no hitter against Emmett?" Bill Mansfield asked. "And I heard that Bob Burgess struck out 15 Emmett batters in another game."

"You know that Bob is my second cousin and George's brother. They are both pretty good pitchers," young John said.

"Tell me John, what are you going to do this fall. Are you going to get a job?" Shorty Brockman asked. "You're not going to mess with high school are you?"

What does he mean, not mess with high school? Why wouldn't I?

"I think you ought to go on to school," Bill said. "Education is pretty important these days."

"Well just look at the money you lose while you're in school. I didn't go and look how far I've gotten," Shorty said.

Yeah, look….

John said, "Both Mom and Dad went to high school and I guess I want to. I might even go to college."

"College? That's a real waste of time. A guy can be a good farmer without all of that. College people are mostly full of hot air and don't know how to work. You stay on that trailer and handle those bales and it will make a man out of you," Shorty said.

What a joke; what does Shorty Brockman know about farming? Then John thought, *He probably wants me to get a field-work car like his.*

Then, "Gentlemen, I think it's time we get started," the boys' dad said. In a few minutes everyone was in action.

As the bales worked their way to John on the trailer, he thought, *I'm going to be glad when this haying is done 'cause then I'll get to go to school. I wonder what high school is like.* He hooked a bale and pulled it toward the back of the trailer.

All the girls from my class at Prairie View are going to high school.

At that point, the bales started bunching up as they came from the baler. He pulled one out of the way and then grabbed another bale and hauled it to the trailer's rear.

What's it going to be like to play football? I won't know most of the kids. Guess I'll have to make some new friends. I wonder what you do in a place that big. Bet it's got over 200 students.

"Hey, John!" Mr. Habluetzel yelled.

"Huh?" *Oops; better pay attention.*

He pulled another bale up and lifted it to start the second tier. *Do you suppose freshmen can go on dates?*

OFF TO HIGH SCHOOL

Finally, the summer's work ended and the briskness of fall settled on the countryside. At that point, young John officially enrolled as a freshman in Wamego Rural High School. George had one more year at Prairie View School before it closed and he transferred to the Louisville Grade School for his 8th grade.

John had fought a royal battle with his mom over getting school jeans instead wearing overhalls. Her final argument was, "John, with your personality you don't need jeans."

Weak.

By the fall of 1948 this was a long forgotten issue.

On the first morning at WRHS, John got up early and charged through his chores with lightning speed. The sun came pouring around the smoke house and through the east kitchen window. His nervous mom cooked a special breakfast. John scarffed it down and hardly knew what he ate.

"Veda, I think you're more wound up than your son," the boys' dad said.

"Oh John, I'm worried Freddy won't like high school."

"Now Veda, remember he loves to learn … and be sure to call him John."

"I know you're right, it's just that …."

Young John felt first-rate, wearing jeans, plain black shoes and a chambray shirt. His dad's old belt, cut to an acceptable length would do just fine. But he had more on his mind.

After breakfast he slicked down his hair with Wildroot Cream Oil. As he combed a special wave in his red hair's front cowlick, his stomach churned.

I can't wait. This is going to be something.

"Let's go, we don't want to be late," his mom said.

Settled in the new black '48 Chevy Stylemaster, John's mom steered the car out through the driveway ruts and started the six mile trip to town. The young high schooler was buried in thought.

How will we know where to go? They'll tell us won't they?

"Now John, be on your best behavior. High school is different than grade school. Don't do anything stupid. The teachers are a lot stricter than at grade school."

"I know, Mom."

The two approached the school and John surveyed the kids coming from all directions. *Look how big that building is. I hadn't paid much attention before. It has three stories.* His mom let his out of the car and the new freshman headed toward the School's front steps.

FIRST IMPRESSIONS

It is a well known fact that most 14-year-olds are self conscious about their looks. Young boys want to look like boys and the girls want to look like girls, and those looks are strongly influenced by magazine pictures and the movies. Dress right and you'll impress the opposite sex … and your buddies won't kid you about being a 'clod.'

I sure don't want to look like a hick. Just look at those girls.

Without meaning to, he assessed his appearance—especially how well he'd squeezed away his zits—and decided he'd do okay, for now. But before he said hello to anyone he held his hand to his mouth and blew softly.

Seems okay. Maybe I'll chew some Dentyne, for good measure.

He walked up the front steps to join the crowd waiting to enter the school. He nodded to Maxine and Louise Straub and they nodded back. In truth, nothing escaped his glance, and he saw things that amazed him.

While most of the boys wore jeans, one guy wore his belt buckle to the side. A few didn't use belts, letting their garments fall below a descent height. Most wore blue Levi's or Lee jeans. The fashion minded wore the more expensive Levi's, with two seams showing down the legs. The cheaper Lee's had three seams.

Everyone's parents had lived through the Great Depression and the austerity of World War II and spent money on kids clothing carefully. Parents who had growing boys bought them jeans far too long because the clothes needed to last the entire school year. So the kids had to cuff their pant legs. One turn, or two? Style.

One wise adult had said that kids hadn't yet established an identity through accomplishments, so they relied on their appearance for their uniqueness. As if to prove that point, one boy wore his wrist watch turned upside down.

What a klutz.

John compared his hair style to the other kids. Some of the boys combed their hair just like his, while others' hair could be best described as disheveled and still others wore burr cuts. If asked, most girls admitted to styling their hair after their favorite movie actresses, as seen in *Silver Screen, Photoplay, Movie Mirror* or *Screen Romances* magazines.

On the way into the Building, a secretary signed in each freshman and told them to meet in the auditorium. She also gave them a set of mimeographed instructions, including locker number, locker combination, class assignments and times, room locations and a myriad of other need-to-know regulations.

The sheet explained the organization and schedule of the intramural sports programs. Everyone had to take gym, but no one had to go out for football, basketball or track.

Walking beside Prairie View classmates Maxine, Louise and Georgette, John said, "How are we supposed to remember all of this stuff? He masked his excitement with a shallow smile.

"I'm really scared," said Louise.

"Don't get all excited," Georgette said. "Everybody figures it out eventually. You'll be alright. We all will."

Louise said. "Can we can chew gum in class?"

Before anyone could answer, the foursome arrived at the auditorium and filed into seats in the second row. About fifty others took seats around them, while on the stage a stern looking man in a gray suit cleared his throat as a way of quieting everyone.

"My name is Clarence R. Spong and I'm the Wamego High School Principal. The teachers and I are here to help you have a good experience while you learn the things you'll need in later life."

Nothing happened for a few seconds and then he asked, "Did everyone get signed in at the door? If you didn't, Mrs. Pitney, the teacher standing in front of the stage, will take your name and you can talk to her when this assembly ends."

Two freshmen held up their hands and the teacher took their names. Again, Mr. Spong spoke, "This is your first day of high school and we want you to feel at home. We're here to serve you and make your time here useful. Now I'd like to turn the floor over to Mrs. Pitney. She'll be one of your Freshman Sponsors, along with Mr. Revitte and Coach Scales."

"Good morning boys and girls. As the Principal said, we want to help you get acclimated to your new surroundings, and learn the ins and outs of high school. First, would you all take out the school map you got and locate where we are right now?"

A rustling of paper and some muted whispers followed, as the students searched in their handouts until they found their maps.

"Now look at your class schedule and find the location of your first class. Then look for the next class and so on."

More whispers followed and a few kids seemed puzzled. "Don't worry if you can't find your first classroom on the map. See me when we finish here. Notice that all freshmen lockers are on the first floor. They are for storing your books—you'll get them at each class—and your jackets and personal items. Don't leave things in your locker that might spoil like fruit and do a good job of housekeeping your area."

The instructions went on for another few minutes and then everyone went to their first class. John walked up the stairs to the second floor.

"Good morning everyone, my name is Miss Bernice Bender and I'll be your English teacher."

The twenty or so wide-eyed fourteen-year-olds nodded still wondering how this would all work out. And in the case of some students, *Why should we study English? We speak it all the time.*

Miss Bender said, "Let's get acquainted. We'll start over here in the first row and go around the room. Tell us your name and something you'd like us to know about you."

Some students slid down, trying to hide behind the slanted writing board on the front of their desks. Still, others looked like rabbits caught in the middle of the road. They just froze in place as if they couldn't remember who they were.

Others sat up and smiled, all the while thinking up clever beginning lines. John could be seen rehearsing what he'd say.

The number of shy folks exceeded the unfazed three to one. It was obvious most of the freshmen felt intimidated.

First to speak was a pretty black-haired girl. She turned in her seat and said, "Oh, hi. My name is Janice Bigford and I went to Wamego Grade School. I want to be a nurse."

Behind Janice sat her red-haired friend, Norma Brockish, and behind her sat two guys John knew from 4-H and the County Fair, Darrell Tanner and Myron Flinn. Both boys lived near Laclede.

In the end seat in the first row sat the shyest, but biggest class member. If John heard him right he said his name was Ross

Worden, Jr. and that people called him Junior. *I hope he plays football … for us,* John thought.

The rest of the introductions went fine, including John's announcing his name and that he hit clean-up for Louisville. Some kids were hard to hear, especially a tall, soft-spoken boy named Robert Grieshaber. John smiled at the unusual name and then grinned some more when Johnny Lichtenhan and Donnie Eisenbies introduced themselves. *What a class this is going to be.*

It turned out to be a fine group and at the end of the morning the freshmen broke for lunch. One whole hour, with eating the only chore.

Wamego High hadn't established a cafeteria yet, so many of the town kids went home to eat. Many like John brought sandwiches in brown paper sacks. Dinner buckets seemed too old-fashioned.

There were drinking fountains on each floor and a Coke machine at the end of the gym. Some ate in the library while others went outside to sit on the grass to eat and talk.

John would quickly learn the rules. Later he'd get to know most of his classmates and many of the older high school students.

I really like high school, he thought that first day. *This should be a lot of fun. It has to be better than tossing hay bales.*

When classes ended for the day, it was time for football. Would this be a good thing for John? He'd find out.

CHARLEY-HORSED FOR LIFE

At 3:30 classes ended, and the football players headed for the boys' locker room. The Head Coach introduced himself as William Scales, though he said everyone called him Dave. Next he introduced his assistant, Head Basketball Coach Sam Butterfield.

"Now I want to welcome our returning players from last year's squad and to give a special welcome to our crop of freshmen. We've got the makings of a good team and should challenge for the Jayhawk League title," Coach Scales said. "We'll continue to use the double-wing formation with an unbalanced line to the right. That should set us up to bust some noggins."

The Coach next asked the lettermen to come to the equipment table to get their uniforms. The returning non-letter squad members followed and picked out their helmets, shoulder pads, hip pads, practice jerseys and practice pants with thigh guards. Soon all but the freshmen were suited.

"Dick and Hank, you take the boys for five laps around the track and then do some calisthenics," the coach instructed team captains Dick Knostman and Hank Graf. "We'll be along as soon as we get the freshmen suited up," he said.

With the returning players gone, John and his classmates went to the table get their equipment from the somewhat ramshackle pile that remained. Several of the smaller football hopefuls ended up with old style leather helmets and somewhat ratty paraphernalia.

"Everyone going out for football was supposed to bring a jock strap and a pair of football shoes and socks. Be sure to wear the strap and lace your shoes up tight. I see most of you bought used football shoes, and that is alright for now, but if you make the B team, you might want to get better ones," the Coach said.

"Okay guys, grab an empty locker for stowing your clothes and put your gear on. Go to the field as soon as you're dressed."

The dozen boys hunted down empty lockers and started donning their uniforms While John sat on a bench lacing up his shoulder pads Coach Scales walked to him and reached down and poked his left thigh. "By golly that is muscle. You might make a good lineman one day if you fill out some more."

Hey, that's great. I can't wait to start playing. I want to bust some noggins, John thought as he pulled on the practice jersey, grabbed his helmet and trotted for his first football practice.

That first workout consisted of a lot of running, some jumping jacks and pushups, plus blocking practice. The freshmen left the field early so the team starters could prepare for the first game.

While the boys undressed, mousy looking Cecil Bernt kept groaning as he took off his pants. "Man that thing has rubbed me raw. I don't see why we have to wear these jockstraps."

"What's wrong, Cecil?" Donnie Eisenbies asked.

"I don't know, but my crotch is all red."

"Is that how you wore your strap?" Donnie asked.

"Yeah."

"You bozo, you wore it backwards. Turn it around."

Chuckles followed, though most everyone realized it could have been him that made such a big mistake. They were far from the football players they hoped to be.

It would have been nice to report that John's dream of heroism came true that first year, but he only made the freshmen team. Junior Worden made the Varsity, proving that as with Baby Beef size mattered. Still John played well when he got into a game. He liked scrimmaging against the Varsity.

All went well for the 135 pounder until toward the end of the season. One day in his role on the practice squad he held his own. The team was working on covering punts. On one play, as John hustled to tackle the punt returner, huge George Worden—Junior's brother—came out of nowhere and flattened John. The collision's crash sounded like a stack of plywood slamming onto the ground. John felt instant pain in his left thigh muscle. He'd just gotten *charley-horsed for life* … as the saying went.

That ended the freshman's football for 1948. But in the coming years as a pulling guard, John would inflict many charley-horses on opposing players. He'd later receive an All-League Honorable Mention.

John turned in his gear and limped on to other activities. He wouldn't make the basketball team, so many of his sporting activities took place away from school, and much of which was with family. None of these events involved a ball, but they nevertheless offered high excitement.

THANKGIVING RABBIT HUNTS

Hunting for some inexplicable reason always seemed be a regular activity on Thanksgiving Day. When the David and Mary Burgess family celebrated at Aunt Helen and Uncle Houston Gordon's, John and George had great fun with the Gordon cousins.

"Look out *rachets*, if you hang out near Adams Creek."

The boys and Cousins Jim, Ben and Roland were usually short of shells. Jim the oldest, divvied up rifle and shotgun ammunition for the hunters' two .22 rifles and three shotguns

"George, you get three shorts and two longs," Jim said. "Rollie, you get the same. And here are the shotgun shells for the rest of us."

At Thanksgiving in 1948, snow covered the landscape with a three inch blanket, sparkling in the crisp November sunlight creating perfect rabbit hunt surroundings. Rabbits left easy tracks to follow. The hunt started in mid-morning and continued right through to midday. Jim and Rollie each bagged a rabbit.

Two cottontails weren't much to brag about, after slogging up and down ditches and creek banks and tracking through the slippery, fast melting snow. But when the leftover turkey was gone, there'd be stewed rabbit on the Gordon table.

Just after noon, the hunters heard Uncle Huston bang on his steel dinner triangle. The boys didn't need to hear it twice. They hurried to the house for the annual Thanksgiving feast.

All five boys squirmed through the blessing that took longer than normal because there was so much for which to be thankful. Family, homes, good health, country and peace. To end his prayer, the boys' dad asked for blessings for the food atop the burgeoning table. A loud chorus of "amens" followed. The smells caused every saliva gland to gush and flow.

Uncle Houston carved the turkey and passed a heaping platter around the table. As young John surveyed the table he thought, *What a meal of turkey, sage dressing, mounds of mashed Irish potatoes—of course!—and turkey gravy flavored with pan drippings and giblets.*

Other traditions included home canned string beans, lumpy sweet potatoes and puckering cranberry sauce.

All 80 pounds of George polished off a one-pound turkey leg. Aunt Helen said with a grin, "I think George has two stomachs. They all do. Just look at those boys eat."

And eat the boys did, and adults as well. Bowls and platters passed around and around the table. Hunting surely developed good appetites for the young men.

Two year old Judy and nine month old Joyce occasionally stopped eating just to watch their brothers and cousins. "That's okay girls, they're just being boys," their mother said.

Dessert consisted of homemade pumpkin and mincemeat pies. Some of the hunters had a piece of each, lathered with homemade whipped cream. Oh for the life in farm country.

"GET THAT COYOTE!"

Hunting wasn't confined to Thanksgiving Day, for in mid-century Kansas farmers faced losses from varmints of all kinds. Hunting was the major method to help eradicate or at least curtail the pests that threatened livelihoods.

Most people considered the coyote the worst of all. They preyed on young calves and lambs, regularly stole poultry and led to the disappearance of many a farm cat and small dog.

Therefore, hunting coyotes was a big-time activity, whether involving a single hunter or dozens of people at specially organized events. Most individuals used high powered rifles with good scopes. During a coyote roundup with lots of people, shotguns were the weapon of choice.

The wily coyote blended into the tall, dry prairie grass. With its camouflaged coat of brown mixed with gray, the coyote could move like a phantom and slip undetected up a draw or around a ridge. This elusiveness frustrated some hunters. As a result, some overly intense hunters did some strange things. Case in point, Uncle Tom's son—and George and Bob Burgess' brother—Charles (Chas).

§

This is the way we heard it.

Chas was out looking for coyotes with his nephew Dwight (of the 4Ds). Some felt Chas had what would now be called, "Davey Crocket DNA." No varmint was going to escape his sights.

At one point that day Chas got overly aggressive and drove his car into a ditch. The car survived and undaunted the two hunters kept on hunting.

Now it must be said that that incident was pale in comparison to what would happen later in the day. Stand by for the real drama.

Chas and Dwight were motoring along on a sand road scanning the hills.

"I see one!" shouted Dwight. "Down the road, over on the right!"

The lanky Chas erupted into action and tromped his new Ford's accelerator to the floor. Tires spun; sand spit.

As the two approached the coyote's position Chas steered up onto the road's centerline ridge. Finally the inevitable happened. He over corrected the car's steering. With one sharp jerk of the wheel the car tipped, barrel rolled and came to rest upright on all four wheels.

Chas shut off the ignition, checked on his passenger—no seat belts in those days—and found that Dwight was okay.

Then Chas hollered, "Dwight, hand me my gun!"

Chas jumped out with his thirty-aught-six, draped his arms across the dented car roof and aimed at the trotting target, now far up the hill.

BLAMM! BLAAM! BLAAM!

Chas hit but only wounded the animal, but a couple of other hunters in the area finished him off.

With the dust still settling all around the banged up Ford, Chas and Dwight surveyed the situation. The paint was scratched in several places, some chrome was bent, one window was cracked and the radio antenna was flattened.

Dwight's uncle shook his head and said, "You know Dwight, next time I go coyote hunting I think I'm going to bring out a car that's already beat up—if I can just find one."

Dwight didn't say a word but thought, *Uncle Charles, I think you just did* ….

§

Most of the wild happenings in the boys' lives took place in the country. However, once John entered high school that year, he'd find there was a *call of the wild* within the city as well. After Thanksgiving Day he returned to the classroom.

The way he lived his life, it was probably inevitable that before the year was out he'd have some dealings with the teachers. Take for instance the flying eraser.

No, we're not kidding.

TWENTY ONE

WATCH YOUR Ps AND Qs, TRIPLE-THREAT COW AND THE LAST OF LAST LEGS

[*Wamego Times – February 17, 1949*] ~ OVER THE FARM FENCE

Mrs. John Burgess of Route 2 went to Topeka Tuesday for a major operation.

A large crowd of Wamego people attended the Highland Park-Wamego basketball game in Topeka Friday evening. Water over the pavement near Topeka made hazardous driving but as far as we know all got home safely.

1949

WATCH YOUR Ps AND Qs

Most people would agree that John's freshman year at Wamego Rural High School moved along at a pretty normal pace. He liked his classes and his teachers and the first semester he got a couple of As and the rest were Bs.

He liked English I, Vocational Ag I and General Science, plus he found gym to be fun and easy, especially when compared to football. One wise guy said, "The purpose of 'gym' is to get you in good enough shape to be able to take … 'gym.'

John wasn't so keen on Algebra taught by Mrs. Pitney. Unfortunately for him, his jokes and quips, maybe to compensate for his lack of understanding, didn't set too well. On several occasions, she scolded him and even tossed pieces of chalk at him to shut him up. *Here comes another one.* Those incidents helped his concentration for a while each time.

Once however, she fired an eraser him. The freshman ducked and the eraser flew out the open third story window—they'd opened it to control the classroom temperature—like an erratic flying pigeon. Guess who went downstairs to retrieve the eraser?

John's biggest run in with Mrs. Pitney occurred just as class was about to start one day. The teacher had yet to arrive, so he moved to stand at the podium and addressed the whole class in a loud and exaggerated voice.

"The night was dark and dreary, the road was slick as glass, along came Mrs. Pitney, sliding on her-r-r-r ... sled."

His teacher walked in as the ditty ended. She glared at young John and informed him that he needed to sit down, and to watch his Ps and Qs. In the end, she gave John a charitable B minus.

Besides interesting classes and good teachers, football had been great—until George Worden flattened him. John was a starter on the freshman squad. And he substituted for one B-Team game against the much bigger Manhattan High's team.

John played pulling guard and reveled in this assignment. On almost every play, he took a half step back and dashed right or left to block the on-coming defensive end. That block was meant to free the ball carrier for a big gain ... and it did, sometimes.

Beyond football, John joined the *Future Farmers of America.* FFA was very popular with farm boys. The FFA motto, "Learning to do, Doing to learn, Earning to live, Living to serve," inspired him, just as the 4-H motto did.

He and Bob Pinet were good friends and did things together, although Bob dated some and John didn't take that plunge until the very end of the year. He liked talking to Donnie Eisenbies and Larry Fechter, and others.

About the middle of April 1949, Mrs. Pitney sent a note asking all freshmen to meet her in the gym during the noon hour. When most were seated, she said, "There is an all-school assembly next Friday and each class is to perform a skit. Does anyone have any ideas?"

There was some mumbling and a lot of head shaking. "Well," she said, "one time I saw someone play an invisible piano. The maestro and his friend pushed the pretend piano on stage and he acted as if he sat down on the stool."

"Hey, I could do that," John said. "But where does the sound come from?"

"We need someone off-stage to do the real playing."

"I could play some boogie-woogie," Georgette said. "Would that work?"

The answer was yes and at the assembly John and his fellow frosh Duane McDaniel appeared to struggle as they rolled out the *piano*. Duane then brought the stool and John crouched into a sitting position.

With great drama, he raised his right hand and pointed up. Down came his index finger and a B-flat note resounded from Georgette's piano. Next, John riffed across the invisible keyboard. Georgette followed. With gusto he began to play the standard, *Scrub Me Mama with a Boogie Beat*.

About half way through the song John raised his left hand and said, "Look Ma, one hand." The music continued unabated. Finally, he roared, "Look Ma ... no hands."

The reaction to these theatrics on the part of the classes, faculty and staff was that the performance was worthy of Broadway. John's class' skit would long be remembered.

FUN AT SCHOOL, FUN AT HOME

John had a good time at school. Of course, when not in school he did his share of farm work. What about the other times at home? Particularly joyous, were the times he spent playing with his two baby sisters.

§

We did indeed enjoy our little sisters and helped teach them important lessons. We helped them learn to walk and talk.

With Judy about three and Joyce age one, we felt very protective, the way older siblings should be. Both girls returned our attention with loving grins and, in Joyce's case, babbling sentences. Our nicknames for them came from what they called each other ... Geedy and Way-ce.

As the spring warmed, Geedy and Way-ce were often bundled up and would join us outside for trips to feed the chickens, look at the new batch of multi-colored kittens or to see a bird's nest. A highlight of the time together might involve Tony the Pony.

Tony the Pony; Joyce in front, George and Judy at the rear

By the way, our horse sensed she was a part of the family. She cared for us, and in some ways, she was more of a pet than a cow pony. She learned to come when we called—oats still helped—and seemed to enjoy our many dashes across the pasture.

Tony appeared proud to parade around the yard with our sisters on her back. With one brother or the other riding along, she would carefully walk where directed with her head held high.

There were times, when the two girls rode double file, laughing and smiling while one brother led Tony around the yard and the other brother walked along side. It was apparent Geedy and Way-ce liked those times.

Sometimes Mom would bring them to the barn to play with the tamest of the barn cats and watch us milk the huge dairy cows.

STAY AWAY FROM THE GRINDER

The fifteen or so animals in our dairy herd, depending on the year, were Dad's pride and joy. He treasured and talked to them.

They came in varying shapes and colors. We've mentioned many of our milk cows before. At one time or another we had Alma, Louise, Ernestine, Hazel, Miss Wilma, Spot, Mabel, Bubbles, Maudie, Helga … and others.

One unfortunate and luckless cow was a very short tailed Holstein nicknamed Bob. During a sub-zero winter night, she must have unwittingly caught her tail between the corn grinder and a barn timber, and in her haste to exit, cleanly broke off the end of that tail. Her name was a no-brainer.

Our biggest cow, known affectionately as Crump, had a gnarly, curved horn stump growing out of the left side of her head after she butted that same grinder.

The only brown and white cow we had was a registered Guernsey named, Claudette. Dad paid a lot of money for her and got little milk in return. She wasn't the only poor milker for the two very spooky Holstein heifers named Tootsie and Helga hardly gave milk at all.

Tootsie was the worst; she was always on guard, glaring at us. Dad believed she'd been abused in her earlier life. And she'd kick us when she could.

During milking, both Tootsie and Helga needed kickers (molded metal grips with a light chain) across the back legs above the knee. With these in place, they couldn't kick, but kickers didn't stop them from doing a two-legged hop, and bucking their skinny rear-ends.

Finally, Tootsie and Helga got to be more than Dad could handle. It wasn't long before he found them new milking parlors through the St. Mary's auction yard—a placement service of sorts. Those heifers had been a pain, but our other cows were much more satisfying to be around.

In fact, one could say most of our cows were All-Americans … that is of mixed and varied heritages like the majority of the country's citizens. We did have some purebred Holsteins, but we had other cows with Hereford, Angus, Shorthorn or even Brahma in their backgrounds. A couple produced creamy milk—great for ice cream—indicating a connection to the Jersey line. Some showed parentage from several breeds which meant those cows had interesting shapes and colors.

One of these multi-colored and funny looking cows developed a real story all her own. Her name was Maudie.

§

TRIPLE THREAT COW

Maudie just showed up one day the boys remembered. Actually their dad had bought her and a couple of other crossbred bovines at auction. Maudie made a big impression right away.

She appeared to be about 4-5 years old and her color was more black than brown. However, the brown seemed to flow over black like spilled paint. She also had some muted, black zebra stripes on her front quarters and part way up her neck, definitely what might be labeled brindle.

Maudie had the largest cow ears the boys had ever seen and the ears drooped downward.

I wonder if she's part Jersey-rahma, like that cow Maggie we had when we lived at Hartford, George thought.

Funny looking maybe, but indeed, Maudie was a triple threat, multipurpose cow. She came to be known for three very different attributes.

Maudie's first assignment was as a member the dairy herd. She had a huge bag that dangled down ponderously between her back legs. "With a bag like that she should be quite a milker," the boys' dad had said.

Maudie was to some extent, though it became clear that Maudie would be a difficult cow to milk after all. No, she didn't buck or jump and she didn't need kickers. And Maudie wasn't a switcher.

No, Maudie's problem was that she had miniscule pinholes from which the milk could exit. The family milking machine strained as it tried to extract the milk through these small outlets so the boys' dad decided they should hand milk her. That wasn't going to be an easy task.

Now we had been milking for several years and could milk well using the strong squeeze and pull, squeeze and pull technique. But, no matter how hard we worked on Maudie, we only generated tiny streams.

Fortunately, Maudie's calves could suckle okay, and because of that, we launched her into her second career. She moved out of the milking parlor and joined the mostly Hereford beef herd.

In this case, we mated Maudie with our genuine, registered all-everything Hereford bull, Domino. Yep he was the same bull that our slingshots sent crashing through the fence. He was the farm's pride and joy. Domino, in retrospect, looked quite squatty and compact and nothing like the upstanding, lengthy, muscled behemoths of today. But, he was all bull.

Domino and Maudie seemed to get along well, because season after season their union produced fast growing calves with funny ears and nondescript colors.

Maudie's third career came to the fore when she led the beef cattle march to the big pasture. She'd developed a lead-cow vocation. Where she led, others followed.

§

Early each spring, Maudie led the herd up the road a total of eight miles from the home place to the quarter section of summer pasture. These cattle drives were hardly death marches, but strenuous enough and used up a good part of a day under normal conditions.

That particular year, the day of the big drive had a nip in the air until the sun came up. Blackbirds, on very friendly terms with the beef herd, flew erratic patterns around the feed lot.

That day the steady supply of cow feed the birds enjoyed through the winter was about to end. There would be nothing more for the free loaders until fall.

"All right, today's the day," the boys' dad said. It was already seven-thirty on a Saturday morning.

"We'll take the herd north to the Louisville-Flush Road, east four miles until we cross Highway 99, and then north again on the Wheaton Road," he said.

"Mom, you take the truck and lead off. The cows are used to it and will follow you," he said. "Go fast enough to keep them hurrying along."

He turned to his number two son and said, "George, you put a couple of buckets of water in the back of the truck in case it overheats at the slow pace."

"You want me to ride Tony?" young John asked.

"Yes, you can ride alongside the herd, and keep any quitters from taking a side road. George, the girls and I will follow in the car. He and I can jump out and yell at any cow that tries to double back home. Hopefully they won't do anything dumb."

George wondered, *I wonder how Shorty's field-work car would handle this job.*

§

We should have focused on the word dumb, for that day several dumb things happened along the way. And, they were partly Maudie's fault, though the careless act of neighbors registered at the pinnacle on the dumb scale.

At eight o'clock, Mom drove the truck out of the feed lot in low gear. Maudie and the herd followed past the barn and our house, out the lane, and down the road north. Maudie seemed to revel in her lead-role, for she shuffled along at a floppy-eared and bag swinging trot. The other cows, their calves, and of course, Domino—sniffing the air—hurried after her.

Pep barked a "so long" to us and laid back down.

After part of a mile we came to the big yard at Louie Riat's place, where for some strange reason Maudie decided to visit. Though Mom drove the truck on by,

275

Maudie wanted to investigate behind the Riat's house—where she found Louie's recently planted garden.

She high stepped across the freshly tilled patch, trampling huge, deep hoof prints into the soil, all the while mashing down early stage peas and spinach. She had company—oh boy—as the herd of cows and their calves joined her.

With the intent to turn the herd back to the road, John and Tony circled in front of Maudie and the others.

But, where do you suppose they made the turn? Yep, right in middle of the new garden. As it was, Louie's garden was a disaster.

Helped by Louie's shouting, Maudie realized her mistake and headed back around the Riat house. For a moment, the cow seemed confused about direction, but then spotted the truck, made a sharp left turn and ambled along as if nothing had happened.

While running toward the car, Dad quickly apologized to Louie, said we'd rebuild the garden.

Louie, shook his graying head and said something about bad luck. We hardly heard him for we were in hot pursuit of Maudie and the rest of the herd, now approaching the rickety Rock Creek Bridge.

Mom slowly drove the truck over the bridge and Maudie ambled up and across—almost. About mid-span she stopped.

§

.

The boys' dad laid on the car horn, George yelled and John and Tony crowded the cows onto the bridge. Maudie realized her error, again made eye contact with the truck and walked off the bridge and the other cows followed

Maudie focused on only the truck for the next four miles. Perhaps she was dreaming of the big blue stem pasture destination, now alive with fresh green shoots, following the early spring burn-over—the Indian way—to encourage new growth.

Maudie picked up the pace. Indeed, she was a triple threat cow. However, through no fault of her own, a threat of another kind awaited just as the herd crossed State Highway 99.

It seems neighborhood character Shorty Brockman and his cousin Tubs had stopped off early at Younge's Store and Tavern in Louisville, just down the way. Apparently, Shorty's 3-4 beer breakfast made him less attentive than usual—hard to imagine—for he drove his wife's Model A Ford right toward the middle of the crossing herd. When he finally saw the cows in front of him he hit the brakes.

Still fixated on the truck, Maudie and some of her friends went on across Highway 99. The laggard cows, and most of the calves turned back towards home, and Domino, for reasons known only to bulls, started north up 99 toward Westmoreland.

Shorty, with Tubs yelling at him from the passenger side of the fish-tailing car, over controlled the steering wheel. Then he hit the brakes again—hard—and drove right into the ditch.

What a mess. Cows were milling, the bull started bellowing, the boys' dad and George shouted, the baby sisters in the car's backseat cried, John astride Tony galloped and their mom stood on the truck's running board with hands on hips, staring in aggravated wonder. Shorty and his cousin Tubs? They were nose to nose cussing at each other inside the mired car.

Finally, the boys' mom honked the truck's horn and eased slowly up the Wheaton road, fortunately well fenced on both sides. Maudie seemed to communicate with the herd and with some hesitation the cattle crossed the highway's blacktop to join her. By this time John and the lathered Tony had galloped past the still running Domino and turned him back to join his ladies.

Unfortunately, the boys and their dad saw they would have to waste several important minutes helping the also wasted Shorty get his car out of the ditch.

The boys' dad thought, *I've said it before and I'll say it again, those Brockmans are the densest group of people I have ever known.*

"Come on boys, let's give them a hand," John senior said with a good deal of sarcasm in his voice.

With everybody pushing, Shorty spun backwards with the back tires smoking. He slammed the gear shift into low and ground forward, then quickly shifted into reverse and spun backwards again, gaining a foot at a time. With the Burgesses helping, Shorty rocked the car back up onto the highway. Shorty mumbled his thanks. As he drove off, Tubs was still cussing at him.

I wonder if Lulu will hear about this. George thought.

With about two miles to go, it was apparent some of the cows … and quite a few calves were tiring. Even Maudie's loping trot slowed to a spladdle-footed walk and it was well after noon when she led her troop through the wire gate into the fresh pasture.

Was she exhausted? Apparently not. She took off running for the pond to take a cool drink. She and the others seemed very happy to return to their summer home.

The boys' dad dropped off a couple of salt blocks, looked the herd over and turned the car around with George alongside him. In the back seat Geedy and Way-ce giggled. George was making faces. The family loaded Tony into the truck and everyone made for home. What a day, no thanks to Shorty Brockman

§

THE LAST OF LAST LEGS

Shorty was a neighbor and a friend, but sometimes he was also down right trouble, and most often he was terribly out of step with common sense farming. For the latter, take one day in April when he made his weekly visit to the St. Mary's livestock auction. Here's what we heard.

It was near midday, cloudy and cool, when Shorty again borrowed Lulu's car. His field-work car wouldn't start, even when he rolled it off the little hill where he always parked it.

In St. Marys, he shut off the Model A right next to the café built into one end of the auction building. He ate a greasy hamburger with a big slab of onion and gulped down two cups of coffee. After a few minutes of jawing with

278

Tubs—they'd made up—Shorty ambled onto the bleachers that circled around the sale ring.

He watched several bunches of dairy calves sell with auctioneer Lawrence Welter doing his best to move them at good prices. While most calves sold in groups, from time to time a single animal might go through the ring.

Soon, just such an event caused Shorty no small amount of grief. As a small, healthy bull calf—it sold for top dollar—left the ring by one door, another single 150 pound crossbred calf entered through the other door and coughed, drawing attention to it.

Welter tried to start the bidding at $20, but not one person nodded, raised a hand, or made any kind of gesture. Everyone just sat there looking at each other and at the somewhat scrawny Angus and Jersey cross calf.

"All right fellows, I know this little steer looks like it's been on skinny rations, but it is still a fairly good calf," Welter said. "We have to start someplace. What am I bid?"

"A dollar!" a grinning rancher across the ring from Shorty yelled. Chuckles swept through the crowd.

That bid sounds low, thought Shorty.

"I bid a dollar fifty," someone called.

Soon bids followed in 50 cent increments until the price reached five dollars. "Hey, this calf is worth more." Welter asked for another bid.

Shorty sat on the edge of his bleacher seat and decided to gamble. However, before the sun went down he'd find he'd made a bum decision.

"I bid six dollars," Shortly yelled. *This is too good to be true.*

No one moved. Time stood still, with the other farmers staring at Shorty. Tubs shot him a questioning glance as well. Then the calf coughed again. Then again.

"Sold! To the fellow with that DeKalb cap."

Welter looked Shorty right in the eye, asked his name for the sale record and then asked, "You know what you just bought don't you bub?"

279

We heard later that Shorty nodded without conviction and headed for the parking lot and Lulu's car. He backed up to the loading chute.

The auction yard hostler, pushed, prodded and partly carried the coughing calf down the ramp, and with difficulty, bent the calf's legs to get it into the back seat.

"Were I you," the hostler said, "I'd stop by the vet's on the way out of town."

Distress slammed into Shorty as he drove away from the yard with the calf nervously sprawling on the back. When Shorty turned into the vet's parking lot, the calf coughed some more … and then some more. Shorty struggled to get it out of the back. He tied the animal to the bumper with his belt.

At Shorty's request, the vet came out to give the calf the once over. He prodded some, poked some, listened and looked it right in the eye.

As if on cue, the poor calf erupted into a series of raking coughs. "That's pneumonia … probably chronic pneumonia," the vet said. "This calf is pretty sick."

"Dad-gum-it," Shorty said. "What should I do?"

The vet shook his head. "Well you should have bought a well calf."

So, Shorty reloaded the calf, paid the vet $18.65 for medicine and drove on home to a less than cheerful reception. Lulu found much fault with the calf, her husband and the smelly mess in her car's back seat. And as she looked the calf over and she just shook her head.

"That poor calf is on its last legs," she said.

And it was … unfortunately….

Last Legs lived only a couple of weeks, in spite of Louella Ethel's care and the vet's costly medicine.

Last Legs cost Shorty $24.65 cash money on the deal—$6 for the calf and $18.65 for the medicine—plus he found his wife's goodwill had drifted, yet again.

"Dang you, Shorty Brockman, you and your crazy ideas cost us money," Lulu said. "If you don't beat all. And, you made me nurse a dying calf. Better call the rendering truck."

Shorty didn't get any special meals for a while, but in the end he got back into Lulu's good graces. Women did have forgiving ways.

In reality, farm animals including Last Legs, did get sick and sometimes there was nothing anyone could do to save them. Even the best doctoring could be of little help as Shorty had found out.

Incidentally, Lulu's car smelled for weeks and Shorty got a constant reminder about it.

TWENTY TWO

MAGIC BY A NOSE, GREAT TRACTOR RACE AND WAKE UP CRIED THE BRUSH PILE

[*Wamego Times – July 21, 1949*] ~ LEGAL LIQUOR IN WAMEGO

Wednesday, July 20th, 1949 marks the date of the first sales of legal liquor in Wamego in over 69 years. Art Herren has met all requirements, is duly licensed and is now ready to serve customers.

Mr. Herren has remodeled his building, even putting down a thick expensive carpet. His licenses, state and city, cost him $400 per year. And Mr. Herren says he will comply with every rule and regulation put out by the State Board.

1949

MAGIC BY A NOSE

The entire population of Pottawatomie County didn't know about George's nose, but a lot of people his own age did. Some relatives and friends swore that he had the mystifying ability to not only detect smells, but catalog them as to type, source, distance and of all things, color. At the County Fair his friends doubted that he could really tell one tractor from the other simply by its smell, but he left them wondering. Some said his olfactory senses rivaled a warthog that could smell a meal six feet underground.

George likewise smelled meals at far greater distances than 'normal' people. And, he could easily tell the difference in odor between a cow plop and a horse's road apples clear down at Cotton's farm.

§

Kids treasured being recognized for their special qualities, real or imagined. All boys valued hearing the adults comment on how much, "those boys could eat," how fast they were growing or how big their biceps were.

We'd swell with pride when being compared to hard working men. Whether singled out for our athletic prowess or farm work, we felt a glow of pride each time we were in the spotlight.

Maybe we created artificial abilities to perpetuate our time in the sun. At any rate, after a while we actually believed in our extraordinary skills. The challenge was, would others?

§

Take the day George plowed in the south field. Though a good half-mile away, he sensed the aroma of smothered pork chops.

Ahhhhhh, food is on the way.

With hope, he glanced down at his left arm and the dirty $12.95 fourteen-jewel Elgin wristwatch he'd purchased with 4-H project sales profit. Once a shiny gold color, now grime covered the tarnished watch. It told the sad story; dinner was a half hour away.

"Ah, dog-gone-it, it's only 11:30," he said out loud, as he rocked from side to side on the tractor's broad vinyl seat cushion. "I don't know if I can make it 'til noon," he told a big gray grasshopper that plopped onto the steering wheel.

Dust darkened his tan and shirtless torso and channels of sweat tiger-striped his back. This was turning into a very hot July day. Only his old straw hat, drooping fore and aft with turned up sides, protected him from the sun. Dirty perspiration layered and marked the sweatband and the chicken feathers stuck in it.

So while meadowlarks trilled and grasshoppers skipped he looked over his right shoulder, watching the wheat stubble turn under. His mind wandered to beyond the sun's heat, the tractor's noise and the empty pit in his stomach.

He drifted to the Kansas Free Fair in Topeka recalling images from before. He sensed the excitement of the carnival, the livestock barns, the machinery displays, and of course, the smell of the food. Hamburgers and buttered popcorn.

He'd never before seen a food vendor cut 16 bars from a block of ice cream, stick in wooden tongue depressors, dip the bars in hot chocolate, and then roll them in cracked nuts.

Beyond the food his mind flashed to the Free Fair's Night Show with its spectacular fireworks and vehicles, including stunt cars. That year, Joey Chitwood's daredevils had driven new Fords at high speeds on only two wheels, maneuvering in crisscrossing figure eights and then whizzing across long wooden ramps.

I wonder if I could do that, in the truck.

George's mind took him to the midway and to the rides. He'd tried out the Ferris Wheel and the Bumper Cars.

Next time we go, I want to do the Loop-de-Loop. He remembered when his brother threw up on that ride, and lost his billfold. George grinned remembering his brother's agony.

In the Fair's heat George had seen a cocky, high stepping Army paratrooper remove his tie and stuff it into a shoulder epaulette. This greatly impressed his girlfriend, but not the two on-duty military policemen. In short order, the tie went back on, and the trooper was again squared away. His girl didn't seem to mind.

Later, George and the family heard a tent singer of very large proportions do her rendition of *"… my Mama done tole me, when I was in knee pants …."* That was his first professional musical performance.

Kind of a dumb song … but I like it.

Suddenly, the daydreaming ended with a slight tinge of pain. Another huge grasshopper crash landed on his bare right forearm and dug its six scratchy feet into his flesh. George frowned at the hopper and gave it a forceful flick that sent the insect flying. Only tiny foot scratches and daubs of tobacco juice remained.

George again watched the slowly turning stubble … and slouched lower onto the rocking tractor seat. The majority of the 40-acre field still needed plowing. A sense of worthlessness settled over him. Was he losing the battle for life? Or just hungry?

With no warning, a massive stomach gurgle answered his questions. He looked at his watch; both hands were near the top. *Hooray!* George raised the plow shares and sent the John Deere flying across the field. As he pulled up to the huge gas tank, he inhaled the pork chop smell that grew stronger second by second.

No question about it, a vast variety of smells motivated George. He did have a superior olfactory sense. And, this trait went beyond food. Far beyond.

GREEN SMELLS FRESHER THAN RED

"Did you know that every piece of farm machinery has its own scent?" George asked his friend Don Flinn at the County Fair.

Don ignored George's question about smells. *What the deuce is he talking about?*

George loved the smell of freshly painted machinery. It gave him a sense of excitement … much like the new car smell everyone raved about.

"And you can tell which girl is in a room at school when you smell her. Plus, it's easy to tell a town girl from a country girl," he said with a nod.

A wide grin crossed Don's face. *Is he going goofy on me?* Don reached down and plucked a grass stem and stuck it in his mouth. *I think that boy is going to need some help.*

"It's easy to tell if a John Deere or a Farmall is driving by. It's all in the smell."

Don shook his head and bit down on the grass. *How about the sound?*

Seeing Don's doubt George said, "I've spent a lot of time around the new tractors, balers and plows. There is nothing like the sweet smell of new paint. I think green paint smells fresher than red."

Don cocked his head again, but stayed mum.

About then, John and Don's brother, Myron, walked up.

"Hey dumbbell, what you doing?" John asked with a touch of self-importance and showing off for his high school buddy.

"I'm checking to see how hard this tractor is to run. I want to be sure that even you can handle it."

What a loon, John thought. "You're just smelling paint."

"Smelling paint?" Myron asked. "What's wrong with 'him?'"

John smirked, tossed his head in George's direction, and said, "I think there was a mix-up when he was born. He says he can tell paint colors by their smell, magic by a nose I guess."

The older boys chuckled and walked away. Not to worry, George *knew what he knew.*

For his part, John would soon be in the twilight zone on this. Just a month after the Fair the two searched in the tool shed for a misplaced Prince Albert tobacco can full of used nuts and washers.

For a number of minutes, John hunted in the dimly lighted space, squinting through his smudged wire rim glasses. Logic told him the missing can was either on the work bench or in the big cedar tool box Grandpa Scott had made. Nothing.

"Hey, I think it's back here under these boards. I smell tobacco from under there," George said. He pointed at a pile of scrap lumber stacked against the shed's far wall.

"Ah, you're crazy," John said as he kept digging through the wrenches, hammers, and saws on the workbench. "You probably smell your grubby straw hat."

Undaunted, George peeled away the top boards. First one board and then another. There lay the missing can with the badly needed hardware. "Here it is."

How did the tobacco can get where it was? John never knew and George wouldn't say.

Well, I'll be a monkey's uncle, the older brother thought as he cleaned his glasses with his shirttail. After that he started bragging about George's miraculous talent.

On the other hand, George knew his nose could get him in trouble. Some girls and older ladies especially didn't like others talking about how they smelled.

But his magic by a nose wasn't the only thing that could get him in trouble. Opportunities and temptations always lurked just around the corner. Some were overwhelming; some downright dangerous.

∫

286

Part of our quandary involved tractor speed. We knew for example, that our Allis Chalmers could make 12 m.p.h. and the John Deere A about 14, while neighbor Wally Hoffman's Farmall M could go 16 m.p.h. The difference made a difference ... to us. Every area boy had a secret wish to drive the fastest tractor, whether pulling a plow or hurrying down the road.

What was the best way to verify tractor speed? A race, of course.

§

Farm boys could make a race track out any place where adults weren't around. On a hot day in late August with the temperatures in the 90s and the humidity about 65 percent, George sat wearily daydreaming at the wheel of the John Deere.

He could see neighbor John Lee (Buddy) Habluetzel plowing a 40-acre field across the road.

I'll bet our A model will outrun his B.

Unhitching his plow, George drove across the road seeking bragging rights. As it turned out later, nobody felt like bragging about anything. However, the event did teach a crucial life lesson.

John continued plowing with the Allis Chalmers and curiously watched the scene. Something was in the wind.

"Hey, Buddy, how's it going?" George hollered as he drove up. Buddy disengaged his clutch, shut off his engine and cupped his hand over his ear.

"Oh, I'm fine," Buddy said, showing a curious grin as he took a swig from his canvas water bag. "It's hotter than a blacksmith's forge isn't it?"

George said, "That tractor looks slower than a snail."

"Hey, it's not the bark in the dog ..." Buddy said laughing.

George looked down the field of wheat stubble. "What you say we race to the far end and back. We'll see who has the bark."

Buddy grinned. He didn't mind a little competition. Anyway, he needed a break. Nodding okay, he unhooked his plow.

287

The two boys parked side by side and each set their throttles wide open.

What are they doing? John wondered.

"Go," yelled George. Both drivers slammed their hand clutches forward. For an instant, the two tractors hesitated, hopping their front wheels off of the ground. Then, the big rear wheels dug in and the race was on.

They flew nip and tuck across the bumpy stubble, with Buddy's John Deere B pop-pop, popping in staccato and George's larger A booming at the slower factory-set rate.

Have you ever heard a pair of two-cylinder John Deere's popping at their maximum revs? That was music to young farmers, like Harley Davidsons are to bikers. Noise echoed from the creek.

The two raced at full throttle, scattering grasshoppers before the green and yellow chariots. By the time they neared the far end of the field, George was ahead by a neck.

When they approached the fence line, they communicated their opposite turn-around directions. In a flash the turnaround proved to be breath-taking and heart-stopping, a lesson of a lifetime, changing blissful grins into shocked fear.

George's turn was conservative. He disengaged the clutch and slowed his tractor. *I'll slow, turn and accelerate again.*

Buddy, on the other hand, challenged the forces of nature by turning without slowing. Cars certainly turned at his tractor's speed, and much higher. With the throttle wide open, he turned his front wheels full right, and then hit his right drive wheel brake hard, expecting to turn on a dime.

What Buddy hadn't accounted for was his tractor's high center of gravity, so as he tried to make his circus turn, the tractor started to roll.

Oh, God no. Not that. George prayed, his eyes bugging in horror. *He'll be killed.*

As the B's right drive wheel rose into the air the tractor tipped. Buddy couldn't breathe, but reacted quickly. He released the brake, straightened the turn, disengaged the clutch and closed the throttle. As quickly as the accident waiting to happen began, it was over.

Oh, thank you Lord.

Oh my ... thank you Lord.

When the tractor settled onto all four wheels with a heavy thump, Buddy took his first breath in a while. He shot a weak smile, and headed back—slowly—to his plow.

George headed back across the road in pale silence. It took half an hour for him to regain his composure. Even John, a quarter of a mile away, seemed shaken by the near disaster.

Later, John would date Buddy's sister Lois, but he never mentioned the race. She might tell her dad. As a matter of fact, it would be many days before the boys even discussed the subject.

§

A few weeks later we saw Buddy in town. By then, we could manage embarrassed grins about it, but we all agreed that we would never race tractors again. And we didn't. And no one even mentioned bragging rights, for we guessed they didn't seem so important after all. We just filed the events into our memories and left them there, until now.

Looking back, farm kids faced danger every day. We worked daily around cows and sometimes an ornery bull. We interacted with horses that outweighed us more than 15 times. We galloped Tony the Pony at breakneck speeds.

We drove tractors over rough ground ... always in a hurry. Sometimes we plowed and disked side hills, drove up steep banks and crossed narrow bridges, each with the means to cause harm. We'd force feed corn through the grinder, dig clogged straw from inside the combine and clear grass away from the mower's cutter bar.

Country youth learned a great deal about natural laws, for farm disasters were continually on the prowl. The truth was we generally tended to use caution, maybe because of lessons learned from events like the great tractor race.

By the way, Buddy turned out to be a highly successful and respected farmer in Pottawatomie County.

Farmers knew that riding a tractor all day could get monotonous, but for those with interest, the beauty of nature around far exceeded the boredom. God's creation was everywhere.

Our folks said that when Mom first came from Michigan to live in Kansas she didn't recognize its beauty. Dad said he'd often pull the car over and point out the magnificent surroundings. Once she really started looking she was hooked. She loved her native Michigan, but she was now a farmer's wife, and from then she never wanted to leave Kansas.

VIEW FROM A TRACTOR SEAT

Field work took concentration. We needed to keep an eye on tractor speed, engine sounds, implement depth, soil conditions and of course steering where we needed to go. Tilling the weeds from young corn and sorghum with a tractor mounted cultivator demanded intense attentiveness.

When we weren't engrossed, either with the work, drawing in the dirt for art's sake or daydreaming about fairs or food ... we watched nature at its finest. We saw rabbits, snakes, ground nesting birds and many other animals sometimes scurrying to safety before our implements disturbed their nests or burrows or invaded their territories.

Every so often we'd say, "Sorry missus, we need to plow here. You'll just have to find another place to live."

§

One tall sky September day, the noise of the AC flushed a covey of 15 bobwhite quail. This explosion of fast winging birds almost under the tractor startled John. His 'knee-jerk' reaction sent his head snapping back and his hat flying.

The birds had burst away with a roar of loudly beating wings. After a few feet, the birds locked their wings and glided many yards before disappearing into the underbrush. Their feathers gave them perfect camouflage.

The boys would sometimes see hawks, circling overhead looking for displaced mice and other rodents. When they spotted a meal these large birds barreled downward, while their prey seemed unaware of the danger until it was too late.

The ever present Kansas wind blew to bend and twist trees and sculpt each to be different from its neighbor. Many seemed like waving fans that cooled the countryside. When an occasional leaf descended haphazardly to the ground, it might become animal nesting material or simply decay and add nutrients into soil.

The boys did take note of these marvelous things.

THE VIEW AT THE SLOUGH

At the ever flowing Slough, fallen tree trunks sometimes bridged scenic pools of clear water. Fallen leaves and tiny branches bobbed on their way toward some unknown destination.

Squirrels with nut-filled cheeks, walked the tree bridges and then climbed upright cottonwoods to the high nests of leaves and sticks. Raccoons, possums and skunks also used the bridges, and so did the boys.

One day John made great fun of his brother after he stumbled and fell from a log, right into the cold Slough water.

"Hey, dork-o, you need practice."

George sat nestled in mud. *Yikes, it's cold.*

While the mud clouded the clear water, the muddy cocktail seeped into his boots and soaked his clothes from the waist down. Meanwhile, John roared with laughter, high and dry on the bank.

After a few seconds the coldish wet spurred George into action and he scaled up the slippery bank. Angry with himself and his brother, he cringed at the mud and water.

"Boy that was a great dive. Did you catch any fish?" John asked, still chuckling.

"No," George replied, "and I didn't catch a water moccasin either!"

John swallowed but didn't reply. *He got me on that one.*

George poured the water out of his brogans and went back to work. The incident was soon forgotten and the Slough continued its normal uses. It had some nice swimming holes, some small fish pools and it watered the cattle. The boys liked that stream, except where they needed to cross it to bring in the cows. Unfortunately, most often as the boys tried to jump across it, they got wet.

If those darned old cows just weren't grazing on the other side ....

This special stream flowed clear, even in the driest years. It crossed through much of the farm and emptied into Rock Creek. There it mixed with the creek water, flowed into the undersized Vermillion River, on to the bigger Kaw, to the huge Missouri River and finally into the mighty Mississippi. In theory, a leaf from the Burgess farm could drift all the way to New Orleans.

The Slough's cooling shade trees called to the boys in hot weather and they sometimes took a cool water swim. What would they find in the water? Crawdads, bullheads, turtles, minnows, floating debris and of course the 14 leeches George encountered one day, much to his surprise. On the occasion when a water moccasin really did come swimming their way—they rocketed out of the water.

Once out, they'd dress and climb back onto their tractors to continue their work, daydream or even sing at the top of their lungs.

In this humdrum of cycling back and forth across the fields, a person might get drowsy or even nod off for a moment. What happened next could have been entertaining—and it was dangerous.

WAKE UP CRIED THE BRUSH PILE.

One afternoon maybe George had stuffed down too much fried chicken at noon. At any rate, once back in the field he started nodding off. Before long he was buried in a bona fide snooze. The Allis Chalmers and cultivator were on their own, heading directly toward a brush pile near the edge of the cornfield.

George awakened in fright when the tractor clawed its way into the pile, screeching like fingernails on a blackboard. Branches scratched off streaks of orange paint and the big rubber tires continued to spin in the loose soil.

What the heck?

Now alert, he pushed in on the clutch and stopped the tractor's grunting and spinning. Everything seemed okay until he glanced over his shoulder. He had cultivated a long zigzag trail across a dozen or more corn rows.

Slowly, he raised the cultivator, backed up and untangled the tractor and cultivator from the brush. With a jolt, he realized luck— and the good Lord—had been on his side. If he'd missed the brush pile, he'd have driven square into the Slough in another 20 yards.

Happily, the mangled corn grew quickly, obscuring the mysterious 'Sign of Zorro' in the field, and if his dad ever noticed the paint scratches, he never mentioned them. This was another close call perhaps, but it definitely taught another valuable lesson about staying alert.

As John said later, "George is just like a horse, he can sleep anywhere, even standing up or on a tractor."

Yes, George could *sleep like a horse*. That country saying was part of the lingo that described real life. And there were many other vivid sayings.

TWENTY-THREE

KANSAS LINGO, ADAGES AND SAYINGS AND PREDICTABLE MOM

[St. George News - October 20, 1949] ~ BASEBALL PLAYING CATFISH LANDED ~ Beans Bleford of St. George caught a 38-pound Yellow Catfish in the Kaw River this week. The giant fish was caught on a willow pole bank line baited with a frog. What made the fish special, in addition to its size, was what it contained in its stomach. It had swallowed a real baseball, which was only partially digested "I think that catfish probably rooted for the St. George town team," Bleford opined.

1949

KANSAS LINGO

A lot of mid-twentieth century Kansans used a curious mix of words in their language. Many words came out in a garbled fashion because of the wrong verb form or pronunciation. Words like *jist* and *git*. To this day Kansans still say things like, *pert near*, *acrost* and *clost enuf.*.

The boys' mom used *pert near*. She'd say, "Boys, hurry up, it's *pert near* time to go." When something didn't happen often, she'd say, "That happens *once in* a *blue moon*."

The boys' Great Aunt Mollie, first generation of Irish descent, used a couple of quaint sayings. The first dealt with her age. When asked how old she was—she seemed elderly to the boys—she always replied, "I'm as old as the hills." That was her stock answer and she never told her secret.

Aunt Mollie spent many years caring for her immigrant parents during their declining years. They lived in a neat and tidy house at the north edge of Wamego. She never married, because, "Men leave the newspaper scattered all over the house."

Much of the lingo of that time involved the weather. Back then, it didn't rain, *it poured*. Sometimes it *came down in buckets* and at other times *it rained cats and dogs*. Then again, the rain might *come down a mile a minute*.

The boys had sayings for animals, too. They didn't hunt ducks but *quackers*. Redheaded woodpeckers were just *peckers*. And of course, the coyote was a *ki-yoat*, not a ki-oat-tee.

Much like today, cars had special nicknames, like *Chevys* and *Caddys*. Oldsmobiles, Pontiacs and Studebakers were *Olds, Poot-ten-aacks* and *Studies*.

§

SPEAKING OF CARS

When icy winter air came through a car window, we would often say we needed to *put some Isinglass in that pneumonia hole*. Incidentally, the flexible translucent mica-compound Isinglass patched many a broken farmhouse window.

People drove a car *lickety-split,* doing a daredevil *Joey Chitwood*. Some might say, *It's all downhill from here.*

While the Model T Ford had been the *tin lizzie* and cars from the 20s were *flivers,* we wanted to drive *big boats* like those long and wide Buicks.

Caddies and Buicks in particular had slow shifting automatic transmissions. We called the cars *sleds,* though we weren't sure why. In fact, there were lots of strange things we encountered but didn't understand.

One Thanksgiving we heard Aunt Helen, Aunt Dorothy, Aunt Dot and our Mom talking as they worked together preparing the Thanksgiving dinner.

THE VERY STYLISH BLOUSE

"Goodness, isn't she the *cat's meow?*" Aunt Helen asked as she watched her younger sister Dorothy enter the room wearing a new outfit. "Is that the fashion in Topeka?"

Aunt Helen sat on the divan, head cocked to the side and waited for the chuckle to follow. It always did.

"Good grief, Dorothy, that blouse is smothered in lace" sister-in-law Aunt Dot said. "So that's what you're wearing these days."

Aunt Dot continued, "Wear that around Wamego and men will *run around like chickens with their heads cut off.*"

"You have to admit that Dorothy looks *finer than frog's hair* doesn't she?" Aunt Helen asked.

At that point, looking at Dorothy's light purple blouse, the boys' Mom spoke in her sister-in law's defense. "I hear that style is all the rage in places like Chicago and Kansas City. She's just trying to be *up town.*"

"I'll have you know," Dorothy said with a toss of her head, "this blouse was a gift from an admirer, and I do feel quite smart in it. After all, *you only live once.*"

For a good while longer the repartee continued. Frequent chuckles and laughs peppered the chatter as the four ladies gossiped and teased each other. Their speech, filled with sayings, quotations and quips, reflected the language of the time. Well chosen words greatly added to the wit and wisdom of the conversation.

"Remember when Louella Ethel Smenke *set her cap on* that Shorty Brockman?" Aunt Helen asked. Then she grinned *like a Cheshire Cat.* "I'd bet Lulu regrets the day she ever put on that outfit."

' Set her cap?"

"Yeah, you know, when a woman is trying to appeal to a guy so he'll marry her. I heard that's what Lulu did."

We heard that some women married because *they weren't the brightest candle on the Christmas tree.* Some had *shotgun weddings.*

"Yeah, Dorothy," Aunt Helen instructed, her face looking somewhat stern although her gleeful eyes betrayed the humor. "You might end up with a Shorty Brockman."

By now Aunt Dorothy's face was as *red as a beet.* Then, without meaning to, she started to grin. All did.

And so the day went with the two sisters and two sisters-in-law, laughing their way through preparing of another huge Thanksgiving meal for the family gathering, again at Aunt Helen's and Uncle Huston's rented farmhouse.

When Uncle Huston, banged on an old pot, we hurried to the back porch to wash up. We hadn't had much luck hunting but tramping around in the melting snow had developed our appetites.

The two of us didn't need any coaxing to come in to eat nor did Jim, Ben or Rollie. We all grabbed a chair and fidgeted through Uncle Alfred's long Thanksgiving blessing, including everyone's mention of, "bountiful blessings."

As platter after platter and bowl after bowl went around the two tables, one for adults and little kids plus one for us boys, we snatched bites when possible. And, with all the wonderful food, we ate and ate.

We hurried and finished off a piece or two of pie. With all of the cousins around, there were more places to explore and more hunting, so out the door we went.

ADAGES AND SAYINGS

At home we used our Irish senses of humor. We could laugh at the *drop of a hat.* Humor worked well because if we could get each other laughing our folks usually followed.

For example we sat at the supper table one cold fall evening and faced the main dish, stewed turnips. This totally disgusting vegetable really capped off a difficult day that had included school, cold and windy corn shucking and an hour of frigid evening chores. By now, our stomachs cried out for hot, robust food … only to be offered mushy, smelly turnips. Judy and Joyce would have nothing to do with them.

We had to do something to get past the turnips so we could fill up on dessert. So we played around with our meal.

First one of us and then the other would splat a spoon into the repulsive glob of soggy turnips. The other would giggle and then smash his turnips.

Finally, Dad just had to say something, though it seemed hard for him to *keep a straight face*. He used a parental proverb to help put us back on track.

"If you boys don't straighten up and eat, I'm going to have to *break your plates*," he said, his voice stern, but not his face. Maybe he wasn't fond of the *good-for-you* food either.

Now we faced a real dilemma, turnips on the one hand—*Why isn't Pep an inside dog?*—and some degree of Dad's displeasure. However, eating the foul smelling stuff was *easier said than done*, so we continued to dawdle. Dad then moved to a second level warning, though it came out as another somewhat playful threat.

"Sit up and eat or I'm just going to *saw your corners of the table off*." This came with a slight smile.

We caught the joke, and in our playful mood, laughed. We looked back and forth at each other and both waggled our heads from side-to-side, then shrugged at the same time and laughed, sliding down in our chairs.

Parents and boys laughed and the girls giggled. It had happened again. Laughter and humor came to our table and into our lives.

Sooner or later, however, the smile left Dad's face and he said with gentle authority, "That's enough now, go ahead and finish up."

Somehow things like turnips tasted better when spiced with family fun and witty sayings.

Sayings and adages of all kinds were a part of our speech—everybody's—and spiced up every conversation, whether among friends and neighbors, at church, at school or even at the feed store.

§

SOME WEATHER

"Some weather we're having," Shorty Brockman said. He stamped snow from his boots just inside the Wamego Elevator's feed store. "Cold enough to *freeze a well-digger's arse*, ain't it?" The four or five farmers crowded around the store's pot belly stove chuckled. "I bet it's never been so cold as this *afore*."

"Why, Shorty, what's the matter with you? Is your rememberer stuck?" Bill Mansfield asked with a pretend frown. "Why it's been a lot colder than this. Don't you remember your dad telling you about that bad winter around World War I? He must have told you there hasn't been any weather to compare with that."

Shorty looked down and then away. He shook his head.

"Yep Shorty, why that winter was so cold here at Wamego that the ole Kaw turned around and went the other way. Started flowing west. It sort of piled up a few miles west of here. Isn't that right, Alfred?"

Bill often drew listeners into the exchange. He eyed the boys' uncle who said, "Well it was pretty darn cold alright. I do remember that for a time the Kaw didn't flow toward Kansas City."

This statement was true, at least in part. That had been a year when the Kaw froze up for a couple of days and the river really didn't flow eastward. The freeze created dams with ice blocks and debris, and the pools got bigger … and the water looked to be backing up.

Shorty looked at Alfred and scratched his neck. "That ain't so, is it? You're just pulling my leg. I think I'm going to go check on my catfish groveling hole to see if the fish are able to move."

As soon as Shorty shut the outside door, the crowd broke into laughter. Once again Kansas weather took center stage in the mirth and merriment.

In fact, a weather observation was part of almost every chat. "*Hot enough for you?*" or "*Cold enough for you?*" Friends and neighbors used these as greetings.

Someone might say, "I'm not moving, '*til hell freezes over*."

"Yep," someone else might answer, "*Be colder than the hubs of hell* if the wind comes up."

Although no one spoke about it, it was a well known fact that every farmer hated visiting his outhouse on a cold winter's night. Why bother discussing the inevitable?

Conversation could include comments about too much rain, too little rain, the chance of snow, sleet or hail and questions about the occasional tornado or threat of one. Wind was good for a couple minutes of conversation, especially when it came with thunder and lightning.

For example, the week after Thanksgiving, the boys' dad met his brother in town. Both were doing some banking at the First National.

"Did you hear what happened to Beans Bleford over to St. George?" Alfred asked. "I hear he lost his barn in the wind yesterday."

"That's too bad. I didn't know it blew that hard. What happened?" the boys' dad asked.

"Somebody said Beans accidentally cracked corner post on his barn last week when he backed his tractor into it. Made it easier for the wind to push the barn down on top of the corn crib. He had corn scattered all over the place."

"Too bad."

The exchange about Beans—or any farmer—losing his barn could continue in one of two ways. If Beans was a respected and well liked farmer, his plight was considered a bit of bad luck.

However, if for some reason, Beans—or whomever—was one of those unfeeling souls who mistreated his animals or couldn't be trusted, then the misfortune might be summed up with *he got what he had coming to him.*

Deserved or not, wind could be a problem and so could the hot Kansas weather that scorched crops. Drought made for plenty of dialog with the wrong verb form often used with *don't* and *come.*

A neighbor might say, "The corn is going to shrivel-up if this wind *don't* quit."

"Sure could use some rain," the other fellow might respond. "How long has it been since the last one *come*?"

Kansas climate made for good conversation, especially its four seasons.

FOUR SEASONS

Kansas weather consisted of rain, drought, hot, or cold. And these seasons could change places on a whim. If *a body* didn't like one weather *spell*, people would say he just had to wait a few minutes and it'd change.

The temperature could be 95 degrees, and an hour later if a storm blew in, the thermometer might drop into the 60's. The 30 or more degree variation could come about in *the blink of an eye*.

Rain storms sometimes seemed to come *out of nowhere* and towering thunderheads poured down huge rain drops and lots of them. At times, drivers pulled off the road because their car's windshield wipers couldn't keep up.

When it rained really hard, intelligent animals like pigs, cows and horses ran for cover, if they could find it. A few on the lower mental scale, especially turkeys, tended to look up with their mouths open—*and drown*. Shorty Brockman believed that.

Heavy rains yielded enough run off to sometimes trap livestock when murky creeks and streams got to bank full. Now and then, a flood swept stock away.

Most folks called the downpours *gully washers* ... and that they were. Little runnels washed away farmland to create small ditches and cut channels that carried away gushing, muddy water ... often labeled as *too thick to drink and too thin to plow*.

After the rains and run off ceased, a thick, silty mud lay in drifts wherever it collected, often on someone else's farm. The flooding changed the soil composition, by adding sand to the loam in some fields and by stripping others to nothing but clay-like gumbo.

Wet gumbo was so slick and sticky that a whole body of stories developed involving it. Some farmers got implements stuck in the springtime—so the stories went—and recovered them when the ground froze in the late fall. Gumbo could *suck a hoof right off a horse* some said.

301

Wally Hofman told Shorty a great gumbo story about how a prized boar hog walked across a big, wet gumbo field with the hog's tail barely touching the muck. As the pig walked, gumbo balled up on the pig's tail.

Wally said the ball got bigger and bigger as the hog travelled. At the far side of the field—swore it was true—the ball was so big that it pulled the pig inside out.

"That's amazing," Shorty said. "How did he eat?"

The boys knew about gumbo first hand. That year their dad and Wally rented an 80-acre field northwest of Belvue. It had dark black gumbo, and after a heavy rain, grew sticky and mucky and nearly did suck off the boys' boots a couple of times. A few weeks later it dried so hard that the tractors had to strain to plow just 2-3 inches deep.

No doubt about it, working gumbo, or any farmland for that matter, took a lot of planning. And some luck. Farming has always been a constant gamble with timing. Just what did the weather have in store and, when was the next big storm?

"After all," Bill Mansfield passed on, "timing has a lot to do with the success of a rain dance."

IF AND WHEN IT WILL RAIN

Kansas farm folks constantly looked for ways to predict weather changes, especially in the days before highly developed forecasting. A big farming question was when to plant.

Waiting for a field to dry out before planting shortened growing season and sometimes hurt the harvest. A farmer whose wheat wasn't ready when winter set in faced reduced results.

Of course, heavy rains after planting might cause seeds to rot before sprouting. Sometimes wet weather caused newly emerged shoots to damp off … and that meant costly replanting.

Weather affected the wheat harvest. When the grain got ripe, immediate harvesting was a must. Delays exposed the crop to the possibility of severe wind or hail. Those storms might flatten a field of standing wheat in as little as an hour and reduce or eliminate the harvest. Continual rain on standing, ripened wheat could drop quality, and the kernels might start to sprout if it stayed wet.

On the other hand, the lack of rain meant some crops wouldn't germinate in the dry soil or, without timely rain, new growth withered and died. Again, the weather seemed all powerful, for it impacted the harvest and frequently put farmers in jeopardy.

§

Dad and most of our neighbors had a pressing ambition to stay ahead the climate. For one thing, they listened to the daily weather assumptions broadcast over radio station WIBW in Topeka or KMAN in Manhattan. The meteorologists did their best, but a lot of time what they aired seemed to be sketchy, best guesses.

One weatherman said, "Predicting weather is extremely difficult, but one day you might get up and have that day's forecast wired—and then a bunch of Christians would get together and start praying for rain."

At our house, Dad listened for crop weather; and we listened for baseball weather. We shared concern, but for totally different reasons.

Not many people really trusted the fairly newly enhanced forecaster profession, and it did lack the radar and other tools used today. Some farmers, short on reliable scientific information, turned to the *Farmer's Almanac* or to some other old fashioned forecasting method.

SO YOU CAN PREDICT IT?

Without much confidence in the radio forecasts, some farmers turned to the intuitive art of prediction. Predictors might use instinct, hunches, old wives tales, and … as some thought at least, divine intervention.

As best as we could tell, the process meant guessing with a dash of common sense. However, we heard of people who relied on getting the forecast message from up on high.

When things got too hot, dry, wet or cold a lot of people did turn to prayer and supplication. Our family did its share of praying and, looking back, we realize most of our prayers were answered.

Sometimes, however, we relied on traditional *horse-sense*. We didn't have to be very smart to know that when huge black clouds rolled in from the southwest, accompanied with thunder and lightning and dropping temperatures, it was probably going to rain.

Shorty Brockman, on the other hand, said he could predict the weather depending on whether his convertible field-work car dripped oil. Shorty claimed that if the sky darkened and it smelled like rain all he had to do was to look for signs of motor oil leaking onto the ground.

"My method sure is reliable. It never rains without my field work car leaking oil."

Good grief, Shorty.

Our world changed color when the storm-laden clouds drew close. First, the sun painted everything with an orange tinge and then the landscape grew incredibly brilliant. Grass and trees displayed a vibrant green.

As the storm got closer, shadows grew longer and colors got deeper. The air became crisp and smelled of ozone. Finally it would darken as if the sun was going down, and then the rains would come. It would usually be a fierce downpour … a deluge … with lightning and thunder *loud enough to wake the dead.*

LIGHTNING YOU SEE WON'T HURT YOU

Zizzz-a-zaaaaaaaaaappp! Right before our eyes the night lit up as bright as day and a mighty, jagged lightning bolt exploded a hedge tree in the pasture. The clouds, the trees and even the back porch from where we watched, grew brighter than sunlight, for an instant. As the flash dimmed, the intense *smell of rain* overflowed our nostrils.

We'd almost *jump out of our skins*, and then an instant later….

Boooooom-de-booooooooooommmmmm-boom.

Pause. Rummmmmble-rummmble-rumble-rumble.

§

"Man that *scared the daylights out of me*. What if it hits the house? I want to go back inside," George muttered.

"Now boys, remember what I tell your mom," their dad said confidently, trying to calm fears about the mighty forces of nature. "If you see lightning, it won't hit you. By the time you see the flash it has already hit the ground. There is no way that it can hurt you."

The boys respected lightning. They'd head for cover when dozens of jagged electrical charges crackled again and again between the clouds and then crashed to the earth while thunderclaps assaulted their ears.

Fortunately, most lightning hit some distance away. A person could tell the distance between where he was standing and where the strike hit. If he counted the seconds between the lightning and the thunder he could calculate how far it was to the storm.

People calculated storm distance by counting, *One Mississippi, two Mississippi, three Mississippi, etc.* "That one's about two miles away," George said one night. "I hope it goes around us."

That storm inched toward the farm and a few minutes later the crackling and the booming occurred almost simultaneously. Finally, a mammoth strike struck and down came the rain—easy to predict—though there was little anyone could have done about it.

§

PREDICTABLE MOM

We thought our Mom was a weather expert. She continually predicted when storms were approaching. Mom had remarkable ways of telling the weather trends. She contended, for example, that if our dog, Pep, started eating grass it was a sure sign of rain.

Mom also said rain was a sure thing when flies congregated en masse on the screen door. When they were there, rains often did come. She felt the best rain forecaster was when a cat laid on its head and back. How Mom knew these things, we didn't know. She seemed to be right.

Mom could predict things other than weather. If, for example, we loudly banged the screen door, Mom would announce that visitors were coming. Perhaps the screen door bang accurately foretold company, but Mom's predictions never dealt with timing.

For some reason a single visitor didn't count toward Mom's forecast. It had to be a couple. If the couple's kids came along we were pleased.

If Mom had an itchy nose it could mean people were on their way to see us, or someone was talking about us. We often wondered who might talk about us.

Mom had two other ways to predict the arrival of visitors. If the house looked unkempt, she would stew and fret, certain that company was on their way. "You wait and see. With this mess, somebody's bound to show up."

We thought she worried more than necessary about how things looked. After all, any visitors were just like us. And anyway, we thought a mess was normal on a farm.

The last way of telling if company was coming was when our dog barked. Now that method was not very reliable, in our opinion. Pep had a tendency to bark at anything that moved.

His Collie and German Shepherd ancestry gave him a guard dog mentality and he took his work seriously. He barked at skunks, errant crows, wandering chickens, and definitely at any snakes found about the place. Like all dogs, he'd bark at passing cars, tractors and trucks.

Ora Bowman came now and then to fill up the 300-gallon tractor gasoline tank, and while he chatted like a family visitor—he was Aunt Dot's brother—he was there on business. We liked Ora and his Chevy oil tank truck with its bold red, white, and blue Standard Oil markings. Did he count as company?

Interestingly, the oddest guest to visit our house wasn't really there at all. Still we knew he'd arrived when the wind blew the front door open.

"Come in Aven," Mom would say and then she'd tell us that Aven Baneloose had come to call and had just opened the door. Baneloose was a Norwegian folklore legend brought to this country by our Grandmother Sigrid Scott.

Mom's mom shared the old country tales and stories of trolls and gods like Odin, Thor, and Loki. When we had a noisy storm Mom would say, "That's Thor, the god of Thunder, banging his hammer on the clouds."

No doubt about it, whether predicting the arrival of storms or visitors, some people believed odd things. For our part, we just went along with Mom.

We heard lots of tales and sayings from most everyone we knew. There always seemed to be something hidden though, that we had to figure out. .

Our job was to be farmers, so we used the lingo and adages t hat we'd learned and went on about our business.

Sometimes we'd be the ones to hook in a friend to teach him about something he may not know. That usually turned into fun.

TWENTY-FOUR

I'LL DO SOME COWBOYING, BAFFLING OPPOSITE SEX, AND COMEDY ON THE COURT

[Wamego Reporter – November 11, 1949] ~ FISH AND GAME NEWS ~ The state's annual quail season gets underway at one-half hour before sunrise on November 16th, and closes at 4p.m. on December 2nd. The season this year is a 10-day staggered season with hunting permitted in all counties on November 16, 18, 20, 22, 24, 26, 27, 30 and December 2nd. The daily legal bag limit is eight with possession limit two days bag limit.

1949

I'LL DO SOME COWBOYING

Cattle's horns grew bigger as the animal matured. Left alone, our herd's horns could have developed into potential weapons, especially when hungry livestock jostled for food at the feed bunk or for space in the barn. To avoid this, it made sense to dehorn our stock. We did it when our calves were about two months old.

At that young age the horn nubs came off easily with a hacksaw or heavy clippers. Dehorning could get messy as horns had plenty of blood vessels and sometimes little arteries got cut along the way. Luckily, the wounds healed quickly.

§

"Sure, I'll do some cowboying Saturday," classmate Jay N. Cook told John as they left class on Tuesday afternoon. "That'll be fun."

John smiled. "It sure will. Be at our place and ready to work at eight in the morning."

J. N. frowned. "Isn't that awful early?"

"Not for cowboys."

A city slicker—his hometown of Belvue had a population of a hundred or so—J. N. knew little of farm life.

He arrived at the Burgess farm Saturday at ten minutes to eight, attired interestingly enough, in new cowboy boots, new jeans and a new western cut light tan cowboy shirt with a colorful desert scene.

John thought, *Maybe I should have told him more about the job.*

The job started off well. The two boys herded about a dozen calves into the barn. Next, John handed J. N. a rope and suggested he lasso Maudie's brown-brindle offspring.

"Rope that calf in the corner and drag him over here so we can get started."

J. N. shook out a loop and flipped it toward the calf's head. The loop collapsed and banged against the barn wall. The second loop stayed open and settled over the calf's nose and one ear. J. N. jerked the rope like he'd seen in the movies. The loop closed, but slipped off.

On the third try, J.N. hit the mark and he now had a substantial calf pulling against him. The startled calf jumped, bucked and hurried in among the other calves where the rope got tangled.

Brown-Brindle jumped and kicked up barn floor dust. Each move dragged the would-be cowboy and finally slammed him flat on the ground. John shouted, "Let go!"

J. N. stood up and shoved his hands onto his hips. His shirt's cacti had changed from light to dark.

"Well now, you did fine." John laughed. "Let 'em calm down and we'll get the calf out of there."

J. N. was probably thinking, *How did I get myself into this?*

After a couple of minutes, John inched toward the tangled calves and pressured them off the rope. A steady pull brought Brown-Brindle toward a barn post. John snubbed him close.

"Okay," J. N. said, "now what?"

"Well, the hard part is over. All that's left is to saw off the horns. You get a good grip on the calf's head and I'll use the saw."

With a worried look, J. N. did as instructed and John hack sawed away a thumb sized horn nub. In less than twenty seconds, the other horn plopped to the ground.

"See, we got that done didn't we?" asked John as he released the calf and roped another.

With the next calf snubbed tight, J. N. said, "Let me do the sawing this time." He grabbed the saw and went right to work.

"Look out. You might be too close to the skull ... there are a lot of blood vessels there." Too late.

J. N. realized his mistake as the horn nubbin dropped to the ground and a severed artery pulsed out red streams of blood. In an instant his cowboy shirt's pastel mountain scene took on a scarlet shade.

John laughed, "Looks like the sun is setting on you."

"Yeah, what a mess," replied the city slicker.

The calf's blood clotted in a couple of minutes and John sponged on some screwworm ointment. The calf came out of the episode without horns, but no more worse for wear.

At the end of the morning, J. N. looked himself over and said, "I'd rather be a drugstore cowboy."

"Well I appreciate your help. You did a good job," John said. "Hope that shirt washes clean. See you at school."

J. N. mumbled something, walked to his car and headed home. Later he joked about his experience. "My problem was I didn't have a clue what dehorning was about. My cowboying days are over, so I won't need another outfit."

Every young man had major learning experiences as he grew up, for dozens of subjects of practical life. And for some they had a lot to learn about something far more baffling than dehorning.

BAFFLING OPPOSITE SEX

For 8th grader George, the subject of 'boy meets girl' was a mystery of major proportions. Although he now attended the consolidated Louisville Grade School with more girls in his class, he still suffered a lack of details on what made girls tick.

He was suspect of any information he had. His parents were no help, for they never mentioned the subject except to maybe tease him about having a girlfriend. Other boys of George's age were equally ignorant, and his brother wasn't about to share anything he knew.

Oddly George found one source of gender information—and a few other subjects as well—in a very unusual place. At age 13, he discovered sayings and jingles scribbled on the men's room walls at the tiny Belvue Truck Stop. Apparently the long-haul drivers enjoyed passing on their wealth of knowledge. "Kilroy was here," caught George's eye. He knew *Kilroy*, a fictitious World War II serviceman, had visited every spot on the globe.

George never missed an opportunity to visit the Truck Stop latrine. These scrawled bits of wisdom were free. He put one jingle to music and sang it as he disked in the field.

I got a girl in Kansas City, She's got freckles on her ... But ... she's pretty.

Every time he voiced the melody a one-hundred-watt grin crossed his face. Then he's sing it again.

George often questioned the spelling in some jingles or quotes, such as *dun* and *brokkin hardted.* On the other hand, he had less and less doubts about what he read.

One saying puzzled him. It stated that if a girl ate a watermelon seed, she would get pregnant. He knew girls got pregnant—*in a family way*, his cousin Rollie called it. Did that mean young ladies ought to avoid watermelons all together?

Another saying really grabbed George. In those days a Coca Cola advertisement stated, *"Coca Cola ... the pause that refreshes."* In one of the toilet stalls in that same Truck Stop he read, *"To heck with Coca Cola, this is the pause that refreshes."* Although not about girls, it was a dandy.

Picture Shows didn't help. In the movies actors never even went to the bathroom. In fact, the movies always cut away to a fireworks display when a couple enjoyed each other's close company.

George and his buddies struggled to know more about girls, and let's face it; girls struggled with the mystery from their side of the fence. However, at some age the boys' and the girls' interests and desires coincided, and the dating game began.

For all young boys, maturing alongside females was the nuttiest part of growing up. Continually trying to figure out the peculiarities of the opposite sex, the boys looked for any opportunity to interact with girls. Besides at school, what better place was there than in 4-H?

§

BUDDY FACES LIFE

For us, 4-H ranked high on our list of things with purpose. 4-H offered us ever so many chances to interrelate with others—including girls—of our own age. We thought a lot about 4-H and talked a lot about it. To us 4-H was alive and exciting. And, we didn't meet any girls on a ball diamond.

In 4-H, we'd learned what it took to do our best with our projects. New and different things kept popping up and afforded us with ways to leave the isolation of the farm.

As it turned out, that particular year we'd get involved in an extraordinary 4-H highlight, a club play. Our Club Leader, Mrs. Stratton, suggested the Louisville Club consider presenting a play in the county-wide competition. She volunteered to be our director.

We liked the play idea, especially since girls would be part of the cast. Several times we'd been in skits at our one-room Prairie View School, often making people laugh.

Laughter had always been a Burgess family tradition. The Play would be a time where we could *act up.*

The Play's title, *'Buddy Faces Life'* seemed interesting. Was this about the rigors of living a hard life? Could Buddy be headed for trouble? What was the story behind that title?

To our relief, the short one-act production turned out to be a comedy involving some eight or nine club members, including both of us.

§

To his chagrin, John had to play the Father and George acted as the son, *Buddy*. George brought wit and humor to his role and was considered the star of the show by those who apparently knew what they were talking about. And even John concluded his brother had the knack for comedy.

To this day George remembers his favorite line. He recalls Buddy saying, "Oh, I am so sublime." Can you imagine a thirteen-year-old saying that? The line stuck with George through the years, although he said he doesn't remember its meaning within the Play.

As well as John and George remember, Nonavee Taylor was Buddy's sweetheart and Phyllis Carley was Mom. This worked well, as John and Phyllis ended up dating for a while. Also in the cast—the boys sort of remember—were Lois Riat, Florence Blankley, Dean Ebel, Donna Stratton and maybe Harold Wilson.

Undertaking a play seemed like a grand event in the little village of Louisville and the play debuted on the raised stage at the tiny Community Center with the audience in chairs on the main floor.

To say the play brought down the house would be an overstatement. However, people—certainly parents—did rave about it and applauded loudly.

How did the play do in competition? Remarkably well, for it won the County contest and brought accolades to the newly formed Club.

The benefit of having the winning play was a free trip to the Annual State 4-H Roundup held at Kansas State College. There the Club members, dressed in the all-white 4-H clothes, lived in dorms and joined over 250 other young people from every county in the state.

Not all of the 105 Kansas Counties had plays, but many did. How did the Play do? *Buddy Faces Life,* placed near the top. A new 4-H club had put its name on the map.

Many commented how the actors worked together and all supported *Buddy*. George did recite nearly half of the show's lines. No wonder he felt 'so sublime.'

Although the play had taken lots of work it had been rewarding. But in short order George would face yet another challenge, at school, and there'd be no acting this time.

313

"Who wants to play basketball?" Louisville Grade School Principal Mr. Floyd Sutherlin asked the assembled group of young people. ."I do!" echoed throughout the old limestone block building that now housed enough students for boys and girls teams.

During that summer of 1949, most tiny country school districts like Prairie View consolidated into larger school districts. George and others would now be bused to Louisville.

For the first time in recent history, the Grade School could field real basketball teams. "We have both boys and girls uniforms on order," Mr. Sutherlin said. "We'll start regular practice soon."

Wow! Basketball uniforms, George thought. *Man, I've always wanted to play on a real team.*

The die was cast, so George and 11 others formed the boys' basketball team. None of them had ever played on a real team.

I've only played against John in the hayloft. Does that make me good?

At last the shiny gold uniforms with raised black numbers arrived and Mr. Sutherlin picked out one of the handsome outfits.

Everyone stared as the coach held up the jersey and smiled. "These really look good. There are only two sizes, so everyone needs to pick out the size and number they want. Boys, you go to the restroom and suit up. You girls can take the other box to the girl's restroom," Mr. Sutherlin said.

Dean Brazzle carried the box into the restroom and put it on the bench along the wall. Bob Riniker, who'd attended Prairie View with George, pulled out No. 22 and slipped it over his head.

"Hey, this jersey fits me fine," he said. "But the pants are small."

"They look okay on you Bob," George said.

The rest of the boys dug into the box and picked out the size they thought would fit them. George ended up with the number 12. As he slipped on the shorts he thought, *Man, these are skimpy. Will people laugh?*

Others had similar questions but just suited up and looked at each other. They were a team.

A short time later the new boys' team dashed along the corridor to Mrs. Straub's room. She looked the players over and said, "My, don't you boys look fine in those uniforms?"

Back Row: Harold Wilson, Bob Riniker, Dean Brazzle, August Dornbusch, John Brazzle, George Burgess, Tom Schumacher. Front Row: Russell Carley, Marvin Havenstein, Raymond Stratton, Tom Carley, Jerry Ubel

The boys said they felt the uniforms gave them status. Bring on the competition. But, there was much work to be done before any game could be played. Beyond daily practices at the playground hoop, the Community Center needed refurbishing.

Mr. Carley, Mr. Stratton, Mr. Blankley and a few other dads installed new Masonite flooring, and they did a great job; however the tiny structure still had to be turned into a basketball court.

"Due to the small size, we're going to have to make some modifications," Mr. Sutherlin said as he and some boys painted the necessary lines on the floor.

"Spectators along the sidelines will have to stand because there isn't room for chairs; we will have seating on the stage at the west end. Because the court is so short, the free throw lines will also have to serve as the 10-second lines."

George thought, *This court is going to be great, although I'll miss the hay bales on the sides.* Some of the opposing teams were equally inexperienced. Wheaton, Westmoreland, Belvue, St. George, Onaga, St. Bernard's and Wamego grade schools had varied skill. All would make the most with what they had.

Louisville basketball was exciting and fun. It was a comedy of sorts, until the Team found its groove. Some of the Team would go on to star on the Wamego High School Team. George would not.

CORNFIELD TO COURT AND BACK

Though George lacked team experience, he'd tossed many a hook shot into the corn wagon and honed a few of his skills on the barn's warped hayloft floor. He thought he could dribble. His long arms kept his older brother from easy baskets … unless John knocked him into the hay.

The season's first game was at the Belvue gym—a huge basketball court when compared to Louisville's. Parents loaded their kids into cars and drove the 10 miles to the equally small town, but with better facilities—much better. After the tip-off, both teams struggled up and down the court, awkwardly dribbling, passing and trying to score with little success. The crowd cheered them on.

It was a comedy of miscues by ten very young players, many of whom touched a basketball for the first time when they joined their teams.

"Double dribble," whistled the referee. George hung his head. He'd taken two steps before dribbling the ball. *I don't understand it, I dribble okay in the barn.*

While he pondered his mistake, a Belvue player passed the ball down court to that team's biggest player who banked in a shot for two points. "Wake up George," Mr. Sutherlin yelled. "Don't stop when you make a mistake. You have to keep on playing."

Louisville now had the ball. Harold Wilson dribbled up court, passed it to Junior Dornbusch, who passed it on to George. *Whistle!* "Double dribble!"

George gritted his teeth and stopped in disgust. When play resumed Belvue guard Jess Wilson easily maneuvered around the frozen Burgess boy and dropped in a basket.

What happened? C'mon George.

In the end, his classmates picked up the slack. They only lost by one point and George reveled after his first game, and easily erased all memory of his mistakes. He didn't score any points.

Over time, George did get a little better and finally reached the pinnacle of his career about a month later. At a home game against Westmoreland, he was high scorer, pounding in five points in Louisville's 12-7 win.

"Keep it up boy," his dad said. "You're doing fine." Even his brother gave him a compliment. Judy and Joyce seemed unsure what basketball was all about, but they cheered along with their parents.

George's parents' praise swelled his chest and he tried harder and harder. Alas, he never scored more than two points in any other game. But then, he was a guard … known for guarding.

George attended every girl's game and watched them struggle just like his team. He enjoyed watching the girls run around on the court. Maybe the Belvue Truck Stop cues were coming to life for the 13 year old.

Late in the season he thought, *I wonder if I'll be able to play basketball at Wamego High.*

Time would show George didn't play high school basketball, for he got cut after his second day of tryouts. That meant his basketball would be confined to intramurals—except for the hayloft games—and of course, he still had corn to shuck.

"George, wanna go up and play a game of Twenty One?" his brother asked.

"Only if you play fair…."

TWENTY-FIVE

DARE-DEVIL DRIVING, SHE KEEPS EYE-BALLING ME AND LET'S COMPETE

[Onaga Herald – August 25, 1950] ~ COUNTY WINNERS: SWINE ~
~ Duroc Fat Pig: John Burgess - 2 Blue and Champion; Myron Flinn - Blue and Red; Dan Burgess - Red; Dwight Burgess - Red; Denny Burgess – Red; Dean Burgess – Red; Donald Flinn – Red; Luther Holloway – Red; Frank Schilling – Red and White; Greta Kolterman – White.
~ Hampshire Fat Pig: Zona Kocher – Blue and Champion; George Burgess – Red.

1950

DARE-DEVIL DRIVING

A few weeks before John started his junior year at WRHS the family debated how best to get him there. During his first two years his mother had driven him the six miles each way on most days, while at other times the youngster used his driver's permit and drove on his own.

After long discussions the boys' folks decided getting a second car would be the best way to solve the problem.

The following day the boys went car shopping with their dad. Used cars were hard to find. In Wamego the three visited Wentz Ford, Kersey Motors and ended up at the Joe Daylor Chevrolet dealership, where they'd bought their new 1948 Chevy Stylemaster. The selection looked promising. After looking through the fleet, they found a gun metal gray two door '37 Chevrolet. A deal was reached.

Young John drove the new purchase toward home with George as his passenger. "Listen to that engine. It runs like a top," John said. "Do you notice that it doesn't bounce around too bad?"

"Yeah, it zips along okay. I guess the inside is kind of beat up though," George said just as his brother double-clutched and shifted down into second gear to slow for the turn from Highway 99 onto the county road. "Maybe some slip-over seat covers?"

318

John nodded yes. Since his dad wasn't in sight, he made some easy swerving turns that kicked up a little gravel and dust. "This thing handles pretty well." He tested the car's handling the rest of the way home, and finally came to a stop in front of the house.

The car would serve its young driver well—for a while. It took him to school, on an occasional date, to ball games and sometimes to church.

One day the rutted and rough unpaved roads finally exposed one of the car's flaws. What John hadn't discovered on the first day was that the used car had shimmy problems. He soon found that when speeding across ruts, the car would shutter.

Many people said all used car shimmied, some mild and some worse. John tried lots of things to cure the problem, but had little success. One day his mom rode with him.

"Jerk the wheel hard … first one way and then the other way," she said.

Young John did as instructed and to his amazement, the shimmy stopped. *How did she know to do that? I guess she knows a lot of things after all.*

John reveled in driving after a rain over slick, muddy and rut-filled roads. Some folks stayed home when it rained. Not John … he had an excuse. He needed to get to school didn't he?

"Gun'er Ace … blast through that lake," John yelled to himself above the noise of the straining car.

He shoved the gearshift into second and jammed the foot feed hard to the floor. 'Splooooooosh.' The muddy water shot higher than the roof, drenching the entire car, browning out the windows.

John flipped on the windshield wipers. They took five swipes to clear the glass. *That was near a record,* he thought.

He shifted back into high and knobbed the steering wheel hard left to compensate for the fishtailing rear end and wildly spinning Goodyear's. Juking and jiving the steering wheel, he worked hard to stay in the pair of six inch deep ruts.

In a few days the ruts would normally dry out. The next thunderstorm—monthly in summer and fall and twice as much in springtime—started the process all over again. In winter, the moisture came down as snow a lot of the time, that moved and piled as shifting drifts for a couple of days and before melting.

Loss of a driver's concentration could send a vehicle into a ditch. Besides the embarrassment, the driver then had to walk in the mud to the nearest neighbor for help—and teasing. Neighbors showed little mercy.

Farm kids started driving tractors and trucks by age 12—some earlier—so moving to a car at an early age wasn't a big deal. John's challenge was avoiding, "over doing it." He often couldn't hold back. As for the used '37 Chevy, it nearly made it through the year.

Its downfall came when construction began on a new east-west Highway 24, moving its route from through downtown Wamego to what would be a concrete highway on the town's northern side. Sometimes John disregarded the barricades and drove onto the road anyway. He'd snap shift and race the engine. Nothing was going to stop the young driver. His car served as a school ride—and a hotrod. That is until the day the transmission blew out.

"What the dickens were you doing on that highway?" His dad asked. "It's months from being done."

"Well, I was running late, and it's a shorter trip to school and that saves gas. You know gas is already up to 17 cents a gallon."

His dad shook his head and looked away. He probably sent up a prayer for patience and for his son's safety.

To replace the now more-costly-to-repair-than-it-was-worth Chevy, a shiny green 1940 Ford flatbed pickup joined the family. With two drivers, it would have its own stories to tell.

THE CHURCH PICNIC

`The newly acquired pickup performed one of its positive duties in mid-June. After Sunday services, the boys and a few others loaded it with ten long folding tables and chairs from St. Luke's Guild Hall. John then drove toward the Annual Church Picnic site about seven miles away, just west of St. George.

There the Arthur Flenthrope pasture offered an idyllic picnic setting under the trees alongside the clear running Blackjack Creek. In the small paddock, several men and boys helped unload and set up the tables while the Women's Guild spread out long table cloths. Bright sunlight, a blue ethereal sky above and a gentle breeze made the scene picture perfect.

§

We assumed the sun always shined for the picnic, because the Good Lord wanted it that way. It filtered through elm, hackberry and cottonwood leaves as they flickered above the small crystal-clear stream. The water gurgled and shimmered over the pale sand bottom while tiny minnows reflected the sun, as they darted to escape when our shadows passed over them.

In the tall trees, a showy pair of cardinals moved from limb to limb. Bluebirds hunted caterpillars among the buckbrush that lined the slope and a couple of cottontail rabbits scurried away flashing their white fluffs when people walked close by.

§

Soon the tables were weighted down with the world's best food. There would be fried chicken, baked ham, potato salad, baked beans, bread, pies, hand-cranked ice cream and watermelon.

Will the girls eat watermelon? George wondered. *I'm going to watch.*

SHE KEEPS EYE-BALLING ME

As he helped set up the tables and chairs, George's eyes caught sight of a girl about his age. He didn't know her. She kept staring at him. Every time he glanced her way, he found her eyes twinkling directly toward him. *Who is that girl?*

John watched the girl flirt with George and shook his head.

When George moved, the girl moved. When he looked, she looked back.

What is this? John thought. *The dumb-cluck doesn't know what to do. He's acting as nervous as a blacksnake crossing the highway.*

As George put his last chair alongside a table, he thought, *She keeps eye-balling me.* He needed to move and luckily saw his mom beckoning him for help. He took one last look toward the girl. Her eyes were locked onto him.

He jerked his head away as his face began to glow. Nerves on edge, he headed toward his mom. Without warning, the assertive girl stepped forward and blocked his path.

"Hello," she said. "I'm Ardith Tenet. I'm here visiting the Burkholders. They brought me to the picnic."

George's mouth zipped shut. His face froze with his only expression, a single frog-like blink. He said nothing.

"What's your name? Do you live in Wamego?"

His heart ticked as loud as a grandfather clock. His mouth dried and his lips glued shut. His Adam's apple pumped out, "SOS, SOS…."

"Maybe you'd like to picnic with me. We could fill our plates and go sit on the grass over under that elm tree by the little stream."

Maybe if I close my eyes she'll go away.

Slowly his eyes squinted open. She was still there.

"George! Hurry up. Where have you been?" his worried mother called. "Father.Boman is going to say the blessing so we can eat before the flies find the food."

The shaken boy trotted toward the tables and stood with his brother and the twins, Bill and Ben Sesler. As he bowed his head for the prayer, Ardith edged up and stood smiling at him. His eyes clattered shut.

While George waited for relief, the Rector gave thanks to God for world peace, the wonderful church family, for the food and for the hands that prepared

George, Joyce, John and Judy, all spiffed up for church.

it. Then he asked the Lord to bring enjoyment to all.

Yeah, right, George thought.

With doubt, he started opening his eyes and then heard his cousin Beverly Burgess say, "There you are Ardith. Mrs. Burkholder said I should take you over with all of us girls. Want to come?"

"Oh, thank you," Ardith said. "Sometimes boys act kind of dumb. Let's go."

George sighed; *I've been saved—because I'm dumb.*

§

We loaded our plates high, and we'd return for seconds. Everything was so good.

When we shoveled down the last bite of pie, we were *stuffed to the gills.* Still, we jumped into the afternoon's activities with gusto. While the little kids amused themselves splashing in the stream, we played a softball game on a makeshift field, and in the shade of some tall elms, several of the older men pitched horseshoes. The ladies talked, about their husbands and kids and asked for each others' recipes. Mom kept a close eye on Judy and Joyce to be sure they got something to eat and not get hurt.

Beverly, Ardith and a couple of other girls hiked along the stream to find a place to wade. Their goal was to be out of sight of the boys—well, maybe.

What joy it was to share the day with our church family, even with Ardith. The wonderful people of St. Luke's, bound together by Christian love, were our friends and mentors. Through the years they encouraged and coached us. When we had our positive moments, they graciously applauded.

We somehow knew that real respect offered freedom and many opportunities. But, we had to earn it.

LET'S COMPETE

We had finished the school year in May and got back to being full time farmers. Besides field work, we did regular chores including milking about 12 cows. With electricity at the barn, the DeLaval milking machine did the job, two cows at a time.

Hogs were now an important source of income and our operation involved 12 sows, mostly Durocs with a couple of Hampshires. They normally each birthed nine or ten offspring and we fattened them for market. We fed them corn and sorghum grains, plus the skim milk that we didn't take into Haas' Dairy.

Our hogs were growing fast. They'd be reaching 240 pounds in eight or nine months. From this batch of young pigs came our 4-H projects.

Because our Mom liked chickens, we had a lot of them. We ate eggs almost every day and for years had delivered 30 dozen to the Stewart Creamery every week. The eggs came from the flock of 75 or so White Leghorn laying hens, reputed to be the best egg producers. This flock changed size as new pullets started to lay eggs and older hens turned into chicken for the pot.

Each spring Mom ordered 100 chicks from Sears-Roebuck and Company in Chicago. Strangely, the chicks came via the U.S. Mail in a three-foot square cardboard box with four compartments … each with 25 to 27 chicks.

§

"Hello Veda. This is Postmaster Jay Hill. Your chicks came in last night and are sounding hungry. Can you come get them?"

"Oh, thank you Mr. Hill. I'll drive in right away. I hope they all lasted out the trip."

"There seems to be a lot of them peeping. My guess is they are alright. They can go a couple of days without feed or water. Pretty amazing, isn't it?" he said.

"It's just wonderful to get them all the way from Chicago."

"Well, the postal workers look out for them."

"Thank you and I'll see you shortly. Goodbye."

The boys' mom left home about fifteen minutes later and within an hour had the chicks secure under a warm brooder lamp, and with plenty of chick mash and water within reach. Only a couple of chicks didn't make it so in the end she'd gotten more than 100 baby Leghorns. They'd add one more job for the boys. Oh well.

Before corn planting time that year the boys' dad said, "Okay boys, we need to work the south field today. George you disk with the John Deere and John you follow him with the AC and the harrow. I'll go look at the beef herd and then to Wamego to shop for seed corn. We'll probably use DeKalb again, but I need to check the price."

Soon George and his brother were doing their assigned jobs. They would spend a good three days preparing all of the farm's row crop ground. Then corn and sorghum planting followed using the formerly horse-drawn, but serviceable two-row Lister planter.

Before the 4th of July wheat harvest commenced. Harvest took a lot of long days with only a five-foot wide combine header. When the combine's grain bin filled, the boys' dad augered the crop into their truck.

I wonder if Shorty Brockman dumps his wheat into his field-work car, thought George.

Young John then drove to the Wamego Grain Elevator to sell the load, each trip taking about an hour. With the truck gone, the boys' dad augered the yellow-brown kernels into the grain wagon. To George's displeasure, his job was to drive tractor and wagon to the granary and shovel the wheat into bins. Happily the task—with all of its hot and sweaty itching and scratching—only lasted a couple of weeks … and then it was on to another task.

"Hey, it's your turn to cultivate the corn," John said to his brother. "I did it two weeks ago. I need to work my 4-H garden project."

George cranked the AC and drove it into the center of the mountable cultivator. Grunting and straining, it took him an hour to attach the implement and clamp it in place.

From the garden John watched his brother struggle with the implement. *I suckered him.*

George's slow work continued while the sun made the world warm and alive. Flowers bloomed and bees buzzed. A bobwhite sent its call from a fence row. George sighed some more and day-dreamed.

In the field the tractor crept along, cultivating two rows at a time. A few hours later his body alarm went off. *Hey it's time for dinner.*

During the next couple of days while George cultivated, John worked with his 4-H projects and then plowed with the John Deere. The entire wheat and oat ground needed turning, but this year the process took a while because with a long, dry spell the ground got dry and hard. When George finished the cultivating he joined his brother plowing.

A few days later the boys, their dad and some of the neighbors started baling hay. And of course, John the younger got to handle all the bales as they came from the baler. "You'll be stronger for football," his dad kept reminding him. "It's good for you."

With the Habluetzel pick-up baler and everyone working together, it wasn't long before all the neighborhood bluestem was baled and stored.

During free time the boys played on the Louisville Youth Baseball team. They also practiced as a team one evening a week.

During 1950, the boys raised 4-H market Fat Pigs again. They did their best to train the animals for the Fair show ring; however, their pigs were pigs.

"Well this isn't getting me anywhere," George said as he watched his self-determining, William, meander. "How am I supposed to be a good showman if he won't cooperate?"

"Don't get mad at the pig. Remember, swine are smart they say."

"Mine is dumber than Bubba, and that's something—or maybe it's me, for trying to show a hog again."

I wouldn't disagree with that, thought John, hiding his smile.

Pigs are obstinate; they go where they want. A line of people couldn't deter a pig with its mind made up. With its low center of gravity and muscle strength, a determined pig can burst through like a torpedo.

I didn't have this much problem with Oscar, George thought. The boys concluded wooden canes had little effect on an independent pig and that the only hope was to develop a kind of interpersonal relationship with their animals. After weeks of working with the animals, they relaxed some and became the boys' buddies.

The boys also worked their other projects. George had collected wheat samples again and John continued to work on his garden project.

Come Fair time, during the Fat Pig judging, the entries wandered every which way. The Judge was constantly looking in different directions trying to pick a winner. In the ring a dozen unruly Duroc, Hampshire, Berkshire and Chester White breeds showed their collective independence. It was too late for the boys to coax their pals with corn. The show was utter chaos, and no animal got a fair shake in the judging.

Thank goodness Bubba stuck with Baby Beef and isn't interfering here.

In the end, John's two Durocs, Red and Rocky, garnered a blue and a red ribbon. George's William won a red.

George thought. *Maybe I'll go back to Baby Beef.*

§

That year the two of us put on a demonstration, extolling the special qualities of leaded paint. We showed painted examples on a chart to make our points. We kept up a steady banter that illustrated and proved that lead based paint was superior and that it covered better and held the color longer. Fortunately, we know today that lead in paint can be hazardous. But we were demonstrating what we had been taught.

Whatever we did, we competed with enthusiasm. Of course most 4-Hers tried hard so that fairs were exciting times. Some contestants won and some lost. We knew both sides of the equation.

The benefit of winning at any competition was the satisfaction of knowing one's best efforts had paid off. This year we'd worked hard, won some ribbons and looked forward to the next adventure.

"Boys, you need to get some new clothes. School starts soon," the boys' mom said.

Look out!

TWENTY-SIX

GREAT SHOE DECISION, WE'LL CALL YOU SUNSHINE AND THE MISSING RED PANTS

[*Wamego Reporter* – October 12, 1950] ~ POTT. COUNTY BILLS ALLOWED ~ … Wm. Falk, jury 5.00, mileage 3.22 = 8.64; La Verne O'Conner, jury, 5.00 mileage .98 = 5.98; Julius Lutz, jury 5.00, mileage2.38 = 7.38; … American Telephone Co. October rental & tolls, 137.80; Crane & Co. supplies, 37.69; … Geo. W. Prinz, meals for Co. jail, 61.00; Clark Estes, salary 140.00 less WT 4.60 = 135.40; Hazel Shaw, salary 140.00 less WT 12.90, Blue Cross, 2.35 = 124.65; … Tom Duncan, 1 coyote, 2.00; John W. Brookens 1 coyote 2.00; C. R. Jenkins 1 coyote 2.00; John McKee 12 coyotes 24.00; Duane Zimmerman 2 coyotes 4.00; Henry Tessendorf 1 coyote 2.00; …

1950

GREAT SHOE DECISION

The boys sold their fat pigs on the Tuesday after the County Fair. The hogs sold at a record price.

The next morning after breakfast they stood in John's bedroom, with their checks. "Man, look at that," John said. "We're flush. It sure is fun to see my name on this."

"Yeah," George said. "I feel great too, but I am going to miss William. Guess you'll miss Red and Rocky, too."

"Yeah I suppose, but right now I want to go put this money in the bank." his brother said. "I can't wait to do some shopping. Let's go to town and look around."

George added, "We have to buy our own school clothes now. But, first we need figure out what we owe for our pigs and their feed. Look at your Project Record to see how much that is. I'll do the same."

They found their dad at the kitchen table. "Dad, this is what we figure we owe you. We're going to head into Wamego and put our checks

328

in the bank," young John said with a grin. "When we come back we'll pay you off."

"Well, thank you boys. You did a good job with your hogs. So tell me, what do you plan to do with the money you have left?"

"I guess we need to go buy some clothes and things." John added, "We're going to be careful how we spend our money."

"Don't forget to put some money back for the Lord."

"We will," George said. *What the heck is tithing anyway?*

As they got into the pickup, John said, "It feels good to feel rich."

Minutes later, John the high school junior and George the freshman-to-be were in town. "We both need to get football shoes, and I want some new school shoes," John said.

In Wamego, they stopped at the First National Bank and made their deposits. Then they headed down the street toward Knostman's Clothing Store. *If they don't have what we need, we can try at Larson's.*

With each step that took him closer to the clothing store, George's concerns about high school grew. *I don't know what color school shoes to get. And do I really want to play football?*

John, on the other hand, had his mind made up. *I need something jazzy, something the girls will like. 'Course, being a football star will help.*

As usual, he tried to use logic to plan his moves. He wanted to wear stylish clothes, like bright colored shirts with bold designs plus flashy shoes. Yep, attention grabbing clothes was the answer. The right pair of jeans, a loud shirt and up-to-date shoes would surely mean success.

Then he thought, *I wonder if J. N.'s cowboy shirt ever got clean.*

John realized he needed trendy footwear similar to that worn by classmates Bob Pinet and Johnny Lichtenhan. *I maybe should get shoes I can shine up to look nice ... like oxbloods. I better get a pair of white bucks ... or maybe blue suedes ... for the dances. I guess if I'm driving the pickup and hauling milk I should have some boots. Can I afford all of this?*

Inside the store, Mr. Harry Knostman greeted them and brought out shoes to try. "Here George," he said, "these blue suedes are quite the rage. Why don't you try them on?"

George slipped his feet into the nearly purple shoes and stood to stare at them in the floor mirror. Sighing, he took a labored walk around the store. Minutes went by. *I wish Mom was here to help me find my toe.* Finally, he realized the shoes did fit, but he wasn't sure about the color.

Without meaning to, he shook his head when Mr. Knostman handed him a box with white bucks. He pulled them on and sat frozen as an Irish Setter. *These look like I'm walking in chicken feathers.*

"Why don't you try on these penny loafers? I sold a couple of pair to freshmen boys this week. I think a lot of kids will have them."

With misgivings, George tried on the black loafers.

"C'mon," his impatient brother said. "Buy something. You can't take all day wondering about one pair of shoes."

That edged George into a decision. His chin moved up and down about a half inch. Like an auctioneer, Mr. Knostman caught the sign. "So you like those, huh, George? Guess I'll wrap them up for you."

George's face went blank … probably meaning yes.

During George's slow walks around the store, his brother bought a pair of white bucks. Now it was time to talk football shoes. John needed a new pair while George decided he'd buy used.

John bought a quality pair of high tops and George left the store with the cheapest, scuffed, well used pair available. They were almost his size. *I wonder if I'll get athlete's foot from these.*

In reality, the fit didn't matter because George didn't play much. Like his shoes, all the football gear initially issued to him was second or third hand. That included a pointed strapless leather helmet without a chin strap. The coaches would find they wouldn't be expecting much out of the school's skinny freshman—and George didn't disappoint them.

YOU CAN'T PUT OFF HIGH SCHOOL

"George David," his mom said through clenched jaws, "there's nothing wrong with you. Quit fretting. You're leaving for school soon, and that's that." She glared some more and added, "Now eat your breakfast before it gets cold."

George understood; when she scowled she was serious. Defeated he forced down a few nibbles lard fried eggs.

"Now just stop worrying," his mom said, as she paced about

wringing her hands. "Go put on your school clothes"

George left the table and shot up to his room. He returned in his new clothes. .

"Oh you look so handsome," his mom said.

Though his stomach churned, he quickly combed a flamboyant loop in the front of his hair and walked toward his ride.

"C'mon, let's go," his brother hollered. "You got a rundown battery or something? High school is like doing the pencil in the swimming pool. Besides, you know some of the kids from Louisville."

"Yeah," said George.

John, the self-important junior, grinned. A *legend in his own mind*, he enjoyed watching his brother struggle. "Stop thinking about dumb stuff; just get in the pickup."

George opened the passenger door and wiped his sleeve across his forehead.

John started the truck and cranked up the radio. From station WIBW in Topeka, singer Johnny Ray sent a tearful song.

Ifff yourrr sweetheartt sends a letter of goodbyeee,
All that's left for you to do,
 Is sit right down and crrrrrrrry…

George stiffened. He could relate to the song. "Turn that thing down, will you?"

His brother switched off the radio and drove out the driveway while their mom watched with bright, shiny eyes.

"When we get to school they'll meet you on the steps and then take you into the auditorium for freshman orientation. They'll tell you everything you'll need to know, including giving you your class schedule, directions and your locker assignment and the lock combo. Pay attention." Then he added, "You'll catch on to how things work."

George nodded.

In short order the three miles of gravel followed by three miles of black top were history and John turned off Lincoln Avenue up into the parking lot behind the school. "Follow me. I'll show you where to go. They'll be waiting for you right up these steps."

George recognized Junior Dornbusch, Tom Schumacher, Laura

Vossloh, Harold Wilson, Phyllis Carley and Nonavee Taylor from Louisville Grade School. *Hey, we're the class of 1954.*

"Hi Augie, do you know what classes you'll get?"

"Not yet, but they'll tell us when we go into the auditorium."

George's stomach flip-flopped.

It wasn't long until the assembled freshmen heard Principal McCormick introduce himself and the faculty sponsors, Mrs. Pitney—also John's freshman class sponsor—Miss Johnson, Mr. Crellin and the Ag teacher, Mr. Stockebrand.

Before long the Class of 1954 had completed its freshman orientation. Everyone then headed off to their first class and to get their books. After what seemed to George to be forever, it was noon.

By lunch time George had learned about the new cafeteria, classrooms, teachers, students, sports teams and had lots of social interaction. For the first time in his life, his limited social graces brought him some uneasy moments.

Since roughly half of George's class was female, he and the other boys experimented with how best to get to know girls they'd never seen before. Some learned, with a little trial and a whole lot of error. The things girls did made for interesting mysteries.

Why do they spend so much time fixing and re fixing their makeup? People say girls spend hours on their hair and that they brush, tease, twist, curl, comb, wash, dry and dye it. How come? Well, at least I know why they don't eat watermelon.

Freshmen boys had much to learn. On the one hand, girls seemed to desire male companionship in an almost frenzied way, while at the same time, they seemed more comfortable giggling among a group of females.

All of this puzzled George. In the end he reckoned sometimes it was better to concentrate on classes and sports and let the girl thing take care of itself.

WE'LL CALL YOU SUNSHINE

Before long George and the other freshmen football hopefuls were on the field finding out what it meant to wear a Red Raider uniform. Practice looked complicated at first, but he would give it a try.

For John's part, he made the first string. John loved football and he played hard and practiced hard. Not physically large for a lineman, about 165 pounds, he took great pleasure in bodily contact. What could be more fun than blocking or tackling an opponent? He was awarded Honorable Mention for All-League that year. Indeed, his day had come. However, the girls didn't seem impressed by his athletic prowess.

Darn, I've got to do something about that.

In contrast, George made an unlikely football player. He could only be listed in the poor-to-awful category, even among the freshmen.

During his time at Wamego Rural High School, George grew from 105 to 145 pounds. Remarkably he only played in varsity games a grand total of five minutes—during his entire four years, at a school with 200 students.

He said he wasn't disappointed. Early on he was convinced he could get mangled playing football. This was proven time after time during practice when his larger than life freshmen classmates, John Simmer and Daryl Campbell, double teamed him and then then piled on.

Eyeing George, Daryl would say to John, "You submarine him and I'll hit him high." George shuddered. *Oh, oh.*

"We'll nail him before he runs down the line," John said with a smile.

Ironically, their efforts to have fun at George's expense, taught him a slide-around movement where he half backed into a block. The form was dismal; still he avoided many bangs and bruises. Did he have great perseverance or was he just a plain stupid? Even George wondered.

He was just a scrub. But he found contentment with his position for he could say he was a football player, even if others might wonder.

The famed big league pitcher and sportscaster Dizzy Dean had a great saying for such situations. "His chances of getting into a game are slim to none."

One blistering hot afternoon, the sweaty Red Raider squad was enjoying a seldom allowed water break. They sat on the dried out grass in the afternoon sun and those who'd been working hard tended to gulp down water to overcome their white, pasty cotton mouth saliva.

"Go easy on the water. Too much can give you stomach cramps,"

Coach Scales said. "We need to work some more on the plays we'll run at the next game. We've got a lot to do, so finish up. I know it's really hot."

"Ah, I like it hot like this," freshman George blurted out. "Yep, I like it hot."

"Oh you do, do you?" the Coach asked, grinning toward his assistant and head basketball coach Butterfield.

"Yeah, the hotter it gets the better I like it," George added.

"Well then, why don't we just call you, 'Sunshine'? And, when we get back to our workout, why don't you take a couple of laps? That'll warm you up some."

So George was branded with a nickname. His outburst brought unwanted notoriety, and didn't help his game a nickel's worth.

Sunshine would earn additional unwanted recognition a couple of weeks later. Though blessed with reasonable intelligence, he sometimes missed the obvious. This time it had to do with his football uniform.

THE MISSING RED PANTS

Before the next to the last game of the season against Highland Park in Topeka, the team held a Thursday practice game under the lights.

"For tonight's scrimmage, wear your khaki practice pants and your red game shirts," the Coach said.

That evening players put on the khaki and red uniforms, then daubed black soot under each eye to cut down on glare. George suited up in his hand me downs. Out of curiosity, he put some soot under his eyes and looked around. *We look classy.*

After calisthenics and for the rest of the evening, he sat at the end of the bench, mostly watching insects fly around the tall light poles, all the while admiring how well the anti-glare black worked. His mind wandered while he sat there for a couple of hours.

The practice game over, George walked lazily into the locker room—not really needing his shower. Unfortunately, that Friday night he came close to getting sent to the shower early, very early.

At the Thursday practice, Coach Scales talked about the Friday game and announced that everyone out for football would make the travelling squad. George couldn't contain himself. "I get to go," he whispered to himself.

A half-grin crossed his face. *And after the game, we'll eat at the Ira Price Cafe in North Topeka.*

Unfortunately, for George, the trip had a down side. It started Friday afternoon while the players chaotically gathered their gear and boarded the bus. In the corner, George aimlessly pulled his gear from his locker and stuffed his socks, shoes, a towel, jock strap, shirt and shoulder pads into the legs of his khaki uniform pants. This made a perfect carrying bag. Most players strapped their helmets to the top of the neat parcel. George had to carry his helmet—no chin strap.

He should have looked around. Unfortunately, he didn't.

No one noticed George was the only one on the bus with khaki pants. In the Highland Park visitor's dressing room again no one noticed one lone Wamego Red Raider player was not wearing red pants. Then the team ran onto the field.

George and his khaki pants stood out like a streaker on the fifty-yard line. When Coach Scales approached with a concrete frown, George's red face matched the missing pants.

The bewildered Coach spoke to George—and not too politely. That would be the last conversation between the two for the rest of the season. "Why in the name of heaven did you bring those khaki pants?"

The pitiful freshman shook his head. In the background he heard chuckles. "I just thought … we had a choice."

Thank goodness, the game was about to start, for George escaped further scolding. Never again would he wear an improper uniform.

In fact, uniforms turned out to be highly important to him, for he spent the majority of his adult life trimmed out in the immaculate uniform of the Unites States Air Force. He had learned, the hard way.

As far as football went, it would be his senior year before George made the traveling squad again. By then Coaches Scales and Butterfield had moved on to other schools. Coach LeRoy Dawson had come and gone and Coach Joe Pollom headed the football program, assisted by head basketball Coach Paul Markham.

What happened to George's off-white, chipped and scratched, elongated, genuine cowhide practice helmet, with no chinstrap? Well, the school finally bought new helmets for the varsity and George got a faded red, chipped and scratched, squatty, genuine plastic practice helmet—with a chinstrap!

His brother's football career bore no resemblance to his. John did well throughout his four years at WRHS.and he got the athletic letters to prove it.

TWENTY-SEVEN

THE FOOTBALL HERO, DODGING THE STRIPES AND THANKS FOR ASKING

[*Wamego Reporter: November 9, 1950*] ~ Wamego Drops Game ~ Wamego High failed to hold the Hayden Wildcats ... in a game that ended 27-12. In the second half, Wamego scored its second touchdown when John Burgess, Red Raider guard, picked up a fumble and carried it to the 8-yard line. John McKinnon then carried it over.

1950

THE FOOTBALL HERO

The highlight of John's football career had to be his junior season. He played first team pulling guard in Coach Scales' double-wing formation. John played in the middle of the line and, unless a play went through his spot, he ran left or right to lead the play and block the defensive end.

He reveled in bursting full speed directly at the defender. John tried to sneak from behind the biggest of Wamego linemen, tackles, and appear with stealth and momentum. A good blocking job sent the defender to the ground with John on top.

Often however, the opponent outweighed him by 20 pounds and made his job tough. Still, the junior liked to mix it up and he often found himself on the ground in a massive pile-up. The tangle of arms and legs might include the defensive end, the ball carrier and perhaps a linebacker or two, and on some occasions, a handful of other players who congregated at the ball. In these cases, since John arrived at the impact point first, he normally ended up at the bottom of the heap.

A good example occurred during the mighty Haskell Institute Fighting Indians game. Native American players from around the country boarded at the Lawrence School.

The star Haskell player was a mature-looking halfback named Skinadore (Skinindore?). Many compared him to the Indian athletic hero, Jim Thorpe, who had attended Haskell for a period. The rumor was Skinadore had played for Haskell a lot more than four years and he looked the part. He had blazing speed and bulging muscles. It was this player who taught John a valuable football lesson.

During the game someone fumbled. John pounced on the ball first. "I got, I got it."

His words were drowned out by loud smacks and thumps as player after player pounced on top. John cradled the ball against his belly, pleased with his recovery. With the play over—he thought—he relaxed. Skinadore grabbed the ball and jerked it away. When the referees got a glimpse they ruled, "Haskell's ball!"

John vowed never to relax again. By the way, the game ended with the Indians scalping Wamego 20-0 … at least that's what the 1951 Wamego High's Yearbook reported.

It should be said that during the season, the Red Raiders won some games and played well enough against Jayhawk League opponents to finish with a 5-4 record.

Besides Haskell, the Red Raiders struggled against two of the Topeka schools with larger enrollments and much bigger players. The Catholic Hayden School had two tackles over 200 pounds, an almost unheard of weight in those days. John's friend and classmate Ross Worden, Jr. was the biggest Wamego player. He played tackle at 190.

At Wamego's home game against Hayden a player fumbled. John, playing defensive linebacker, he grabbed the ball on a bounce and tore for the goal. The run was about 40 yards. As he labored along, several faster Wamego players caught up with him. A couple passed him.

Fullback John McKinnon ran alongside for a few yards yelling, "Hand me the ball, Burgess. Hand me the dang ball."

What if we muff it? I'm almost there.

Whack!

A Hayden player crashed John to the ground on the eight yard line. He didn't fumble, but neither did he score.

For three plays in a row, the irritated McKinnon slammed into the Hayden defense, gaining about two yards per play. On the fourth try he plunged toward the small hole John and Junior opened in the big Hayden line. McKinnon rammed ahead. Colliding helmets and pads whacked and crashed together amid the sounds of "Oofs," "Uuuhs" and "Ahhhhs."

Pulling guard John, set and ready to bust some noggins....

"Touchdown!"

McKinnon, nose bleeding, face scratched and helmet knocked over his left ear, had indeed scored by inches. Wamego now had a touchdown and the big fullback had words.

"You bonehead, why didn't you hand me the ball? Everybody can out run you, backwards."

"I thought I could make it"

McKinnon wiped the blood from his nose on his sleeve, shook his head, glared and walked away.

There would be other occasions when John could be left red faced on the football field. Interestingly, off the field he had even more.

A RIDE BACK

During that year, John had the privilege of driving the slick, green '40 Ford flatbed pickup to school every day. His folks gladly let him drive. Each day he delivered some 35-45 gallons of milk to the Haas Dairy Plant. At the plant, across from the Wamego city park, he and his brother would leave the milk and pick up four or five empty 10-gallon milk cans to take home. These empties cut short one of John's most delicious pranks.

During one noon hour, he and Myron Flinn drove the pickup downtown and had a hamburger. They then cruised Wamego's downtown a couple of times and spotted classmate Janice Bigford walking up the hill.

John pulled over to the curb. Myron said, "Hey, Janice c'mon and hop in. We'll take you back to school."

"Oh, goody," she said.

Myron let Janice slide into the center. John drove north when Martina Elder and Jo Ann Macht flagged him down.

"Can you give us a ride back to school? We're in a hurry."

"Sure, hop in the back. There's isn't room inside," John said.

The two climbed up to stand beside the array of empty milk cans for the two block ride. John drove right past the school. After about a half mile, he turned up the Old Louisville road with Martina and Joan voicing increasing irritation and doing a steady tom-tom on the top of the cab.

John sped on, grinning at his success. In the side mirror he could see that Martina in particular seemed quite animated. She kept shaking her fist at him and mouthing hard to understand words.

"Take ... us back ... or toss ... these ... cans," she yelled.

It's a bluff. He grinned and shifted into high gear. In the back, Martina started tossing off the ten gallon cans.

John slid the pickup to a halt and ran back to pick up of the cans, one of which had lost it lid and another now displayed a badly flattened side. The young driver quickly reloaded the cans and said "Dad is going to kill me. I'll take you back. Can't you take a joke?"

"Well," Martina said, "pull that stunt again, and I'll be the one doing the killing."

John turned around while Martina and Joan fumed. Janice gulped and Myron grinned.

Reckless driving? Not exactly, but—

DODGING THE STRIPES

Driving the pickup home after school John and George headed north out of Wamego on Highway 99. The low afternoon sun shone on fields of ripened corn and turning leaves. The puffy clouds moved slowly across the blue sky. A big bay horse looked across a fence toward the pickup. John eyed the highway.

I wonder if I can drive between those dotted lines. With a crooked smile, he nodded toward the centerline. "Bet I can drive between these dashes."

"What are you talking about? What if a car comes along?"

"There isn't a car in sight. If someone shows up, I'll slow down. Bet I can do 60 between 'em."

He slowed to 20 miles-per-hour and gently turned left. The pickup passed precisely between to two sets of short, white strips. A right turn sent it adjusting through the lines in the other direction. He added speed and turned left and then right.

"Hey, this is a gas."

Increasing speed to 30 he did a successful quick left-right-left-right. John then tried it at 35; this time the pickup rocked slightly and tires gave a gentle tomcat's call.

With a laugh, he eased into another series of zigs and zags. "Wooie., look at that. Should I go faster?"

George kept silent. *He's nuts.*

"Ha, that was easy. Now watch this."

As he revved to about 45 mph the pickup started rocking and rolling. The tires now sounded like a pair of laughing hyenas.

"Slow down you primate," George shouted.

John ignored the warning. He stepped on the accelerator to over 50 and the light pickup careened left and right. No longer missing the white stripes, it rolled up on two wheels just short of tipping. The tires screamed and laid half-moon rubber strips.

George dropped to the floorboard. *He is off his rocker.* "Slow down you goof ball. You're going to turn this thing over."

To George's relief—maybe John's too—the speed dropped and the pickup settled down on all four tires. At that moment, Ora Bowman came out of nowhere heading in the opposite direction. He'd seen the whole stunt.

As he drove by he stared at John, as if to say, "Are you an idiot or something?" George would have answered.

"Shoot, that was Ora. Could he tell who we were?"

"Do you know anybody else who drives a light green pickup?" George grumbled, climbing back into the seat. "And what's this we stuff? Take me home."

Ora must not have mentioned this to the boys' dad. In any event, John's only scolding came from his brother.

John was growing up fast, but was his maturing keeping pace? And as for George, he was maturing slower, and as such had his own growing problems—maybe more serious.

THANKS FOR ASKING

Should I get a date for the Pigskin Prom?

The school schedule forced his hand. The first prom of the year was coming up. George procrastinated.

Fate stepped in a week later. Hurrying to class, he turned a corner and literally knocked down another freshman. Smack! "Whoops!" On the terrazzo sat a ruffled Patty Klinkenbeard.

"Oh my gosh," George said. "Are you hurt?"

"A little," Patty said with a wounded look. "Why don't you look where you're going?"

"I didn't mean to run into you. Can I help you?"

Patty shook her head. She rose and smoothed out her dress. George picked up her books. "Here are your things. I'm really sorry."

Patty said, "I'm guess I'm alright. It wasn't your fault."

Without warning she batted her brown eyes and tossed her head in a half-circle up and to the right. Her brunette hair fluttered, not unlike Tony the Pony's mane at full gallop.

"Do you want to take me to the Prom?" Patty asked.

George's heart jumped. *Is this the way it's supposed to work?*

Patty said, "I guess I'd like to go. Thanks for asking."

Did I?

When the day came, George sat beside his mom as she drove them to Patty's farmhouse. "Go get your date," his mom said.

George did as instructed and soon returned with Patty. He opened the '48 Chevy's door and tipped the front seat forward. He joined Patty in the backseat.

The fourteen-year-old noticed that Patty was studying her fingernails; so he studied his shoelaces. Finally he spoke, "So, Patty, did you all have a good wheat harvest?"

George got a hurried glance from Patty … and a similar one from his mom. *Maybe she didn't get the question.*

"You know George, Patty might like to talk about something besides farming," his mom said. "Where did you get that pretty dress?"

"Oh," Patty said, "my Mom and I made it from material we got in Manhattan. It took us a couple of weeks."

"Well, it certainly is pretty. What do you think, George?"

"Huh? Oh yeah … it's pretty."

By the time the couple entered the gym they were mouthing words, although Patty struggled to deal with his strange comments. Then all of the sudden she said, "I liked making cauliflower soup in Home EC. My favorite class is English."

"English, huh?" George asked. *English?*

Before Patty could reply, someone turned on the phonograph and the dancing started. George and Patty danced with mistimed steps to the lilt of *Moonlight Serenade.* By the time the couple figured out how to avoid tripping each other the music ended.

The next song might have signaled how the date was going. *Comin' In On A Wing And A Prayer*, fit George's feelings to a Tee.

As they sat down George carried the conversation to the *rigors of acne.* By now, Patty decided a clumsy dance was preferable to a discussion about face pustules. As another tune started, she jerked George to his feet and led him out onto the floor.

After the dance, his mom drove them back to Patty's home. The torture ended with another quick "thanks for asking" and a quiet "you're welcome." George's mom had little to say.

George and Patty had no more dates but became friends.

On the positive side, George gained some confidence. He'd broken the date barrier for sure. And, it wouldn't be long until he'd meet the girl of his freshman dreams.

TWENTY-EIGHT

DATING ADVICE, SWEATY CHOICES AND BOGUS SHIN SPLINTS

[*Westmoreland Recorder* – March 26, 1950] ~ MISSING HORSE FOUND ~ Bob Paxton has recovered his pinto horse. Believe it or not the animal came home after an absence of eleven days. Named Betty, the mare turned up missing on March 10th and though Bob drove the area, he found no sign of her.

"I can't imagine where she was for all that time, but she was skinny and had scraped legs and knees. I don't know, but maybe she fell down an old well or into a hole and had to dig her way out," Bob said. "Still, I don't see how a horse could do that."

1950

DATING ADVICE

Man, I really acted dumb with Patty, George thought.

"You just have to be a gentleman," said the smiling Melvin Wille. Standing nearby Jim Bates nodded his agreement.

The next day when George walked back into the school after Ag class, freshman classmate Nonavee asked, "Do you know Regina Kuhn from English class?"

"Yeah, she sits behind me."

"Well, she kind of likes you," Nonavee said. "Why don't you ask her to go out?"

After his friend walked away George thought, *Regina is sure pretty and she lives here in town.* His psyche flip-flopped. *But I feel awkward.* .

At a class assembly, the very prim and proper Mrs. La Vern Griffeth, the freshman English and Speech teacher solved part of his problem. "Today, we're going to learn how to formally introduce one another. There is a proper way. You'll see."

Most of the class looked at each other and shook their heads. Others listened with great interest.

George's mind drifted. *Look at that, Steve Bressler has a self-winding watch. Who ever heard of such a thing? Wonder if we'll ever have battery powered ones.* His teacher spoke again. She instructed that the gentlemen be presented to the ladies by saying; "Bobsy, may I present Delbert Eckart, and Delbert this is Bobsy Brockish."

She then explained how to ask for permission to speak to someone. "You say, 'Excuse me, may I please speak with you?'"

George, now back to the subject at hand, joined his classmates as they practiced the words, and then role played the introductions. *This is going to be something.*

He watched Judy Sebring introduce Walt Foresman to RaEtta Chrest. Then Connie Wilburn introduced Bill Ewing to Barbara Shane and Jerald Wille introduced Kenneth Dinger to Ann Hosler. Ray Vogl introduced Paul Hansen to Bernardine Weixelman. They did reasonably well.

Kay Enlow introduced John Riat to Patty Brant, Jerry Ross introduced Gailyn Hinson to Lois Johnson and Ruth Ann Guilfoyle introduced Don Eichem to Marianne Holdren.

"And now George, why don't you introduce Jake Hecker to Mary Sable? And, Paul Wayne Henningsen to Florence Blankley."

Oh no! Feeling flush, George did his best but stumbled through the task. *I wish someone would introduce me to Regina.*

After class, Marilyn Tibbetts, Peggy Fouraker, Yvonne Hieger and LaRita Dinger walked by and he desperately wanted to ask them to make the introduction, but he didn't have the nerve. Behind them walked Joanne Throop, Bernice Thomas and Jaenetta Rowe but again George thought, *I can't ask for help; I'll make a fool out of myself.*

Finally George mustered his courage and walked down the hall toward Regina's locker. His breath was ragged, but he plowed ahead. "Excuse me; may I please speak with you for a moment?"

Regina looked surprised, and pleased at the same time. She'd been in the class. She nodded yes. George continued.

"Er … would you like to meet me at the theatre Saturday afternoon? We could sit together. *My Blue Heaven* with Betty Grable and

Dan Dailey is playing, and there'll be another episode of the Dick Tracy serial."

"Oh, thank you," Regina said with a smile. "The movie sounds like fun. I'll meet you there for the matinee."

George nodded and walked away. *I'm afraid to look back. Wow, I've gotten another date. She is such a lady.*

When Saturday rolled around he needed a ride. *It's getting late; I should have talked to the folks sooner. I feel like a sap.*

Luckily young John had year book duty so he said he'd drop George at the theater and he could ride home with the folks that night.

His brother said, "I hear you have a date with Regina Kuhn. Is that right?" George nodded yes.

"Well let's get going. You don't have much time. I'll do your chores tonight."

Whew. Maybe he isn't such an ogre.

Soon the green pickup charged down the road.

"That's swell of you for taking me in. Thanks."

John nodded and said, "You'll be able to see your chums after you walk Regina home."

As they arrived in front of the movie house, there was Regina. When George hopped out, she smiled. The two turned to the admission window and when George plunked down the 24 cents for two afternoon tickets, Regina smiled again.

The ads had started as the two entered the darkened theater and an FTD Floral commercial explained how easy it was to wire flowers to love ones. *Do you suppose girls like flowers?*

As the serial began, the couple sat like totem poles—eyes straight ahead.

Finally the feature film started. *Should I have bought her Milk Duds?* An hour and a half later, the movie ended with a love scene during which George and Regina sat like lumps. In the end the rendezvous went well. George thought, *I like the way she smells.*

Freshmen George and Regina went to more picture shows, sometimes had ice cream and attended a couple of dances. He'd ride into town with his brother, but there was a drawback to this.

Since George's dates didn't last as long as his brother's, George often had to sit on the curb in front of Murphy's Drug Store long after he'd walked Regina home. On one occasion, George spent two hours, watching the moths circle the Lincoln Avenue street lights while Dude Cutright, the town constable, slowly circled downtown in the tan police car. Other times George dozed in freezing temperatures until his ride returned to pick him up. *I don't understand why he does this to me. He makes me downright sore.*

Unfortunately for George, before the school year was out, Regina and her family moved away from Wamego. He was sad when Regina left, but he would always have fond memories of her.

SWEATY CHOICES

As dating progressed for John and George during the next couple of years, concerns about how to dress surfaced. What clothes were best and in what colors? Jeans and slacks with a snappy sport shirt worked well on regular dates.

"So George, where did you find your hand-me-downs?" Bubba Brockman asked the night George showed up at a dance wearing muted green checked pants and a light yellow striped shirt. "You look like you've been in a paint mixer."

"Yeah," George answered. "Guess I made a mistake." *Why didn't Mom say something?*

For the rest of his first two years he wore jeans and his favorite red shirt. Some of the boys solved the problem by wearing their blue corduroy FFA jackets with a white shirt and black tie. That was about as dressy as it could get.

George wearing his red shirt, rolled up Levi's and his argyle socks.

347

For dances like the Junior Senior Prom—no tuxedos allowed in tiny Wamego—boys wore sport coats and ties and the girls wore inexpensive formals. Many boys showed up in blue suede shoes, gray trousers and navy blue jackets. All girls had some kind of long dress.

George went to some dances after football games. At the Junior Senior Prom, his brother wore his very first sport jacket, purchased for $15 off the sale rack at Larson's. It had a dubious color perhaps, but its owner felt he looked handsome in the light chocolate brown coat, wearing a white shirt, with a dark brown tie, tan slacks, and of course, brown socks and white buck shoes. Just great.

Fortunately, the prom would turn out to be low-key. He'd dragged his feet about asking for a date, but finally realized classmate Burma Brothers—she'd just broken up with somebody—was available. She said she'd be glad to go. John had his clothes and only needed to go to the florist for what turned out to be an expensive corsage. Burma got him a carnation boutonniere.

When John entered Burma's home to pick her up she wore a beautiful pale-purple, delicate looking floor-length dress. He stared as she came forward and pinned on his flower. His brown jacket decreased the value of the flower. Proudly, she stepped back to receive her corsage

Why do girls wear so little on top and a skirt all the way to the floor?

With relief, Burma helped him pin on the corsage and soon the couple grandly entered the well-decorated gym, resplendent with crepe paper streamers and lights showing red and blue through tissue paper. The long anticipated prom featured the grand Matt Benton Band, all the way from Manhattan. The music was great and so were the dances. The John and Burma date—their only one—included plenty of laughter and unusually pleasant conversation. The twosome had fun and before they knew it the Prom was over.

In the lot behind the gym, John opened the pickup door for Burma and helped gather her long dress. When he hopped in the driver's seat he asked, "You want to go get a coke? I think the Café is still open."

Burma agreed. Minutes later they walked in on a colorful scene of other prom couples. John slid into a booth and Burma followed, pulling her gown behind her. Burma ordered a cherry-coke and John had a green river. Neither said much; time seemed to drag.

"Let's go take a ride," John said as he slurped up the last of his soda through his straw.

His date nodded her approval and soon the pickup headed north on Lincoln Avenue. Just before the high school, John turned left and a few blocks later they cruised along the Wamego Cemetery. With a grin, John turned in and drove slowly around the several curving lanes between the tombstones.

Finally, he pulled into a well used parking spot across the street from the town's water tower. Both boy and girl stared toward the golf course. *I wonder what George would think if he saw my inertia.*

Without too much enthusiasm, John scooted closer to Burma. As he did, a revelation hit. *Too much light.*

Without missing a beat, he turned his face into a sad scowl, and waited for Burma to react. In a whisper he said, "We just can't stay here. See that tombstone right next to your door? It belongs to a relative."

The engine came to life and the pickup slowly inched on down and around the lane, finally stopping in a much darker location, shadowed by a banking family's giant stone mausoleum. It also appeared to be far from deceased relatives. Now was the time for intimate conversation.

It must be said that the Burma-John tryst was far from outstanding. Neither felt any sparks. In fact, it wasn't long before John said, "Burma, I hate to tell you this, but my relatives have taken the fun out of this. Do you mind if I take you home?"

Burma quickly replied, "It is kind of creepy here. Let's go."

So the date, while pleasant over all, didn't progress into romance. The two remained friends and always had happy greetings for each other.

Over time, while John developed more and more confidence about dates and dances, George still had a mind full of questions.

Are you supposed to dance every dance?

Like most, George enjoyed the slow songs like *Stardust* or *Moonlight in Vermont.* One, two, one. One, two, one.

Cheek to cheek is for steadies. This is my first dance with Anna Harmer, so I'd better not step on her feet. Timidly he led them around the dance floor and watched some boys dip their partners.

George liked to dance, better than the wallflowers that sat like frozen roosters on one side of the room while across the floor a bevy of the girls waited. Many of the boys were chewing Double Bubble and showing off their skills with their freewheeling yo-yos. But not dancing.

All the while, Wamego Photography owner, Harry 'Beag' Beagler kept snapping pictures for the school's yearbook, the *Wa-Kaw*. Beag photographed all manner of events—often with his camera's lens cap on.

While the photographer took pictures, boys and girls interacted, sometimes with good results.

Happily, for the Burgess boys and their friends, they'd eventually find the answers. George still frequented the Belvue Truck Stop.

Beyond finding a girl that liked him, a real test for a boy was finding a girl who would have empathy with him and his many problems.

Can I find a girl to nurse my football aches? John wondered.

THE PAIN OF SPORTS

"Ouch," John said, a little louder than necessary. "Man oh man that hurts. It's like old Dracula bit into my back and legs."

He bent in apparent pain to reach his chemistry book at the bottom of his locker. "Oh this is painful."

With big compassionate eyes, Bonnie Cornelius looked his way. "Oh, you poor fellow; football is so rough."

"Do you hurt a lot?" Janice Sauer asked? "Your face looks scratched, too."

Many other junior class girls looked on with sympathy. However, Martina Elder—who knew the score—said "Ladies, stay away from that guy, he's on the prowl." Several girls laughed and walked away.

John sighed. *They just don't know how much I'm suffering.*

He limped along the hall toward class. *I have to look dismal. The girls need to know how badly I got banged up Friday night against the Washburn Ichabods.*

Wamego had won so the bruises and aches were minor, but why not milk the situation?

In truth, some of Wamego's football players did get really hurt and sustained season ending leg injuries or ankle sprains. Track runners could get bruises and sprains as well.

Runners wore shoes with sharp needle spikes under the front sole, with no heel spikes, which forced the trackmen to run totally on the balls of their feet, in the realm of Wanda's Blackjack 4-H Club toe-dancing.

After football and basketball seasons ended it was time to hit the cinders. During his first season, shin splints did hit George like a ton of bricks and lasted about two weeks, but he learned to live with the pain.

John said, "I'll do field events. Who wants to run all day anyway?" He chose the javelin.

BOGUS SHIN SPLINTS

The first Saturday morning after a full week of track, when he got up John bumped his way down the stairs.

"Yoweee," he said when he reached the first floor where his folks listened. He limped into the living room. His sisters gasped.

"Dad, I don't know if I can help with chores this morning. My shins are pretty sore."

"That is just part of sports," his dad said. "Let's go."

His mom said, "Walk it off."

Well, darn. Maybe I'll get some sympathy when I get to school on Monday.

A couple of days later, George watched his brother hobble toward class with girls on each side. *I don't believe what I'm seeing.*

John limped and groaned. "Oh, you look hurt. May I help you?" longtime friend Georgette Talley asked.

"It is okay, Georgette," John said. "It's just my legs and calves. Track takes a lot out of you."

"What can I do?"

"Do you want to sort of massage the calf muscles?"

Kindly Georgette knelt beside him and began rubbing. Joan Machin walked up and said, "Poor guy. Is that helping?"

"It's better, but I'm having trouble keeping my balance."

"Here let me steady you," Joan said.

"What are you two doing with that jerk?" Martina asked when she walked by. "He's just putting you on. You know he's a big show off."

Why does she always have to show up at moments like this?

"Oooh, Teeny, you just don't know my suffering." In short order he overacted and his nurses started going off duty.

However, within a couple of weeks, John started limping again. He suffered shin splints on three separate occasions that track season—as a javelin thrower!

§

We had our share of work and sports related injuries. They lurked everywhere, for humans and for animals. Coyotes continued to be a menace for our small animals. Chas and Bob Burgess and their nephews did their best to cut down on the varmint numbers, but it would take a mass of hunters to reach real success, and that could be dangerous as well.

TWENTY-NINE

COYOTE ROUNDUP, FLOOD OF THE CENTURY AND ST. SOMETHING OR OTHER

[*Wamego Times-May 12, 1951*] JUNE HILL SERVING LAST YEAR

Miss June Hill looked around the high school study hall as she said, "My job? Well, I guess you'd call it herding kids!"

June, now in her last year at WHS, started out in the old school building. She first kept records, later kept study hall, and then was librarian. June has served in the new high school building since 1938, ever since it was built.

The student body holds June in high esteem. In 1949 the WaKaw staff dedicated the annual to her.

1951

COYOTE ROUNDUP

One way to rally the troops was through the coyote roundup. It drew many avid hunters on many a Sunday afternoon. A Roundup was simple. It began with teams of hunters surrounding a section of land—one mile in each direction—who then walked toward each other. As they moved forward, they pressured the coyotes into a smaller area. When the animals tried to run for it, they could be dispatched safely with shotguns.

During one February Sunday afternoon, John decided to join in a roundup. He drove over to Bob Smoot's farm and parked among the many cars and trucks. A couple of older neighbors nodded hello and others voiced greetings. His schoolmate Bubba Brockman, however, wanted some answers.

"Hey lunkhead, you gonna mess up this hunt like you usually do?" Bubba asked as he wiped his runny nose on his sleeve.

"I'll be fine. As for you, don't forget we're hunting coyotes."

A dozen others climbed into a one and a half truck bed. The truck drove into the crisp afternoon. A brown thrush flew across the road at eye level and a group of fall Hereford calves raced along inside Smoot's pasture fence trying to outrun the slow moving truck.

About then the truck started dropping off people every few yards. Soon all the hunters were on the ground and the entire four mile perimeter was covered. In the distance, someone fired and the hunt was on.

Just as the John's group crossed through the pasture fence, a farmer yelled, "There goes one down that draw!"

Someone else hollered, "Stay spread out so it can't double back."

The hunters worked their way forward. As they did a few shotguns popped, not necessarily at coyotes, but at rabbits, hawks and even meadowlarks. A few impatient oddballs seemed predisposed to kill. Name calling and frowns didn't stop the bad apples.

The unnecessary shooting did slow as the square got smaller. Soon the shots were aimed at coyotes and a few did fall.

Besides coyotes, many other pests helped themselves to the feed farmers had for other animals. Creatures like rats, mice, blackbirds, starlings, and sparrows thrived. Blackbirds and starlings multiplied when they had access to cattle or hog feedlots. They would swoop down by the hundreds to feast on the grain meant for livestock. Sparrows always found their way into the granary.

Future Farmers of America (FFA) chapters held contests for eradicating pests. There was a bounty of a penny a sparrow. The reasoning was that there were hungry people in the world and that those individuals needed feeding before rats and birds. Farmers did their part.

It was time consuming and a constant battle of man against pest. However, something occurred that year that turned community focus from normal work, eradicating pests and enjoying leisure time to … survival.

FLOOD OF THE CENTURY

The summer of 1951 was noteworthy for a lot of reasons, but rainfall in particular. There was rain, rain and more rain. Many farmers planted late, lost stands of corn to standing water and couldn't get into wet fields to cultivate.

Toward the end of June, rain fell in torrents within the Smoky Hill and Republican River watersheds that drained thousands of square miles. By the time these two rivers joined to form the Kaw near Junction City, they neared flood stage … and the water kept on rising.

More rains came and as much as 16 inches fell in the days from July 9th to July 13th. On the latter date, the Kaw reached its highest level on record and turned out to be the most destructive flood in Kansas history. The waters rose high enough to crest *above* all the official flood gauges located along its banks at places like Manhattan, Wamego, Topeka, Lawrence and Kansas City. In many locations, the water exceeded old high-water marks by more than five feet.

In Manhattan, fifteen miles west of Wamego, the muddy water flowed eight feet deep along the downtown's main street and for years afterward businesses featured high-water lines painted on their walls. One picture of the time—sometime after the crest had passed—showed a fellow in a boat feeding a parking meter.

On July 13, 1951 a total of 1,074,000 acres in Kansas and 926,000 acres in Missouri were flooded. Topeka evacuated about 24,000 people and at Kansas City water poured over the top of levees and some houses had water to their eaves. There, around 15,000 people were sent to higher ground. The flood devastated the Kansas City Stockyards. The facility would be reconstructed in part for a few more years use.

At the Burgess farm, Rock Creek flooded the lower fields and swept away or mashed down a sizeable acreage of corn and sorghums. The promise of good crops diminished each day.

"If we can't get in to cut that wheat it's all going to be lost," the boys' dad said. "Lord … we thank you for the rain, but you know we don't really need this much."

Some dry days did follow. On one of those days the boys' dad said, "Let's go try to combine the hillside of that acreage by Wally's. That should be the driest ground. The low part is probably still too wet."

Once young John pulled the combine the mile and a half to the rented ground, his dad took over and drove into the top part of the field with the combine running full blast. After a few feet he stopped and shut things down. He reached into the combine's grain bin and scooped up a handful of newly threshed wheat.

"This grain is still a bit damp," he told his sons.

"How much will they dock the price?" John asked his dad.

"Hard to say, but, they'll have to. It'll need some drying."

"Are you going to go ahead and cut?" George asked.

"Yes, and after I fill the combine bin the first time, you pull the trailer up so I can empty it. Then take that home and shovel it into the empty granary and come back. That wheat will be hog and chicken feed."

"Okay," George said. *Here we go again, I shovel and John rides.*

"John, after I get George going, I want you to do the combining. We'll fill up the truck and I'll take the grain to town and see if I can get us the best price."

For the rest of the day the harvesting continued with the hot sun now drying the grain a bit more each hour. By the third day, the entire hillside was stubble.

"Okay John, let me take it around this low section. I walked out in there a ways and the ground seems pretty solid for the most part."

The John Deere and combine duo made a pass along the outside of the patch of uncut wheat. So far so good. Another trip followed and then more. Then it happened.

Not far from the center of the patch, the combine tandem dual wheels started to ball-up with mud and straw. Soon the left wheels locked up and started to drag along. The load got heavier and the John Deere's big 38" rear tires started to spin and dig in. Soon the heavy combine settled onto its frame and tractor mired to the drawbar.

George, sensing what needed to be done, backed the lighter AC to about twenty feet in front of the John Deere. He hooked a log chain— every farm had one or more—between the two tractors.

With a nod from his dad, both tractors tried to move forward with no luck. By now the mucky-wet soil was even with the top of the John Deere's rear axle and the AC was mired as well.

"Hold it. Come help me unhook the combine and we'll try to get the tractors free."

Without the combine, the two tractors tried again. No luck. Both just mired deeper.

Fortunately, across the road, John Habluetzel and his son Buddy had just finished cutting one of their fields—the same one in which the *Great Tractor Race* had run. They came over, one driving the John Deere B and the other with their AC.

"Let us give you a hand," said Mr. Hableutzel. "Keep your AC chained to your John Deere and we'll chain our two ahead of that."

It worked and within ten minutes the line of four tractors was on solid ground. Next the foursome pulled the combine at right angles and brought it to dry ground. Hooray … except for the seven or eight acres that never got cut that year.

The boys' dad thanked the Hableutzels and said, "We owe you."

The summer of 1951 was a disaster for many towns. Manhattan was devastated and would take months to get back to normal. The same in Kansas City. Gloom surrounded the communities for a hundred miles. The Burgess family got off light, but they had empathy for the less fortunate, and helped neighbors where they could.

Still, for some there were good things to report. The County Fair was held on schedule although many potential participants couldn't leave their farm work.

John and his friend Myron Flinn didn't have projects in '51; however, at the Fair they garnered prizes of far greater value than all of their precious blue ribbons.

FAIR GIRLS

Early evening of the third day of the Fair, Myron drove his family's maroon Ford sedan over to pick John up. Off they went, saying they were taking a break from farming and planned to enjoy the Fair.

The two boys headed over to Highway 99 and then headed north. They eased off north on the Wheaton Road, turned east on the Hartwich Road and then north again on the sanded Onaga Road.

"So you think there will be any good looking dollies up there?" Myron asked.

"Maybe. There are bound to be some."

"What's our plan when we meet 'em?" Myron asked.

"Well, we'll check them out and go from there."

For the next few minutes both boys seemed lost in thought. Then John asked, "How much money do you have?"

"Six dollars and six bits," Myron answered.

"I have five dollars and eighteen cents," John said.

A few miles later as Myron parked he said, "Dang. I just realized this is the last night. It's do-or-die."

So the hunt was on for a couple of young looking Betty Grables. John and Myron left the car and walked toward the carnival. Winking fireflies surrounded them as they neared the midway, a sea of booths and rides, lights and the movements of people. Summer dust lingered in the slowly cooling air.

The scene vibrated with loud speaker music, voices and laughter. The smell of popcorn, and frying onions and hamburgers mixed with the dust. From the far end of the midway came the sound of an engine powering the Ferris Wheel, at first revving up and then dropping back when the ride braked to a stop.

The boys walked the area for a few minutes, half-heartedly checking out the booths, though mostly checking for girls.

Several girls strolled up and down the midway, each pretending to find the same attractions ever so interesting.

"Those two over there look pretty good. Do you think they'd fill the bill?" Myron asked.

John spotted the two well groomed girls near the Tilt-A-Whirl. *Both might be close to senior prom quality*. "Yeah," he said. "I'll take the one with the black hair and the smiley one is yours."

Myron made a slow nod and said, "Uh, okay. That smiley one looks mighty nice."

The game of cat and mouse was underway. The boys followed as the girls wandered past four rides and then walked in front of the carnival booths. Smiley made eye contact with Myron, flashed a shy grin, and then did a quick look-away. Next, she and Black Hair found a booth with an array of very interesting beads. They *ignored* the boys.

Finally the boys stopped next to the girls.

"Excuse me," John said in a soft voice, "Do you happen to know the direction to the pig barns?" So much for finesse.

The girls seemed unfazed, pretending the question was well intended. "Yes, the Swine Barn is over there," Black-Hair said.

"Why don't we show you the way," Smiley said.

Later, back at the midway's Milk Bottle Toss, each boy plunked down a dime and started chucking baseballs at pyramids of wooden milk bottles. With grand execution they showed off their pitching abilities. For their part, the girls "oohed" and "awed" at each mighty heave.

"You can sure throw hard," Black-Hair said. In response, John hummed another high hard one toward the bottles. The ball just grazed one bottle. Nothing fell.

"Darn it," he said, "it must have been the wind."

"That's too bad. Why don't you try another one?" Black-Hair asked as she blinked her dark eye lashes.

Down went another dime. Hum went another fastball, and finally bottles shot in all directions.

"Hot dog. Look at 'em fly." *Whew. That was about time.*

John plunked down another dime. Three more tosses knocked the pyramid down again. "Oh, that was wonderful," Black-Hair said.

John dropped another dime and fired away, again with success. "Oh, you're really something," Black-Hair said. "You're won enough tickets to get me that pretty stuffed ape with green eyes and yellow teeth."

John handed her the prize.

"Oh thank you."

"I hope you like it," John said.

"Why, I've never had an ape before."

John smiled and thought, *I hope she's worth it.*

Meanwhile, Myron finally won Smiley a prize, a fine set of laughing teeth in a lidded box. The laughing teeth chattered, and everyone laughed.

The night wore on with lots of walking, talking, and laughing. The moon rose and added light to the scene. The two couples enjoyed cokes, cotton candy and a couple of rides. By now the boys were low on money.

John developed enough courage to ask Black-Hair to go out on real date. Myron asked Smiley and both girls accepted … for the next Sunday afternoon.

Driving home later, Myron agreed to talk his dad out of the Ford again. The trip would be to the girls' hometown of Blaine. The tiny village sat north of Westmoreland on Highway 99.

ST. SOMETHING OR OTHER

Sunday was a warm, cloudless day as the car headed toward Blaine. "Where are they going to meet us?" Myron asked.

"They'll be in front of the big Catholic Church. It's called … uh … St. Something or Other."

"There it is down the street. The girls are sitting in front."

John said, "Look, that mighty steeple is reaching for heaven."

Myron angle parked and Smiley and Black-Hair sauntered toward the car, whispering. Smiley hopped in the front seat beside Myron. John and Black-Hair settled in the back.

Myron started the car and backed out from the curb. He drove around a few blocks until they passed by the Church. After two of these circular trips, John noticed that every time the car cruised in front of the Church, the girls made a sign-of-the-cross.

John found this religious activity intriguing. He knew some Catholics at high school like Donnie Eisenbies, Larry Fechter, Jerry Riat and Johnny Lichtenhan, but he had never seen them doing this.

Humm, he thought. *Better give Myron some driving instructions.*

"Why don't you just drive around another time?"

You guessed it. The girls crossed themselves every time the car passed in front of Church. Myron caught on, put the car on autopilot and drove around and around every 2-3 minutes.

The boys' soon started chuckling and on the 6th or 7th trip, couldn't hold back. John and Myron laughed uncontrollably. This tipped off Black-Hair, who apparently had good sense; so with precise firmness, she suggested it was time to end this *memorable* date.

So with the gigantic St. Columbkilles Catholic Church in the background, Myron headed toward Black-Hair's folks' farm, some two miles from Blaine. Smiley, not so put out about the laughter, rode along for support. Black-Hair scooted far from John, Smiley found Myron's side of the seat preferable.

About half way along on the two-mile trip, Myron reached out for Smiley. The car lurched and looped wide into the ditch. Stuck.

Now the troubled double-date's problems really got exciting. Here sat two guys and two girls inside an immovable car.

Myron looked longingly at Smiley. She frowned. Finally, Black-Hair said, "Jacob Dubinsky's farm is just down the road. He's a good neighbor and will pull you out."

Myron sighed, Smiley frowned, John fidgeted and Black-Hair said, "One of you fellows needs to go ask him for help."

John thought. *I'll feel a pretty dumb, but I guess I should go.* He walked the quarter mile and asked the friendly farmer for assistance. With a smile the farmer fired up his old Farmall and headed toward the stranded car.

"I'm glad you're back," Myron said. "The girls are in a hurry."

John hooked a chain around the Ford's back bumper, and in a minute the car was on the road.

"It is amazing how many boys have problems on this curve … especially when young girls are with them," Mr. Dubinsky said as he left.

Myron drove down the road toward Black-Hair's place with Smiley now scowling from her side of the front seat.

"Thanks," John said as she climbed out.

"For what? I've had more fun cleaning the hog pen."

Guess that didn't work out so well, John thought.

With a defeated look, Myron drove back to Blaine. While John watched from the back seat, he saw his friend grin at Smiley. She returned a scowl. *Better avoid Blaine in the future.*

Meeting Black-Hair and Smiley at the Fair had yielded two angry lasses, a set of laughing teeth in a lidded box, one green eyed stuffed ape and yellow teeth—and two crimson faced baboons!

Oh well, there would be other girls in other places; in the mean time the boys would just have to find something else for amusement.

THIRTY

THE OUTFIELD SWIM, PLAYING IN THE SEWER AND YOU GOTTA SOAK IT

[*Wamego Times* – August 16, 1951] ~ TO TOPEKA MEETING ~

Eustace Trivett, president of the Wamego Chamber of Commerce, and A. E. Garansson, chairman of the Wamego Flood Control Association were among those present for the Flood Control Council of the state C. of C. in Topeka Tuesday. Principles of flood control aimed at uniting different points of view were adopted by the council.

1951

THE OUTFIELD SWIM

While the torrential rains and floods of 1951 forced many activities to play second fiddle, the boys' Louisville youth baseball club again fielded a team though with a short schedule. Still, there was baseball.

On the way home from church on an August Sunday, George stared out the car's open back seat window at the dark and brooding clouds. The air felt muggy and hot and sweat dripped from his nose.

Wiping his nose on his bandanna, George asked, "Dad, do you think our field is going to be dry enough to play on today?"

"Maybe, but that shower during the night didn't help. We'll just have to go check it out. We want to try to get the game in if we can. My guess is we'll have to make special ground rules."

Once home their mom prepared dinner while the boys hung up their church clothes and got into their baseball uniforms—blue jeans and T-shirts. Five-year-old Judy got the bread and three-year-old Joyce carried the butter to the table. Family small talk ceased during the meal.

Once dinner was over, John drove over toward Louisville. "Those clouds look kind of bad, don't they?" he asked.

"Yep, we might end up getting a thunderstorm out of this. If it rains any at all we won't be able to play," his dad said.

At the field, the three got out of the pickup and walked to where their dad's cousin, George Burgess, and his oldest of the 4Ds, Danny, trickled lime from a bag to mark the foul lines. Two other sons, Denny and Deane, raked dry dirt from under the bleachers into a low spot near third base. The work continued with more players arriving, including a carload of the day's opposition from Wamego.

"This field is probably alright to use," the 4Ds dad said. "My boys have dried out the low spot at third and the rest of the infield is okay. But there is quite a little standing water near the right field foul line."

"Yes, it looks okay," Wamego manager Virgil Haas said. "There won't be many balls hit in that direction, and if one does hit the water, we can just go ahead and play it."

"Okay by me," the boys' dad said. "However, I don't think we should play if we get any lightning."

"No, we don't want to take the chance," Mr. Haas said.

"Okay boys, some of you go out into right-center and I'll hit you some flies," the boys' dad said. He tossed a much used baseball up and whacked it out into right. "I got it," Denny said. He threw the ball toward the infield where the Louisville pitcher Crawford Ubel caught it.

Dick Chrest of the Wamego team shagged the next practice fly and his teammate, first baseman Ace Armbrust caught the next one. It was the fourth fly ball that caused the problem.

The boys' dad undercut the ball and it soared higher and higher, reached its peak, veered and started earthward, right above the watery right-field pool. George looked at Denny, at Dick and at Johnny Lolley standing beside him. Nobody moved.

"Okay," George said. "It's mine." After a couple of steps he waded into the puddle. Water soaked his shoes and socks as he steadied himself to make the catch.

Was it the water, the slick, muddy grass or bad lighting? The usually sure outfielder misjudged the ball as it plummeted from the heavens. At the last moment he instinctively dove for the ball.

'Splash.' "Got it!"

As George belly-flopped into the standing water the tidal wave spurted up and away to wet down a couple annoyed players

At arm's length George held up his glove with the ball. He wiped muddy water from his face and wiped his hands on the on the back of his pants.

The rest of the players? They laughed

Cowards, thought George

About ten minutes later it started to pour—another washout.

When George got home his mother asked, "Goodness George, did you fall into a lake?" *If she only knew.*

Even with rainouts that summer, both boys, cousins and friends, enjoyed the baseball they did get to play. They didn't win many games, but they competed. It should be pointed out that George took his *outfield swim* as part of the game. *It could have been worse*, he thought.

§

PLAYING IN THE SEWER

Looking back, the summer of 1951 had been memorable with the flood and saturated soils, the ravaged wheat crop, damped off corn—Black-Hair and Smiley!—and a limited baseball schedule. Still, our family got much of the grain cut—albeit battling the mud—baled bumper crops of hay and alfalfa and brought in an abundance of garden produce. As the summer wound down, only the corn and sorghum crops remained in the fields to mature. Meantime we needed to prepare the ground for next year's crops, but that didn't take three of us to drive two tractors.

§

On one particularly wet day, without hurry or rush, the family sat at the breakfast table. Everyone seemed calm, except for young John. While the others ate popped wheat and milk, he sighed and wiped his brow. Finally he put down his fork and said, "Well, we're pretty well caught up here on the farm, and I was wondering if I could go get an outside job and earn some cash. That way I won't have to ask you for money all the time."

"Yes, I guess that would be nice," his dad said.

His mother stirred her cereal and said, "You need to spend less."

Her son replied "You're right on that, but if I got a job it wouldn't cost you so much."

"Well," his mom said with shining eyes, "Just how are you going to help on the farm and work an outside job, too?"

"I can help on weekends and evenings. If I could get a job to help clean up the flood damage in Manhattan, I'd go to work early."

"Now you listen here young man," his mom stormed back, "You can't burn the candle at both ends. Good grief."

"Now, now you two. Don't get all worked up," John's dad said. "Let's think this thing out."

John and his mom folded their arms across their chests and pursed their lips in obstinate gestures. The two red-heads in the family were at loggerheads again. The girls sat, alarmed, and George kept eating.

"Suppose John did get a job until school starts," his dad said. "It'll only be for a few weeks. George and I could finish the plowing without him. John can help pick corn on weekends if he's needed."

John's face softened, his mom breathed deeply and his dad continued. "Anyway, his having a job would save us some money."

"What about me? George asked. "How do I get some money?"

"We'll give you money for your work here on the farm. Now let's see, how much would that be after we deduct for the cost of your room, your clothes and all the food you eat, and the hole you ripped in the wagon? You know, Veda, that boy might owe us in the long run."

So George got teased and John got permission to go to work for a paycheck for the first time in his life.

The boys' mom thought, *I'm always just amazed how my husband handles these situations.*

That evening John's dad made a phone call to Morton Hollis' dad, Jim, a long time acquaintance who lived in Wamego. Hollis was foreman of a clean-up crew for Walter's Bros. Construction of Manhattan where flood damage had been high.

Yes, Jim said, he needed more workers and would be glad to have young John on his team until school started. The next morning, John met Hollis near St. George at the very early hour of 5:00 a.m. He joined a couple of other Wamego fellows in the back of the Jim's pickup.

The City of Manhattan had contracted with Walters Bros. to clean-out and repair the damaged sewer lines that ran behind the stores and shops underneath the downtown's alleys. Before the flood, the City's storm sewer system had worked well enough. However, when the storm sewer overloaded the excess was diverted into the regular sewer pipes. The most destructive flood of the century had overpowered all drainage.

The surging flood waters had burst the sewers in dozens of places, leaving behind many 10-15 foot deep craters. The huge holes remained like open sores. Now, a month later, at the bottom of these washouts, the sewer effluent flowed, dotted with ugly looking waste. The company's job was to install new sections of sewer pipe, fill in the holes and repave the alleys. First, however, debris and silt needed clearing away.

"Okay Burgess, you, Heckman, Colwich and Jones get them *(expletive)* shovels moving and get rid of the crap the flood washed in here. When the truck has a load you drive it out and unload it," Hollis said.

"Where do I take it?" John asked.

"To the City Dump you dumbbell. It's just across the bridge in Pott. County. You'll find it. And don't take too long. We need to clean this end of the alley so we can get that digger in here."

John and the other laborers did as directed and shoveled drifts of silt, bits of damaged building materials and woody debris into a Reo dump truck. An hour later Ernie Colwich rode along as John drove to the refuse center and dumped the load. Upon return, John backed the truck into the alley where a medium sized Bucyrus-Erie cable shovel worked. It scooped up bits of broken concrete and trash from the washout holes and deposited them into the truck.

Before long, John and Ernie again made the trip to offload the Reo. Back at the site, the cable shovel resumed the loading while workers cleaned up the small rubble.

The work went on and for the first time in his life, John witnessed something he'd never considered. The boss didn't lift a finger to help out.

"Hey," John asked Ernie from the little town of Leonardville, "how come Jim doesn't pitch in? He just stands there all day."

"He's the foreman," Ernie said. "That's what foremen do. They don't do any labor, but just holler and cuss at you. And think up work to keep you busy. It must be a hard job, 'cause foremen get paid extra."

The foreman did indeed keep the crew busy and did a lot of cursing. Finally, in early afternoon, while he leaned against the truck, foreman Hollis pulled out his pocket watch and said, "Okay you sorry yokels, that's it for today. It'll be two o'clock by the time we get to the yard with the truck and gear." He paused, chewed on a wad of Beech Nut Chewing Tobacco and mumbled, "Then you nincompoops can go home."

A half hour later, John dozed off in the back of the pickup on its way east. That became routine for the next several working days. He had reason to be tired. His job was physical and a lot more demanding than driving a tractor. Still, he found the work new and different … and of course he liked the thought of paychecks.

John's new found wealth went for important things like dates. And he bought himself a new cowboy hat.

As his mother had cautioned him not to do, he appeared to be burning the candle at both ends. He worked for Walters Bros. all day, followed that with a couple of hours riding the tractor, did chores and then went out for the evening. Still, the stamina of youth, his enthusiasm for life and his will to achieve kept him going … with catnaps.

One day near the end of the second week, he emptied his sack lunch and curled up in the dump truck's cab for a nap. Just as he dosed off, the heavens opened up and the rain fell in torrents.

The rest of the work crew ran for cover and huddled in doorways. They watched heavy rain splash craters in the many puddles and runoff water surge down the alley several inches deep. Soon the excess water overwhelmed the storm sewer system sending the excess into the main sewer line.

After about 20 minutes, the thunderstorm passed and sunlight gave everything an eerie light. The water roared through the broken sewer line until something blocked the flow.

Foreman Hollis yelled a few expletives and said, "We gotta unplug that pipe." He looked at his four-man labor crew:

"All right, Burgess," he roared, "pick up a length of that rebar and get your sorry rear end down there. Unplug that *(expletive)* hole before we lose our *(expletive)* concrete framing."

"Me?"

"Yes you. Now get going afore that water gets deeper. Don't worry; I'll slip you a little extra come payday."

John grabbed a six-foot rebar and slid down the muddy bank to end up standing in water near knee level. As the runoff swirled around him, he poked the bar into the debris-clogged pipe. Nothing.

He poked and poked but nothing opened up. The water rose up to his pants pockets soaking his wallet. Around him more and more water gushed in, along with unsightly and putrid sewer waste.

Baby Ruths!

Ignoring the floating filth, John rammed and shoved the long rebar into the jammed sewer as he hard as he could. Sweat further dampened his face and shirt in the warm, humid air as the water kept rising. Soon he had water to his belt.

He poked and poked with all his might with no results and by now, the sewage-infused water rose on the front of his colored T-shirt where it read, "Don't sweat the small stuff."

C'mon, c'mon.

"Get a move on," Hollis hollered. "We ain't got all day."

"I'm trying, but …."

"Look, if you wiggle that *(expletive)* rod from one side and to the other it might break the junk free. Hurry up or that *(expletive)* water's gonna be in your face."

John bent down again. This time he had to raise his chin. He poked and poked in a wiggling fashion. The water kept rising.

Stretching his neck up one last time, he gave a mighty jab … and with that the dam broke loose. Almost instantly the water dropped. *I got to get out of here.*

John pointed the end of the rebar toward Ernie Colwich. Ernie grabbed the bar and hauled John up and out of the hole, leaving the unpleasantness, except for his clothes.

The rest of the story is the crew shut down for the day and on the way back toward Wamego in the back of the Hollis' truck John's clothes dried out and some of the smell flew away. At home, John undressed on the back porch and took a bath.

Did the foreman take care of him for his soaking? Well, John got three hours of overtime pay in his paycheck.

But … speaking of soaking ….

YOU GOTTA SOAK IT

Cowboy hats and rural life seemed to go together and when John used part of his paycheck to buy a new J.C. Penney straw cowboy hat, his action fit that mold. The pale tan hat with a high crown had a broad, flat brim and a narrow band of imitation snake skin.

John's hat wasn't the 10-gallon variety but it fit the bill. In the spirit of a real cowboy, he planned to style his hat like Red Ryder's.

"You know what you need to do with that new hat, John?" younger cousin Dwight Burgess asked?

"What?"

"Well, I read in a barbershop magazine you have to soak new hats before you shape them."

"What do you mean soak?" John caressed and admired his hat.

Dwight scratched his chin and said, "I don't rightly know, but it seems to me the more water the better. You could use a bucket, but if it was mine, I'd put her in the horse tank overnight so it got lots of water."

Maybe Dwight's right.

That evening about the time the barn swallows finished catching mosquitoes on the wing; John sank his new hat to the bottom of the horse tank and anchored it with rocks. In the morning, he'd give the brim the needed roll and crease the top to achieve perfection.

The next day John reached down to retrieve his properly soaked fedora. *What the heck?*

It had absorbed water alright, but that wasn't all. Green algae slime wrapped around the crown and clung to edge of the brim.

Sadly, the tank's denizens, tiny catfish minnows, apparently liked the flavor of the dyed straw. There were little nicks and holes in several places. The new stylish hat now looked wear worn and shabby.

Darn.

John tried to rub off the slime, and in the process, imbedded much of it permanently. What was planned as trendy was now discolored with green polka dots. So much for Dwight's advice about hats.

In what screwy barbershop did he find that magazine article anyway?

Shaking his head, John rolled up both sides of the brim and set the hat out to dry. Over time, the green spots blended into the tan straw and the little nicks added charm. As for Dwight's advice, John teased him about believing everything he read and Dwight teased back about John's funny looking hat. In any event, Dwight wasn't through. He also had good advice about boots.

"You need to soak your cowboy boots the same way. However, I'd recommend a five-gallon bucket of water." Then he added, "Put the new boots into a bucket overnight, and in the morning pour out the water and wear them dry."

That worked, for after all, there were no minnows in the five gallon bucket. Dwight, who always seemed long on advice, used the same method to form-fit many pairs of his own boots. While he contended his lifetime of ranching and farming was an expensive hobby, he wore his cowboy boots proudly. In fact, he liked the boots so well he entitled his first book of cowboy poetry, *My Old Cowboy Boots.*

THIRTY-ONE

OVER 90,000 MILES, THE GREAT JAVELIN THROWER AND CHIROPRACTIC DANCING

[*Wamego Times:* September 2, 1951] ~ A WHEAT HAREST ~

Approximately 490,000 bushels of wheat were harvested in Pottawatomie County this year, according to the State Board of Agriculture. The average yield was 11.6 bushels per acre. In Wabaunsee County the production in bushels this year was 344,200 and the average per acre was 10.2.

Wheat prospects continued to decline during July with the 1951 crop now estimated at 126,732,000 bushels, according the August Crop Report. Heavy, continuous rains and extensive flooding surely damaged Kansas field crops during July. In many sections hail and wind caused further damage.

1951

OVER 90,000 MILES

"Well, it is using quite a bit of oil and the transmission feels pretty sloppy. We probably need to get rid of it," the boys' dad said. "After all, that pickup has over 90,000 miles on it."

And so the shiny green 1940 Ford pickup with its flathead V-8 engine headed to a dealer and perhaps to the junkyard. Vehicles from the 40s and 50s were traded when their speedometers neared 100,000 miles.

Cars and light trucks in those years didn't rack up miles very fast. Towns were small, jobs were close and every Eastern Kansas farm had a small town within 5-10 miles for shopping and equipment purchases. Schools were nearby and buses hauled most kids. A lot of families had just one car and that vehicle only went shopping and to church on a weekly basis. Shorty and Lulu had two cars, but usually only one would run.

The quality of automobiles and pickups of the period wasn't too far advanced from the old Model Ts of the '20s. The vehicles lacked precision parts. An accessory like safety glass was seldom seen.

§

The two of us had ridden the pickup pretty hard and were responsible for most of its abuse. We loved the feel of the Ford's light rear end swinging wide. This may sound daring, but in fact, we really approached driving with quite a bit of caution. We never lost control—close a time or two—although now and then the driver drew a gasp from his brother in other seat.

Driving on country roads, we liked to come out of the turn in second gear and then see how fast we could rev the engine before shifting into high. We paid little attention to the moan from under the hood as we fish-tailed and bounced onward.

This kind of driving put the vehicle's tires under stress. Fortunately, since the end of WWII we drove on real rubber tires instead of those of synthetic composition. With real tires we could confidently ride the galloping truck across ruts and rocks. However, with our abuse the pickup finally hollered 'uncle.'

Dad said it was time to trade.

§

What eventually joined the family was a 1946 Harvest Tan colored Hudson Super Six Deluxe. It had cost about $1,500 new and was rated at about 100 horsepower. Its revolutionary styling—according to its maker— looked a bit like a teardrop. From a narrow appearing front end, the car widened as it worked its way to the rear.

The hood hinged in the front and opened from the rear. If the youngsters forgot to latch the bonnet, at about 25 mph aerodynamics would lift it to eye level, but not blocking the driver's view. *Disconcerting.*

In teenager's eyes the car was pretty ugly; however, it would pick up the slack and take the boys to school. This was John's senior year. And he wanted to…"show his stuff." The Hudson would get him where he needed to go and the rest was up to him. He did have a few avenues to lift him above the Hudson's image.

With fall came football and John and George rejoined the Red Raider team. Football delighted John, while George questioned his own sanity. John again made varsity's first team while 'Sunshine' continued practice duties as a low value target. .

John was a *senior stalwart*, according to the yearbook, on a woeful team that won one game and lost eight. Why the futility?

One could point fingers in many directions. Seventeen players had graduated the year before. Counting John and Junior Worden, only five other senior classmates joined the 1951 team.

The very successful coach of the previous year, Mr. Dave Scales, had moved on, and in his place came LeRoy Dawson, a brand new graduate from Kansas State in his first coaching job. Dawson brought in the Split-T offense, designed to open the game for more passing and more speed.

"Man, I sure hope this formation works," John said, as he pulled off his shoes in the locker room after practice.

"I don't see how it's going to," left guard Darrell Tanner said. "How can we block and open a hole when we're a yard apart. The defensive guys will just run between us won't they?"

"Yeah," Center Myron Flinn said. "We're so far apart I can hardly see the tackles."

Junior Wordon asked. "What do you think, Guy?"

"As an end, I'm sure a long ways from everybody. I feel lonely out there," Guy Bishop said.

"We won't know how it'll work unless we give it a try. Anyway, that's what the Coach wants. What can we lose?" John asked.

So the team leaders tried their best to adapt to the new system and, for his part, the new Coach did his best to teach the intricacies of the Split-T. After a week of practice, some optimism surfaced.

Still, there was a problem. The Red Raider team lacked speed and size. Besides the seven seniors, a hand full of juniors made the team, including Cousin Danny Burgess.

George's sophomore class made up the rest of the positions. These younger players were good athletes. Still, they lacked experience. However, as the upper classmen got sidelined with injuries, the sophomores played more and more.

For the season's first game the Red Raiders journeyed to Chapman and struggled to score. The extra wide gaps between offensive blockers made it hard to keep the opposing players away from Wamego's backs. The main Wamego ball carriers, seniors Johnny Lichtenhan and Jim Shea, did their best, but had little success.

The Red Raiders battled, but Chapman's Fighting Irish won 7-0. The uncomfortable bus ride home on through Junction City, Ft. Riley, Ogden, Manhattan and St. George took 'forever.'

Council Grove won the next game with Lichtenhan scoring the lone Wamego touchdown. The next opponent, the bigger Highland Park squad, blew the Red Raiders apart, 31-0. After the three games Wamego had scored a lone touchdown.

The fourth game against Haskell Institute yielded three Red Raider scores and the season's only victory 21-12. Sadly, Johnny Lichtenhan got hurt and that ended his season. Jim Shea was also sidelined. By now the several sophomores from George's class had to step into the breech.

Wamego lost the next two games to much bigger Topeka schools. The next game pitted Topeka's large Hayden High Wildcats, against the lowly Red Raiders.

The Hayden game had hardly started when the Wildcats scored. Over and over their giant line opened holes, their skillful runners made long runs and their defense shut down the Wamego offense completely.

"C'mon you guys," John growled at his friends during a timeout. "We have to try. Let's block those guys. They're not that big."

"Oh, yeah? Those two tackles outweigh Junior by 20 pounds each. He can't even move them. Anyway, my shoulder is heading out of joint again," Myron said as he flexed his right arm and winced in pain.

"Dang you Flinn," John said. "Don't you go getting hurt again. We need you. We gotta try. C'mon guys."

During the next play John rolled his right ankle and tore the ligaments. And that was the season for him. With tears in his eyes he limped off the field and sat on the bench, gritting his teeth in pain and hanging his head in frustration. *Darn, I couldn't even protect our quarterbacks. I bet they'll have words later.*

George looked into the stands to see his folks. *They're not even paying attention. And this time it's not bogus shin splints.*

About then Myron Flinn's shoulder went out again and he joined his pal on the sideline. That was that, a 73-0 loss.

Yes, John had played his last high school football game and that ended a somewhat vexing year. Still, he felt he and his friends had done their best. Junior was named to the Jayhawk League's Second All-Star Team and John and Myron earned Honorable Mention again. But honors didn't win games.

George summed up his brother's final football game. "He charged onto the battlefield, he clawed and scratched in the trenches and he limped off with the walking wounded."

John thought, *Where are my nurses?*

THE GREAT JAVELIN THROWER

John enjoyed football and baseball, but avoided running. *Why would I want to be a runner? It tires me to think about it. George can have it*

So come track season, John again opted for the javelin. His only running needed was the approach to the throw line. He could walk back for another try. He almost craved the times he could fire a baseball, a football, a rock, and in this case a javelin.

To throw a javelin, John would fling the spear with a mighty whip of his arm. Alone on the practice field behind the Ag building—the coaches still didn't trust him throwing near others—he admired his tosses.

During the early season, John's practice tosses would wobble through an arc and land some 100 feet away. He was far from emulating his hero, Bud Held, who won the javelin event at the NCAA Track Meet three years in a row for Stanford University. Held's throws were around 270 feet or more.

Neither Coach Dawson nor Coach Butterfield did much more than encourage John. If they happened to wander by the practice area they might say, "Keep working. You're getting the hang of it."

When the first meet came along at Council Grove, John managed 130 feet and that earned him third place among the three javelin throwers entered. In later meets he reached 135 feet.

Finally during a practice—alone of course—he began his trot to the throw line, lost concentration and without strain tossed the javelin 186 feet. The coaches took him with the squad to the Kansas University Relays in Lawrence. There, as Wamego's lone javelin thrower, he hobbled forward to toss a woeful 139 feet. There would be no back slaps.

Still, in his mind, John had risen to the status of a mighty thrower, though he was his only witness. When he tried to explain his achievement, the comments were always the same, "Oh yeah? Another fish story, huh? I'll believe it when I see it."

The physical challengers of football and track were behind him. But it wouldn't be long before he'd discover how important four years of football calisthenics, handling hundreds of hay bales and tossing the javelin would be.

CHIROPRACTIC DANCING

During his last weeks at Wamego High, John stayed attentive in class and was Sports Editor of the *Wamego Buzz*.

He took a course called Career Development, hoping to get an idea about his future. His good friends, Bob Pinet and Al Kaine, knew what they were going to be after high school. Bob did become a lawyer and later a Judge. Al Kaine became an electrical engineer and owner of more than one company. In contrast, all John knew was he didn't relish the uncertainties of farming as his life's work.

On the plus side, John liked journalism and thought maybe he'd become a newspaper sports reporter, or maybe a minister, though that was a distant second. When he spotted the Career Development class on the schedule, he assumed that might clue him in about possible choices.

Coach Dawson taught the course and his method of instruction left a lot of time for self learning, where students would study on their own and turn in reports … much like online learning today. Some days the classes met only long enough to turn in papers … which gave students like John time to do other things. And he did.

In fact, the last half of John's senior year was spotted with absences. Several were for farming projects that needed his assistance. It turned out John's grades for the term were good. Graduation grew closer.

Before John would don his red robe and walk across the stage to receive his diploma, there were school activities to attend, like the Wa Kaw Dance, sponsored by the yearbook committee. It arrived near the end of school and would be a time for fun and lots of dancing.

From his freshman year, John had learned a great deal about dancing! He'd learned that waltzing seemed to be an attempt to spin each other until both got dizzy, and the foxtrot seemed best left to the foxes.

Over time he'd developed his own style. He could perform twists and spins, often with the music. He pumped and dipped and turned. Girls always said nice things about his dancing; he presumed these were tributes.

"You surely have an unusual step," one said.

"I've never danced that way before," said another.

Still another said, "Where did you learn that?"

As the Wa Kaw Dance progressed, John and some of his friends leaned against the gym wall. Most wore clean Levi's, a white shirt and, those who had played sports, had on white Letter Sweaters with big red Ws. How sweet it was ….

Their bodies smelled of generous quantities of cologne, deodorant and hair tonic.

The group stood watching a hand full of dancers swaying to the music of Matt Benton and his Orchestra under a canopy of crepe paper streamers, balloons and artificial flowers. The speckled stick-dancer drawings reflected from poster boards hanging from the balcony rails and multicolored strobe lights created a dreamlike atmosphere.

John proudly wearing his letter sweater

"Hey guys, look at that," John said with a laugh. He nodded to where classmates Maxine Straub and Rita Peddicord danced together.

"What's with girls anyhow?" Bob Gable asked. "They want to dance every dance, even if they have to dance with each other."

"Girls dancing with other girls is a mystery all right, like aliens and UFOs," Jim Kastner said. "No guy would dance with another guy."

"Hey, John, I'll bet you don't have the guts to dance with Queenie over there," J. N. said, smiling toward the tall and husky upper classman.

All eyes looked at Queenie. She outweighed most of the boys in school. Even in flats she stood three inches taller than John.

"We'll give you five dollars if you dance with her, won't we guys?" J. N. asked. Several nodded approval and dug in their pockets.

John looked at Queenie in the distance, then at the money up close, hastily collected from Junior, Myron, Jim, Donnie, Darrell, and Larry.

John accepted the challenge. Five dollars was five dollars. Later he would admit he may have made a poor choice.

As John walked toward Queenie, sitting alone under the lights, the band came to the end of the slow ballad *Stardust*. The next song started with a loud tar-ump, tar-ump and swung into the jerky Latin beat of *Hernando's Hide-away*.

Good gosh, not that one.

He looked toward his friends signaling he wanted off the hook. J. N. shook his head and Junior pointed toward Queenie. The rest just crossed their arms.

John's heart skipped. *She might kill me.*

Perhaps it was his friends' ridicule, or maybe the challenge, or maybe his full-speed-ahead attitude. At any rate he chewed his gob of Juicy Fruit, and stepped forward.

"So, do you want to dance?" John asked in a weak voice.

With a husky voice, Queenie said, "Charmed, I'm sure. I'm tired of dancing with girls. I'll take a whack at you."

John shuttered. He'd soon learn what she meant. With a feeble smile toward his friends, he followed her onto the dance floor.

It's just one dance. It's going to cost those yoyos.

378

His smile immediately turned to shock. Queenie yanked him close and quick stepped into a wild version of the Hokey Pokey. Months of lifting bales, shoveling corn and construction work hadn't prepared him for this.

She's strong ... real strong.

With an iron grip, Queenie hauled the 170-pound football lineman like Raggedy Ann. As Hernando got closer to his hide-away, the music tempo picked up. At that point Queenie adjusted John's femur with greater ferocity than George Worden's blindside tackle.

Ouch!

It was left foot left, right foot right, push, pull, pump up and down, up and down. Queenie's muscles overpowered him.

Oh boy, when's this train going to stop?

Across the room, the guys belly laughed.

John was by now having his fourth vertebrae realigned, his rotator cuff repositioned, his fibula adjusted and his sternum rearranged. He vaguely sensed the music slowing, for Queenie kept right on drawing water a few beats after the song ended.

Whew!

John limped back to his laughing buddies.

"Where's my five bucks?"

They handed him his money and asked, "Where's your gum?"

"Uh, when I was gasping for air, I swallowed it."

J. N. laughed and said, "Was that like doing some cowboying?"

I get his point. At least I didn't get my shirt bloodied. Then he checked to be sure.

From then on, John ducked every time Queenie came his way. Luckily he was spared that night. His bones were still connected, and aches slowly went away—with the help of one of George's remaining tins of salve.

Dances under the right circumstances were fun. Junior Senior proms in particular had a delightful excitement about them.

But, who would you ask for a date? What would you wear? What kind of corsage would you buy? How much would your date want to dance? Would your folks let you have the family car?

It had only taken one dance to convince him that he liked gentler women. Fortunately, the girls he wanted to date liked to dance—and let the boy lead! As the Junior Senior Prom night approached, John had stylish clothes, some ability to dance and a good rapport with the girls. Now who should he ask to the dance?

Norma Brockish accepted his invitation. That night she wore a pretty taffeta dress replete with the Junior Class' flowered lei, and John's corsage.

The Juniors took the Seniors on a Hawai'ian Cruise, with music by the Carl Johnson talented Orchestra.

John and Norma take a break during the Prom

The highly proficient K-State Hawai'ian Club performed typical Island chants. The night was worthy of a *Bali Hai* setting, and would leave many fond memories.

The Prom ended the organized social year and soon it would be Graduation Day. The seniors were excited and yet sad. After four years together they'd be leaving their friends and going separate ways.

But they'd had a good senior year with many fascinating side events.

THIRTY-TWO

CAR CULTURE, GRADUATION DAY AND OFF TO DETROIT

[*Topeka Capital* - June 4, 1952] Gen. Dwight D. Eisenhower announced his candidacy for the Republican Party nomination for President of the United States.

1952

CAR CULTURE

The boys loved cars. For one thing they by living in the country they needed a car to go to anywhere. The family had traded the Hudson for a '50 Plymouth and the '48 Chevy for a new '51 Ford. What caused the Hudson's demise? Trying to squeal the tires, George blew the spider gears out of the car's rear end. "Dad, I think I blacked out," George explained.

For the umpteenth time the boys' Dad just shook his head.

I don't think he bought it.

§

Early on we tested the new Ford and found it would fly. The speed was faster than we wanted to drive, but we literally came to cherish the Ford's ability to accelerate. From a dead stop we could hit 60 mph in a flash. The car gave us status.

"You are what you drive," was the saying in those days.

Many kids customized their rides. Schoolmate Gary Atkinson repainted his car with jagged lightning streaks. Others painted on Hotrod Magazine tongues of fire. Just riding in one of those buggies gave us points with the girls.

Other distinctive modifications included special seat covers, lighted hood ornaments, modified taillights, windshield visors, fender skirts and spotlights. Don Eichem repainted his car's dashboard—with a paint brush.

Many swapped regular stock mufflers, for deep sounding Hollywood types. What could be better than cruising Wamego with your engine gurgling along like an amplified Stradivarius? Of course everyone hung evergreen air fresheners on their rear view mirror alongside their furry dice.

Some cars displayed raccoon or muskrat tails on the radio antennas. Often Catholics had miniatures of their patron saints on their dashboards.

We had a 'California speed knob' on our steering wheel. Much easier—no power steering—to muscle around a corner. We also knew of some cars that needed no modifications to be unique. Daryl Campbell's light green Crosley was the size of a chemistry table. On one occasion it was found in a High School hallway. Don't ask us ….

§

MISTER HOLLYWOOD

That school year, much to the disgust of Mr. Beagler, a suave California photographer showed up to take the yearbook pictures. "Mr. Hollywood," as the kids called him stood out like a sore thumb in small-town Wamego. Even more than the Carnival Big City Dancers.

He wore cowboy shirts, pleated gabardine trousers, pointed Italian leather wingtip shoes and a metal belt buckle resembling a silver saddle. He wore long slicked back hair and a pencil thin mustache. High society or a shyster?

He wore double shaded movie star sunglasses with his initials engraved on the lens. Diamond chips surrounded his Wittnauer watch. His fingers seemed heavy under the weight of expensive jeweled rings.

His persona was as foreign to Wamego as if he'd come from Mars. But he had an air about him that fascinated students and the faculty. But his biggest attraction was his car.

His light blue customized 1950 Chevrolet hatchback had a chopped '50 Oldsmobile Rocket 88 grill and '51 Cadillac taillights.

Of course he had a Cherry Bomb muffler. The car's interior could only be described as gaudy, but no one complained.

He indicated he knew every starlet in California. After three days he departed. He was gone but hardly forgotten. Incidentally, his pictures turned out well.

GRADUATION DAY

The big day arrived at last and excitement filled the air. Families, friends and younger schoolmates packed Wamego High's Auditorium for the ceremony honoring the graduating Class of 1952.

Seated in the first three rows, the candidates wore the traditional Red Raider all-red robe with a red mortarboard decorated with a white tassel draped over the right side of the brim.

The boy's mom could hardly contain herself. *Oh, I'm so proud of him. John has done so well in school.*

"On behalf of Wamego Rural High School, I welcome you graduating seniors, your families and friends," Principal George R. McCormick said. He stood behind the podium in the middle of the stage and continued, "It is a great honor to host this graduation ceremony for one of the finest classes ever at Wamego High. First, let's stand, while the Reverend Samuel Boman, Rector of St. Luke's Episcopal Church offers the invocation."

Upon completion of the prayer, Principal McCormick joined others in saying, "Amen." He surveyed the crowd and said, "Let us continue standing and sing our *National Anthem.* Our Music Teacher, Mr. Charles Elliot will lead us."

All sang strongly. The cavernous room rang with harmony and reverence. Several of the graduating class smiled at each other; others drew tears.

When the anthem ended, Senior Class President, Al Kaine, went to the stage. "We, the Class of 1952, wish to thank you for coming to witness our graduation. We are honored by your presence and thank you for your support during the last four years. Please know we appreciate all your help. As graduates, we know the challenges we face with our Country engaged in the Korean Conflict. But we pledge ourselves to do our best to make this a better world. Again, we are honored by your presence."

There were short talks by Mr. McCormick and Mr. Virgil Haas, Chairman of the School Board. Next Mrs. Pitney introduced Anna Schleif as the Valedictorian and Al Kaine as Salutatorian.

The Principal handed out scholarship awards. John was sixth in the class. Finally, it came time to award the diplomas.

The seniors rose together and in alphabetical order marched up the steps onto the right side of the stage. There, Mrs. Pitney met them and shook each graduate's hand. Principal McCormick handed out the diplomas and Mr. Haas welcomed each student into the larger society.

Tears flowed easily from students, parents and even a couple of teachers. The new alumnae stood together for the last time as Mrs. Pitney said, "Graduates, switch your tassels."

As the fluffy white ornaments moved from the right to the left side of the brim on each hat, a cheer broke out and some graduates tossed their mortarboards high into the air. Booming applause shook the auditorium. The Class of 1952 had done it.

The Class would say this had been a joyous day, and yet a sad one. But life must go on, so John left the Auditorium that night eager to head to Kansas State College in the fall—but first summer work.

SUMMERTIME

With John graduated and George finished with his sophomore year, the boys awaited a summer with potential opportunities.

With young John returning to his construction job, that left George and his dad to do most of the farm work. Together they cultivated, disked and completed all manner of farm projects. The boys' dad bought five Angus heifers to augment the beef herd, by bringing in new blood lines.

In a few weeks George's dad said, "I might have made a mistake buying those heifers, they're skittish. I guess all Angus are hard to tame, but these seem downright edgy."

That statement turned out to be a prophecy of sorts, for the very next Saturday morning as George finished milking, he spotted the Angus in the alfalfa field. *Dang those heifers, they broke through the fence.*

"Dad, Dad!" George yelled, "The Angus are in the alfalfa."

Young John—no construction work on a Saturday—and his dad dropped the new cutter bar they were installing onto the Massey Harris combine and came running. The trio stared at the five heifers munching on the fresh green shoots.

"That alfalfa could be deadly for them. Even though cattle have four stomach compartments, these five could still end up suffering from bloat," the boys' dad said. "If they balloon-up too far it will be fatal. C'mon, we'll have to hurry."

"How do we handle it?" John asked.

"Let's see. George, you run down through the meadow and circle around behind them. Pressure them toward the gate." George took off at a half-miler pace.

Responding to the gentle encouragement, the heifers, already too bloated to run, meandered to the corral. In minutes, the swollen heifers stood heads down near the barn. Now what?

"We'd got to get some soda down them," the boys' dad said. "We've got to counteract the alfalfa effects."

He hollered toward the house, asking the boys' mom to mix up a pail of water with baking soda. "The soda will neutralize the stomach acid that's causing the bloat. We don't have time to call in the Vet. John, go get the mixture and we'll drench them. Let's get these Nellies into the barn."

The three men worked the heifers into the barn, locked them in stanchions and wrestled the solution down each animal's throat. The good news was they all recovered from what could have been a lethal amount of alfalfa. In the end, the Angus were none-the-worse-for-wear. Over time, they also turned out to be gentler, and the beef herd did improve. Another challenge met and managed.

On the ball field the boys continued to work toward their perceived goals of becoming big leaguers. *I think I'm getting better with my pitching. I can throw a 70 MPH fastball,* John thought. Playing ball seemed to be on everybody's mind.

The boys continued playing with the group from Louisville. Although George would never be confused with a speedy outfielder, he somehow always seemed to make the catch. He'd often slide and fall and stretch and reach out, and would come up with his Joe Gordon autographed glove, holding the ball.

George's ability to reach the ball, on the fly or bounce, did put him in jeopardy at times, especially in places like Paxico and Emmett. There, the ball fields doubled as cow pastures. The infields might have hoof prints … and many other hazards lay plopped in the outfield.

One late Sunday afternoon, a Paxico batter slapped a line-drive single toward centerfield. It hit the grass well beyond second base and skipped and bounced … right into a huge, fresh and warm cow pattie.

George rushed the ball, picked it up, looked it over and threw it toward home plate. Infielders jumped out of the way.

As another Paxico player rounded third and headed home, so did the ball … past one player, then another. Finally as the ball bounced toward catcher Danny at home plate, he pulled his hand back at the last instant. The ball continued its slow roll until it hit the backstop, sending a small amount of residual night soil toward the front row seats.

"Safe!" Paxico had another run. George had a smelly hand. Everyone else had a grin.

"What's the matter with you guys, afraid of a little manure?" roared a guy from the Paxico dugout. "That's high quality stuff from my best cow, Zelda."

The crowd, mostly Paxico fans, went wild. Nobody from either side or the umpire came to the ball's rescue. George? He wiped his hand on the grass and his jeans, looked toward his team and thought. *Cowards.*

When the Louisville team left for home, the badly stained baseball lay at the foot of the backstop. The ride back home seemed to take forever and inside the car an unpleasant stench floated in the air. *I'm glad we're not in our car,* John thought. Denny turned to George and said, "Don't touch anything."

"You know George, that was a dirty throw you made today," Danny laughed as he drove his dad's Ford toward Louisville. "Next time throw the ball into Paxico's dugout."

"Good idea," George replied. "Next time we'll let the chips fall where … we throw them!"

In baseball as in all aspects of life, people have always had to expect the unexpected. Out of the blue one day, John and George were caught off guard when their parents laid out a proposition. One that would make the summer special, and educational. It shifted their thoughts from work and play toward a new adventure of major proportions. What was this?

§

OFF TO DETROIT

"Boys, you've been working pretty hard, and John you need a break before going off to college," Dad said. "Your mother and I have been thinking it might be okay if you went up to Detroit to see your Grandmother Scott and the Andersens."

Could we be hearing this? We had no inkling that the folks would let us do such a thing.

"Yeah," Mom said, "You can drive the Ford up and spend a few days in the big city. It will be wonderful for you to see Uncle Luther, Aunt Ann, Nellie Ann and Nick, too.

Wow!

So, after careful planning we got breaks from the constructions job and farming. We figured a 16-hour trip, if we traded off driving and drove straight through.

With no air conditioning, every time we stopped for gas or for some eats we'd let the backs of our shirts dry and then press on. The folks gave us each $2.00 a day for food. "Make do!"

they said. We could have spent two bucks for breakfasts, but we knew there wouldn't be any more money coming.

We crossed eastern Kansas, Missouri, Illinois, Indiana and Ohio before arriving in Detroit. *Just look at this city.*

After facing heavy traffic we pulled up to the Andersen's home at 8:00 p.m. We were beat, but excited.

Aunt Annabel, Mom's sister, fixed us something to eat and then we tried to sleep. Before we knew it we were immersed in a whirlwind of activities.

During the next few days we attended Nel's high school graduation and party, Nick's grade school graduations and made it to a Detroit Tiger game in the old Briggs Stadium. What excitement for young ballplayers.

We drove across Fleming Channel into Windsor, Ontario and spent an afternoon on Belle Isle. We had the time of our lives.

Nick showed us how big city 'cool cats' dressed, combed their hair and strutted. What an eye opener for us.

Then we got another surprise. "We've talked to your folks on the phone," Aunt Ann said, "and we've agreed to let Nel and Nick go back to Kansas with you for the summer. It'll be good for them to see how farm life is."

Wow, that'll be great.

§

So the four teenagers drove southwest toward Wamego and the farm—another 16 hours. This would turn out to be a great summer for all.

While John went back to Walters Bros. Construction, Nick helped out with chores and field work, and Nel helped in the kitchen and played with Judy and Joyce.

John and Nel often went off in the Ford to join his friends for social events. Sometimes Nick and George were relegated to the stock truck for transportation.

Not to worry, George and Nick thought, *a ride is a ride.*

388

There were many things to keep everyone busy, like work, family time, church, movies and parties. The four youngsters fished, played catch, shot bows and arrows, shot the rifle and a whole lot more. And there was lots of baseball along the way.

After a few weeks Nel's and Nick's folks drove down to pick them up. Everyone would have something to talk about for years. Nick, who would later become a school superintendent said, he often used those summer experiences to relate to his rural kids.

After the Andersens left, the boys returned to their normal routine. "You know, Mom, it was fun having our cousins here," George said. "And to top it off, we got to see a big league game."

THIRTY-THREE

SEPARATE WAYS, SUPER SENIOR SNEAK AND LEAVING THE FARM

[*WAMEGO BUZZ – 1954*]
SCHOOL TRACK RECORDS TUMBLE;
DENNY BURGESS, HAROLD WILSON SHINE

The 1953-54 track season was highlighted as records fell to the determined Wamego trackmen. Four all-time records were banished for new marks. Ray Vogl tossed the javelin 152 feet to outdo the old mark of 146-10 set by Jim Sackrider in 1947. Jake Hecker also bettered the 146 foot mark when he threw the javelin 149-1½.

The 880-yard relay team lowered the mark as they knocked off .7 of a second. Darold Rischer, Jack Lonsinger, Larry Linton and Harold Wilson ran in the relay. Delbert Eckart replaced Rischer at the Jayhawk Meet in Ottawa, where they again broke the old record. Probably the highlight of highlights was when Denny Burgess lowered the old mile mark of 4 min. 46 sec. to 4:40.6. He broke the record twice, once at the K.U. Relays and once at the League Meet.

Harold Wilson, who had been eyeing the 880 mark for three years, set a new mark of 2 min. 4 sec. which replaced Ted Fleck's 2:06. Incidentally, this record was the longest one held at Wamego High School; it was set in 1924. George Burgess also broke the old 880 mark with his 2:05 running. Ralph Nelson ran 2:06 to tie Fleck's record.

Eight boys qualified for the State Meet. They were Denny Burgess (mile); Rischer, Eckart, Linton and Harry Haas (medley); Wilson and George Burgess (880); Larry Bahner (pole vault). Rischer also qualified for the 220.

1952-54

SEPARATE WAYS

Well it's nearing time to wrap up our story. We've come to the point in our account where we'd soon be going our separate ways.

Happily, we matured, though slowly at times. We learned to work hard and do our best. We enjoyed our leisure time. Our faith in God gave us moral strength and led us to try to treat everyone the way we'd like to be treated. And living the country life gave us opportunities for self-sufficiency.

Looking back, we recognize the years we spent together were especially memorable and helped shape us into who we would become. Recalling activities of our young lives in (FRESH FEATHERED EGGS – Infinity Press, 2005) and now in BEYOND FRESH FEATHERED EGGS has helped us recall even minor events.

§

In the fall of 1952, young John left home and enrolled in Journalism at Kansas State and joined the Pi Kappa Alpha Fraternity. In four years he'd receive his degree, serve his military commitment, with more than a year in Italy and return to Manhattan to begin his first career, in financial services.

While his leaving left a hole in the farm's labor force, there was an even bigger issue and that involved John the elder which brought about a major change in the Burgess farming operation.

§

Our folks had started with nothing, struggled through the depression and World War II, and by 1952 owned a 185 acre farm, plenty of machinery, a small dairy herd and a 160 acre pasture full of beef cattle. All of this took planning, perseverance and a lot of physical labor. It was that labor that took its toll on Dad. He'd developed back pain in a childhood accident, and it dogged him throughout his life.

Finally, the doctors said no more heavy manual labor. So, what next? "What are we going to do, John?" Mom asked. "If you can't farm, how will we live?"

"I'll have to find something else to do. In the meantime, George can do most of the field work and heavy feeding and I'll be available to help with milking and chores. If things get too difficult, we'll have to leave the farm."

"Oh John … would we really have to?" Mom asked.

Dad shrugged and then shook his head. "We'll have to see won't we? Let's be patient. Maybe the Good Lord has something in mind."

§

So they prayed and waited. What was in store for the farm and the family? Could George achieve all that was being asked of him? John was in college; Judy and Joyce were young, so what were the choices?

At a church conference the boys' dad met a district agent for the Northwestern Mutual Life Insurance Co. With a little encouragement, the Kansas farmer took the necessary courses and in early 1953 joined the Company as a special agent.

George's farm duties increased just as he started back to Wamego High School for his junior year. In his brother's absence and with his father's health issues, he shouldered the load until his graduation in 1954.

He still found time for school work, sports, dating, and cars, plus he filled high school governing positions, debated, had roles in the plays, and was on the Wa Kaw Year Book staff.

In sports George had never rose above bench warmer in football and he didn't make the basketball squad. But he did have some first-rate achievements in track.

GEORGE AND SPORTS

No, George wasn't a football star. But neither was he a quitter. His parents had taught him to stick to the job until the job was done. It could be said his football caper was up the first day on the playing field. In truth, he was a pitifully slow light weight.

George never suffered a football injury, so unlike John, he had never been *charley-horsed for life*. He did envy the guys wearing leg or arm casts, as the girls swarmed around them.

George's senior year was a good one for Wamego High School sports. Under Coach Joe Pollom, the football team posted a 7-2 record. Coach Paul Markham led the basketball squad to 15 wins against eight losses.

The Class of '54 had many quality players who garnered athletic letters, and some were selected for the Jayhawk League All-Star squads. George did get a football letter his senior year, probably for 'participation.' Thank goodness, by then his *missing-red-pants episode* had long been forgotten.

George training in the pasture

George earned two track letters. In 1954, he placed third in the Regional Meet, which sent him to the State Meet. He said that as he rounded turn four on the second lap of the State 880 yard run—far back in the pack—he thought, *This has got to be the dumbest thing I've ever done in my life. This hurts.* Luckily, the season was over.

In the summers George turned to American Legion Baseball sponsored by the local Legion Post. The Legion provided each player with a classy uniform, plus bats and balls.

At Wamego, the mix of small town and farm boys blended well. The teams—one time or another—included Dick Chrest, Ray Vogl, Harry Haas, Ace Armbrust, Larry Larson, Bill Gieber, Jim Kastner, John Lichtenhan, Delbert Eckart, Raymond Wilson, Val Bussart, Ed Delk, Denny Burgess, Don Eichem, George and others. Jack Delp, a former St. Louis Browns player, managed the team. Jack's favorite comment about his major league career was, "I went up to the Browns for a cup of coffee."

During one summer the Wamego team beat the much larger towns of Manhattan and Emporia at the American Legion Regionals and that qualified them for the State Tournament in Olathe.

In the double elimination State Tourney, Wamego lost in the first round to Larned and the next day to Olathe and that was that for

Wamego. Topeka Mosby-Mack won the Tournament and went on to take second place in the Nationals. They were led by pitcher Jim Golden who ended up as a pro with the Houston Colt .45s and the LA Dodgers.

On the way back from Olathe, the Wamego teammates discussed the tournament losses. "I don't know what to say," Ray Vogl moaned, "those guys hit everything we threw at them."

George said. "I spent most of my time running toward the outfield fence. But, we did make it to *State*."

As the Team pulled into Wamego and headed down Lincoln Avenue, Don Eichem said, "Hey, let's stop in at Murphy's for a coke."

MURPHY'S DRUG AND THE POOL HALL

Year after year Murphy's Drug Store served as the favorite high school hangout. Mr. and Mrs. Murphy treated everyone well and the young people showed proper respect in return. Many athletes had the habit of stopping at Murphy's for treats after sport practices.

At Murphy's the pin ball machine constantly clanked and flashed in the background. It endured so much play that every few months it'd wear out and a new machine would show up. Legend has it that Class of '49 basketball star Dick Knostman—later a K-State All-American—was a whiz at pinball. Some said he'd often leave dozens of games he'd won on the machine's register when he left for home.

Yes, Murphy's held a special position as a Wamego hangout. However, there was another was another one that offered other opportunities. Across from Murphy's and up the street was a much different business.

Marv Herman ran the Wamego Pool Hall on the east side of Lincoln Avenue where the Friendly Cooker restaurant is today. After school, if a person wasn't at Murphy's, he'd probably be at the Pool Hall.

Some would say Marv acted quite tough, though he treated all of his patrons well. He had a slow manner of speaking and a nice touch of wit. At his establishment, people could shoot pool or shoot the breeze. Most resisted using the restroom facilities, for they seemed to only get an annual cleaning. If a person desperately had to go, he didn't linger.

Marv sold 3.2 beer to anyone age 18 or older. So those in high school stuck with soda pop. George was a fan of Dad's Root Beer laced with peanuts.

Marv also sold spicy hot polish sausages in a huge jar on the bar. That might have been a beer drinker's protein for the day.

Watching beer drinkers fascinated the kids. Some might drop a raw egg into his beer, while others might pour in tomato juice. Some would stir their beer with a beef jerky stick.

THE HAYRACK RIDE

George's Class of '54 entertained themselves. They'd get together just for the heck of it. One night they took a hayrack ride.

Now hayracks weren't exactly practical by the 1950s, so on a spring night in 1953 one classmate got his dad's ton and a half stock truck. Add a few bales of hay, some young people, Daryl Campbell and his ukulele and the hayrack ride sprung to life.

About 20 of the class met at the City Park and climbed aboard the truck. It drove south across the Kaw River bridge into Wabaunsee County. Everyone knew that singing should take center stage. So Daryl strummed and led the singing while the rest of the group joined in. They warmed up with *Down by the Old Mill Stream* and then sang popular tunes like *Don't Fence Me In, Glow Little Glow Worm, Beautiful Dreamer and Chickery Chick Cha-la Cha-la.*

They drove some 30 miles that night, serenading farmers, livestock, wild animals and the moon. Their songs and laughter stopped an unsuspecting Barred Owl in midstream as it sounded its familiar hoot, "Who cooks for you, who cooks for you all?" The Class of '54 sang and laughed and had fun at the cost of less than a buck's worth of gas. The hayrack ride was just plain fun.

As their senior year drew to a close, one activity waited and would cost a healthy sum of money. The Class of '54 had earned and saved for four years. But it was worth it and the Senior Sneak would become a highly memorable experience for George and his friends.

SUPER SENIOR SNEAK

As was the custom at Wamego High School in those years, each class earned money in anticipation of a week-long senior sneak. Every student considered this to be a great way to cap off four years of hard study. John's Class of '52 had traveled by train to St. Louis.

Months before graduating, the Class of '54 decided to bus across several states to the great city of Chicago. There they'd visit museums, stay in a hotel—some kids had never done that—see shows and enjoy many other exciting sights of a real metropolis.

So, on the evening of April 23, 1954, they boarded two buses on Lincoln Avenue in front of the School, along with their chaperones—if memory serves correctly—Principal C.A. Christ and teachers Chris Langvardt, Marilyn Hart, Bill Scott and Mary Starner.

Excitement? You bet. *Windy City, here we come!*

As the buses pulled out euphoria filled the air. The long trip—few could sleep—wore everyone out, but when the buses pulled into Chicago all eyes opened wide.

"Will you look at that?" George asked as he looked across the aisle. "Those buildings are reaching the clouds. And look at that elevated train."

Several classmates nodded and chatter erupted as those seated near the windows pressed their noses against the glass, while those in the center seats draped themselves over their classmates. The bus drivers smiled. Had they taken their own senior sneak when they were young?

Some of the class had seen a small amount of art. They'd seen the giant memorial Eagle at the southwest corner of the City Park. In the Columbian Theatre hung huge paintings of bigger-than-life ladies that Walter P. Chrysler had brought back from the 1893 Chicago's World Fair.

However, by comparison, what the class saw in Chicago seemed unreal. The size of the Chicago Art Institute building with its two oversized concrete lions on the steps dazzled them. Inside they saw room after room of paintings and sculptures by artists from around the world.

How can anybody paint like that? How can you make a boulder turn into a bear? George thought, and then smiled. *This is better than agricultural art.*

The well planned Sneak moved from one activity to another: the history museum, the natural history museum and the Annual Chicago Auto Show … where the Class got a glimpse of one of the earliest Chevrolet Corvettes. *Who'd buy something like that?*

One night the class went to the Aragon Ballroom. The huge room's ceiling looked like a starry evening sky with wispy clouds passing overhead. On the floor, the kids danced to the music of an 18-piece orchestra and felt grown up while fox-trotting amid dozens of the dancing Chicagoans.

At a theater the next day the Class was entertained by the popular *Spike Jones and his City Slickers* orchestra that punctuated songs like *Cocktails for Two* with gunshots, cow bells, wash boards, whistles, outlandish vocals and wild costumes. Next they saw the popular singer, *Frankie Laine* do his show with his driving, jazzy style. He finished with his very moving version of *That's My Desire*.

George, impressed by the performance, could only say, "I am so sublime" All of his classmates were.

The last night, the class attended a professional wrestling match. This was the real stuff, none of that phony Wamego 4th of July *GREAT MOUNTAIN MAN* wrestling *THE LOCAL BOY*. Back in the hotel some of the boys practiced the professional moves on their beds, until the chaperones put a stop to it.

In the morning everyone loaded onto the buses. Most carried some kind of souvenirs. George had a small Army look-alike radio. He'd paid $2.99 for it and it turned out to be a bum deal. It played more static than music. *I should have bought those polished rocks from that street vendor.*

Many hours later the buses with the worn out Class arrived back in Wamego. The Sneak had surely influenced each person's understanding of, "things beyond a small rural town." As they'd leave high school to join the work force or move on to college, they'd have a new foundation on which to build their lives.

Even the teachers seemed to have enjoyed the sights.

§

KANSAS STATE

A household word most of our lives, Kansas State Agricultural College and Applied Sciences (later Kansas State University) nestled fifteen miles west of the farm in Manhattan. Since Dad loved K-State sports, it grew to be our favorite school.

Dad listened to all of the ball games over the radio. For hours on end, he'd sit beside the Philco with his head cocked toward the sound; a K-State fan indeed.

In 1951, the purple and white clad basketball team, coached by the legendary coach Jack Gardner, along with All-American player Ernie Barrett, played for the NCAA National Championship, though they lost 78-68 to the University of Kentucky.

On one occasion Dad took us to a K-State football game and we remember going to a basketball game. We knew the campus some since we'd attended 4-H Roundups there.

One thing that made K-State attractive was the cost. Neither of us had much money and since our family—Dad was beginning a new business—wasn't able to help financially; K-State was our obvious choice. It was a good decision, though it meant beside classes, we had to work part-time jobs 25 hours a week.

§

In journalism John was learning, but he also had many questions. *Will I become a sports writer like Red Smith or Grantland Rice or Jim Murray? Wouldn't it be something to see my name on a sports page?*

John had found out soon enough that college involved more than journalism. He had to take courses that covered things like science and literature. *Why does a sportswriter need to know biology or English literature?* Needless to say, some of his studies baffled him.

Happily, beginning his second semester he took a real journalism class and that tweaked his interest as he learned the techniques of newspaper reporting. Later, he wrote sports stories, feature articles and helped edit the *Kansas State Collegian*, the campus newspaper published by the Journalism Department five days a week. It had a circulation of 5,000.

John stayed busy, with classes from 8:00 a.m. to noon six days a week and work during the afternoon and evenings. A couple of semesters he had three part-time jobs at once.

Meanwhile, George worked the farm. His days were full with chores, school and sports. His dad bought a tractor mounted corn picker to help him bring in his "twenty bushels after school." And by now, it was he who rode behind the baler … stacking every bale.

I can't wait for graduation.

Like his brother's ceremony two years earlier, George's graduation day began with great eagerness. That evening it didn't take long for a huge crowd to assemble in the auditorium. The place buzzed with excitement.

The graduating seniors of the Class of '54 squirmed in their caps and gowns, their parents beamed not unlike those who'd just brought in a good harvest and the teachers exhibited a great sense of satisfaction knowing they'd successfully carried another class through high school. From now on it would be up to the graduates.

There was a down side on George's graduation night—in reality a minor but sad one—when John Simmer accidentally sat on Daryl Campbell's ukulele, and made a two-pommel side-saddle out of it. Although the classmate's singing days were over, they were saddened by the instrument's demise. But then as the saying went, all good things must come to an end. And this year, that also included ending the Burgess farming operation.

LEAVING THE FARM

That spring the boy's dad decided to move from the farm and work full time in the insurance business. At the farm sale, the family sold the dairy herd, the tractors, all of the farm implements, and some miscellaneous items like feeders and the milk separator. Some household items went as well.

The boys' parents bought a small house in Manhattan and started a new life in the city. In the fall, Judy and Joyce enrolled in

Bluemont Elementary School and made friendships that have lasted through the years. George enrolled in K-State and following his brother, pledged the Pi Kappa Alpha Fraternity.

Herman Elder and his family moved onto the farm as tenants and would remain there for many years. They were honest, God-fearing folks that could be relied upon to do the job right.

With the move to Manhattan, both boys lived at home while attending college. George had joined the Naval Reserve in the spring of 1954 and was committed to two years on active duty. Following three semesters he flew to San Francisco, CA and boarded the aircraft carrier USS Yorktown, home ported in Alameda, CA.

Two years of watching the airplane operations enticed him to return to school, earn his degree and an Air Force commission, and in March of 1961 he entered undergraduate pilot training in Georgia.

§

AS A FAREWELL

Well, we've tried to give you a look at a special time in Midwest history. We've colored our story with personal experiences showing life as it was in mid 20th century.

You've seen our family and farm life, shared our dreams, failures and triumphs … and how much we trusted in the Lord. We weren't unique, as countless young people have done comparable things. Our hope is that maybe in all of this you will have noticed similarities to your own growing-up days.

This story has been based upon real people and events. And thanks to the fictitious Brockmans and a few others, we've sheltered some folks from embarrassment. We hope that sixty years after the fact we have dates and events in order. If we've misplaced a date, event or person, for that we deeply apologize.

To this end, we always tell people, "All of the events in this Book actually happened … or could have." Thank you for reading our tale.

EPILOGUE

Looking back on our youth as Kansas farm boys, we cherish our experiences and achievements.

We weren't rich back then, but neither were we poor. We had little money but lots of love and encouragement. Many would envy us for that.

We hope this Book has shown in a humorous way a couple of brothers who often stumbled and had lots of disappointments, but always picked themselves up, ready to face their next challenge. Our firm foundation taught us that we could overcome even the toughest obstacle.

After college and his Army stint, in 1959 John married Susan Cooley. They have two sons and six grandchildren.

Following a move to Portland, Oregon, John earned an MBA and a Doctorate of Business Administration and began his career in educations as Professor of Business and Economics at Concordia University. He co-authored three editions of the *Small Business Management Fundamentals* text book and developed a degree completion program for adult learners.

In 1961, George married Carol Minturn. They have three sons and three grandchildren. Their family has lived in eight states and two overseas locations during his 29 years in the United States Air Force. Additionally, George spent a year overseas without his family. He was a command pilot and a commander, earned a masters degree in international affairs and rose to the rank of colonel. The family treasured most his three-year assignment to the American Embassy in Canberra, Australia. There they shared life with the Aussies and he flew the Ambassador, "… all over God's creation."

Farm life gave us the groundwork for success, and once we graduated from college, we found that we were tailor made for our future careers.

One cousin asked us, "How in the heck do you guys remember all those things?"

Our reply was quick and easy, "How could we forget them?"

I identify with the Burgess boys. What a great way to depict rural Kansas in the mid 20th Century.

D.F. Cox, Cedar Vale, KS

Don't miss this one. A great read with plenty of laughs as brothers, Freddy and George, grow up on a Kansas farm in a time when faith and family made our country strong.

Mary Ann Stohlmann, Murdock, NE

The Burgess Brothers show how it was back then … lots of work and loads of fun.

"Jim" Brewster, Sun Lakes, AZ

A humorous and exciting portrayal of the challenges and rewards of farm life. Bravo Freddy and George….

Karen Meek, Manhattan, KS

The Burgess way, the Kansas way, the Christian way … it makes your heart sing!

Gordon and Rosemary Crilly, Wamego, KS